AN HISTORICAL AND ARCHAEOLOGICAL SKETCH OF THE CITY OF GOA

AFFONÇO DE ALBUQUERQUE.

AN HISTORICAL AND ARCHAEOLOGICAL SKETCH OF THE CITY OF GOA

PRECEDED BY A SHORT

STATISTICAL ACCOUNT OF THE TERRITORY OF GOA.

WRITTEN BY THE AUTHORIZATION OF THE GOVERNMENT

BY

JOSE NICOLAU DA FONSECA,

PRESIDENT OF THE SOCIEDADE DOS AMIGOS DAS LETRAS.

ILLUSTRATED WITH A MAP, A PLAN, AND LITHOGRAPHIC PLATES.

THE ARCH OF THE VICEROYS.

GYAN

Published by

Gyan Publishing House
5, Ansari Road
Daryaganj, New Delhi-110002
Phone: 011-47034999, 9811692060
E-mail: books@gyanbooks.com

Distribution Network
gyanbooks.com
India, USA, Canada, UK, Australia, France

ISBN : 978-81-212-4566-1 (HB)
First Published, 1878

2nd Impression 2020

Printed at: Gyan Press, Delhi.

An Historical and Archaeological Sketch of the City of Goa
Author: Jose Nicolau Da Fonseca

PORTUGUESE HISTORICAL RECORDS.

TO THE EDITOR OF THE TIMES.

Sir,—With reference to this subject and to the letter of your correspondent "A Portuguese" upon it in your Saturday's issue, let me add that there is, and has for many years been, in progress, under official Portuguese auspices, a magnificent issue in folio of Portuguese records, which may be useful to the India Office in its quest. Its title is "Portugaliæ Monumenta;" and we have a copy of so much of it as has been published in our library at Lincoln's Inn.

Your obedient servant,

RICHARD HORTON SMITH.

Looe, Cornwall, Aug. 16. 1891.

"THE history of the Portuguese in India would point the moral and adorn the tale of a philosophical historian who should write of the decline and fall of the empires. . . . It (the city of Goa) is a place an Englishman ought to visit. It is a place which an English Prince especially may visit with great profit. If we are proud of our deeds and of our history in India, and if we are elated by the greatness of the doings of our race, we may be led by the aspect of the ruins, such as those which the Prince of Wales has been gazing upon, to turn our thoughts to the investigation of the causes which sap the foundation of mighty states, and lay the work of statesmen and soldiers in the dust."—*Dr. Russell.*

PREFACE.

THE present work is written, by the authorization of the Bombay Government, in connection with the local and imperial Gazetteer. The materials have been gathered from the most reliable sources—such as the writings of many eminent authors and of distinguished travellers who visited Goa at different times, official documents and records preserved in the Secretariat of the Government of Goa, ancient inscriptions recently deciphered, and the information supplied to me by the heads of several Public Departments in Goa.

The plan of the city appended to this work is taken from D. L. Cottineau de Kloguen, and the outlines of the Map of Goa from that of Lieutenant J. F. d'Assa Castel Branco.

The proper names, except the Portuguese, are spelt according to the Hunterian system.

I have to thank Messrs. Joaquim Heliodoro da Cunha Rivara and Eduardo de Sá Nogueira P. de Balsemão, the late and the present Chief Secretary to the Government of Goa, for having kindly placed at my disposal some of the most important records of the Secretariat; as well as several other public authorities and literary gentlemen of Goa, who have favoured me with valuable information on different subjects, and whose names will be mentioned in the more detailed work on the territory of Goa which is under preparation.

I also avail myself of this opportunity to acknowledge my obligations to several other gentlemen for their kind assistance, especially Messrs. James Macnabb Campbell, C. S., Ganpat Sadashiv Rao, M. A., and Julio Lucas Brito.

Bombay, 16th December 1878.

CONTENTS.

PART I.

A short Statistical Account of the Territory of Goa.

CHAPTER I.

CHAPTER II.

CHAPTER III.

CHAPTER IV.

CHAPTER V.

CHAPTER VI.

CHAPTER VII.

CHAPTER VIII.

CHAPTER IX.

PART II.

An Historical and Archæological Sketch of the City of Goa.

CHAPTER I.

CHAPTER II.

CHAPTER III.

CHAPTER XV.

CHAPTER XVI.

LIST OF ILLUSTRATIONS.

ERRATA.

For " 1497," at page 37, line 7, *read* " 1498."

For " 1814," at page 70, line 2, *read* " 1812."

For " 21st May," at page 70, line 2, *read* " 16th June."

For " the latter part," at page 83, line 9, *read* " about the middle."

For " transparency," at page 292, line 9, *read* " brilliancy."

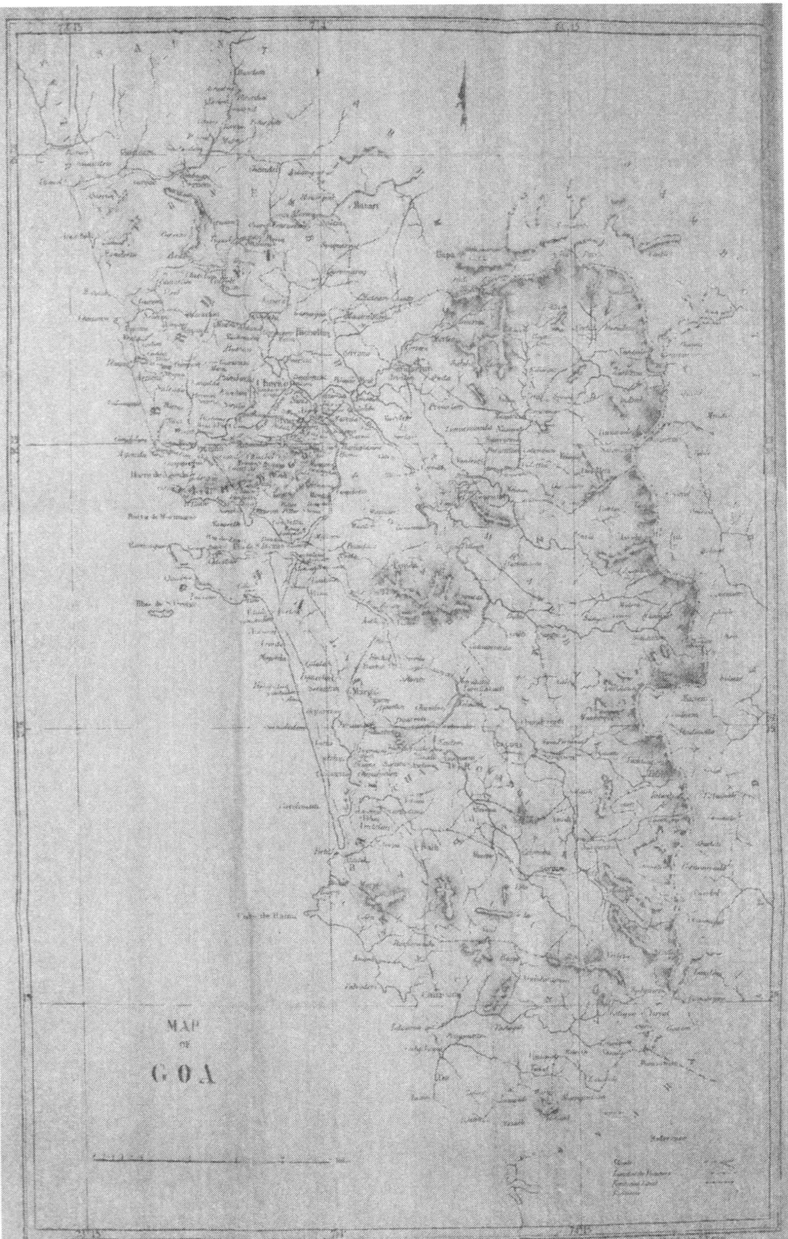
MAP
of
GOA

PART I.

A SHORT STATISTICAL ACCOUNT OF THE TERRITORY OF GOA.

CHAPTER I.

POSITION AND AREA—BOUNDARIES AND DIVISIONS—PHYSICAL FEATURES—RIVERS—HARBOUR—ISLANDS—CLIMATE—MINERALS—TREES AND FORESTS—ANIMALS.

Position and Area.—The territory of Goa lies on the Malabar Coast between 15° 44′ 30″ and 14° 53′ 30″ north latitude, and 73° 45′ and 74° 26′ east longitude, and is distant about 250 miles SSE. from Bombay. Its extreme length from north to south is 60 miles, its greatest breadth from east to west 30 miles, and its entire area 1060 square miles.

Boundaries and Divisions.—On the north the territory is bounded by the Tiracol or Araundem river, which separates it from the Sávantváḍi State, on the east by the Western Gháṭs, on the west by the Arabian Sea, and on the south by the district of Kanará. It is divided into the *Velhas* and *Novas Conquistas*, or the Old and New Conquests. The former, which came under the Portuguese sway at an early date, comprise the three provinces of the Ilhas, Salsette, and Bardez, with an area of 48, 102, and 72 square miles respectively. The latter, conquered at a comparatively recent date, consists of four divisions composed of the following provinces :—Pernem, 73 square miles ; Bicholim or Batagrama, 67 square miles ; Sátari, 144 square miles ; Pondá or Antruz, 79 square miles ; Canacona, 113 square miles ; Embarbacem,

1 *g*

186 square miles; Cacorá, 5 square miles; Chandrovádi, 37 square miles; Balli, 57 square miles; Astagrar, 77 square miles. The last five are collectively known under the name of Zambaulim, or Panch-Mahál. The island of Anjediva and the district of Tiracol, having each an area of one square mile, are also, for administrative purposes, included in the territory of Goa.

Physical Features.—Goa is a hilly country, especially that portion which is known as the Novas Conquistas. Its most distinguishing features are the Sahyádri mountains, which, skirting a considerable portion of its north-eastern and eastern boundary, branch off into numerous spurs and ridges westwards across the district, the valleys between them forming the beds of rivers. Of the isolated peaks with which this range of mountains is studded, the most conspicuous are on the north Sonsogôr, 3827 feet above the level of the sea; Catlanchimauli, 3633 feet; Vaguerim, 3500 feet, and Morlemchogôr, 3400 feet, all in the Sátari mahál or province. On the east and west Sidnato at Pondá, Chandarnáte at Chandrovádi, Consid at Astagrar, and Dudsagôr at Embarbacem are no less prominent, but their exact altitude has not yet been determined.

Rivers.—The territory is intersected by numerous rivers, which, being mostly navigable, are, in such a hilly country, the natural highways of communication between its most distant provinces, only requiring here and there a few small canals to complete the system of internal navigation. Beginning with the north the principal rivers are the following:—

1. The Tiracol or Araundem river, so called from the fortress of that name guarding its estuary, has its source in the Western Gháṭs in the Sávantvádi State, flows south-west for a distance of 14 miles, and, forming the northern boundary of Pernem and of Goa itself, discharges its waters into the Arabian Sea.

2. The Chaporá or Colvalle river, 18 miles long, rises at Rám Gháṭ, and after separating the provinces of Bardez, Bicholim, and Sanquelim from that of Pernem, takes a zigzag

direction to the south-west through the villages of Salem, Revorá, Colvalle, &c., and empties itself into the sea close to the village of Chaporá.

3. The Bága river, only a mile long, rises in Bardez, and, passing by a redoubt of the same name, falls into the Arabian Sea.

4. The Sinquerim river, 3½ miles long, also rises in Bardez, close to the village of Pilerne, and, after describing almost a right angle westwards and southwards and forming the peninsula of Agoada, falls into the bay of the same name.

5. The Mandovi, 38½ miles in length, is the most important river in the Goa territory, both the ancient and the modern Portuguese metropolis being situated on its banks. It rises in the Parvor Ghāṭ in the province of Sátari, first runs north-west of Pondá, and then south-west of Bicholim and Bardez, and, after forming some islands and passing Pangim or Nova Goa, discharges its waters into the bay of Agoada. Its principal branches drain the villages of Mapuçá, Tivim, and Assonorá, and the provinces of Bicholim, Sanquelim, and Zambaulim, and are named after the localities through which they flow.

6. The Zuari is the longest river in Goa, exceeding the Mandovi by half a mile in length. It rises at the foot of the Digni Ghāṭ in the province of Embarbacem, runs northwards, separating Salsette from Pondá, and falls into the bay of Mormugão. Like the Mandovi, it has numerous tributaries, one of which joins that river between Marçaim and São Lourenço after forming the island of Tísváḍi.

7. The Sal river, 15 miles long, runs close to the town of Margão and through some neighbouring villages, and discharges itself into the Arabian Sea near the fort of Betul.

8. The Talpona river, 7 miles long, rises at Ámbughāṭ, in the province of Astagrar, and, running westwards through the province of Canacona, falls into the sea near the small fort of Talpona, from which it derives its name.

The boats by which these rivers are navigated are called *hoddê* or *tonas*, and the ferries across them, of which there are more than a hundred, are designated *tari* or *passagens*.

Harbour.—Goa has a fine harbour formed by the promontories of Bardez and Salsette. Intermediately between these extremities projects the Cabo (Cape) from the island of Goa, dividing the harbour into two anchorages, those of Agoada and Mormugão. Both are capable of safely berthing the largest shipping from September to May; but Agoada is virtually closed to navigation during the south-west monsoon, owing to the high winds and sea, and the formation of sand-banks in the estuary of the Mandovi at that period; while Mormugão, where these causes act with less or no force, is accessible at all times.

Islands.—The necessary consequence of the intersection of numerous rivers is the formation of many islands, of which the principal are the islands of Goa (Tísváḍi), Chorão, Divar, Cumbarjua, Jua or Santo Estevão, De Ratos, Acadó or De Mota, Toltó, Doṅgorim, De Capão or Vanxim, De São Venancio, Panelem, Corjuem, Dos Ranes, São Jacintho, Quelossim, and Vanxó.

Climate.—Except in a few localities, the climate of Goa is generally salubrious. The seasons, being the same as in the neighbouring Koṅkaṇ districts, call for no special remarks. The rainfall for the three years ending 1875, as registered by the Meteorological Department, was 79·96, 118·58, and 102·12 inches respectively. The prevailing endemic diseases are intermittent and remittent fevers, diarrhœa, and dysentery. According to a statement published in the *Boletim do Governo*, epidemics, chiefly of fever, have, on several occasions, raged in the following places:—In the old city of Goa in 1570; in the villages of Pomburpá and Sirulá, in Bardez, in 1775; at Taleigão, Santa Ignez, Pangim, Murdá, in the Ilhas, in 1781; at Margão, in Salsette, at Colvalle and Revorá, in Bardez, in 1782; at Talaulim, Goalim, Moulá, Batim, Gancim, Mandur, Ázossim, Carambolim, Corlim, and Neurá, in the Ilhas, in 1783; at

Loutolim, Mormugão, Chicalim, Vaddem, and Bogmaló, in Salsette, in 1785; at Rachol, in Salsette, in 1787; at Malvara, Agaçaim, Goa-velha, Neurá, and São Lourenço, in the Ilhas, in 1790; at Sancoale and the neighbouring villages in Salsette in 1792; at Divar, in the Ilhas, and at Sinquerim, in Bardez, in 1840; at Chimbel, in the Ilhas, in 1842; at Mormugão, Vaddem, and Chicalim, in Salsette, in 1843. In addition small-pox and cholera have on various occasions prevailed with more or less virulence, the outbreaks of the latter in 1775, 1845, 1849, 1853, and in the middle of the present year being specially worthy of notice.

Minerals.—Laterite is the stone most abundant throughout the district. Iron is found at Bága, Sátari, Pernem, and especially in the provinces of Zambaulim. Though no other mines or quarries are worked, the above by no means represent all the geological resources of the country, which are very imperfectly known, owing to the soil not having yet been scientifically explored.

Trees and Forests.—Goa is rich in trees, shrubs, and plants. Stately forests are found in the Novas Conquistas. The reserved and other forests,—which are scattered over an area of 30,000 hectares, or 74,133 acres,—of the aggregate value, according to the report of the Forest Committee of 1871, of £700,000, are divided into four zones, corresponding with the four provinces of Pernem, Sátari, Embarbacem, and Canacona. The principal timber trees are Nánon (*Lagerstrœmia parviflora*), Asson (*Briedelia spinosa*), Márthi (*Terminalia glabra*), Bábúl (*Acacia arabica*), Hedú (*Nauclea cordifolia*), Kinzol (*Pentaptera paniculata*), Sailó (*Tectona grandis*), and Sissó (*Dalbergia latifolia*).

Honey, lac, and other forest products do not appear to be utilized for revenue purposes. The pernicious practice of *kumri* or wood-ash cultivation, till very lately prevalent in the forest tracts, greatly denuded them of valuable trees. More attention is now paid to this important branch of public administration, and the conservation is entrusted to a special department. In 1874 the forest revenue amounted to £1040-7-6, and the expenditure to £426-16-0.

Animals.—The *feræ naturæ* are the tiger (*Felis tigris*), bison (*Gavæus gaurus*), monkey (*Presbytis entellus*), black bear (*Ursus labiatus*), jackal (*Canis aureus*), common grey jungle cat (*Felis chaus*), &c. The domestic animals consist of buffaloes, oxen, cows, pigs, dogs and cats, as well as of turkeys, fowls, and ducks. The forests abound with the various species of birds common to the Koṅkaṇ, while the rivers and estuaries are plentifully stocked with fish, which forms an important element in the diet of the country people.

The following is an official return of some of the domestic animals in Goa in 1877 :—

Domestic Animals, 1877.

	District.	Horses. No.	Horses. Value. £ s. d.	Assés. No.	Assés. Value. £ s. d.	Oxen. No.	Oxen. Value. £ s. d.	Goats. No.	Goats. Value. £ s. d.	Sheep. No.	Sheep. Value. £ s. d.	Pigs. No.	Pigs. Value. £ s. d.
Velhas Conquistas.	Ilhas ...	29	207 10 0	1	0 3 4	6,835	4,004 5 10	210	49 9 2	43	5 3 4	9,940	2,507 10 10
	Bardez ...	24	48 0 0	...	...	15,204	7,602 0 0	429	10 14 6	33	1 4 9	23,951	1,682 3 10⅔
	Salsette ...	34	87 4 5⅛	2	0 16 8	19,873	15,267 8 4	542	95 11 6	2	0 10 4	45,346	15,460 15 6
Novas Conquistas.	1st Division...	20	77 12 6	...	...	12,186	5,739 11 8	676	93 17 6	...	...	1,400	271 0 0
	2nd do. ...	37	21 12 6	2	0 13 4	15,530	5,908 18 4	1,003	171 19 2	...	...	890	49 8 4
	3rd do. ...	11	18 18 4	...	...	13,305	5,233 13 9	487	51 13 9	...	...	3,891	624 7 6
	4th do. ...	2	1 6 8	...	...	12,615	11,725 5 10	578	80 11 8	...	...	1,976	304 4 2
	Total......	157	522 4 5⅓	5	1 13 4	102,548	55,481 3 9	3,925	553 17 3	78	6 18 5	87,394	20,899 10 2¼

CHAPTER II.

POPULATION—CLASSES AND CASTES—BIRTHS, MARRIAGES, AND DEATHS—IMMIGRATION AND EMIGRATION—LANGUAGE—HOUSES—FOOD—DRESS AND ORNAMENTS—GAMES AND AMUSEMENTS—DAILY LIFE—VILLAGE COMMUNITIES.

Population.—The total population of Goa in 1800, not including the Novas Conquistas, was estimated at 178,478, of which 91,436 were males and 87,042 females. No sufficiently detailed statistics of the whole population of the Velhas and Novas Conquistas have been published since 1851, the census for which year gave a total of 363,788 inhabitants, or a density of 342·54 to the square mile, being an increase of 1044 over that of 1848, when the aggregate was returned at 362,744 souls. By the enumeration of 1851 the population was classified under the following heads :—

I.—Sex :—Males 180,240, females 183,548.

II.—Age :—Males and females from birth to five years of age 52,387 ; from five to fifteen 73,633 ; from fifteen to twenty-five 85,895 ; from twenty-five to fifty 104,856 ; from fifty to a hundred 47,006 ; above a hundred 11.

III.—Races :—(A) European males and females and their descendants 1851, (B) Asiatic males and females 361,241, (C) African males and females and their descendants 696.

IV.—Social Condition :—Married males 81,522 ; married females 81,682 ; widowers 16,753 ; widows 35,202 ; unmarried males 81,965 ; unmarried females 66,664.

V.—Religion :—Christians 232,189 ; Hindus 128,824, Muhammadans 2,775.

The present population of Goa, as gathered from the statistics published in the *Boletim do Governo,* is as follows :—

Population, 1877.

	District.	Men. Under 14 years.	Men. Unmarried above 14 years.	Men. Married.	Men. Widowers.	Men. Total.	Women. Under 14 years.	Women. Unmarried above 14 years.	Women. Married.	Women. Widows.	Women. Total.	Grand Total.
Velhas Conquistas.	Ilhas	5,811	4,511	11,040	949	22,311	5,390	3,696	11,059	3,651	23,796	46,107
	Bardez ...	14,165	9,086	23,242	3,068	49,561	12,849	4,978	23,541	10,898	52,266	101,827
	Salsette ...	15,688	15,251	22,212	3,332	56,483	15,944	11,959	22,347	10,073	60,323	116,806
Novas Conquistas.	1st Division ...	4,504	1,360	6,505	409	12,778	3,639	306	6,402	2,038	12,385	25,163
	2nd do. ...	4,428	3,228	7,626	1,026	16,308	3,294	1,774	7,923	2,279	15,270	31,578
	3rd do. ...	4,229	3,197	9,974	1,093	18,493	2,856	1,068	9,535	2,435	15,894	34,387
	4th do. ...	4,730	3,169	9,279	1,478	18,656	4,129	1,304	9,286	2,991	17,710	36,366
	Total...	53,555	39,802	89,878	11,355	194,590	48,101	25,085	90,093	34,365	197,644	392,234

The total population of Goa was in 1877, according to the preceding statement, 392,234, against 178,478 in the year 1800 in the Velhas Conquistas alone. But supposing that the population was in both these years the same in the Novas Conquistas, about which nothing is known as regards the latter year, there would appear to have been an increase of 86,262 in 1877, or a density of 369·335 to the square mile.

Classes and Castes.—The inhabitants of the country are divided into three classes—Europeans, Eurasians, and natives. The natives are again subdivided into Christians and pagans. The former, who constitute about two-thirds of the entire population, are the descendants of Hindus converted to Christianity on the subjugation of the country by the Portuguese, and can still trace the caste to which they originally belonged. The predominating caste among the Hindus is that of Shenvís, or Sarasvati Bráhmaṇs. The Chitpávans and Kárádás are also to be found, as well as the low or depressed castes, as Mahárs, Chambárs, &c., who are generally distinguished from the former by their darker complexion. There are a few Muhammadans in the territory, who, as a class, are in a poor condition.

Births, Marriages, and Deaths.—The average number of births to each marriage is from four to six children. The native Christian males generally marry between the ages of twenty and twenty-five, and the females between thirteen and eighteen. The Hindus of course, as everywhere in India, marry earlier. On the occasions of marriage, the native Christians invite all their relatives and friends, even those living in distant villages, and continue to feast for two or three days, the rich giving balls and sumptuous entertainments, and their less favoured brethren contenting themselves with homely but profuse dinners, followed by their country dance called *máṇḍó*. On the occasion of a death, the relatives and friends of the deceased meet at his house, and all the males accompany the funeral to the last resting-place. The family for a few days after the event keep strictly to the house, and abstain from every kind of work. So closely is this rule carried out in some villages that they do not even cook at home, the neighbours sending them food at the usual hours for meals.

The following tabular statement shows the number of births, marriages, and deaths in each district of Goa in 1876 :—

District.	Births.	Deaths.	Excess of Births over Deaths.	Marriages.
Ilhas	836	689	147	473
Bardez	2264	1809	437	896
Salsette	2887	2424	463	782
1st Division of Novas Conquistas ...	220	155	65	172
2nd Division of do. ...	508	316	192	225
3rd Division do. ...	471	188	283	221
4th Division do. ...	473	235	238	270
Total... ...	7641	5816	1825	3039

Immigration and Emigration.—In the zenith of its prosperity, Goa was the centre to which the enterprising people of almost all the countries of the East flocked for commercial purposes. Hence it was for a long time one of the most populous cities in India during the Portuguese ascendancy. At present, however, there is little occasion for immigration, and, with the exception of a handful of Gavalís who annually resort from British territories to Sátari for grazing cattle, scarcely any people think of fixing their abodes permanently in the once flourishing settlement of Goa. On the other hand, for the last forty or fifty years it has been noticed that a vast proportion of the natives of the place, principally belonging to the menial classes, annually emigrate to British India in search of employment. The total number of such may be estimated at 25,000 or 30,000. Their stay is, however, temporary, for after some years they return to their native country. In 1874 the number of those who returned to Goa amounted to 6938, and of those who left it to 5969.

Houses and Furniture.—According to the statistical report of Captain Kol published in 1850, the following was in that year the ratio of the number of houses to the population in each district of Goa:—In the Ilhas the houses stood in the same relation to the population as 1 to 3·626, or 989 souls to every square mile; in Salsette they were as 1 to 3·368, or 945 souls to the square mile; in Bardez, which is by far the most cultivated and thickly populated province of the whole territory of Goa, as 1 to 3·457, or 1331 souls to the square mile; and in the Novas Conquistas, the most extensive but least populous and cultivated, as 1 to 4·598, or scarcely 144 souls to the square mile.

The present number of houses—or rather *fogos* (hearths), as they are generally styled—amounts in the Velhas Conquistas to 42,972, or 191·839 per square mile, and in the Novas Conquistas to 15,323, or 18·285 per square mile.

The better class of houses, which are built of stone and covered with tiles, are of two kinds, two-storied and one-storied. The former, found especially in the city, contain on the upper floor all the requisite accommodation, such as a hall, which is generally spacious, a passage, a dining-room, two or more sleeping apartments, and a few other rooms intended for various purposes, the groundfloor being ordinarily used as shops, granaries, storehouses, etc., or converted into habitations for the poor. The latter, more numerous, and seen chiefly in the villages of the Velhas Conquistas, have the groundfloor elevated to a height of three to seven feet, in consequence of which they are called *meio sobrados* or half-storied. Most of the houses of either description have windows with thin and transparent oyster-shells instead of glass. They cost from £100 to £1000 each. Those of the humbler classes, chiefly in the Novas Conquistas, are built of mud and covered with tiles, palm leaves, or grass, and cost from £5 to £10 each. Scarcely any house is let to tenants in the villages; but in the city and towns a house can be hired at from two shillings to three pounds a month. Most of the indispensable and even ornamental articles of furniture that constitute the internal appendages of a modern European household may be seen in the dwellings of the well-to-do citizens.

Language.—All classes of the people speak the Koṅkaṇi dialect, except the Europeans and educated natives residing in the capital and the principal towns and villages, who use Portuguese, which is also the official language. French is understood by some, and English chiefly by those who have resided for a long time in British territory.

Food.—Rice is the favourite article of diet, supplemented among the upper and middle classes by various dishes of meat, fish, and vegetables, dressed in the modern European style, and among the poor by fish and vegetables, meat being indulged in on Sundays or festive occasions alone. The meals are generally wound up by a course of fruits and sweets by those who can afford these luxuries. Owing to the comparative cheapness of the necessaries of life, the ordinary monthly expenses of a family of five persons would be among the rich from £5 to £10, among the middle class £3, and among the poor from 10*s*. to £1.

Dress and Ornaments.—The males among Christians for the most part adopt the European costume; while a great majority of the females still adhere to the primitive *sári* known as *óll* or *panpaló*. This dress for domestic purposes is very simple and chaste, consisting of a simple web of cloth seven or seven and a half yards long, and a bodice or *choli*. The former is worn as it comes from the loom, and can be arranged in such a manner as to cover the whole body. It is first wrapped twice or thrice round the waist and the lower part of the body, and then one of its ends is drawn over the back and shoulder and brought down again over the breast, the remaining portion being gathered into small folds which are fixed, or tied with a string. This web of cloth has at each end a narrow border of silk or common thread, and two others of greater width at the extremities lengthwise, called *pâloum*. On festivals and occasions of marriage the dress is very costly and gaudy. The church attire consists of the above garments made of materials of a superior description, and a long piece of cloth, called *hôl*, which serves to cover the whole body *cap-à-pie*. Besides this dress there is another much used, called *bájú-toropo*, composed of two articles, one of which covers the lower, and the other the upper part of the body, respectively known as *toropo* and *báju*. The former is wound several times tightly round the waist and the nether part of the body, and one of its ends is collected into a number of uniform folds. The latter, which forms the complement of this dress, covers the shoulders and breast, and being loose resembles the upper part of a chemise rather than the Hindu *choli* or bodice ; its sleeves are short, loose, and ornamented with frills, while round the neck narrow pieces of silk or rich embroidered velvet are stitched, according to the taste or means of the wearer. The church attire of this class of women is identical with that of those who wear the *óll*, described above. Both of these dresses, however, are gradually giving way to the European costume, which is being introduced now-a-days amongst the rich and educated classes. On an average the outlay on dress in a middle-class family is said to amount to about £15 a year.

The principal ornaments worn by men belonging to the lower classes are a girdle called *munz* or *gôf*, and round the neck a small quadrangular green stone (*fatór* or *pedra verde*) encased in gold and suspended from a piece of thread, or a chain made of the same material. Round the loins of children immediately after birth is tied a piece of thin blue cord, for which are afterwards substituted coral and gold beads intermixed and strung together. To these are added, after some time, gold or silver anklets, chains of either metal, and other trinkets of various shapes. Those of the females who appear in the costumes described above wear during their infancy earrings and small pendants, and on reaching the age of womanhood three gold *carab* or *cravos*, flower-shaped ornaments, fixed in the ear by means of a short screw, or sometimes joined by a small chain usually drawn over the ear and fastened to the hair; a short chain about the neck with a green stone encased in gold; a necklace, *fugudôr*, consisting of a gold brooch (with three small pendants) surmounted by an image of Christ, appended to a species of chain made up of minute gold beads skilfully arranged on fine threads; and glass bangles. On festivals they wear, in addition to these, a *fugilad*, or neck ornament made up of thin, flat, and small quadrangular pieces of gold hooked together, a rosary of coral and gold beads, costly chains of exquisite workmanship, bracelets, pendants, and a large gold comb. On occasions of marriage a more brilliant display is made of the numberless personal decorations sanctioned by long established usage. The educated and advanced classes are, however, more moderate in the use of jewellery.

Amusements and Games.—It is a circumstance worthy of notice that the people of Goa, as a rule, possess a peculiar taste for music; but it is only amongst the upper and educated ranks that the principal European musical instruments are in use. The humbler classes still adhere to the national musical instruments, such as *gumhot*, a quasi-semicircular earthen vessel ending in a small open tube, and covered in the front with lizard skin; and *madlem*, a cylindrical earthen vessel covered on both ends with the same skin. The former is played with the right hand, and is specially used as an accompaniment to the popular country dance of *máṇḍó*, and the latter with both. The chief games and amusements among the educated are cards, backgammon, and chess. Of those in vogue among the lower ranks the following may be mentioned :—(1) *Tabolã* are a kind of draughts played on a quadrangular board divided into four rows of twelve squares each. The squares in the lateral rows are filled respectively with pebbles and small shells. The players consist of two or more persons, and the game is played by throwing four flat and thin pieces of bamboo, called *tabolas*, whence its name, on the ground, and removing the pebbles or shells from the squares which they occupy into the inner rows according to the number of points indicated by the fall and position of the *tabolas*. (2) *Circundió* is a species of game in which one boy stands with a piece of stick on the ground at the foot of a tree whose boughs are not very high, and other boys climb up the tree and perch on its various branches. The latter endeavour to descend and touch the stick, while the boy guarding it tries not only to prevent them from doing so, but also to climb the tree in order to touch his comrades. Should the boy below succeed in his efforts, he is relieved from the task of guarding the stick, while the boy touched is compelled to take his place at the foot of the tree. (3) *Follió* is played thus :—A large parallelogram is formed on the ground and divided into many others which are intersected by a line parallel to the sides of the parallelogram. Each cross line is guarded by a boy. Two or more boys stand out of the parallelogram and endeavour to enter the inner ones without being touched by their adversaries, and again, after entering and passing them, to return to the place whence they started. (4) *Appa-lippa* is identical with the English 'hide-and-seek'; and (5) *Andrubôia* is the same as 'blind man's buff.' The last two games are also played by the children of the upper classes.

Daily Life.—The daily routine of life in the villages of Goa varies, as everywhere else, according to the sex and the social status of the members of each class.

The males of the rich and middle ranks, who are mostly landed proprietors (*báthkarás*), advocates, doctors, and priests, pursue a somewhat similar course of life, modified in some degree by the pecularities of their respective avocations. The *báthkará* is the very type of a Goa country gentleman, simple in his tastes but of a cultivated mind. He rises in the morning about seven, and after finishing his toilet and sipping a cup of tea or coffee starts for church or the nearest chapel to hear Mass. After Mass he joins in a familiar conversation with his friends, either in the parochial hall or the church corridor, for some time; then he returns home for breakfast, which he takes at nine o'clock. Many, however, do not go to church, but after taking tea sit in their balconies, either poring over a newspaper, or talking with their neighbours. After breakfast, owing to lack of occupation, some while away their time in card-playing, or reading novels and other light literary works, till one or two o'clock, when dinner is served. This is followed by a short *siesta*, and at four o'clock by tea, with sweets or fruits, after which they sit in the balcony or parlour talking with their families till sunset, when they go for a walk, meeting their friends at various places of rendezvous. At nightfall they return home, recite the rosary with their families, bathe if they have not already done so at noon, sup at nine, and retire to rest at ten. The landed proprietors of the middle class, being generally unable to engage the services of an inspector or *mukádam*, to superintend the agricultural operations in their fields, look after this business themselves till noon or evening, when they return home if their property is not situated at a considerable distance from their dwelling-places; otherwise they make temporary arrangements for living in their fields till the harvest-time. The rich, on the other hand, seldom or never visit their fields, all the work being performed by their dependants and servants.

Advocates commanding a large practice generally reside in the city, or in towns where courts of justice are located. Many, however, have their abodes in adjoining villages, and attend the courts twice a week, or oftener when necessary. Medical practitioners are found equally in towns and villages, though comparatively in less numbers in the latter than in the former. The members of these professions are mostly rich landed proprietors, and therefore care little for practice, their aim being solely to obtain diplomas, and with them a higher social status. Their mode of living is almost identical with that of the landed proprietors described above.

The number of priests is considerable in all the districts of the Velhas Conquistas, which contain a vast proportion of Catholics. Some of them, preferring the paternal roof, continue to live in the bosom of their families, but their mode of living is in perfect harmony with their sacred calling. The rest are employed either as vicars of churches, curates, or professors in public and private schools.

The females of the rich and the middle ranks also rise early, and, after finishing their toilet, generally go to church. After breakfast their attention is directed for some time towards the management of the household. Amongst the middle class, however, some women perform no small part of the duties usually devolving on servants. The rest of the time before and after dinner is passed in sewing, knitting, playing on the piano or guitar, reading romances or religious books, or teaching their children.

The poorer classes, composed chiefly of cultivators and day-labourers, rise with the dawn, and after a light breakfast set out at about seven, with coarse blankets (*kánblím*) on their heads and agricultural implements on their shoulders, for the fields rented by them, or for those of their masters. There they toil very hard, enlivening the work at times with an interchange of views on their landlords' character, or talking about affairs relating to the parish and the village communities. At noon they obtain a short intermission for the midday meal, which is usually preceded by a visit to the nearest liquor-shop for a dram of *urráka*, or distilled toddy. The meal, consisting of a large quantity of coarse rice and curry, is either taken at home, if their dwellings are near the scene of their labour, or brought to the place by a female member of the family. After partaking of it heartily and taking a smoke, they stretch their weary limbs on bamboo mats, enjoying rest for about an hour. Work is then resumed with redoubled energy, and finished at six o'clock, when they are seen once more wending their way, in small groups, to the favourite tavern, where they spend an hour or so in drinking and wrangling on topics that are at the moment uppermost in their minds. Thus refreshed, they return home with their comrades, sit talking for some time, chiefly regarding the prospects of the harvest, then recite the rosary with their families, take a warm bath followed by supper, and, after saying the night prayers, go to rest at eight o'clock. This dull and monotonous routine has, however, a good many diversions in the year—on the principal festivals of the Church and on Sundays, on which occasions, the primary duty of attendance at Mass being accomplished, they devote the rest of the time to sauntering, and amusements suitable to their tastes and walks in life.

With the agricultural classes the burden of toil falls generally most heavily in the ploughing season, which continues through the months of March, April and May, when they plod through their work from early dawn till late in the evening, and often after dusk. This is, however, compensated for by the lightness of work in the monsoon, in which season gossip and games occupy a large share of their attention.

The Kunbís belong to the lowest ranks, and generally obtain work by contract. They have to undergo greater toil than their brethren of the other classes, and sometimes even sacrifice their hours of sleep for the sake of gain. The toddy-drawers (*rendeiros*), fishermen, and some other people of this description lead a comparatively easier life, working only for a few hours in the day, but their lives are often exposed to the danger inseparable from the nature of their occupations.

Amongst the rural population and the poor classes generally, all the domestic duties devolve on women, who rise at four, when the first streaks of light begin to glimmer, and the church bell invites Càtholics to recite the angelic salutation to Mary, and before sunrise go through a great part of the household work, such as washing tho earthen cooking utensils, cleaning the brass plates and all kinds of vessels, sweeping the house, fetching water from the wells, feeding the cattle if any, looking after the poultry and pigs, and cooking food. When the men and children awake, the women serve them first with breakfast, and then take it themselves.

Thus fortified, they either go at seven o'clock to labour in the fields, or are hired to carry stones and other materials necessary for building houses, or to do any other work. In the forenoon they obtain a short recess for taking the midday meal, and, having partaken of it, resume work, continuing to perform it till evening. On returning home, they fondle and caress the children,—who stand near the door anxiously watching for their mothers' return,—fetch water, cook their food, and, after washing themselves and the children, sit in front of the door, teaching the young ones catechism, till the arrival of the men, when they recite the rosary and take supper. After this, they clean the pots, put them in safe places, fasten well the doors and windows, shut up the poultry and pigs, and after reciting the night prayers go to bed.

In households containing a great many females, the daughters-in-law perform the hardest work, the elder women only superintending the culinary business and amusing themselves with the children. The elder girls take the cattle to pasture, and collect firewood for preparing the day's meals. When the women have leisure, they busy themselves with grinding grain, washing clothes and cutting grass, the rest of the time being employed in gossip.

The routine of daily life in the city and towns does not vary much from that in the villages, the chief point of difference worthy of notice being the change in the hours of breakfast and dinner, which necessarily arises from the fact that most of the residents of the former places being Government servants have to attend to their avocations for a specified number of hours from 9 A.M. to 2½ P.M.

Village Communities.—At the time of the conquest of Goa by Affonso de Albuquerque in A.D. 1510, its inhabitants were found to be divided into village communities, enjoying certain special rights and privileges. Unwilling to destroy their time-honoured institutions, that wise and able ruler determined not to disturb the constitution of these communities, or to impose on them any other taxes than those exacted by the Muhammadan rulers. The policy thus chalked out was followed by his successors, and in 1526 a register, called *Foral de Usos e Costumes,* containing the peculiar usages and customs of the communities, and the privileges enjoyed by them from times immemorial, was compiled. This register served as a guide-book to subsequent rulers. But in course of time the communities were burdened with additional imposts, and placed under certain restrictions. In the 17th century, being unable to meet the pecuniary demand made by the Government for the defence of the State, then attacked by the neighbouring chieftains, they were constrained to sell certain shares which they held, called *tangás, mélagas,* etc., to persons alien to their association, whence arose a class of individuals known as *cuntocares* or *interessàdos.* These, notwithstanding the interest they naturally had in the welfare of the communities, were not allowed to participate in their régime. About the same time several other alterations were effected in the administration of the communities, which in 1735 received a fresh set of regulations, generally called *Regimento das Communidades.* At present they are under the control and supervision of the Government, which appoints in each district (*conselho*) of the Velhas Conquistas an officer called *Administrador das Communidades* to keep a sharp eye on their proceedings, and in each division of the Novas Conquistas a functionary entitled *Administrador Fiscal,* who is entrusted with the same task in addition to his other duties. Thus circumstanced, the communities are precluded from spending even the smallest sum without the sanction of Government, and have to pay certain contributions to the parish churches, as well as for the construction and repair of roads, the maintenance of schools, etc. Amongst their other functions, they are entrusted with the collection of the Government taxes in the villages to which they respectively belong.

The staff of village officials and servants is not uniform everywhere, but in most places it comprises the following members—the tax-collector (*sacador*), the clerk (*escrivão*), the carpenter (*carpinteiro*), the barber (*barbeiro*), the shoemaker (*alparqueiro*), the washerman (*mainato*), the crier (*parpoti*), and the Mahár (*faráz*); there is, however, no head-man. These, especially the last, live apart from the other villagers. On questions affecting the interests of a whole village, a sort of *panch* or council is held, composed of one or more members of each clan (*vangor*), and the decisions are regulated by the majority of votes given. In the Velhas Conquistas a great portion of the lands is held by the village communities, which, after paying the usual rents and other Government taxes, divide the annual produce amongst them-selves; while in the Novas Conquistas the lands are distributed among the *vangors*, who cultivate them and enjoy their net produce. The total number of village communities is 394, of which 137 are in the Velhas Conquistas, and 257 in the Novas Conquistas. The aggregate revenue of the villages comprehended in the Velhas Conquistas amounted in 1872 to £77,111-6-0, and their expenditure to £26,436-6-8.

CHAPTER III.

COMMERCE AND INDUSTRY—AGRICULTURE—COINS, WEIGHTS, AND MEASURES—MONEY-LENDING, WAGES, AND PRICES—ROADS AND MEANS OF COMMUNICATION—CONVEYANCES—TELEGRAPH AND POST OFFICES.

Commerce and Industry.—Prior to the close of the fifteenth century the Venetians enjoyed a monopoly of the whole trade of Europe with the East, receiving the produce of the Eastern countries through Syria and Alexandria. But the discovery of a new route to India by the Cape of Good Hope, and the conquest by Albuquerque of Ormuz and Malacca, the two chief ports to which the Arab traders, who principally supplied the Venetians with merchandize, resorted, worked a complete revolution in the commercial world, and contributed to enhance the importance of Goa by rendering it the principal emporium of trade between the East and West. From this time goods were conveyed to Europe by new hands and by a new track. The Venetians were supplanted by the Portuguese, while the goods, instead of being transmitted through the ports of the Levant and the Mediterranean Sea, were exported, on a considerably larger scale, from Goa to Lisbon, which had at this time become the greatest mart of Europe. Claiming the sole right of using the new route, and the absolute command of the Eastern seas, the Portuguese prevented, by means of their powerful navy, the vessels of every other nation from navigating therein, unless they possessed duly authenticated passports.

Purchases were usually effected either in retail at the various ports visited by the Portuguese vessels, or by means of regular contracts entered into with native princes and merchants; and the rich commodities thus obtained were annually conveyed to Europe in a fleet of about twenty sail. The King reserved to himself the monopoly of the trade in spices, which were transmitted every year to Portugal to the extent of about 30,000 *quintaes* (3,840,000 lbs.). The profits accruing therefrom have been estimated at about £45,000. Other goods were also largely imported, yielding a profit of at least thirty per cent., or in other words, the sum of £150,000. In 1587 the royal monopoly of the spice trade was sold to a company of merchants denominated the *Companhia Portuguesa das Indias Orientaes*, which, however, owing to the strong competition of the chief authorities at Goa, who were also engaged in the same traffic, did not realize the expected profits. Nevertheless, in accordance with the stipulations made with the Portuguese Government, 20,000 quintaes (2,560,000 lbs.) of pepper, costing £100,833, were yearly conveyed to Lisbon towards the close of the 16th century, a quintal being purchased at the rate of 10*s.* 1*d.* About the same period private trade had increased to such proportions that fleets composed of several ships were successively sailing to various parts in search of merchandize on private account. One of these fleets is related to have consisted of 240 merchantmen. In 1697 another company was started under the designation of the *Companhia do Commercio da India*, which received the royal charter on condition of paying a yearly contribution to Government of £2,763-17-6; but, meeting with the same obstacles which its predecessor experienced, it was dissolved four years later. This was followed in 1788 by a third trading company, which was equally unsuccessful. Meanwhile the power of the Portuguese in the East had been almost completely crippled, and, as a natural consequence, their commerce sustained a serious blow. Nevertheless Goa continued to trade for some years with the mother-country, Brazil, and Mozambique, but the returns were very small. In 1847 a company was organized to revive the decayed commerce, but its efforts proved abortive.

At present, Goa, which was once the chief entrepôt of commerce between the East and West, has dwindled into insignificance. There being scarcely any enterprise amongst its inhabitants, few manufacturing industries of any importance are encouraged. Yet the country is not devoid of excellent and skilful artizans, such as goldsmiths, carpenters, blacksmiths, shoemakers, etc., who, however, have few inducements to work more than is sufficient to ensure a bare livelihood. Some of the articles produced are disposed of privately, while others are exposed for sale at the weekly and annual fairs held in various places. The principal exports are cocoanuts, betelnuts, mangoes, water-melons, jack and other fruits, cinnamon, pepper, salt-fish, gum, coir-work, firewood, fowls, and salt. Of these the last forms one of the principal sources of profit, the numerous salt-pans that exist in the country yielding a large quantity of salt over and above the local demand, in consequence of which it is exported for foreign consumption.

The following is a table of the manufacture and consumption of salt in 1876, a *khaṇḍí* being equal to about 266 lbs. :—

	District.	No. of Villages.	No. of Salt-pans.	No. of Labourers working in Salt-pans.	Manufacture.	Consumption.	
						For Domestic use.	For Manure.
					Khaṇḍís.	Khaṇḍís.	Khaṇḍís.
Velhas Conquistas.	Ilhas ...	11	104	546	160,415	40,210	40,210
	Salsette ...	12	197	466	46,117¼	20,000	10,000
	Bardez ...	8	64	339	78,400	2,820	11,600
Novas Conquistas.	1st Division	5	21	380	8,440	3,000	955
	2nd do.	......	......	......	......	11,001	3,000
	3rd do.	......	......	......	......	10,472	7,627
	4th do.	......	......	......	......	13,140	2,620
	Total...	36	386	1,731	293,372¼	100,643	76,012

The chief articles imported consist of rice, cloth, refined sugar, wines, tobacco, glassware, hardware, and other miscellaneous things. The value of the imports always exceeds that of the exports, thus causing a great drain of money, which is, however, replenished by a large stream constantly flowing into the country out of the savings of those of its inhabitants who reside temporarily in British India. In 1874-75 the imports amounted to £119,912-1-8, and the exports to £90,354-6-6. The total number of vessels of every kind that entered the port of Goa in the same year was returned at 2,271, with 113,729½ tons of cargo; and the number of those that left at 2239, with 122,411½ tons. The customs revenue is reported to be £31,317-14-0, and the expenditure £6,275.

Agriculture.—For upwards of two centuries and a half since the conquest of Goa by the Portuguese, agriculture met with little or no encouragement from Government, but continued to demand, as heretofore, the solicitude of the village communities. About the same period the religious orders, and preëminently amongst these the Jesuits, who had now become possessed of large landed estates, imparted some impulse to the cultivation of land, especially to the planting of cocoanut-trees, on which subject the latter have left an excellent treatise, entitled *Arte Palmarica.* As the lands subjected to culture were, however, limited in number, the production of rice was always found to be insufficient for the maintenance of the entire population of the country, which was, besides, now and then visited by a famine. To supply this deficiency, and, above all, to mitigate the terrible sufferings attendant on seasons of scarcity, the Government, though remiss in matters relating to agriculture, evinced its concern for the comfort of the people by importing large quantities of grain from the neighbouring places at the expense of the municipal chambers, and storing it in public granaries (*celleiros*), as well as by imposing on the village communities the obligation of supporting the poor people residing in their respective districts. The celebrated Marquis of Pombal was the first Portuguese statesman who took seriously into consideration the subject of improving the agriculture of Goa, and with this object issued in 1771 the necessary instructions to the local executive authorities. Five years from this date the post of Superintendent of Agriculture (*Intendente da Agricultura*) was created, whose duties were to suggest and carry out such improvements in the cultivation of the lands in each village as were deemed most essential. The result did not, however, answer fully the expectations entertained, but still it was satisfactory to find that the produce had palpably increased. In 1729 the quantity of rice grown in the Ilhas, Salsette, and Bardez was 9,843 *khumbos* 16 *khaṇḍís* 17 *kurós* (41,342,038½ lbs.); in 1777 there was an increase of 1327 *khumbos* (7,673,400 lbs.), and in 1805 of 2,350 *khumbos* 3 *khaṇḍís* and 15 *kurós* (9,870,787½ lbs.).

Since this time agriculture has made steady progress in the country, and forms at present its chief industry. Of the entire territory of Goa, a comparatively small portion, consisting of 234,754 acres, is stated to be under cultivation. Out of these rice occupies 122,566 acres; other cereals, vegetables, etc., 77,066; cocoanut-trees 33,194; areca palms 565; and fruit trees the remainder. The soil is chiefly argillaceous, but also contains light sand, and more or less of decayed vegetable matter. In many parts it is full of stone and gravel. Its fertility varies according to the quality and situation of the land, the supply of water, and the employment of labour. Manure, consisting of ashes, fish, and animal excrement, is largely employed as a fertilizer of the soil. As a rule, the Velhas Conquistas are better cultivated than the Novas Conquistas, owing chiefly to the want of personal security in the latter, which are exposed to the frequent depredations of dacoits. In both these divisions a holding of fifteen or sixteen acres is considered to be a pretty good farm, though the majority of holdings are of smaller extent.

The staple produce of the country is rice (*Oryza sativa*), of which there are two crops—one the winter crop, called *sorodio*, and the other the summer or *vangana*, raised by means of artificial irrigation from the rain-water accumulated in reservoirs, ponds, and wells. As to the former, the field is generally ploughed before the commencement of the monsoon, the seed scattered in May or June, and the crop harvested in September; while as regards the latter the ploughing operations begin in October, the sowing in November, and the harvesting in February. Rice is cultivated on low lands, *cazana* or *cantor*, situated near the banks of rivers; the slopes of hills, *molloy* ; stiff grounds, *dulpam* or *dulip* ; and sandy soils, *quero* : in consequence of which various kinds of seed are sown. The ratio of the produce to the seed is as follows :—Near the banks of rivers it is 10 to 1, in dry and stiff soils 6 to 1, and in other places 8 to 1, more or less. The quantity of rice produced is sufficient to meet the local demand for only two-thirds of the year. The cost of cultivation is calculated in some places at one-third, and in others at one-half of the value of the produce.

The following statement shows the quantity of rice produced in each district of Goa in the rainy season of 1876, a *khaṇḍí* being equal to 266 lbs. :—

		Khaṇḍís	kurós.
Velhas Conquistas.	Ilhas	120,809	0
	Salsette	109,153	10
	Bardez	121,419	0
Novas Conquistas.	1st Division	34,297	0
	2nd Division	28,949	0
	3rd Division	17,155	16
	4th Division	11,388	11
	Total...	443,171	17

Next to rice, the culture of cocoanut trees (*Cocos nucifera*) is deemed most important, owing chiefly to the variety of uses to which their products are applied. They grow abundantly in beautiful groves on all lands not hilly, or serviceable for the production of rice, and along the sea-coast, which is finely fringed with them. Hilly places and inferior soils are set apart for the cultivation of such cereals and pulses as *náchni* (*Eleusine Coracana*), *urid* (*Phaseolus radiatus*), *culit* (*Dolichos uniflorus*), *oriô* (*Panicum miliaceum*), *mug* (*Phaseolus Mungo*), and *tori* (*Cajanus indicus*) ; of fruit trees, the most important of which are the mango, *ámbó* (*Mangifera indica*), the jack, *ponós* (*Artocarpus integrifolia*), the cashew, *caz* (*Anacardium occidentale*), and the plantain, *quelmó* (*Musa paradisiaca*) ; of oil and fibrous plants, as *till* (*Sesamum indicum*), *sôn* (*Crotalaria juncea*) ; and of various kinds of vegetables, as potatoes (*Convolvulus Batatas*), radishes (*Raphanus sativus*), yams (*Dioscorea sativa*), *beṇḍé* (*Abelmoschus esculentus*), melons (*Cucumis Melo*), water-melons (*Cucurbita Citrillus*), cucumbers (*Cucumis sativus*), pumpkins (*Cucurbita Pepo*), bottle gourds (*Cucurbita lagenaria*), and snake gourds (*Trichosanthes anguina*). Besides these, chillies (*Capsicum frutescens*), ginger (*Zingiber officinale*), turmeric (*Curcuma longa*), onions (*Allium Cœpa*), and certain vegetables of daily consumption are extensively cultivated in some villages. In the province of Sátari enterprising foreigners rented some years ago from Government certain plots of ground for starting coffee plantations. Several experiments were tried, but the result did not prove very encouraging.

The chief agricultural implements in use in the country are the plough, hoe, reaping-hook, rake, and mattock.

Goa is seldom visited with great floods. Some of its provinces, indeed, occasionally suffer from partial inundations, especially during heavy rains, but no great damage results therefrom to the crops. In times of drought the agricultural classes sustain heavy losses, but the people at large are supplied, though at great cost, with rice from British territories. It is only when a famine occurs in these territories that palpable signs of distress are visible amongst the inhabitants of Goa. Formerly this country suffered frequently from famines ; the years 1553, 1570, and 1682 particularly are said to have been seasons of great scarcity. In subsequent years the constant incursions of the Maráṭhás, who on each occasion ravaged and plundered the territory of Goa, occasioned great distress, misery, and want amongst the people. The condition of the agricultural classes in the Velhas Conquistas has of late improved considerably, owing partly to the general rise in prices of all kinds of agricultural produce, and partly to the want of labourers, caused by the large emigration of people to British territory. In the Novas Conquistas, however, the cultivators have been reduced to great want and misery, through the oppression of the land-owners on the one hand, and their own insolvent circumstances and general poverty on the other. As a rule, the tillers of the former district are much more honest and regular in their habits than those of the latter.

Coins, Weights, and Measures.—One of the earliest institutions established by Albuquerque in Goa was a mint, and the first coins which it turned out were of gold (*manueis*), silver (*esperas* and *meias-esperas*), and copper (*leaes*). These were brought into use with great pomp and solemnity, and superseded the coins then in force, except a few, such as the gold *párdau*, worth 360 *reis* (1*s*.), which still remained in circulation. During the administration of Nuno da Cunha and of Martim Affonso de Souza new copper pieces were successively coined, while Garcia de Sá, who was at the helm of the government in 1548-49, issued a gold coin called *São Thomé*, of the value of 1,000 *reis* (£0-2-9½), followed by a silver piece of the same designation. Dom Luis de Athaide, some years afterwards, not content with the existing currency, sent into circulation another silver coin, valued at about 300 *reis* (10*d*.) and called *bastião*, after St. Sebastian, whose impress it bore. Subsequently other pieces of money were coined from time to time, including *párdaus* or copper *xerafins*, *bazarucos* of tutenag, silver and pewter, and gold coins. In 1713 the most important gold coin was the *São Thomé novo* ('new São Thomé'), as distinguished from the earlier piece of the same metal and designation already mentioned. This coin was of three kinds, called double, single, and half São Thomé, valued respectively at 3,000 (8*s*. 4*d*.), 1,500 (4*s*. 2*d*.), and 750 *reis*

(2*s.* 1*d.*). Silver rupees, each worth 600 *reis*, were for the first time circulated in 1720, followed by silver *párdaus* of 300 *reis*, *meios-párdaus* of 150 *reis*, *tangas* of 60 *reis*, and *meias-tangas* of 30 *reis* each. In 1726 some small brass pieces were coined and issued, viz. two *tangas*, one *tanga*, *meia-tanga*, one *vintem*, fifteen *reis*, ten *reis*, five *reis*, and two and a half *reis*. These coins have been renewed, with slight variations in their form, on different occasions, the last of which was during the government of the Viscount of São Januario in 1871. At present, besides the coinage of the Bombay mint, and that of some other foreign countries, the following are the coins chiefly current in the country. The public accounts, however, are generally kept in *reis*.

	£	s.	d.
Gold.			
Peça or meia-dobla (15,000 reis)	2	1	8
Meia-peça (7,500 reis)	1	0	10
Silver.			
Rupia (720 reis)	0	2	0
Meia-rupia, xerafim or párdau (360 reis) ...	0	1	0
Um quarto de rupia, meio-xerafim, or meio-párdau (180 reis)	0	0	6
Copper.			
Xerafim or párdau, 5 tangas (300 reis) ...	0	0	10
Tanga (60 reis)	0	0	2
Meia-tanga or *ortang* (30 reis)	0	0	1
Vintem (20 reis)	0	0	0⅔
Rubo (15 reis)	0	0	0½
Vis duddu (12 reis)	0	0	0⅖
Dá res (10 reis)	0	0	0⅓
Polemvintem or pondra duddu (9 reis) ...	0	0	0$\frac{3}{10}$
Panch dombdio (7½ reis)	0	0	0¼
Dá duddu (6 reis)	0	0	0⅕
Ordem vintem (4½ reis)	0	0	0$\frac{3}{20}$
Panch duddu (3 reis)	0	0	0$\frac{1}{10}$

Of weights and measures, the following are chiefly in use. They, however, vary in some provinces.

Weights for solids.

Khaṇḍi	=	20 mans.
Man	=	32 lbs. for copra.
Man	=	26 ,, for sugar, bees' wax.
Man	=	24 ,, for onions, garlic, iron, &c.
Man	=	4 dorás.
Dorá or Doddó	=	$6\frac{1}{2}$ lbs. for almonds, coffee, saffron, ginger, etc.; sometimes it is equivalent to 8 lbs., or about 4 lbs.
Pavonxeri or Painxeri	=	4 ratto.
Ratto	=	1 lb.
Pavonratto	=	$\frac{3}{4}$ lb.
Ordoratto	=	$\frac{1}{2}$ lb.
Pauratto	=	$\frac{1}{4}$ lb.

Weights for liquids.

Xero	=	$12\frac{4}{5}$ ozs.	
Ordoxero	=	$6\frac{2}{5}$ ozs.	
Pausero	=	$3\frac{1}{5}$ ozs.	For oil and butter.
Noutango	=	$1\frac{3}{5}$ oz.	
Ordemnoutang	=	$0\frac{4}{5}$ oz.	

Measures for solids.

Khumbo	=	20 khaṇḍís.
Khaṇḍi	=	20 kurós.
Kuró	=	2 pailis.
Paili	=	4 poddis.
Poddi	=	2 ordipoddis.
Ordipoddi, Solguem, Natti	=	2 ordnattis.
Ordnati or Ardnati	=	2 guirnatis.
Guirnati	=	2 solahós.
Solahó or Solavem	=	2 bothisavós or bothisolavem.

The *pôr*, which may be taken as a basis of these measures, consists of 48 cubic inches.

Measures for liquids.

1 khaṇḍi	=	20 mans or almudes.
1 man	=	2 caloẽs or colsós.
1 calão	=	6 canadas ; in Salsette 4 canadas.
1 canada	=	2 meias-canadas.
1 meia-canada	=	2 quartilhos.
1 quartilho	=	1 xero. The sub-divisions of the xero are similar to those in the table of weights for liquids.

Roads and Means of Communication.—Goa is devoid of railway communication, and till 1846 was intersected by few roads of any importance. Since then many projects for connecting the provinces by means of roads have been made and carried into execution. Thus, there are at present thirty-one lines of roads, some of which are still in course of construction. According to the data furnished by the Chief Engineer in 1876, the following are the principal lines, with their length actually completed:—

(1) A road, 14 miles long, runs northwards in the province of Bardez from Verem, opposite Pangim, through the villages of Pilerne, Saligão, and Parrá, to Mapuçá, and thence proceeding through Cunchelim to Colvalle, where it is interrupted by the river of the same name, continues its northward course from Macasana, in the province of Pernem, to Naebaga, on the confines of the Sávantváḍi State.

(2) A line, 10 miles long, begins at Cunchelim, where it meets the above road, and threading Tivim, Assonorá, and Doromarogo towards the north-east, terminates at Sanquerval, in the province of Bicholim, also on the borders of Sávantváḍi.

(3) A road, $22\frac{1}{3}$ miles in length, runs eastward from Sanquelim, in the province of Sátari, and joins it with Codival, in the same province.

(4) A road, 5 miles, commences at Sanquelim, and, taking a north-eastern direction, stops at Chorlem, also in Sátari.

(5) A road joins Dona Paula, in the island of Goa, with the capital, and thence running to São Braz or Gandaulim, in the same island, where it is interrupted by a branch of the Mandovi, continues its course through Usgão, in Bicholim, to the Tinem Ghâṭs in Embarbacem. It is 35 miles long, and proceeds first from south-west to north-east, then from west to east, next from north-west to south-east, and again from west to east.

(6) A road, 23 miles in length, commences from the capital, and after being interrupted in its course by the river Zuari, continues in a southward direction, passing through the villages of Cortalim, Verná, Margão, Navelim, Dramapur, and others in the province of Salsette, and terminating at Polem, in Canacona, on the borders of Kanará.

(7) A road, $9\frac{1}{2}$ miles, runs north-eastward from Durbate, in the province of Pondá, to Piliem, in Embarbacem.

(8) A road, $4\frac{3}{4}$ miles long, going in a south-western direction, joins Raia with the town of Margão, both in the province of Salsette.

(9) A road, $2\frac{1}{2}$ miles in length, running westward in the province of Chandrováḍi, joins Mulem with Parodá.

(10) A road of the same length, taking a northward course, connects Colem with Molem, in the province of Embarbacem.

The total length of the roads already constructed is about 128 miles, and their cost has been estimated at £108,800.

Conveyances.—There are scarcely any bullock or horse carriages in Goa, the principal conveyances consisting of palanquins of various shapes, known as *macas*, *catres*, *cadeirinhas*, etc. These are carried by four men, called *boyas*, belonging either to the Mahár, Kunbi, or Śúdra class. The Mahárs carry them on their shoulders, and the Kunbis and Śúdras on their heads; the latter are generally preferred for their activity and bodily strength. There being no fixed fares, the bearers often demand exorbitant rates, besides troubling the passengers, in long journeys, with frequent calls for '*tanga*' (about 2*d.*), in order to refresh themselves with liquor, at almost every shop. But the ordinary rate is four or six shillings a day, and if the conveyances are hired for a month three and a half to four pounds. The conveyance formerly used was the *machilla*, which, owing to its inconvenience, has now gone out of fashion.

The water conveyances are rather wretched, consisting of boats, called *hoddē* or *tonas*, of two or four oars. They are ill-constructed, and have very common awnings, and can be hired for about four to six shillings a day for long, and sixpence for short distances.

Money-lending, Wages, and Prices.—Except a branch of the *Banco Ultramarino*, there are no banking establishments, or professional money-lenders in this country. But in cases of necessity money can be borrowed from wealthy proprietors and religious confraternities at five per cent. In districts inhabited by Hindus, however, the current rate of interest is about ten per cent. Owing to the litigious propensities of the people, and the difficulty of obtaining speedy redress in courts of justice, lenders seldom enter into large transactions without good security. Nevertheless some land-owners not unfrequently advance petty sums, or their equivalents in kind, without interest, to such of the cultivators or labourers as are their dependants, or live in their oarts (*bátt* or *palmares*), deducting these amounts by monthly instalments from the wages due to the latter. In the Novas Conquistas, however, the rate charged for an advance of grain is generally half as much as the value of the advance, and sometimes more.

Owing to the want of labourers, and the comparative increase in the price of grain, wages have of late risen considerably. Formerly they varied from two to three pence a day, but at present a male labourer earns as much as sixpence, and a female twopence halfpenny. Agricultural labourers generally receive their wages in kind, either daily or weekly. Good masons and carpenters are paid at the rate of a shilling a day; and male servants at about four shillings a month, besides food. Wherever female servants are employed, they, as a rule, receive no fixed wages, but it is usual to give them periodically some suits of clothes, and some jewels at the time of their marriage.

The average price of a good cow is about one pound, of a pair of oxen or buffaloes five pounds, of a pig sixteen shillings, of a score of fowls ten shillings, and of a score of ducks one pound.

Rice (*Oryza sativa*) was sold in 1874-75 at 26 lbs. for two shillings, Urid (*Phaseolus radiatus*) at 30 lbs., and Culita (*Dolichos uniflorus*) at 50 lbs.

Telegraph and Post Offices.—There is only one telegraph office in Goa,—at Pangim, the capital of the country,—maintained jointly by the British and Portuguese Governments, the latter contributing yearly the sum of £160, besides paying £3 monthly as house-rent. During the year 1874-75 the total number of messages sent was 1,294, and of those received 1,869. The total receipts amounted to £198-3-9, and the expenditure to £256-11-6¼. The head-quarters of the Post Office are also at Pangim, but it has some branches established at Margão, Mapuçá, Pondá, Bicholim, Chinchinim, and Pernem. Letters sent from Goa to any part of British India, or *vice versâ*, bear respectively the postage stamps issued by the Portuguese and English Governments. The delivery of letters in Goa is made by a staff of carriers paid by the local Government. The total receipts were in 1876 £1,114-2-11.

CHAPTER IV.

NAVAL AND MILITARY ESTABLISHMENTS—FORTRESSES.

Naval and Military Establishments.—The Portuguese owed the foundation of their once extensive dominion in the East to their powerful navy. Their *armadas* or fleets, then reputed the best in the world, regularly crossed the Indian Ocean, of which they had the sole command, subjected towns and cities, and monopolized the entire commerce of Asia. From 1497, the memorable year in which Vasco de Gama opened out a new way to India, till 1612, it is computed that 806 ships of various sizes, under 107 chief captains (*capitaès mores*), left the shores of Portugal for the Indian waters; out of which 425 returned safely to Europe, 285 were permanently stationed in the East, and the rest were lost. The expense of fitting up these armadas varied in each year. In 1588 a fleet of five ships is said to have cost the contractors £11,926-15-0, in 1589, £14,125-15-7, and in 1590, £15,483-2-10. Usually the construction of a single vessel intended for India, the pay of the captain and crew for one voyage, and the purchase of the necessary supplies for them, cost together nearly £4,076-18-10.

In 1525 there were in India six ships, eleven galleons, and a very great number of other vessels, measuring from 100 to 550 tons, and armed with several guns. The *Madre de Deus*, seized in 1592 by the English, was 165 feet long from the beak-head to the stern, and 46 feet 10 inches broad on the second close deck. She drew 31 feet of water, and had three close decks, seven storeys, a main orlop, a forecastle and a spar deck of two floors; her keel was 100 feet long, her main-mast 121 feet, and her main yard 106 feet. Besides those sent from Europe, there were some built in Goa and Daman, the most celebrated being the *Constantina*. This vessel was constructed about the middle of the 16th century, and doubled the Cape of Good Hope seventeen times, having brought from Europe five viceroys, and lasted for twenty-five years in a perfectly good condition.

To guard the western coast of India against pirates, the Portuguese stationed a fleet called *Armada do Norte* to the north of Goa, and another called *Armada do Sul*, to the south of it, which cruised along the Malabar Coast down to Cape Comorin. In the beginning of the 17th century these two armadas together consisted of sixty small vessels called *galeotas*, and a couple of large ones called *galés*. Besides these, in cases of emergency special fleets were occasionally despatched from Goa to several places in the East. Each large ship thus employed in the Indian service had on board two or three hundred soldiers, and each small vessel forty or fifty. All these soldiers were enlisted at the India House in Lisbon, and served generally for seven years. From an early period embezzlement on a large scale was practised in this department, for while only four thousand soldiers were actually in service the pay abstracts exhibited for some years the names of seventeen thousand, and the extra money thus obtained naturally found its way into the pockets of the persons in charge of that department.

During the ascendancy of the Portuguese in the East, armadas consisting of five to ten ships were annually sent to Goa and other settlements in Asia, but about the beginning of the 17th century their power began rapidly to decline, and with it also their once superb and splendid navy. The chief cause of this was the sudden appearance in the East of the Dutch and the English, who had by this time become great naval powers, and were, by their superior skill, endeavouring to undermine the influence of the Portuguese. The latter, meeting with opposition on all sides, and finding the returns of their trade on the decrease, could hardly maintain a large naval armament. In 1744 it consisted of two men-of-war with 64 and 48 guns respectively, three frigates with 48, 38, and 30 guns, one *palla* with 24 guns, two corvettes with 14 guns each, and twenty-one small vessels. The sum spent on account of this naval force amounted annually to £7,555-13-4. In 1841 this force was reduced to two corvettes, with 22 and 18 guns respectively, and a few small ships; but the State had nevertheless to set apart for this purpose more than double the amount mentioned above, viz., £18,139-4-9. Later on it could hardly count more than one *gallia,* called the *Torres Novas.* At present, there is no naval force at all in Goa, but the settlement is made to contribute yearly a large sum of money towards the maintenance of the Portuguese navy. In the year 1874-75 this charge amounted to £9,815-15-0.

While the Portuguese were the undisputed masters of the sea, and their navy was the object of dread to their enemies, they stood in no need of a large fixed army in Goa. In 1566, however, a militia was for the first time organized, to be employed in cases of emergency, and in 1630 a regular company, called *Terço,* of 2,500 men, and a battalion of 5,000 men were employed to defend the country against foreign invasion. In 1671 two extra *terços* were added, which had, however, no special work in time of peace. In 1683 a body of cavalry was raised for the defence of Salsette and Bardez, which was disbanded in 1732, but soon after re-established. In 1708 a subsidiary regiment was added, consisting of twenty-three companies, seven of which were composed entirely of native sepoys. Several changes were in subsequent years made in the military department. In 1768 the total number of persons in military service amounted to 6,532, which was reduced in 1840 to 4,291. In 1860 the total force consisted of 4,294, but, owing to a rebellion which broke out eleven years after, it was disbanded, and a battalion composed wholly of Europeans despatched from Portugal. This force consisted in 1874 or 313 men, including officers. The entire strength of the police was in the same year 970, distributed proportionally in the city and the principal places in the districts. The village police is little more than nominal. It receives no payment and is unable to protect life and property. The total expenditure for the public force was in 1874-75 £49,687-6-0.

Fortresses.—After their settlement in Goa, the Portuguese erected from time to time several fortresses for the defence as well of the city and the harbour as of their newly acquired provinces. Besides these, many others, originally built by the neighbouring chieftains, came successively into their possession by the right of conquest. All of these being once strongly garrisoned, and mounted with 1,204 guns, presented an imposing aspect of the military strength of the country; but at present many have fallen into ruin. The following is a list of them, with the number of guns found therein both previous to, and about, the year 1870, accompanied with a brief descriptive sketch of their position. The first two, from their importance, belong to the first order, and the rest (such of them at least as still remain) to the second and third orders.

1. *The Fortress of Agoada* encloses the whole peninsula at the south-western extremity of the province of Bardez, and forms the northern extremity of the Goa bay. It was erected in 1612, as appears from an inscription on its main gate, which runs thus:—

"Reinando o mui Catholico Rei D. Filippe 2º de Portugal, mandou a Cidade faser esta Fortaleza do dinheiro de um por cento para guarda e defensão das Náos, que á este Porto vem, aqual foi acabada pelos Vereadores do anno de 1612, sendo Vice-Rei Ruy de Tavora."

Translation.

"In the reign of the Most Catholic King, Dom Filippe II. of Portugal, the Municipality ordered the construction of this Fortress with the money realized from the one per cent. duty for the protection and defence of the ships coming to this Port, which fortress was completed by the members of the Municipality of the year 1612, Ruy de Tavora being Viceroy."

Its circumvallation skirts the sea-shore, and ascends the summit of the bare and rocky headland called the Agoada Point, which is 260 feet above the level of the sea. On this point stands a castle or citadel with a lighthouse in the form of a circular tower, about 36½ feet in diameter and 42 feet in height, which exhibits a light revolving once in seven minutes, and supports a huge clock with a bell, the largest in Goa, once belonging to the Convent of St. Augustine. Contiguous to this lighthouse are a flagstaff and semaphore. Within the citadel lies a large square cistern measuring 115⅓ feet across, and capable of containing about 2,376,000 gallons of water. It is divided into five compartments by sixteen columns supporting its vaults. This fortress has two powder-rooms, two magazines, two prisons, four barracks, a chapel dedicated to Our Lady of Good Voyage, and several buildings for the residence of the commandant, the chaplain, the surgeon, and other officers. At present no traces remain of the buildings erected by the Bombay Government in 1808, when British troops occupied the fortress. Within its precincts are also seen several fountains and wells, which have from olden times been supplying the shipping with water; in consequence of which circumstance the spot has derived its name of Agoada, or watering-place, from *agoa*, 'water.' One of these fountains was cut out of a rock in 1624, during the administration of Dom Francisco da Gama, grandson of Vasco da Gama, as seen from an inscription over it, which is as follows :—

"Reinando o mui Catholico Rei D. Fillipe 3° de Portugal, e sendo segunda vez Vice-Rey deste estado o Conde de Almira, D. Francisco da Gama, mandou a Cidade faser esta Fonte do dinheiro de um sporeo, para nella faserem agoada as Náos deste Porto; a qual mandaram faser os Vereadores do anno de 1624."

Translation.

"The Most Catholic King Dom Filippe III. reigning in Portugal, and the Count of Almira, Dom Francisco da Gama, being

Viceroy of this country for the second time, the Municipality ordered this fountain to be made out of the money of one *sporeo* for the purpose of providing the ships of this port with water, which fountain the Municipal Officers of 1624 caused to be built."

This fortress contains 79 guns, and is defended by a guard with four officers. Close to it, on a hill, stands the Church of St. Lawrence, facing the harbour, and commanding a distant view of the beautiful scenery around. The construction of this edifice was begun in 1630, under the auspices of the Count of Linhares, the then viceroy of Goa, and completed in 1643, as testified by the following inscription on its main door:—

"Reinando em Portugal o Catholico Rei D. Filippe 3° N. Sr. e governando este Estado o Vice-Rei D. Miguel de Noronha, Conde de Linhares, mandou faser esta Ermida do Bemaventurado S. Lourenço, com parte do dinheiro do dito Sancto, e parte do seu, no anno de 1630."

Translation.

"The Catholic King Dom Filippe III. our Lord reigning in Portugal, the Viceroy, Dom Miguel de Noronha, Count of Linhares, who governed this State, ordered this Chapel of the blessed St. Lawrence to be made, partly with the money of the said Saint, and partly with his own, in the year 1630."

Here annually towards the close of the monsoon is celebrated with great pomp and *éclat* the feast of St. Lawrence, amidst a large gathering of people who traditionally believe that after his feast the port can safely be opened for ships and country craft.

2. *The Fortress of Mormugão* lies to the south of the port of Goa, in a peninsula at the extreme north-western point of Salsette. Its construction was commenced in 1624, as appears from an inscription over its gate, which runs thus:—

"Reinando em Portugal o Catholico Rei D. Filippe III. deste nome, sendo Vice-Rey deste Estado 2. vez D. Francisco da Gama,

4. Conde De Vidigueira e Almirante da India, do Conselho d'Estado de Sua Magestade e seu Gentil-homem da Camara, fez esta Fortaleza. E lançou a 1. pedra aos .... de Abril de 1624 a qual se fez C .... tas Terras concederam per .... dellas."

Translation.

"The Catholic King Dom Filippe, the third of this name, reigning in Portugal, Dom Francisco da Gama, fourth Count of Vidigueira, Admiral of India, a member of His Majesty's Council and a Gentleman of the Royal Household, being Viceroy for the second time, this Fortress was begun, the first stone being laid on ... April 1624 ...."

This fortress, which is upwards of two leagues in circumference, and in a good state of preservation, contains twenty bulwarks, three magazines, five prisons, a chapel, and quarters for the guard. There are, besides, still traceable at Mormugão, some vestiges of the edifices erected in 1684, when the Government contemplated transferring the capital to that end of the country. The fortress possesses two beautiful fountains with abundance of water, one of which, "Fonte de Malabar," surmounted with the royal arms, is popularly believed to obtain its supply from a spring in a gold mine; and the other, "Fonte de Santo Ignacio," also well-built, from a spring in a sulphur mine. It derives its significance from the protection it affords to the entrance of the port, and hence in a military point of view it is the most important fortress on the western coast. It has 53 guns, and a garrison with four officers.

3. *The Fortress of Cabo* is situated on the western extremity of the island of Goa. It was once a large structure supplemented with a citadel, and crossed fire with those of Agoada and Mormugão, from the latter of which it is distant three miles. But it is now in so ruinous a condition that scarcely anything remains to indicate its former size and greatness except a few vestiges, amongst which the most interesting are three large cisterns. The project of erecting a fortress on this site, which

might supersede that standing at Pangim, originated in 1540 with the governor, Dom Estevão da Gama, but it was not realized till some years later. Prior to this, however, a chapel dedicated to the Blessed Virgin Mary, under the invocation of "Nossa Senhora de Cabo," had been raised within the space subsequently comprehended in the fortress, and to this was attached a convent of the Reformed Franciscans during the administration of the Viceroy Mathias d'Albuquerque in 1594. Of these two edifices, which still exist, the latter deserves special notice. Owing to its salubrity and the panoramic view with which it is surrounded, the building was selected in the seventeenth century as a temporary residence of the archbishops. Subsequently the Count of Rio Pardo, who evinced a great predilection for the Franciscans, made some improvements to the convent, and was wont to spend there some months every year. After the abolition of the religious orders in Goa, it was placed in charge of a friar, and once more served as temporary quarters to the archbishops. It was subsequently repaired by the Count of Torres Novas and his successor, at an outlay of about £1000, and has since then been converted into the summer palace of the Governors of Goa.

About the beginning of the present century, this fortress was occupied for a time, with the consent of the Portuguese Government, by the British, who erected there a hospital, barracks, and some other buildings, which in 1848 were demolished by the Portuguese so completely that hardly any traces of them are now visible. A cemetery is the only monument which still attests this occupation, and for its preservation and safe custody the Government of Bombay allows the sum of six rupees monthly to a guard posted there. Of the thirty-eight tombs found in the cemetery, six only bear epitaphs.

4. *The Fortress of Reis Magos* is situated on the south-eastern extremity of the table-land on the right bank of the Mandovi, in the province of Bardez, about two miles to the north-east of Agoada. It was constructed in 1551, enlarged

subsequently on different occasions, and finally re-erected in 1707, as is shown by the following inscription on its gate:—

"No anno de 1707 foi re-edificada esta Fortaleza governando o Vice-Rey Caetano de Mello e Castro, e se poseram estas armas sendo Capitão della D. Aleixo de Almeida."

Translation.

"In the year 1707 this fortress was rebuilt, during the administration of the Viceroy Caetano de Mello e Castro, and these arms were placed when Dom Aleixo de Almeida was Captain thereof."

Though far inferior in size to the fortress of Mormugão, yet, standing on an eminence, it commands a splendid view around. It is in a good state of preservation, and is defended by 33 guns and a small garrison. Towards the east, at a little distance from it, flows a spring with abundance of excellent water; while at its base rises the Church of the Reis Magos, ascended by a beautiful flight of steps. This edifice was built on the ruins of a pagoda in 1550 by the Franciscans, with the sum allowed them by the Government, and bears a crown on its façade, and the royal arms on its sanctuary and other places. The pavement is dotted with inscriptions, the most important of which, found in the sanctuary, indicates the spot enclosing the remains of Dom Luis de Athaide, Count of Athoughia, who twice held the sceptre of India as viceroy. In this church is celebrated annually on the 6th January the feast of the Epiphany, or Reis Magos, with great pomp, and near it is held a popular fair. Side by side with this sacred edifice stood the College of the Franciscans, now decayed, where the viceroys resided for a time on their arrival in India, previous to assuming charge of their office.

5. *The Fortress of Gaspar Dias* is situated in the island of Goa on the left bank of the Mandovi, one and a half miles to the north-east of the Cabo, and faces the fortress of the Reis Magos. It was erected in 1598 by the

viceroy, Dom Francisco da Gama, on a site owned by one Gaspar Dias, from whom it receives its name. It was considerably damaged during the military revolt of 1835, but was restored to its primitive condition in 1842. At present, however, it is in a dilapidated state.

6. *The Fortress of Rachol* lies to the east of the province of Salsette, at a distance of about four miles from Margão, on the left bank of the river Zuari, and opposite the village of Sirodá, in Pondá. Wrested from the king of Bijápur in 1520 by Kṛishṇaráv, Rájá of Vijayanagara, it was shortly afterwards ceded by the latter to the Portuguese, under the administration of Diogo Lopes de Siqueira. This fortress, once the chief bulwark of defence in Salsette, was frequently attacked by the Muhammadans and the Maráṭhás during their incursions into Goa. The damage thus caused called for frequent repairs, which were executed successively in 1604 by the governor Ayres de Saldanha, in 1684 by the Viceroy the Count of Alvôr, and afterwards by other Viceroys. The last occasion on which it underwent important repairs appears, from the following inscription on a gate of its citadel, now in ruins, to correspond with the period following its investment by Sambáji :—

"Sendo o Conde de Alvôr, Vice-Rey da India, mandou reformar esta Fortaleza, depois de se defender do cerco de Sambaji, 22 Abril 1684."

Translation.

"The Count of Alvôr, being Viceroy of India, caused this Fortress to be repaired after its defence from the siege of Sambáji, 22nd April 1684."

In 1745 the Marquis of Alorna had some additional works erected, and a ditch dug. From its having been the head-quarters of the general of Salsette and his troops, the residence of the chief authorities, and a place of refuge for those of the inhabitants of the province who, on the approach of the enemy, flocked thither to save themselves and their property from the impending danger, the fortress of Rachol once enjoyed a high celebrity. It was defended by more than a hundred guns, which number was reduced in 1832 to sixty-five. It was abandoned ten years later, and lies now in utter ruin. Of all the elegant buildings, both public and private, with which this renowned fortress was in its palmy days embellished, the parochial church and the Royal Seminary with its church have alone escaped destruction. The parochial church was built in 1576, and dedicated to "Nossa Senhora de Neves," but, being of weak construction, was rebuilt in 1596, the foundation-stone of the new edifice having been laid twelve years previously. It has a pretty appearance, and is remarkable chiefly for some of the epitaphs which are to be seen in it. Two of these are particularly interesting. The first, being in the sanctuary, indicates the spot where the martyrs of Cuncolim were at first interred, and runs thus :—

"Debaixo desta campa grande foraõ depositados os corpos de cinco Religiosos da Companhia do Jesu, Rodolfo Aquaviva, Affonço Pacheco, Antonio Francisco, Pero Berno, Sacerdotes, e Francisco Aranha, Irmaõ Leigo, aos quaes os idolatras mataraõ em Cuncolim aos quinse de Julho de mil quinhentos oitenta e tres, e cujas reliquias foraõ tresladadas para o collegio de S. Paulo de Goa em Julho de mil quinhentos noventa e sete."

Translation.

"Under this large slab were deposited the bodies of five members of the Society of Jesus, Rodolfo Aquaviva, Affonso Pacheco, Antonio Francisco, and Pero Berno, Priests, and Francisco Aranha, a Lay Brother, whom the idolaters put to death in Cuncolim on 15th July 1583, and whose relics were removed to the College of St. Paul, of Goa, in July 1597."

The second inscription is over the grave of the famous Captain Diogo Rodrigues, who destroyed a large number of the Hindu pagodas in Salsette, and is as follows :—

"Aqui jaz Diogo Rodrigues o do Forte, Capitão desta Fortaleza, o qual derrubou os pagodes destas terras. Falleceu á 21 de Abril de 1577 annos."

Translation.

"Here lies Diogo Rodrigues, (called) 'o do Forte,' Captain of this Fortress, who destroyed the pagodas of these territories. He died on the 21st April of the year 1577."

The seminary, formerly a college of the Jesuits, was originally founded at Margão in 1574, but the building having been reduced to ashes by the Muhammadans in 1579 the establishment was removed to Rachol in the following year. Subsequently it was retransferred to Margão, and eventually to Rachol, where it now stands, the latter being regarded as a place of greater security. The foundation-stone of this building was laid on the 1st November 1606, under the auspices of King Dom Sebastião, whose portrait on horseback hangs in the principal room, called after his name. While under the Jesuits it possessed a hospital for the destitute, a school for poor children, a house for catechumens, a printing-press, and classes for teaching theology and the Portuguese and Canarese languages. At Margão it was called the College of the Holy Ghost, but on its removal to Rachol its name was changed first to the College of all Saints, and subsequently to that of St. Ignatius of Loyola, patron of the church attached to it. After the expulsion of the Jesuits from the Portuguese dominions, the college was converted into a seminary for the education of the clergy. This institution, the only one of its kind extant, is supported by the Government. Its lower classes are designed for preliminary training, and the higher for studies indispensable to the clerical calling. The curriculum in the former comprises Maráṭhi, English, Latin, moral and mental philosophy, and the elements of literature; while that in the latter embraces a complete course of theology, moral and dogmatic. The seminary is provided with a library containing upwards of five thousand volumes.

The church attached to the seminary is, as stated above, dedicated to St. Ignatius of Loyola, and is pretty large and well built. One of its side altars bears an image of the Infant Jesus of exquisite workmanship, which, according to a legend, was found by a Jesuit Father, Bento Ferreira, seated on a rock on the coast of Africa, and brought to the church of Colluá, of which he was the vicar. Subsequently it is said to have been removed by the Jesuits to the college, though the inhabitants of Colluá hold that a similar image in their church is the original one.

Close to the chief door of the church lie the relics of São Constancio, martyr, placed in a special chapel, with a vial marked with his blood. He is represented in a military uniform, like a soldier of Christ. These relics, brought from Rome to Goa in 1782, were arranged in the form of a body by Archbishop Dom Fr. Manoel de Santa Catharina, and exhibited publicly on the 18th October 1783. A certificate of their genuineness is affixed to the walls. The saint is said to have worked many miracles.

The parish of Rachol, which in the beginning of the 16th century had more than 6000 parishioners, counts at present only 1555 souls, the greater part of whom belong to the agricultural class.

7. *The Fort of Naroá,* situated in the island of Divar, which is opposite the old city of Goa, in the Ilhas, was originally built by the Muhammadans. It was abandoned in 1834, and is now in ruins.

The island of Divar, the ancient Dipavati, is one league in length, and a quarter of a league in breadth. Celebrated in ancient traditions for its sanctity, it was the site of a *tírtha* and of a Hindu temple which existed up to the time of the Portuguese conquest. This island became subsequently the residence of many of the noble families of Goa, but now, on account of the unhealthy character of the locality, its population is much reduced. Besides three parochial churches, it possesses a chapel containing two images of Christ held in great veneration by the Catholics of the place. The ruins of the fort are discernible on the northern part of the island, called Naroá; and opposite to them, on the bank of a tributary of the Mandovi, lies the modern *tírtha,* to which the Hindus annually flock in great crowds to perform their ablutions.

8. *The Fort of São Bartholomeo* lies on the north-east of the island of Chorão, in the province of the Ilhas. It was probably erected at the same time as the preceding fortress, and having been abandoned in 1811 is now in ruins.

The island of Chorão is next in size to that of Goa, being more than a league and a half in length, and three-quarters of a league in breadth. It had once many villas owned by Portuguese grandees, and a novitiate belonging to the Jesuits—a superb edifice, converted in after years into a seminary for the training of the clergy. The ruins of the building are still visible from the old city. The island is now almost deserted, on account of its insalubrity. It possesses two churches, and a population of 2200 souls.

9. *The Fortress of Alorna* lies on the north-east limit of Pernem, on the right bank of the Chaporá or Colvalle river, about three miles from the British frontier. It was taken from the Bhoṅsles on the 4th of May 1746 by the Marquis of Castello Novo, for whom this acquisition earned the title of Marquis of Alorna. It was, however, restored to the Bhoṅsles in 1761, in consequence of a royal mandate; but the Portuguese, under Dom Frederico Guilherme de Souza, found occasion to recapture it on the 25th of August 1781. It has four guns, and is at present in a dilapidated condition.

10. *The Fort of Chaporá,* eight miles to the NNW. of Agoada, is situated on the western extremity of Bardez on a high bluff point on the south side of the mouth of the river of the same name. Its erection was commenced in 1717 by the Count of Ericeira, viceroy of Goa, and completed, during the administration of his successor, Francisco José de Sampaio e Castro. This fort was dedicated to St. Anthony, and was intended not only for the defence of the mouth of the river, but also as a place of refuge to the population of Bardez when harassed by the Maráṭhá freebooters or the Bhoṅsles. It was taken in 1683 and 1739 by Sambáji and the Bhoṅsle chieftains respectively; but the former retained it only for a month, and the latter were, after a precarious tenure of two

years, forced to surrender it to its former owners. This fort began to be of less consequence after the acquisition of the province of Pernem by the Portuguese, and is now in a somewhat decayed condition. It has nine guns and a small garrison, whose commander resides in a newly built house near it.

Chaporá possesses a chapel, a custom-house, and some springs, of which the best is situated on the slope of the hill to the south of the fort. It is destitute of a bazaar, and its inhabitants are very poor.

11. *The Fortress of Colvalle,* standing on the northern frontier of Bardez, on the left bank of the river of the same name, was erected in 1681 by the Count of Alvôr as a barrier against the inroads of the Maráṭhás and Bhoṅsles. It was taken by the latter in 1739, and recaptured by the Marquis of Louriçal on the 13th of June 1741, and had a small garrison, besides a regiment, posted about the same time in a convenient situation. The regiment was removed to Mapuça in 1841, while the fortress, which had been abandoned and neglected a few years previously, went to ruin, and now presents but few traces of its former condition. Nor has the decaying influence of time spared any of the buildings which graced its interior. Colvalle has a population of 3800 souls, a church and two schools. It is said to have been once selected as a place of residence by a Hindu prince.

12. *The Fortress of Tivim,* which lies to the east of the fortress of Colvalle, was originally intended to answer the same purpose as the preceding. It was constructed by the Count of Linhares in 1635, as seen from the following inscription on its gate:—

"Reinando o Catholico Rei D. Filippe 3°, governando este Estado o vigilantissimo D. Miguel de Noronha, Conde de Linhares, foi feita esta obra no anno de 1635."

Translation.

"During the reign of the Catholic King Dom Filippe III., and the administration of the most vigilant Viceroy Dom Miguel de

Noronha, Count of Linhares, this structure was finished, in the year 1635."

This fortress was called *Forte Novo de Tivim*. Subsequently in the same village in 1681 two auxiliary forts were raised by the Count of Alvôr, respectively named *Forte de Assumpção de Tivim* and *Forte de Meio de Tivim*, which were connected with one another and with that of Colvalle by a strong wall protected by a deep ditch, originally dug for joining the river Mandovi with that of Chaporá. The ditch, however, was not completed so as to effect that purpose. The two forts mentioned above were taken by Sambáji in 1683, who retained them only for a short time. In 1834 they were forsaken, and the nineteen guns found in them removed to the arsenal. The Forte de Meio stands in a precarious condition, and the rest are in total ruin. The village of Tivim has a population of 6000 souls, a church and a school.

13. *The Fort of Quitula,* erected in the village of Aldoná, on the north-eastern frontier of Bardez, owed its origin to Vasco Fernandes Cezar de Menezes, who was at the head of the government from 1712 to 1717. It was abandoned, together with some other forts, in 1834, and there is now hardly any trace of it left. In the same year it had three guns. Aldoná is a flourishing village with an industrious population, and has a church and schools.

14. *The Fort of Corjuem* lies in the island of the same name in Bardez, to the east of the village of Aldoná, from which it is separated by the Mapuçá river, a branch of the Mandovi. It was taken from the Bhońsles by Caetano de Mello e Castro in 1705, and was subsequently rebuilt. In the beginning of the present century it was assigned to the students of the Military School as a place for being initiated in military manœuvres. Abandoned in 1834, till which time it was defended by four guns, it is now in a somewhat decayed condition. The island of Corjuem is two miles long, and a little less than half a mile wide, and is very fertile, with an industrious

population. It has a chapel, which is subordinate to the parochial church of Aldoná.

15. *The Fortress of Bicholim,* situated in the heart of the province of the same name, on the bank of a small tributary of the Mandovi, was owned by the Bhonsles till its capture and partial demolition by Caetano de Mello e Castro, Viceroy of Goa, in 1705. But it was soon retaken and rebuilt by the Chief of the Sávantváḍi State, who continued, except for a very short period, in its possession till the 17th of May 1746, when it fell once more into the hands of the Marquis of Alorna. Subsequently, however, a royal decree ordered its cession to the native chieftains, from whose feeble grasp it was eventually snatched in 1781 by the Portuguese under Dom Frederico Guilherme de Souza. In 1834 it was abandoned, and the eight guns which defended it were removed to the arsenal, in consequence of which the fortress fell into ruin. Nevertheless the Government stationed a regiment at Bicholim till 1871, for whose use military quarters, a bazaar, and some private buildings were erected. Tradition points to the existence of a Hindu city on the site occupied by this fortress.

16. *The Fort of Sanquelim,* standing on the left bank of a river of the same name, a tributary of the Mandovi, was conquered in 1746 by the Marquis of Alorna, and was regarded as a very important military point. There were eight guns in it in 1817; but it is now in a ruinous condition. At present Sanquelim boasts of a custom house, a bazaar, a church, and the residence of the *Administrador Fiscal* of Sátari, as well as that of a Desái. Through it runs also the important road leading to the Queulá Gháṭ.

17. *The Fort of Nanuz* occupies a central position in the province of Sátari, and lies on the right bank of the river Madey, a branch of the Mandovi. The date of its construction remains yet to be ascertained; it was probably erected, or re-erected, by the Portuguese after the conquest of the same province, but it is only of late that it has found a place in the official

list of fortifications. There is nothing in it that deserves special mention save a spring close by.

18. *The Fort of Arabó* is situated towards the south-east of Pernem, on the right bank of the Chaporá river, and faces the village of Colvalle at Bardez. It was taken from the Bhońsles in 1746 by the Marquis of Alorna, and having been lost was recaptured by Dom Frederico Guilherme de Souza in 1781. It is a small fort, and in 1842 bore seven guns. It was deserted shortly after, and is now in ruins. Near it is the residence of the Desáí of Arabó, the population of which place, consisting chiefly of Hindus, is very poor.

19. *The Fortress of Tiracol,* situated six miles from Chaporá, stands on the brow of a hill on the right bank of the river of the same name, which, as already stated, forms the northern boundary of the territory of Goa. It was taken from the Bhońsles in 1776, and is particularly known for a horrible massacre which took place there on 27th May 1835, during a military revolt. It is tolerably well preserved, and has twelve guns, a barrack and a chapel. The village of Tiracol is poor and devoid of interest.

20. *The Fortress of Cabo de Rama,* situated towards the south-west of Goa, at Collá, on a high, bluff headland bearing the same name, was taken from the prince of Sunda, by whom it was retaken shortly afterwards. It fell, however, again into the hands of the Portuguese, during the administration of the Count of Ega, on the 1st of June 1763. It is in a somewhat decayed state, and has twenty-one guns. Besides the military barracks, it contains a chapel, and quarters for the use of the commandant and other officers. Within its precincts is to be seen a quadrangular well, while in its vicinity flow two springs. One of these lies to the NNE. at a short distance from the fortress, and has, according to an official report, two stone spouts, through which issues water of unequal temperature—the cold being used for drinking purposes; and the more tepid, which is said to be sulphureous, for

bathing, by people suffering from cutaneous diseases, especially during the hot season.

Besides the above fortresses there are some small forts or redoubts, viz. those of Collá, in Salsette ; of Uguem, Doromarogo, Canacona, and Collem, in the Novas Conquistas ; and of Bága, in Bardez. The last-named place is now much resorted to during the hot season. The above list does not include the fortresses built for the defence of the old city, as they are mentioned elsewhere.

CHAPTER V.

EDUCATION—PRINTING PRESSES—NEWSPAPERS AND LITERARY ASSOCIATIONS—HOSPITALS—CHARITABLE AND OTHER INSTITUTIONS.

Education.—Having placed the administration of Goa, after its final capture, on a firm basis, Albuquerque cherished, even at that early period, the desire of diffusing the light of education in the newly conquered city, and indeed established a rudimentary school for this purpose; but his hasty departure from the settlement, on a military undertaking, possibly prevented him from fully carrying out his plan. His successors, too, amidst the more weighty and onerous cares and anxieties of government, had hardly any leisure to give attention to this subject, and thus the glory of inaugurating a systematic and mature scheme of education in Goa belongs chiefly to the religious orders, especially the Franciscans and Jesuits. These indefatigable missionaries not only applied themselves with zeal and energy to the work appertaining to their sacred ministry, but also endeavoured to confer on the natives those "vast moral and material blessings which flow from the diffusion of useful knowledge." At first their efforts in this respect were restricted to teaching the catechism and imparting rudimentary instruction, but as early as the year 1541 an educational institution, the first of its kind in the country, called the *Seminario de Santa Fe*, or the Seminary of the Holy Faith, was founded, to which not only the youth of Goa, but also those of other countries of the East, flocked to be instructed in the languages and sciences of the West. Such indeed was the usefulness and fame of this institution, which was placed under the direction of the Jesuits and was pompously called the University, that the Government endowed it with the large funds accruing from the landed properties confiscated by the State on the demolition of the Hindu pagodas to which they once belonged. In 1545 the system of instruction became more popular, elementary schools having sprung up in almost all the parishes. These schools exist up to this date, in increased numbers, and maintain the same course of study which was then introduced and which embraced, among other things, sacred music. By this time almost all the religious orders possessed colleges of their own, and vied with each other in promoting the spread of education, but foremost amongst them was the Society of Jesus, which, in addition to the abovementioned Seminary, owned a college at Margão, which was transferred in 1610 to Rachol. This institution is still kept up, under the superintendence of secular priests, and is devoted to the training of candidates for the priesthood. After the expulsion of the Jesuits, their Novitiate in the island of Chorão and their House of Bom Jesus were converted, by order of Government, into public seminaries, but the latter was of short duration, while the former continued till 1858, when it was closed. Besides these, there existed special schools for the benefit of the neophytes and of the fair sex. The latter, though limited in number, were brought up in the convent of Santa Monica, and in the retreats of Nossa Senhora de Serra and of Santa Maria Magdalena. In 1773 the Government, resolving to give an impulse to education, established in various parts of the country public grammar-schools, for the support of which a special cess was imposed, and founded two other institutions intended to teach the military and naval arts; these were followed in 1812 by a Mathematical School. In 1817 the three latter institutions were amalgamated into one, under the designation of *Academia Militar de Goa,* which name was subsequently changed to *Escola Mathematica e Militar*. In 1844 a Medical School was founded, in 1854 a Normal School as well as a High School, called *Lyceu Nacional de Nova Goa,* and about the same time a class for teaching chemistry. In addition to these higher-grade establishments, there were 49 public lower-grade schools. Of late education has been comparatively better cared for in

Goa than formerly. In 1869-70 there were 137 lower schools, with 6027 pupils of both sexes, of which 52 were public and 85 private; 29 higher schools,—including the *Lyceu Nacional* or High School, with 2433 pupils, all males,—of which 21 were public and 8 private; the Medical School, with 60 pupils; the School of Chemistry, with 48 pupils; the Mathematical and Military School, with 137 pupils; the Seminary for priests, with 92 pupils. Besides these there were three public schools for girls. The Military School is, however, now closed, and a college for experimental sciences, called *Instituto Professional*, has been created in its place. The total expenditure for public instruction in 1874-75 was £3319-8-10.

Printing-Presses, Newspapers, and Literary Associations.—The art of printing was first introduced into Goa by the Jesuits. Not long after the foundation of their educational institutions, they brought from Europe two presses, which were located in their colleges of St. Paul and Rachol. The earliest book printed by them of which any record exists was a catechism composed in 1557 by the great Apostle of the Indies for the use of children. Subsequently on various occasions many other pamphlets, chiefly religious tracts and hornbooks, in Portuguese, Tamil, and Koṅkaṇi, were printed in the Roman character, those in Tamil having been prepared in 1581 by João de Castro, a Jesuit who had acquired great proficiency in that dialect. These presses continued to be worked till 1683, as evidenced by the books which issued from them up to that year. Since then little or nothing has been heard of them, and no record remains to show why and how they ceased to exist.

From a document bearing the date of 1754, it appears that the Home Government was averse to the establishment of printing-presses in the territory of Goa, either by the local Government or by private individuals, and that accordingly, instructions were issued to the then viceroy, the Count of Alva, recommending the adoption of stringent measures in the matter.

For nearly a century this narrow-minded policy was rigidly followed, regardless of the intellectual and moral advancement of the inhabitants of the settlement; and it was only in 1821, the same year in which the constitutional system of government was introduced, that a Government press was established for the first time.

The following is a list of the newspapers and other periodicals which have from time to time been printed at this press :—

Gazeta de Goa, a weekly official paper, continuing from 22nd December 1821 to 1826.

Chronica Constitucional de Goa, also a weekly official newspaper, from 13th June 1835 to 30th November 1837.

Boletim do Governo do Estado da India, commenced on the 7th December 1837, and continuing still; formerly a weekly, since 1856 a bi-weekly paper.

Echo da Lusitania, weekly, from 7th January 1836 to 5th March 1837.

O Vigilante, weekly, from 13th July to 22nd October 1838.

O Observador, fortnightly, and afterwards monthly, from 15th February 1839 to 31st October 1840.

O Correio de Nova-Goa, weekly, from 4th January 1844 to 8th March of the same year.

A Voz dos Povos da India, weekly, from 3rd July 1845 to 3rd March 1846.

O Defensor da Ordem e Verdade, fortnightly, from 24th August 1852 to 31st August 1853.

Jornal da Santa Igreja Lusitana do Oriente, a religious periodical of irregular issue, continuing from 22nd May 1844 to the end of the year 1845, and again from January 1846 to March 1849.

O Defensor do Real Padroado, both religious and political, from 1st September 1853 to March 1854.

Till 1859 the Government press was the only one of its kind; but since then several private presses have been started, and the following periodicals have issued therefrom :—

O Ultramar, begun on the 6th April 1859 and continuing still.

A India Portugueza, commencing on the 4th January 1861 and continuing still.

A Phenix de Goa, from 6th April 1861 to 30th December 1862.

A Harmonia, from 12th April 1862 to 27th October 1864.

A Aurora de Goa, from 6th January 1863 to 1st July 1865.

A Sentinella da Liberdade, from 7th October 1864 to 31st December 1869.

Jornal de Noticias, from 1st October 1868 to 30th April 1869.

A Imprensa, from 18th November 1870 to April 1876.

A Gazeta de Goa, from 16th July 1872 to 30th December 1873.

O Mensageiro, from 16th August 1872 to 12th December 1873.

O Paiz, from 4th February 1873 to 27th October 1874.

O Progresso, from 7th April to 21st June 1873.

A Opinião Publica, from 2nd July 1873 to 22nd September 1875.

O Oriente, from 7th March to 27th November 1874.

A Gazeta de Bardez, begun on 17th October 1874 and continuing still.

Nova-Goa, from 15th July 1876 to 1877.

A Patria, started on 10th January 1877 and continuing still.

The *Dexassudharanetxo* (Maráṭhi) lasted from July to September 1876. This paper was again started, in Maráṭhi and Portuguese, in January 1877. It was followed by two others, *A Civilisação* and *Imparcial,* published respectively in 1877 and 1878, and continuing to this date.

With the exception of the last, and of the *Dexassudharanetxo,* which was a monthly periodical, and the *Imprensa,* at first hebdomadal, and subsequently irregularly issued, all were weekly papers treating of politics and literature. The *Jornal de Noticias* was, however, confined, as its name imports, to giving the news of the day.

Besides these, the *Oriente Catholico,* a religious paper issued fortnightly, was published from 15th March 1866 to 31st December 1870; at present its place is supplied by the *Cruz,* which was started on the 15th July 1876.

At the above presses a number of literary and scientific periodicals have also been printed. Of these the following may be mentioned :—

O Encyclopedico, published from 31st July 1841 to 30th June 1842, monthly.

O Compilador, from 7th October 1843 to 28th December 1844, weekly. And again from 15th July to the end of December 1847, fortnightly.

O Gabinete Litterario das Fontainhas, from January 1846 to December 1848, monthly.

Jornal de Pharmacia e Sciencias Medicas da India Portugueza, monthly, from 15th June 1862 to 15th December 1863.

Archivo de Pharmacia e Sciencias Accessorias da India Portugueza, from January 1864 to December 1871, monthly.

Revista Medico-militar da India Portugueza, monthly, from October 1862 to January 1864.

Periodico Militar do Ultramar Portuguez, from 16th March to 16th October 1863, monthly.

Illustracão Goana, from 30th November 1864 to 31st December 1866, monthly.

Goa Sociavel, from 1st March to November 1866.

Harpa do Maudovi, from 7th June 1865 to 20th November of the same year; this paper did not appear at regular periods, and only contained poetry.

O Chronista de Tissuary, from 1866 to June 1869, monthly.

Jornal de Pharmacia, Chimica e Historia natural medica, from January 1872 to December 1873, monthly.

Instituto Vasco da Gama, from January 1872 to December 1875, monthly.

Album Litterario, from 1875 to 1876, monthly.

Estreia Litteraria, from April to July 1877.

There are at present two or three literary associations, founded by some educated young men for mutual improvement.

Hospitals, Charitable and other Institutions.—Of the two hospitals in Goa, one, called *Hospital Militar de Goa*, is situated at Pangim, and is intended for military men; the other, called *Hospital da Santa Casa de Misericordia*, or Holy House of Mercy, situated at Ribandar, for poor and destitute natives. The former, which is supported by Government, admits also, by special sanction, Government servants on forfeiting a portion of their pay, and in 1871 contained 2232 patients. The latter had in the same year on its roll 290 patients, of whom 153 were males and 137 females.

The most important charitable institutions are the *Santa Casa de Misericordia*, or the Holy House of Mercy, at Chimbel; *Sociedade da Caridade*, Charitable Society, at Pangim; *Hospicio de Sagrado Coração de Maria*, Asylum of the Sacred Heart of Mary, at Margão; and *Asylo de Nossa Senhora de Milagres*, Asylum of Our Lady of Miracles, at Mapuçá. The first dates almost from the conquest of Goa by the Portuguese, and supports the hospital of the same name, and two establishments for the improvement and education of females. In 1874 these two houses contained thirty-eight and ten inmates respectively. The receipts and expenditure of the *Santa Casa* were lately estimated at £2608-8-2½.

Besides these, there is in Goa an association of great usefulness called *Monte Pio*, or Family Pension Fund. It was established in 1862, and now possesses a large fund.

CHAPTER VI.

RELIGION AND RELIGIOUS INSTITUTIONS—LIST OF THE ARCHBISHOPS AND BISHOPS OF GOA.

The propagation of the Christian religion was one of the main objects which the Portuguese had constantly in view in carrying their successful arms into the distant countries of Asia. Hence, when Goa passed into their hands, they soon turned their attention to the conversion of the natives, inviting for this purpose from time to time several pious missionaries; and such was their success that the settlement became in course of time the centre of all their religious institutions in the East, as it was of their power and commerce.

The first missionaries, sent to India after the discovery of the new route, were some Dominican friars, who came out as chaplains of the fleet brought by Albuquerque. They landed at Goa immediately after its second capture by that great captain in 1510, and, in the absence of a proper building consecrated to Catholic worship, celebrated Mass for some time in a suitable place in the castle of the city. Not long after, a church was built through the piety of Albuquerque, and dedicated to St. Catherine, owing to his having taken the city on the day of her festival. These friars, however, made scarcely any conversions at that time. The glory of sowing the first seeds of Christianity in Goa belongs to the Franciscans, who arrived in 1517. For nearly a quarter of a century they alone prosecuted the work of evangelization in the East, preaching the Gospel not only in various parts of India, but also in some of the neighbouring islands and places. Within the first eight years after their arrival, they held as many general baptisms in Goa, during which seven thousand natives were received into the Catholic Church, and spread the glad tidings of the Gospel with almost equal success throughout Daman, Agassaim, Bassein, Tanna, Karanja, Cannanore, Calicut, Cochin, and some parts of the Dakhan. In 1530 they preached in the Molucca islands, in 1540 in Porca, Quilon, Travancore, and Manaar, and in 1542 in Ceylon, Pegu, and other places. Pope Paul III., delighted with these successes of the missionaries, raised the city of Goa to an episcopal see on the 3rd November 1534, placing under its spiritual jurisdiction all the Portuguese possessions from the Cape of Good Hope to China. It was, however, made suffragan to the archbishopric of Funchal, in the island of Madeira, to which ever since 1515 all the foreign missions founded by the Portuguese had been subordinate. The first bishop appointed to the see of Goa having died before his departure from Portugal, the Pope invested with episcopal authority a Franciscan friar, named Dom Fr. João de Albuquerque, who took charge of his diocese in 1538, and established a chapter in the same year. This prelate was celebrated for his sanctity, and imparted a fresh impulse to the spread of Christianity in the East. During his administration the Seminary of the Holy Faith was founded, through the efforts of two priests, Miguel Vas and Diogo Borba, for the education of young neophytes, the revenues of the properties once belonging to the demolished pagodas in the Ilhas being employed for its support. By this time the voice of the missionaries had already resounded even in the palaces of some of the Eastern princes, and had won many a member of royal blood to Christianity. Among these the most noteworthy were the king and queen of Tanore, the brother of the king of Manaar, the queen of Jaffnapatam, and some other princes of Ceylon.

In 1542 St. Francis Xavier, a member of the newly founded Society of Jesus, came to Goa. He was the most zealous and successful of all the missionaries ever sent to the East. Xavier began his mission by attempting to reclaim the Portuguese from their dissolute habits, and inducing them to lead a purer life. He next proceeded to preach the Gospel not only in Goa, but also southward as far as Cape Comorin, in Malacca, Amboyna, Ternate, Java, and Japan; and such was his success that in the short space of ten years he is said to have brought within the pale of the Catholic Church one million two hundred thousand people, of both sexes and of every age and condition. During this period he endured with astonishing patience the greatest privations and hardships, faced with unexampled courage the most appalling trials and difficulties, and performed with marvellous energy the most arduous duties connected with his pious mission. Nor was his mission confined to the work of evangelization. He visited and tended the sick in the hospitals, helped and consoled the poor and destitute, looked after the orphans and widows, and directed the religious and secular education of the young converts in the Seminary of the Holy Faith, or the College of St. Paul. The career of this great apostle was brought to a close in 1552. The other members of his Society, who had followed him to the East and who had also been employed in a similar work, preached in the Ilhas, where they baptized up to 1560 thirteen thousand and ninety-two persons. In the same year they proceeded to evangelize in the province of Salsette, which became thenceforward the chief field of their labours, the village of Cortalim being the first to witness the celebration of mass by them. The conversion of the inhabitants of this province was indeed very rapid, hundreds and thousands of them being baptized almost every year. Owing to this, several churches were erected on the ruins of the Hindu temples, two hundred and eighty of which are said to have been razed to the ground in 1567. Some of the churches thus erected were, however, burnt by the Muhammadans during their inroads into the territory of Goa in 1571 and 1578, but they were promptly rebuilt.

The Jesuits employed themselves not only in proselytizing, but also in educating their young converts, for which purpose they opened a college and schools. Besides these they founded a hospital, established a printing-press, published catechisms and divers tracts in the vernacular dialect, and held public discussions with the Hindus on religious subjects.

While the Jesuits were thus employed in Salsette, the Franciscans successfully prosecuted their work in Bardez, and evinced almost equal zeal and activity. They too erected, in 1555, a college and church at Reis Magos, the first of this kind in the province, gradually founded several parishes, the population of which amounted in the beginning of the 17th century to 32,000 souls, and imparted education to the people.

The court of Lisbon manifested a lively interest in the labours of the missionaries, and directed the executive authorities of Goa and other settlements to coöperate with them in the prosecution of their pious work. In accordance with these instructions, the viceroys and governors allowed considerable sums of money from the public treasury for the erection and support of their institutions, and gave every encouragement to the converts. The latter enjoyed, moreover, several special privileges, in preference to their pagan brethren, who were excluded from every public office, deprived of some of their rights, and prohibited from publicly performing their religious ceremonies and erecting new temples. For the benefit of the Christians the Government created the office of a curator called *Pae dos Christaons*, or 'Father of the Christians,' who was entrusted with the task of advancing their spiritual and temporal welfare. In 1560 the tribunal of the Inquisition was also introduced into Goa, and subsequently into other Portuguese possessions. Besides its other functions, this tribunal kept a strict surveillance over the proselytes, lest they should relapse into paganism.

Pleased with the interest thus taken, and the sacrifices made by Portugal, the Holy See honoured its sovereigns with the title of Patron of the Catholic Missions of the East, conferring on them at the same time several other privileges. It also elevated Goa to the dignity of an archiepiscopal see by a Bull dated 4th February 1557, and placed under its jurisdiction the bishoprics of Cochin and Malacca. Subsequently, owing to the progress of Christianity, these dioceses were subdivided into those of Macao on 23rd January 1575, Japan on 19th February 1588, Angamale (called also the archbishopric of Cranganur) on 4th August 1600, Meliapur on the 9th January 1606, Pekin on 10th April 1690, and Nankin on the same date. Mozambique with the whole eastern coast of Africa was also formed into what was called a *prelazia*, or a district subject to a prelate with episcopal jurisdiction, but without episcopal dignity. The bishops of all these places were suffragan to the archbishop of Goa, who assumed from 1606 the title of Primate of the East. When the archiepiscopal see, however, was vacant, the bishop of Cochin was entrusted with its administration, and in his absence the archbishop of Cranganur, and next to him the bishop of Meliapur.

Goa, being the chief diocese in the East, became the seat of five provincial councils, which were attended by the suffragan bishops, the superiors of the religious orders, several doctors of divinity, and other distinguished theologians, as well as by a representative of the viceroy. The first and second councils were convened and presided over by the archbishop Dom Gaspar de Leão Pereira, in 1567 and 1575 respectively; the third in 1585 by the archbishop Dom Fr. Vincente de Fonseca; the fourth in 1592 by Dom Fr. Matheus de Medina; and the fifth in 1606 by Dom Fr. Aleixo de Menezes. In these five councils 316 decrees were framed relating to ecclesiastical discipline.

The large number of Catholics subject to the archbishop of Goa and the suffragan bishops were under the immediate care of the Franciscans, the Jesuits, and the members of the other religious orders which had from time to time settled in Goa. These orders possessed their own convents in the city, and founded in various countries missions supported by public and private contributions, and by revenues derived from the landed property belonging to them. The Franciscans from the beginning of the 17th century were divided into two communities, one of which followed the old rules of the Observantines, and the other those of the Reformed Franciscans. The former founded missions in Bardez, Quilon, Cochin, Ceylon, and Japan, as well as on the Coromandel coast. These friars, having in course of time greatly relaxed in their primitive zeal, were removed from Bardez in 1766, and replaced by the secular native clergy. The Reformed Franciscans had charge of the missions of Mozambique, Diu, Daman, Tanna, Cochin, St. Thomé, Malacca, and Ceylon.

The Jesuits possessed missions not only in Goa, but also in several countries in the East. These missions were divided into four provinces. The first two were called the provinces of the north and south of Goa, the third the province of China, and the fourth that of Japan. The number of Jesuit Fathers in 1636 was 1710, and their houses were more numerous and magnificent than those of the other orders. They were expelled from Goa and the other Portuguese settlements in 1759, when 221 of them were imprisoned, and their missions divided among the other religious communities.

The Dominicans were, as already stated, the first missionaries who came to Goa, but they did not settle there as a community till 1548. They established missions in Eastern Africa, the Ilhas (Goa),—which were divided between them and the Jesuits,—Jaffnapatam, Malacca, China, Solor, and Timor.

The Augustinians followed the Dominicans in 1572, and possessed houses in Mombaça, Bassora, Muscat, Persia, Bengal and several other parts of India.

The Barefooted Carmelites established themselves in Goa in the first quarter of the 17th century, and established missions in Surat and Bombay, as well as in several places subject to the Moghul emperor. They were expelled from the Portuguese settlements in 1707, owing to their refusal to take the oath of allegiance to the King of Portugal. In 1750 the Carmelites of the Third Order established a convent at Chimbel, in Goa, and sent their brethren to Quitur, Kanapur, and Tamaricopa.

The Theatines, or Friars of the Order of St. Cajetan, arrived in Goa in 1640, and after founding a convent there established missions in the Dakhan, Malabar, Golkonda, Sumatra, and Borneo.

In 1681 the Order of St. John of God was introduced into Goa, and its members served in the hospitals not only of that place, but also of Daman, Diu, &c.

The Congregation of the Oratorians, or Priests of St. Philip of Neri, was founded in Goa in 1683. They were chiefly entrusted with the missions of Ceylon.

There was only one nunnery in Goa, called the Monastery of St. Monica, founded in 1606 by Dom Fr. Aleixo de Menezes, archbishop of Goa. It followed the rules of the Order of St. Augustine.

All the religious orders mentioned above were in a very flourishing condition during the ascendancy of the Portuguese in the East, and began to decline gradually after the collapse of their power. The large funds once belonging to them, and the number of their members, were considerably reduced towards the beginning of the present century. The following tabular statement, framed in 1804 by an order of Government, shows the number of the convents then existing, and of their inmates, together with their respective funds :—

Religious Order.	No. of Convents.	No. of Inmates.	Capital.			Income.		
			£	s.	d.	£	s.	d.
Franciscans (Observantines)	3	63	3,649	15	0	598	14	$10\frac{2}{3}$
Reformed Franciscans ...	7	72	4,325	13	$5\frac{1}{5}$	281	7	4
Dominicans...	10	61	29,929	6	$11\frac{7}{10}$	1,592	6	$2\frac{1}{10}$
Augustinians	9	79	21,971	4	2	1,362	19	$5\frac{7}{10}$
Carmelites	1	28	6,018	6	8	292	0	$2\frac{7}{12}$
Theatines	1	13	3,399	4	$2\frac{1}{2}$	144	4	$1\frac{3}{5}$
Members of the Order of St. John of God ...	4	30	2,595	0	10	373	2	6
Oratorians	2	61	13,420	4	$11\frac{17}{30}$	663	13	$10\frac{7}{30}$
Nuns of St. Monica ...	1	61	11,070	0	0	568	7	4
Total ...	38	468	96,378	16	$2\frac{29}{30}$	5,876	15	11

The tribunal of the Inquisition, already mentioned, was abolished in 1814 by a royal decree of the 21st May, and the same fate overtook the religious orders in 1835. The convents and other buildings belonging to these orders were consequently abandoned, and their property, both moveable and immoveable, of the aggregate value of £122,566-4-0, was appropriated by the Government. The number of friars who were turned out of their monasteries, and who received a moderate pension from the State, was 248, viz.:—Franciscans (Observantines) 27, Reformed 31, Dominicans 41, Augustinians 59, Theatines 16, members of the Order of St. John of God 15, those of the Order of St. Philip of Neri 36, and Carmelites 23. Their extensive missions were transferred to the secular clergy, while some of the parishes comprised in them had already been occupied by the missionaries of the Congregation *De Propaganda Fide.* According to the Concordat of the 21st February 1857 made by the Holy See with the King of Portugal, the ancient right of patronage of the Portuguese sovereigns was restricted to the metropolitan archbishopric of Goa, the archbishopric of Cranganur, the bishoprics of Cochin, Meliapur, Malacca, and Macao. At present besides the archbishop of Goa there are two suffragan prelates, viz. the bishop of Macao and the prelate of Mozambique. No other suffragan bishops have of late been appointed in the other dioceses, which, together with the other missions, are under the direction of vicars-general appointed by the archbishop.

According to the Government Budget of 1873-74 the State contributed towards the maintenance of 110 missionaries the sum of £2145-16-8. The annual salary of the Archbishop is £666-13-4, of the Dean of the Cathedral £55-11-1⅓, of each of the four chief dignitaries £33-6-8, of each Canon £27-15-6. The total expenditure on the ecclesiastical establishments in the above year was £4955-14-0.

The majority of the present population of Goa profess the Roman Catholic religion. They are divided into ninety-three parishes, having as many churches, the chief being the Cathedral or metropolitan church, called the *Se Primacial de Goa.* These churches are under the care of secular priests, all of whom are natives of the place.

The total number of Catholics in Goa in 1722 was reported to be 181,565. The present number is estimated at 245,415.

The Hindus and Muhammadans enjoy perfect liberty in the exercise of their religions, and have their own places of worship. The chief Hindu temples are those of Mangesh, Málshá, Sántádurga, Kapileśvar, Nágesh, and Rámnáth, all of which are situated in the Novas Conquistas. The Muhammadans have mosques, but none worthy of notice.

Archbishops and Bishops of Goa.—These prelates ranked next to the viceroys and governors, and once vied with the latter in magnificence and ostentation. The archbishops especially have always been treated with the high honour due to their dignity. As already stated, in the event of their death or absence the temporary administration of the diocese devolved by right of precedence on the bishop of Cochin, and next to him on the bishops of Cranganur and Meliapur.

The following is a list of the archbishops and bishops who have governed the diocese of Goa, from the date of its foundation to the present time:—

(1) Dom Fr. João de Albuquerque, the first bishop of Goa, arrived in India in 1538, and died in 1553; when the government of the diocese was taken by a vicar capitular chosen by the chapter, and from 1558 the episcopal functions were discharged by Dom João Nunes Pereira, patriarch of Ethiopia.

(2) Dom Gaspar de Leão Pereira, the first archbishop of Goa, arrived in India towards the close of the year 1560, and resigned his office in September 1567.

(3) Dom Fr. Jorge Themudo, bishop of Cochin, governed, *sede vacante*, in Goa from 1567 to 29th April 1571.

(4) Dom Gaspar de Leão Pereira was again appointed archbishop of Goa, and assumed charge of his see in 1574. He died on 15th August 1576.

(5) Dom Fr. Henrique de Tavora, bishop of Cochin, having been transferred to Goa in 1578, owing to the death of the preceding archbishop, governed the diocese for three years.

(6) Dom Fr. Vicente da Fonseca came as archbishop of Goa in 1580, and died six years later, on his return voyage to Portugal.

(7) Dom Fr. Matheus de Medina, bishop of Cochin, was transferred to Goa in 1588, and resigned his office in 1592.

(8) Dom Fr. Andre de Santa Maria, also bishop of Cochin, was entrusted with the administration of the diocese in 1593, which he held till 1595.

(9) Dom Fr. Aleixo de Menezes, archbishop of Goa and first Primate of the East, assumed charge of his diocese in 1595, and governed till 1610, when he returned to Portugal, entrusting the administration of the see of Goa to one of his coadjutors, Dom Fr. Domingos de Trindade, bishop of Sale, who held the office till his death on 30th December 1612.

(10) Dom Fr. Christovão de Sá e Lisboa, bishop of Malacca, was transferred to Goa in 1616, and governed till his death on 31st March 1622.

(11) Dom Fr. Sebastião de S. Pedro governed as bishop of Meliapur from 1623 to 1625, when he was appointed archbishop of Goa. On his death on 7th November 1629 the chapter assumed the government of the diocese, and delegated its functions at first to the dean, Gonçalo Velloso, and afterwards to Dom Fr. João de Rocha, bishop of Hierapolis.

(12) Dom Fr. Miguel Rangel, of Cochin, took charge of the diocese in 1634, and governed it for some time, in consequence of the death of Dom Fr. Manuel Telles de Brito, the newly appointed archbishop of Goa, on his voyage to India.

(13) Dom Fr. Francisco dos Martyres, archbishop of Goa, took charge of his diocese on 21st October 1636. After his death, which occurred on 25th November 1652, the see of Goa remained vacant for twenty-two years. Dom Fr. Christovão da Silveira was appointed archbishop of Goa in 1672, but died on his voyage to India.

(14) Dom Fr. Antonio de Brandão, archbishop of Goa, arrived on 24th September 1675, and died on 6th July 1678.

(15) Dom Manuel de Souza e Menezes, archbishop of Goa, governed his diocese from 20th September 1681 to 31st January 1684.

(16) Dom Alberto do Silva, archbishop of Goa, arrived in India on 24th September 1687, and governed the diocese till 18th April 1688.

(17) Dom Fr. Pedro de Silva, bishop of Cochin, was transferred to Goa in 1689, and continued to govern the see till 15th March 1691.

(18) Dom Fr. Agostinho de Annnnciação, archbishop of Goa, arrived on 1691 and died on 6th July 1713.

(19) Dom Sebastião de Andrade Pessanha, archbishop of Goa, governed his see from 24th September 1716 to 25th January 1721, when he resigned his post.

(20) Dom Ignacio de Santa Thereza, archbishop of Goa, governed his diocese from 1721 to 1739, when he was transferred to the bishopric of Algarve, in Portugal. He was succeeded by the bishcp of Macao, Dom Fr. Eugenio Trigueiros, who died on his way to Goa.

(21) Dom Clemente José, bishop of Cochin, took charge of the diocese after the death of the foregoing, and governed it till 1742.

(22) Dom Francisco Vasconcellos, bishop of Cochin, succeeded on 20th December 1742, and governed the diocese till his death on 30th March 1743.

(23) Dom Fr. Lourenço de Santa Maria, archbishop of Goa, governed his see from 1744 to 1750.

(24) Dom Antonio Taveira da Neiva Brum da Silveira, archbishop of Goa, arrived 23rd September 1750, and governed till 4th March 1775.

(25) Dom Francisco da Assumpção e Brito, archbishop of Goa, took charge of his diocese in March 1775, and governed it till 5th February 1780.

(26) Dom Fr. Manoel de Santa Catharina, at first governor of the archbishopric, and subsequently archbishop of Goa, took charge of his diocese in February 1780, and died in February 1812.

(27) Dom Fr. Manoel de São Galdino, archbishop of Goa, governed his see from 18th February 1812 to 15th July 1831. After his death the chapter, *sede vacante*, appointed succes-

sively four vicars-capitular, one of them being Dom Antonio Felcciano de Santa Rita Carvalho, who was appointed archbishop, but was not consecrated.

(28) Dom José Maria de Silva Torres, archbishop of Goa, took charge of his diocese on 7th March 1844, and governed it till 26th March 1849, when he returned to Portugal. For thirteen years the see of Goa remained vacant, being governed by vicars-capitular, one of them being Dom Joaquim de Santa Rita Botelho, who held the office for a long time.

(29) Dom João Chrysostomo d'Amorim e Pessoa, archbishop of Goa, arrived on 3rd January 1863, and returned to Portugal on 5th February 1869; he did not, however, resign his office till 1874.

(30) Dom Ayres de Ornellas e Vasconcellos is the present archbishop; he arrived in Goa on 27th December 1875.

CHAPTER VII.

JUDICIAL ADMINISTRATION—CIVIL ADMINISTRATION—MUNICIPALITIES—REVENUE AND EXPENDITURE.

Judicial Administration.—The administration of justice in Goa has, since the conquest, been mainly regulated according to the laws obtaining in Portugal, but in certain respects modifications have been introduced to suit the peculiar circumstances of the country, especially those relating to the Hindus, whose usages were codified, for the first time, in 1526. In the early days of the Portuguese rule, justice was dispensed by a judicial functionary called the *Ouvidor Geral*, who exercised both civil and criminal jurisdiction in the settlement. In 1544 a High Court, presided over by a Chancellor, was organized under the appellation of the *Relação das Indias*, having its seat in Goa, but its jurisdiction extending over all the Portuguese possessions in the East. Subsequently several alterations were effected in its constitution, the chief among them relating to the number of the judges, which in 1587 amounted to ten, in 1628 to five, and in 1748 to six. It continued in existence for upwards of two centuries, having been abolished in 1774, when again the *Ouvidor Geral* was solely invested with all the powers conferred upon and exercised by this defunct tribunal. In addition to his other duties, he was empowered to hear appeals from the decisions of the judges in the districts of the Velhas Conquistas, who were called *ouvidores*. In 1763 the Novas Conquistas were placed under an officer invested with judicial powers called *Intendente Geral das Novas Conquistas* (Intendent General of the New Conquests). This arrangement came to a close in 1778, and was superseded by the aforesaid High Court. This tribunal was completely reorganized in 1837, previous to which it was twice closed temporarily, on the first occasion its place having been taken by a Bench called *Junta da Justiça*, which lasted from 1822 to 1827, and on the second by a court called *Tribunal da segunda instancia*, which continued for only two years, from 1835 to 1837.

At present Goa with its dependencies in India, viz. Daman and Diu, and with Mozambique, Macao, and Timor, constitutes, for judicial purposes, but one district. This district is divided into *comarcas*, which are subdivided into *julgados*, and these again into *freguesias* or parishes.

Each parish is superintended by a justice of the peace, whose duty it is to arbitrate between litigants in civil suits, except those affecting the interests of minors, lunatics, idiots, etc., as well as those relating to mortmain. It is also incumbent on this functionary to institute preliminary inquiries into criminal matters previous to their submission for trial before the competent judicial authorities, to try municipal offences, and decide petty suits not exceeding in amount or value 2500 *reis fortes*, or a little above 12*s*. Against his decision an appeal lies to the court of a judge of higher jurisdiction called *Juiz ordinario*. The office of justice of the peace is honorary.

In every *julgado* there is one *Juiz ordinario*, with an establishment consisting of a sub-delegate of the Attorney General, two clerks, two or more bailiffs, and a translator or interpreter. All these officials are paid by Government and are besides entitled to fees, except the clerks, who receive no fixed compensation from the public treasury, but only certain fees sanctioned by law.

The *Juiz ordinario* holds his sittings twice a week for the purpose of deciding such civil and criminal cases as are within his jurisdiction. The former are chiefly suits concerning landed property not exceeding the value of 8000 reis (£2), or moveable property of not more than 12,000 reis (£3), and the latter relate to offences for which no higher punishment can be awarded than a fine of 3000 reis (15*s*.) or three days' rigorous imprisonment. Against these decisions no appeal lies to any tribunal. In almost all other cases this officer cannot exercise judicial functions beyond making certain preliminary investigations in regard to those cases which are heard by a *Juiz de direito*, who, besides his own duties,—which will be specified below,—hears appeals against the decisions of a judge of ordinary jurisdiction.

The rank of *Juiz de direito* is identical with that of District Judge in British India. He is placed in charge of a *comarca*, and has a staff composed of a delegate of the Attorney General, three clerks, one interpreter and translator, an accountant, and four or five bailiffs, all of whom, except the clerks and accountant, receive, in addition to certain fees, fixed salaries. A judge of this class exercises ordinary and extraordinary jurisdiction in matters both civil and criminal. He holds his ordinary sittings twice a week, and extraordinary, in cases of emergency, on any day. He has, moreover, to go on circuit annually to the *julgados*, where he receives and hears complaints against the judicial functionaries subordinate to him, examines their proceedings, and registers and sometimes tries those suits within his competence which may not have been submitted to his tribunal by the judges of ordinary jurisdiction. His decision in suits relating to landed property exceeding in value £10, and moveable property above £15, may be appealed against in the High Court of Goa. Within the limits of the *julgado* where the seat of his tribunal is fixed, this officer exercises the functions both of a judge of ordinary jurisdiction and a district judge (*Juiz de direito*), but in other places within the *comarca* over which he presides he performs the duties proper to his office.

The supervision over the above judges is entrusted to a High Court (*Tribunal da Relação*) which is located at Nova Goa, in consequence of which it is called *Relação de Nova Goa*. This court consists of the chief justice (*Presidente*) and three puisne judges, with a staff consisting of an attorney general, an assistant, a registrar, two assistant registrars, an accountant, and two bailiffs, all drawing salaries from the public treasury besides certain perquisites.

The High Court has jurisdiction, both ordinary and extraordinary, in all cases, whether civil or criminal, and is invested with appellate powers. Its decisions are final in all suits except those relating to immoveable property exceeding in value £150, and moveable property above £250, in which an appeal lies to the Supreme Tribunal of Portugal.

Besides the High Court, there are in Goa three courts of the *Juiz de direito*, established in the three *comarcas* of the Ilhas, Bardez, and Salsette. The Ilhas are divided into two *julgados*—those of Pangim and Poudá; Bardez into four— the first of Mapuçá, the chief town of the *comarca*, the second of Calangute, the third of Pernem, and the fourth of Bicholim; and Salsette into three—those of Margão, Chinchinim and Quepem.

The offices of the Judges of the High Court and of District Judges are filled by Europeans, and those of Judges of the *julgados* by natives.

The annual salary of the Chief Justice is £416-13-4, of each Judge of the High Court and of the Attorney General £312-10-0, of the District Judges £260-8-4, and of a *Juiz do julgado*, or Subordinate Judge, £58-6-8.

The total sum spent on judicial administration amounted in 1873-74 to £5551-16-0.

In 1874 there were in the High Court 167 civil and 164 criminal cases, total 331.

Civil Administration.—After the discovery of the new route to India, the Portuguese entered on a career of conquest by subjugating various parts of the East, and thus gradually established an empire comprising a great number of the most important towns and commercial ports, from Sofala to Ormuz, and from Cambay to China. The whole of this vast empire, of which Goa was the metropolis, was subject to one chief authority, with the title of Viceroy or Governor. Under his supervision were placed five governors, who ruled over Mozambique, Malacca, Ormuz, Muscat and Ceylon, besides the captains of several fortresses exercising, within their respective jurisdictions, civil and military authority. The Viceroy, whose tenure of office was generally limited to three years, was invested with almost absolute powers, and had the entire control of all branches of the administration. In military, naval, and civil affairs his authority was held supreme; in civil suits his court was of final resort, and in criminal matters his power extended even to the passing of capital sentences, except in the case of Portuguese noblemen, whom he could not order to be executed without the royal sanction. He was assisted in the government by two councils, the one called the "Council of the State," and the other the "Council of Three Estates." The former, composed of the highest functionaries, was intended to act, in certain respects, as a check on the Viceroy, but practically its action was hampered by his influence. The latter was composed of the representatives of the three principal classes, viz. civil, military, and ecclesiastical, and amongst other functions it had the power, which appears to have been seldom exercised, of selecting an interim Governor in the event of the death of the Viceroy and in default of a person previously appointed by a royal patent.

About the year 1570 the empire had attained the climax of its grandeur, and owing to its expansion was divided into three governments, one of which extended from Cape Guardafui to Ceylon, the second from Pegu to China, and the third embraced the territories situated on the eastern coast of Africa. The first of these was immediately under the Viceroy, and the other two under separate governors; but this arrangement prevailed only for a short time, and the Viceroy reassumed the government of the whole empire. In course of time a great portion of this empire was wrested from the Portuguese by the Dutch, and in 1752 the province of Mozambique became a direct dependency of the Crown. In 1844 Macao and Timor also severed their connection with Goa, thus leaving only Daman and Diu subordinate to it. Many reforms were also intro-

introduced successively in the administration of Goa; while the title of the Viceroy, which was once changed into that of Captain General, was soon altered to Governor General. Since 1821 the State of Portuguese India has been enjoying the same political rights as the mother-country, and has been represented in the Cortes by deputies, many of whom are natives of the place.

At present Goa is regarded as an integral portion of the Portuguese empire, and with Daman and Diu forms for administrative purposes one province. This province is subject to a Governor General, who is appointed directly by the King of Portugal, and holds his office for five years. Besides his ordinary functions, he is invested with the highest military authority in the province. His personal staff consists chiefly of two Aides-de-camp and a Secretary, styled the Chief Secretary of the Governor General of Portuguese India, and likewise appointed by the King. Though the chief executive functionary, the Governor General cannot, except in cases of emergency, impose new taxes or abolish the existing ones, contract loans, create new appointments or reduce the old ones, retrench salaries, or even incur any expenses not sanctioned by law. Nor can he, under any circumstances whatever, leave the province without the special permission of the Home Government. In the administration of the province he is aided by a council composed of the Chief Secretary, the Archbishop of Goa (or in his absence the chief ecclesiastical authority exercising his functions), the Judges of the High Court, the two highest Military Officers in Goa, the Attorney General, the Secretary of the *Junta da Fazenda Publica* (Council of Public Revenue), the Health Officer, and the President of the Municipal Chamber or Corporation of the capital (*Camara Municipal de Capital*). As a rule, all the members give their opinions and votes in every matter on which they are consulted by the Governor General. Besides this, there are three other councils called *Junta Geral da Provincia* (General Council of the Province), *Junta da Fazenda Publica* (Council of Public Revenue), and *Conselho de Provincia* (another Council of the Province). The first is composed of the Chief Secretary, the Archbishop or his substitute, the Attorney General, the Secretary of the *Junta da Fazenda Publica,* the Director of Public Works, the Health Officer, a Professor of the Medico-Surgical School, a Professor of the *Instituto Professional,* a Professor of the Lyceum, a Professor of the Normal School, and a representative of each of the municipal corporations of the province. This *Junta* discusses and decides all questions relating to public works and the expenses necessary for their execution, the preservation of public health, the establishment of schools, the alteration of customs duties, etc. When, however, the Junta passes any illegal or hasty resolution, the Governor General is empowered to suspend its operation pending a reference on the subject to, and final decision by, the Home Government.

The second consists of the Governor General as President, the Attorney General, the Secretary of the same Council, and the Accountant General. This *Junta* exercises a direct and active control over the public revenues, making the requisite provision for their proper collection and expenditure; and no payment can be made without its sanction.

The third council is not important, and does not, therefore, call for special remark. In addition to the above machinery of civil administration, there are subordinate agencies employed for the local government of the different districts. In connection with these agencies, Goa is divided into Velhas and Novas Conquistas. The former is subdivided into three districts (*concelhos*), viz. the Ilhas, Salsette, and Bardez, and each of these again into parishes, of which there are 93 in all. Every district has a municipal corporation, and is placed under the charge of a functionary called *Administrador do Concelho.* This officer is appointed by the Governor General, and is entrusted with duties of an administrative character, besides those connected with the public safety and health, and the due collection of taxes sanctioned by law. Every parish has likewise a minor council called *Junta da Parochia,* and has a magistrate called *Regedor,* whose duties are to inspect and direct the police establishment of the parish, keep a strict surveillance over liquor-shops, gaming-houses, etc., open wills and testaments, and report generally every important occurrence within its limits to the *Administrador*, to whom he is subordinate.

Similarly in each of the four divisions into which the Novas Conquistas are subdivided, there is an officer called *Administrador Fiscal,* who combines the duties usually performed by the *Administrador do Concelho* with those of the *Administrador das Communidades.* The functions of a *Regedor* are here exercised by a village Kulkarṇi. Of the abovenamed four divisions the first consists of Pernem; the second of Sanquelim or Sátari and Bicholim; the third of Pondá and Embarbacem; the fourth of Astagrar, Balli, Chandrováḍi, Cacorá and Canacona, with Cabo de Rama. Each of the subdivisions of the Velhas and Novas Conquistas is also known by the name of province.

The offices of Governor, Chief Secretary, Attorney General, and some other important functionaries are almost invariably filled by Europeans, while those of *Administrador do Concelho* and *Regedor* are held by natives.

The annual salary of the Governor is £1,250, and that of the Chief Secretary £305-11-1⅓.

The total expenditure for administrative purposes was in 1873-74 £27,069-2-0.

Muncipalities.—As stated above, there are three municipalities, the chief being that of the Ilhas. The receipts and expenditure of this in 1874-75 were estimated at £1232-15-0.

Revenue.—The total revenue of the State in 1873-74 was £112,473-18-10, and the expenditure £110,059-15-2. The chief sources of revenue are tithes on rice, cocoanuts, and salt; customs and postal dues; seal and stamp duties; tobacco licenses; licenses on liquor shops, etc.

CHAPTER VIII.

HISTORY—LIST OF THE VICEROYS AND GOVERNORS.

History.—The ancient history of Goa is involved in obscurity. The accounts handed down by the Puráṇas teem with legendary tales on which little historical reliance can be placed. Some of the inscriptions lately deciphered, however, show that Goa had long been the metropolis of a vast kingdom under the sway of the Kâdambas, whose first king, Trilochanakâdamba, is supposed by some antiquarians to have flourished in Kali Yuga 2601, or about B.C. 500. This dynasty continued to rule there till the latter part of the 13th century, when Goa became subject to the Yádavas of Devagiri. In 1312 it fell for the first time into the hands of the Muhammadans, who were, however, compelled to evacuate it in 1370, on their defeat by Vidyaranya Mádhava, the prime minister of Harihara of Vijayánagara, under whose successors it remained for about one hundred years. In 1469 it was conquered by Muhammad Gawan, the general and vizier of Muhammad II., the 13th Báhmani king of the Dakhaṇ, and incorporated into the dominions of that sovereign. After the downfall of this house, Goa became subject to the Adil Sháhi dynasty, reigning at Bijápur, about the time that Vasco de Gama landed at Calicut in 1498. This family retained possession of the city till the 17th February 1510, when it was captured by Affonso d'Albuquerque. But shortly afterwards Yusuf Adil Sháh, king of Bijápur, marched against the place with a considerable force, and retook it on the 23rd May of the same year. Reinforced, however, by the large armament that opportunely arrived from Portugal about this time on the coast of India, Albuquerque hastened back to Goa with the Portuguese fleet, and conquered the city a second time, after a sanguinary contest, on the 25th November. Immediately after this event, he occupied himself in fortifying the place, embellishing the city, and establishing there the Portuguese rule on a firm basis. From this time Goa began rapidly to rise in importance, and eventually became the metropolis of the Portuguese empire in the East, which is said to have been about 4000 leagues in extent. In 1543, during the governorship of Martim Affonso, who came to India along with the celebrated St. Francis Xavier, the two important provinces or *mahâls* of Salsette and Bardez were ceded to the Portuguese by Ibráhim Adil Sháh, who however, not long afterwards attempted to recover them, but, being foiled in his endeavours by the intrepidity of Dom João de Castro, had to abandon the project. To guard against any future invasion on the part of the Muhammadans, a scheme was formed to protect the eastern part of the island of Goa by means of a long wall, but before it was realized Ali Adil Sháh had marched against the city with an overwhelming force of a hundred thousand men and laid siege to it, in 1570; so bravely and effectively, however, was it defended by the little band within, under the Viceroy, Dom Luiz de Athaide, that the Muhammadan army, greatly thinned in numbers, retreated precipitately after a tedious siege of ten months' duration. This gallant defence of Goa, and the other important successes gained by the Portuguese over their foes in other parts of India, contributed to raise considerably their reputation as a military people, and to deter their enemies from attempting to attack their possessions. But about this period they were greatly alarmed by the appearance, on the coast of India, of a new and very formidable enemy. The Dutch, having shaken off the yoke of Spain, assumed a warlike attitude towards them on account of their connexion with that country, and began to annoy them in every quarter of the globe. Having come over to India with a large armament, this people blockaded Goa in 1603, but soon withdrew from the place. In other parts, however, they were more successful, wresting from the Portuguese several of their important possessions. These losses, together with the constant attacks to which the latter were exposed from the enemy, tended in a great measure to paralyze their once flourishing trade in the East, and from this time Goa began rapidly to decline. During the administration of the Count of Alvôr, this settlement was visited in 1683 by the predatory hordes of the Maráṭhás, but was, it is believed, preserved from falling into their hands by St. Francis Xavier. Subsequently the Bhonsles, from the Sávantváḍi State, invaded the territory, and though at the outset partially successful they were eventually defeated by the Portuguese, who took from them the islands of Corjuem and Panelem, and destroyed their fortress at Bicholim, besides inflicting on them other serious losses. To defend the place against the future inroads of these troublesome neighbours, the Viceroys who then governed the state built a fortress on the frontiers of Bardez, and another at Chaporá, between the years 1712 and 1717. Notwithstanding these defensive measures, the Bhonsles continued to harass Goa by their frequent inroads, but the Viceroy João de Saldanha da Gama successfully repelled their attacks, conquering from Phond Sávant the fortress of Bicholim, which was, however, offered to his son Nág Sávant, who had rebelled against his father. During the administration of the Count of Sandomil, which commenced in 1732 and ended in 1741, the Portuguese became once more involved in a war with the Maráṭhás, and lost some of their most important possessions towards the north of Goa. In the same year (1741) the latter renewed hostilities, and invaded the peninsulas of Salsette and Bardez, threatening the city of Goa itself, with a powerful body of horse. At the same time the Bhonsles, seeing the Portuguese thus hard pressed, availed themselves of their critical situation to overrun their settlement. While these things were going on, a new Viceroy arrived in Goa, the Marquis of Louriçal, bringing with him from Europe a reinforcement of twelve thousand men. With this army he encountered and overthrew the Maráṭhás at Bardez with great slaughter, captured the celebrated fortress of Pondá and other minor forts, and compelled them to retire from Goa. He then marched against the Bhonsles, and after a crushing defeat forced them to sue for peace, making their Chief, Khem Sávant, a tributary of the Portuguese. Not long afterwards, however, the Bhonsles renewed hostilities, but were on this occasion also overthrown by the Marquis of Castello Novo, who conquered Alorna (whence his later title), Tiracol, Neutim, Rarim and Sanquelim or Sátari. In 1750 the Maráṭhás and Bhonsles jointly attacked the fortress of Neutim, which they closely invested both by sea and land. The Viceroy, the Marquis of Tavora, hastened to the relief of the place with all the available force at his disposal, and compelled the enemy to raise the siege; after which he turned his arms against the king of Sunda,—who, like the Bhonsles, was continually annoying and ravaging the settlement of Goa,—and captured the fortress of Piro (Sadáshivgaḍh). His successor, the Count of Alva, prosecuted successfully for a time the war against the Maráṭhás, but eventually lost Rarim and Neutim, and was killed at the siege of one of the fortresses which had fallen into the hands of the enemy. These reverses of the Portuguese would most probably have been followed by others, had not the Maráṭhás become by this time involved in a war wlth another people, which necessitated the withdrawal of their forces from Goa. About this period the Court of Lisbon sent peremptory orders to the Viceroy, the Count of Ega, to restore the fortresses of Piro and Ximpem to the king of Sunda, and of Bicholim, Sanquelim, and Alorna to Khem Sávant II. Subsequently, however, the former allowed the Portuguese to possess themselves of Pondá, with the adjacent territory of Zambaulim, Cabo de Rama, and Canacona, during the time that his dominions were invaded by Haidar Ali. After some years of repose, Khem Sávant again attempted to disturb the Portuguese, but, being defeated, had to surrender to them Bicholim, Sanquelim or Sátari, Alorna, and Pernem. From 1794 to 1815 the territory of Goa and other Portuguese settlements in India received little attention or help from the Court of Lisbon, owing to various causes, the chief of which was the invasion of the Iberian peninsula by the French. To protect the former, however, against any contingency, an English auxiliary force was allowed to garrison the two fortresses commanding its port till the general peace in Europe after the battle of Waterloo. In 1817 the Viceroy, the Count of Rio Pardo, repelled the inroads of the predatory forces from the Sávantváḍi State, capturing the fortresses of Uspá and Rarim. This Governor was, however, deposed in consequence of a revolution which took place in 1821, in which year a constitutional system of government was proclaimed in Goa. In 1835 a native of the place, named Bernardo Peres da Silva, was appointed Governor or Prefect of the Portuguese State of India by Dona Maria II., in return for his loyalty and adherence to the house of Braganza during the usurpation of Dom Miguel. But his reforms in Goa during the seventeen days of his government provoked a disturbance, fomented by his adversaries, which ended in much bloodshed and his own flight to Bombay. For about sixteen years after this event Goa, except a military rebellion in 1842, was undisturbed either by external foes or internal dissensions. During the administration of Pestana, however, the insurrection at Sávantváḍi, and the shelter afforded in Goa to the rebels who had fled thither, threatened at first to bring about a rupture between the governments of Bombay and Goa. But, owing to the prudence of both governments, their differences were in a short time satisfactorily settled. In 1852 the Ráṇes of Sátari, headed by Dipú or Dipáji, raised the standard of revolt, which was quelled with difficulty after an obstinate and protracted resistance. In 1871 a rebellion of the military force at Goa broke out, in consequence of the refusal of the Government to grant their exorbitant demands. To suppress this insurrection the Court of Lisbon despatched a reinforcement, accompanied by the King's own brother, Dom Augusto. On the restoration of peace the regiments that had revolted were disbanded.

List of Viceroys and Governors.—During the Portuguese ascendancy in the East the Viceroys and Governors displayed much of the pomp and pageantry characteristic of Oriental courts. The first title was, comparatively speaking, conferred on a few of those sent to Goa, as a mark of special favour from the King, while the other was more general. Both of these were changed in 1774 into that of Captain General, but soon afterwards were restored. They were finally replaced by that of Governor General, which is still in use. At first on the death or in the absence of a Viceroy or Governor the administration of the State vested generally in the persons mentioned in a royal patent called *Via de Successão*, or 'The Way or Patent of Succession,' but nowadays it devolves on a Council composed of the chief functionaries of the country. The following is a list of the Viceroys, Governors, &c., from the earliest times to the present date:—

1. Dom Francisco de Almeida, the first Viceroy, left Lisbon on 25th March 1505, arrived in India on 12th September following, and after four years of administration was murdered on his return voyage by some negroes at the Cape of Good Hope, on the 1st of March 1510.

2. Affonso de Albuquerque succeeded the preceding Viceroy, with the title of Governor, towards the end of October of the year 1509, and on his return from Ormuz died in the harbour of Goa on 16th December 1515.

3. Lopo Soares de Albergaria succeeded Albuquerque on 8th September 1515, and returned to Portugal on 20th January 1519.

4. Diogo Lopes de Siqueira, the next Governor, arrived in Goa on 8th September 1518, and remained there till 22nd January 1522.

5. Dom Duarte de Menezes took charge of the government in January 1522, and left Goa for Portugal in December 1524.

6. Dom Vasco da Gama, Count of Vidigueira, came as 2nd Viceroy in September 1524, and died in Cochin on 24th December following.

7. Dom Henrique de Menezes assumed the government, according to a patent of succession, on 17th January 1525, and continued to exercise his functions till his death, on 21st February 1526.

8. Lopo Vaz de Sampaio succeeded the foregoing in virtue of a royal patent of succession, and governed till 18th November 1529, when he was sent to Portugal in chains.

9. Nuno da Cunha left Lisbon on 18th April, arrived in Goa on 22nd October, and took charge on 18th November 1529. He governed till 14th September 1538, and died on his voyage back to Portugal.

10. Dom Garcia de Noronha, the 3rd Viceroy, arrived in Goa on 14th September 1538, and died on 3rd April 1540.

11. Dom Estevão da Gama, son of Vasco da Gama, succeeded the foregoing by a patent of succession, and governed till 6th May 1542, when he returned to Portugal.

12. Martim Affonso de Souza took charge on the day following his arrival from Portugal, on 7th May 1542. His administration lasted till 10th September 1545.

13. Dom João de Castro, who came out as Governor on 10th September 1545, was promoted to the rank of Viceroy in 1547, but died on the 6th June of the following year.

14. Garcia de Sá assumed the government in virtue of a royal patent of succession, and died on 13th June 1549.

15. Jorge Cabral also took charge in virtue of a similar patent, and governed till November 1550.

16. Dom Affonso de Noronha, the 5th Viceroy, arrived in Cochin in November 1550, and took charge immediately. His administration lasted till 23rd September 1554.

17. Dom Pedro Mascarenhas, the 6th Viceroy, arrived in Goa on the 23rd September 1554, and governed till the 16th June 1555, when he died.

18. Francisco Barreto assumed the government in virtue of a patent of succession, and ruled till 8th September 1558.

19. Dom Constantino de Bragança, the 7th Viceroy, came out to India on the 3rd September 1558, and governed till 7th September 1561.

20. Dom Francisco Coutinho, Count of Redondo, the 8th Viceroy, left Portugal on 15th March, arriving in Goa on 7th September 1561. He died on the 19th February 1564.

21. João de Mendonça governed till 3rd September 1564, in pursuance of a patent of succession.

22. Dom Antão de Noronha, the 9th Viceroy, arrived in Goa from Portugal on 3rd September 1564, and governed till 10th September 1568.

23. Dom Luiz de Athaide, the 10th Viceroy, came out to India and assumed the government on the above date. His administration lasted till the 6th September 1571.

24. Dom Antonio de Noronha, the 11th Viceroy, arrived in Goa from Portugal on the 6th September 1571; he was relieved of his office on 9th December 1573 by a royal letter.

25. Antonio Moniz Barreto succeeded the above on the same date, and governed till September 1576.

26. Dom Diogo de Menezes succeeded the foregoing in virtue of a royal patent of succession, and governed till 31st August 1578.

27. Dom Luiz de Athaide came out to India a second time as Viceroy on the 31st August 1578, and died in Goa on the 10th March 1581.

28. Fernão Telles de Menezes assumed the government after the death of the above, and continued in power till 17th September 1581.

29. Dom Francisco Mascarenhas, Count of Villa da Horta, was the 13th Viceroy. He arrived in Goa on 16th September 1581, and governed till November 1584.

30. Dom Duarte de Menezes, Count of Tarouca, the 14th Viceroy, arrived on 25th October 1584, and died on 4th May 1588.

31. Manuel de Souza Coutinho assumed the government in virtue of a patent of succession. His administration lasted till the 15th May 1591.

32. Mathias de Albuquerque, the 15th Viceroy, arrived on the 15th May 1591, and governed till 25th May 1597, when he returned to Portugal.

33. Dom Francisco da Gama, Count of Vidigueira, and grandson of Vasco da Gama, arrived on 22nd May 1597, and took charge immediately afterwards. His administration lasted till 25th December 1600.

34. Ayres de Saldanha, the 17th Viceroy, came out to India on 25th December 1600, and governed till the middle of January 1605.

35. Martim Affonso de Castro, the 18th Viceroy, arrived in January 1605, and died in Malacca on 3rd June 1607.

36. Dom Fr. Aleixo de Menezes, Archbishop of Goa, held the reins of government, in virtue of a patent of succession, till 27th May 1609.

37. André Furtado de Mendonça governed three months and eight days, when he returned to Portugal.

38. Ruy Lourenço de Tavora, the 19th Viceroy, commenced his administration on 5th September 1609, which continued till about the close of 1612.

39. Dom Jeronimo de Azevedo, the 20th Viceroy, assumed the administration of the State on the 15th December 1612, and governed till 18th November 1617.

40. Dom João Coutinho, Count of Redondo and 21st Viceroy, took charge on 18th November 1617, and died on 10th November 1619.

41. Fernão de Albuquerque succeeded the above, in virtue of a patent of succession, on the 11th November 1619. His administration terminated on the 19th December 1622.

42. Dom Francisco da Gama, Count of Vidigueira, came out to India as Viceroy for the second time on 19th December 1622. His government lasted till the end of January 1627.

43. Dom Fr. Luiz de Brito, Bishop of Meliapur, succeeded the above as Governor by a patent of succession, and died on 29th July 1628. After his death the affairs of the State were entrusted to a committee.

44. Dom Miguel de Noronha, Count of Linhares, the 23rd Viceroy, reached Goa on 21st October 1629, taking charge on the next day. He governed till 8th December 1635, when he returned to Portugal.

45. Pero da Silva, the 24th Viceroy, came out to India on 8th December 1635, and governed till 24th June 1639.

46. Antonio Telles de Menezes assumed charge on 4th October 1639, and governed till 21st September of the following year.

47. João da Silva Tello de Menezes, Count of Aveiras, the 25th Viceroy, arrived on 20th September 1640, and governed till 1646.

48. Dom Filippe Mascarenhas, the 26th Viceroy, took charge in Goa on 30th December 1646, and governed till 31st May 1651. Pending the arrival of his successor, a committee was entrusted with the administration of the State.

49. Dom Vasco Mascarenhas, Count of Obidos, came out as 27th Viceroy on 3rd September 1652; he was deposed, in consequence of a rebellion which took place on 22nd October 1653, the government having been usurped by Dom Braz de Castro, who fomented and headed the rebellion.

50. Dom Rodrigo Lobo da Silveira, Count of Sarzedas, the 28th Viceroy, left Lisbon on 23rd March, and arrived in Goa on the 19th August 1655. He died on 3rd January 1656. In the interval between his death and the arrival of his successor, the government was provisionally entrusted to several persons.

51. Antonio de Mello e Castro came out to India at first simply as Governor, and was subsequently raised to the rank of Viceroy. He governed till 1666.

52. João Nunes da Cunha, Count of St. Vincent, the 30th Viceroy, arrived in India on the 11th October 1666, and died on 6th November 1668. After his death the government was entrusted to the persons appointed in the patent of succession.

53. Luis de Mendonça Furtado de Albuquerque, Count of Lavradio, 31st Viceroy, arrived in Goa on the 20th May 1671, and took charge on the 22nd. His government lasted till 30th October 1677.

54. Dom Pedro de Almeida, Count of Assumar, came as 32nd Viceroy on 28th October 1677, and left Goa on 27th January 1678, having been ordered to proceed to Mozambique, where he died in March following. In his absence the government was entrusted to the persons appointed by a patent of succession.

55. Francisco de Tavora, Count of Alvôr, 33rd Viceroy, go-

verned from 12th September 1681 to 3rd December 1686, leaving for Portugal on the 15th of the same month.

56. Dom Rodrigo da Costa governed, in virtue of a royal patent, from 1686 to 1690, when he died.

57. Dom Miguel de Almeida held the reins of government, in pursuance also of a patent of succession, from June 1690 to January 1691, when he died. The administration devolved for a time on the nominees of a new patent.

58. Dom Pedro Antonio de Noronha, Count of Villa Verde, came as 34th Viceroy on 26th May 1693, and continued at the head of the government till 20th September 1698.

59. Antonio Luiz Gonçalves da Camara Coutinho, 35th Viceroy, assumed charge on 20th September 1698, and governed till 17th September 1701, when the persons mentioned in the patent were placed at the head of the administration.

60. Caetano de Mello de Castro, 36th Viceroy, governed from 2nd October 1702 till 29th October 1707, when he returned to Portugal.

61. Dom Rodrigo da Costa succeeded the above as 37th Viceroy on the same date, and governed till 21st September 1712.

62. Vasco Fernandes Cesar de Menezes, 38th Viceroy, arrived in Goa on 16th September 1712, and took charge five days afterwards. His government lasted till 13th January 1717.

63. Dom Sebastião d'Andrade Pessanha, Archbishop of Goa, became Governor, pursuant to a royal patent, on 13th January 1717, continuing as such till 16th October following.

64. Dom Luiz de Menezes, Count of Ericeira, came as 39th Viceroy on 9th October 1717, and took charge seven days after. His government lasted till 14th September 1720.

65. Francisco José de Sampaio e Castro, 40th Viceroy, came from Lisbon on 12th September 1720, and assumed the government two days after. He died on 13th July 1723.

66. Dom Christovão de Mello was Governor, in virtue of a royal patent, from 13th July to 3rd September 1723, when the administration devolved on the nominees of a new patent.

67. João de Saldanha da Gama, the 41st Viceroy, was at the helm of the State from 28th October 1725 to 23rd January

1732, on which date he made over the government to the persons named in a royal patent.

68. Dom Pedro Mascarenhas, Count of Sandomil, 42nd Viceroy, directed the affairs of the State from 7th October 1732 to 18th May 1741, when he returned to Portugal.

69. Dom Luiz de Menezes, Count of Ericeira, and afterwards first Marquis of Louriçal, was the 43rd Viceroy, and governed from 18th May 1741 to 12th June 1742, when he died. After his death the government became vested in the persons named in a royal patent.

70. Dom Pedro Miguel de Almeida e Portugal, Count of Assumar, and first Marquis of Castello Novo, and afterwards Marquis of Alorna, came out to India as 44th Viceroy on 24th September 1744, and returned to Portugal on 27th September 1750.

71. Francisco Assis, Marquis of Tavora, and 45th Viceroy, took charge on his arrival in Goa on 27th September 1750. He returned to Portugal on 18th September 1754.

72. Dom Luiz Mascarenhas, Count of Alva, came as 46th Viceroy on 18th September 1754, and governed till 28th June 1756, when he was killed by the Maráṭhás. Pending the arrival of his successor, the government was entrusted to the persons mentioned in the royal patent.

73. Manoel da Saldanha de Albuquerque, Count of Ega, was appointed 47th Viceroy, and assumed the government on 23rd September 1756. He returned to Portugal, giving over charge of the administration to the nominees of a royal patent.

74. Dom João José de Mello was Governor from 12th March 1768 to 10th January 1774, when he died.

75. Filippe de Valladares Souto Maior was at the head of the State, in pursuance of a patent of succession, from 13th January to 24th September 1774.

76. Dom José Pedro de Camara, Governor and Captain General, took charge on 24th September 1774, and governed till 26th May 1779, when he returned to Portugal.

77. Dom Frederico Guilherme de Souza took charge on 26th May 1779, and remained in office till 3rd November 1786.

78. Francisco da Cunha e Menezes succeeded as Governor and Captain General on the last mentioned date, and managed the affairs of the State till 22nd May 1794.

79. Francisco Antonio da Veiga Cabral, at first Commander in-Chief of the Goa Army, took charge of the government of the State on 22nd May 1794, and continued in office till 30th May 1807. He was subsequently created Viscount of Mirandella.

80. Bernardo José de Lorena, Count of Sarzedas, came as 48th Viceroy, and took charge on the above date. He governed till 29th November 1816.

81. Dom Diogo de Souza, Count of Rio Pardo, 49th Viceroy, entered in office on 29th November 1816, and was deposed in consequence of a military rebellion on 16th September 1821. After his deposition, two provisional committees were successively entrusted with the administration till 18th November 1822.

82. Dom Manoel de Camara, 50th Viceroy, governed from the last mentioned date till 16th November 1825, when he died. The administration consequently devolved on a committee presided over by the Archbishop.

83. Dom Manoel de Portugal e Castro, the 51st and last Viceroy, governed from 9th October 1827 to 14th January 1835.

84. Bernardo Peres da Silva, a native of Goa, came from Portugal with the title of Prefect on 10th January 1835, and took charge four days afterwards. He was deposed, in consequence of a military rebellion, on the 1st February following. Several provisional committees were successively entrusted with the government till 22nd November 1837.

85. Simão Infante de Lacerda, Baron of Sabroso, appointed Governor General, assumed charge on 23rd November 1837, and died on 14th October 1838. A council composed of the chief authorities managed the affairs both during his illness and after his death.

86. José Antonio Vieira da Fonseca acted as Governor from 5th March to 14th November 1839.

87. Manoel José Mendes, Barão de Candal, arrived in Goa on 12th November 1839, and died on 18th April 1840, a council assuming in consequence the administration of the State.

88. José Joaquim Lopes de Lima acted as Governor from 24th September 1840 to 27th April 1842, being compelled to leave Goa owing to a military revolt. A council assumed consequently the reins of government.

89. Francisco Xavier da Silva Pereira, Count of Antas, took charge on 19th September 1842, and governed till 25th April 1843.

90. Joaquim Mourão Garces Palha governed from 25th April 1843 to 20th May 1844.

91. José Ferreira Pestana assumed the reins of government on the last mentioned date, and ruled till the 15th January 1851, returning some time after to Portugal.

92. José Joaquim Januario Lapa, Baron and afterwards Viscount of Villa Nova de Ourem, governed from 15th January 1851 to 6th May 1855, leaving the administration in the hands of a council.

93. Antonio Cesar de Vasconcellos Correia, Viscount and afterwards Count of Torres Novas, took charge on 3rd November 1855, and governed till 25th December 1864.

94. José Ferreira Pestana, appointed Governor General for the second time, directed the helm of government from the last mentioned date till 7th May 1870.

95. Januario Correia de Almeida, Viscount of St. Januario, came as Governor General on 5th May 1870, and took charge on the 7th idem, governing till 12th December 1871.

96. Joaquim José Macedo e Couto succeeded the above on the same date, and continued as Governor General till 10th May 1875.

97. João Tavares de Almeida took charge on 10th May 1875, and died on 24th July 1877. The administration devolved after his death on a council, presided over by the Archbishop.

98. Antonio Sergio de Souza, Viscount, came as Governor General, and assumed charge of his office on 12th November 1877. He died on 3rd May 1878, when a council, presided over by the same Archbishop, again assumed the administration.

99. Caetano Alexandre de Almeida e Albuquerque was appointed Governor General by the royal decree of 9th May 1878. He has not yet arrived from Portugal, but is expected shortly.

CHAPTER IX.

THE CITY AND TOWNS—POLYMETRICAL TABLE OF DISTANCES OF IMPORTANT PLACES FROM THE CITY AND FROM EACH OTHER.

The City.—PANGIM lies in 15° 30′ N. Latitude and 73° 53′ E. Longitude, on the left or southern bank of the river Mandovi, at a distance of about five miles from its mouth. It has one mile of river frontage to the north, and occupies a narrow strip of the village of Taleigão, which is bounded on the east by a causeway connecting it with Ribandar, on the south by a hill, and on the west by an esplanade. Pangim with Ribandar and the old city of Goa constitutes the modern capital of Portuguese India, called Nova Goa or New Goa, though this name is commonly applied to Pangim alone. Its population numbered in 1827 about 9,000 souls; in 1851, 9,800; and in 1865, 14,134: at present it is estimated at 15,000. In the vernacular dialect of the country it is called *Pongi*, meaning probably 'arable land that cannot be inundated.'

Pangim was once a miserable place full of stagnant pools, and inhabited principally by fishermen and other poor people dwelling in huts. During the Muhammadan sway it was only remarkable for the castle of Yusuf Adil Sháh, which is now transformed into the viceregal palace. At some distance from it stood a fort or bulwark on the neighbouring hill, amidst a dense forest, from which in after years during the Portuguese rule, firewood, according to a document of 1524, was cut and sold. This bulwark was but ill constructed, while the castle was strongly built and defended by fifteen guns and a garrison of about three hundred soldiers. It was from the castle that the Muhammadans under Yusuf Gurji offered a vigorous resistance to Albuquerque on his first invasion of

Goa in 1510, and it was within view of the castle that his fleet lay at anchor during the rainy season following his expulsion from the city by the overwhelming forces of the king of Bijápur.

After the second capture of Goa by the Portuguese, Pangim was selected as an important military station, in consequence of which a new bastion with a breastwork was erected, and the castle of the Muhammadans, which had been partly burnt by Albuquerque, was repaired. The castle was placed under the command of Captain Pero de Freitas, who was stationed there with two hundred sepoys to guard the city against any foreign attack on that side of the river. As a precautionary measure, all the ships that entered or left the river were subjected to the inspection of the Captain, and obliged to obtain passports from him. In course of time a few houses were built in Pangim, in one of which a brother of the famous king of Cambay, Bahádur Sháh, is said to have lodged during his sojourn in Goa in 1533. About the same period a chapel dedicated to *Nossa Senhora da Conceição* was erected there at the public expense, and was the first sacred edifice raised outside of the old city of Goa. This chapel, endowed in 1541 with an annual sum of £1-13-4, accruing from the rents of the property once belonging to some Hindu pagodas, was converted thirteen years later into a parish church. About this period an asylum was also built there, and then a college. The former afforded, till 1567, shelter to such ladies as had offended their husbands by their guilty conduct and fled from their homes to avoid being put to death. The latter, founded in 1584 and called *Collegio de São Thomé* (College of St. Thomas), stood on a hill adjoining the above church, but was transferred in 1596 to Banguenim.

Except these, Pangim possessed at this period few buildings worth mentioning, and was almost an isolated and secluded spot. Yet, owing to its convenient situation, it was often selected as a place for embarking troops or fitting out expeditions to various parts of the East, and during the first century of the Portuguese ascendancy it formed a temporary residence for the Viceroys and Governors on their arrival from, or departure to, Portugal. Ordinarily, it was the rendezvous of fishermen and native sailors, who went thither to haul up their boats on the margin of the river. In the middle of the 16th century a great portion of this margin was bestowed as a grant on a lady named Isabella Fernandes, who raised thereon a wall, causing so much inconvenience to its inhabitants that the Government, in consequence of their repeated complaints, cancelled the grant and transferred the place to the custody of the municipality of the city. This corporation erected there a causeway, of which few or no traces now remain.

During the 17th century Pangim continued still to be inhabited chiefly by fishermen and ordinary artizans. Yet there were many country-houses owned by Portuguese grandees and other wealthy persons. In consequence of the terrible epidemic which was then raging in the old city of Goa and its suburbs, the viceregal residence was transferred to this place in 1759, from which year dates its gradual rise. In 1811 the Custom-house was also removed thither, followed soon after by the Accountant General's Office, the High Court, the Chancery and other public offices, so that its population began steadily to increase. Several well-to-do people, and amongst them many public servants, fixed their habitation there. During the administration of Dom Manuel de Portugal e Castro (1827-35) Pangim was raised to its present conspicuous position, at an expense of £36,607-5-0, having been reclaimed from the stagnant pools with which it formerly abounded, and considerably improved by the construction of new roads and public edifices. In 1843 it was formally declared by a royal decree to be the capital of Portuguese India, and is now the seat of the Governor, the Archbishop, and all the chief authorities of Goa. From the river the appearance of the city, with its row of public and private buildings all along the principal road, called *Rua de Boa Vista,* is picturesque. The public edifices are double-storied and of a simple style. Most of the private buildings are also double-storied and are neatly painted.

The first edifice that meets the sight on touching the principal pier is the Custom-house (*Alfandega*). This is the highest building in Pangim, and is 108 feet long and 72 broad. Its upper story consists of somewhat spacious halls, and is occupied by the office establishment, while the groundfloor is used as a warehouse. Close to the Custom-house, on its eastern side, is seen the Governor's Palace. As already stated, it was originally a Muhammadan castle, and was transformed into the viceregal residence about the middle of the 18th century, as is shown by the following inscription on the gate facing the river :—

> "Rege Fidelissimo Josepho primo,
> Pro Rege Comite ab Ega,
> Senatus ex informi formavit. 1760."

Translation.

"During the reign of the most faithful King Joseph I., and the government of Viceroy the Count of Ega, the Senate transformed the building [into the viceregal palace]. 1760."

It is a double-storied edifice, facing the south, and commanding a beautiful view on the river-side. The entrance hall is adorned with the portraits of the Viceroys and Governors of Goa. The principal hall, which is towards the north, is called *sala de docel*, where a large portrait of the reigning King is hung and the chief state ceremonials take place. On the groundfloor there is, besides the civil and military departments of the Secretariat, a chapel in the vestry of which is seen the image of Christ which once belonged to the famous tribunal of the Inquisition.

Opposite the Palace lies the *Contadoria Geral*, or the Accountant General's Office. It is a large building, 249 feet long and 128 broad, and possesses good accommodation. Some rooms on the groundfloor are occupied by the Post Office.

A few paces further lie the Jail, the Telegraph Office, and, at the end of the road called *Rua da Relação*, the High Court, the last of these being a building 88 feet long and 82 broad, and accommodating also the District Court and the Supreme

Military Tribunal. To the south of the High Court is situated the most populous and extensive quarter of Pangim, designated *Fontainhas*. The chief road leading to it is called *Rua de 4 de Abril*. It commences almost opposite the fish bazaar, and terminates near a well-built fountain called *Phœnix*. Bordering on the eastern edge of the *Fontainhas* runs the road, still under construction, called *Rua Nova de Ourem*.

Returning to the principal road already mentioned (*Rua da Boa Vista*), and proceeding south-west from the square in front of the Governor's palace through a street called *Rua de Conceição*, we come to the parochial church of *Nossa Senhora da Conceição*, standing prominently on the slope of a hill: though inferior in size to many other churches of Goa, yet its interior is well decorated. Close to the church lies a cemetery, the walls of which are adorned by pictures formerly belonging to the convents of the old city. On the summit of the hill stands a banyan tree, which serves as a pilot's mark to the entrance of the port, and near it there is a semaphore. From this standpoint a beautiful panoramic view is enjoyed not only of Pangim, but also of the sea, the river, and the surrounding fortresses and villages.

At the foot of the hill a few paces to the south are seen a mosque which is a small and wretched building, and a Hindu pagoda built in 1818 and dedicated to Mahálakshmí. Close to this temple is a pretty fountain known as *Cabeça de Vacca*, so called from an artificial spout shaped like a cow's head, through which the water flows.

To the north-west of the Muhammadan mosque, in the square called *Praça das Flores*, is the Town Hall (*Camara Municipal*), 72 feet long and 105 broad. In its principal hall, which is pretty large and adorned with the portraits of the King of Portugal, Vasco da Gama, and Affonso de Albuquerque, the chief municipal corporation of Goa holds its meetings, and in another hall the *Camara Agraria*, which represents all the village communities of the district of the Ilhas. In the latter is seen the portrait of Bernardo Peres da Silva, the only native of Goa who held the post of Governor. The lower rooms are occupied by the offices of the two chief *Administradores* or collectors of the Ilhas. Facing the building lies a square with a garden, named after the reigning sovereign, Dom Luis.

Proceeding a few paces further from the northern extremity of the garden, we come back to the Custom-house, in the principal street or *Rua de Boa Vista.* To the east of this building is seen the Archbishop's Palace; it was lately fitted up for this purpose, and has not the imposing aspect of the three ancient palaces in which the Primates of the East formerly resided. Connected with it towards the south is the Public Works' Office.

To the west of the Archbishop's Palace are the Barracks, the largest building in tho city, erected in 1832 at a cost of £13,006-17-7. It is of a quadrangular form with an open space in the middle, and is 498 long by 521 broad. On its principal door is read the following inscription :—

"Naõ vos hade faltar gente famosa,
Honra, valor e fama gloriosa,
No bom e feliz governo do
Illmo. e Exmo. Sr. D. Manoel de Portugal e Castro V. Rei da India,
Anno de 1832."

Translation.

"You will not want distinguished persons, honour, valour and glorious fame during the good and prosperous government of the most illustrious and excellent Dom Manoel de Portugal e Castro, Viceroy of India, 1832."

Besides the accommodation for the military force stationed in the capital, as well as for a chapel and a theatre, the eastern wing of the building is occupied by the High School or *Lyceu Nacional,* by the *Instituto Professional,* where chemistry, agriculture and other practical sciences are taught, and by the Public Library. The daily attendance in this library is considerable. There are many old books brought from the convents, but none of them are of great importance, except some manuscripts—Indian vocabularies, a Portuguese and

Tamil grammar and dictionary, also grammars of the Tamil and Malayalam languages, and a *Dictionarium Malabaricum.*

The square facing the barracks is graced by a life-size statue of Albuquerque, the same which formerly stood in a niche in the façade of the Church of *Nossa Senhora da Serra* in the old city. The present monument consists of a cupola supported by large columns which once adorned the convent of St. Dominic; in the middle stands on a high pedestal the conqueror of Goa in an imposing attitude. It was set up there amid great pomp, on 29th October 1847, by the Governor, José Fereira Pestana, who recited on the occasion an appropriate panegyric in verse to the memory of the Portuguese hero.

Close to the barracks to the west are the new Bazaar and the Government Printing Office, and a few paces further the Military Hospital with its chapel, and adjoining it the Medical School, which have nothing in them worth mentioning. At the furthest limit of the city to the west lies the esplanade, called since 1838 *Campo de Dom Manoel;* it was formed by orders of the Viceroy Dom Manoel de Portugal e Castro, from whom it derives its name, and is a fashionable resort for evening recreation. It is enclosed by a small wall from north to south, having two piers on both sides, and a semicircular seat in the middle between two pillars. On the northern and southern extremities of it there are two bridges, those of Minerva and Santa Ignez, both seats and railing, as well as pillars, bearing the arms of the Senate and several inscriptions.

To the south-west limit of Pangim, on a spot where the Road of Santa Ignez begins, are seen the ruins of one of the ancient palaces of the Archbishop. The same road leads through Caranzalem, a place much frequented during the hot season by the higher classes, to enjoy the sea-breeze, to the extreme point of the island called *Cabo,* where is the summer palace of the Governor.

Towns.—MARGÃO lies in 15° 18′ N. Lat. and 74° 1′ E. Long., in a beautiful plain in the centre of the province of Salsette, and in the proximity of the Sal river. It is about 16 miles distant from the capital. The population of Margão in 1851 was 13,193, but has now increased to 15,178, of which 13,128 are Christians, 2,000 Hindus, and 50 Muhammadans. The number of houses is 3,298. Its revenue is estimated at £13,096-2-6, of which rice yields £9,314-7-6, cocoanut plantations £3,335-4-0, salt £118-16-9, and cereals and fruits £327-14-3. Margão, according to a Hindu tradition, was one of the early seats of the Aryan settlers of Goa, and the site of the chief *maṭha* or convent, whence its name *Maṭhagráma*, or 'the village of the convent,' which was corrupted into *Margão*. The village is connected with Paraśuráma's legend, and during the Hindu and the Muhammadan rule appears to have been considered a place of great importance. At the time of the Portuguese conquest it was in a flourishing condition and contained many well constructed buildings, the most remarkable of which was a Hindu temple. It is described by an old Portugese chronicler as being so large and strongly built that the Muhammadans, when they invaded Salsette, occupied it as a good military post. According to a tradition, this temple was consecrated to the memory of a native of Margão, by name Makáji Dámodar, who having met a tragic death on the spot with his newly married spouse received the honours of a god. There were besides nine other pagodas in the same village, all of which were destroyed by Diogo Rodrigues, captain of Rachol, who was rewarded with the revenues of the lands belonging to them.

Christianity was introduced into Margão by the Jesuit Fathers about the year 1560; and in 1565 a church was erected there, on the ruins of the chief pagoda just mentioned, at the desire of the first Archbishop, Dom Gaspar de Leão Pereira, the idol of Dámodar being removed to Zambaulim. This church was burnt by the Muhammadans during the government of Dom Luiz de Athaide, and was rebuilt in 1585; and having afterwards fallen into decay was reconstructed in 1645 as it is seen at present. It is one of the largest and best constructed churches of Goa, and has a beautiful façade and eight altars. The chief of these is dedicated to the Holy Ghost, the patron of the Church, and one of the side ones is adorned with the image of St. Roch, through whose intercession the village is said to have been delivered from a fearful epidemic which raged there from 1772 to 1776. There are some epitaphs in the pavement of the church, and under the chief altar there is said to be a slab of black stone which covers the grave of a native child killed with some Jesuit fathers at Cuncolim.

The Jesuits had also built a college at Margão in 1574, which was subsequently removed to Rachol; they had also in 1575 an hospital where poor men, no matter of what creed, were treated with great care.

Margão, though for some time exposed to the incursions of the Muhammadans and Maráṭhás, was always in a prosperous state, and inhabited by many rich families. Of late it has been considerably improved; many public and private buildings have been erected, which impart to it a beautiful aspect. It was raised to the rank of a town by a royal decree of the 3rd April 1778. There are at present five chapels, one of which, built in 1595 at Nuvem, is particularly mentioned by the author of the *Oriente Conquistado.* The Town Hall (*Camara Municipal*) is a double-storied edifice facing the east, built in 1770 and rebuilt in 1873; here the Municipal Corporation of Salsette holds its meetings. Near it is the Jail, with its chapel, built in 1817. The groundfloor is reserved for the prisoners, and the upper storey set apart for the Agrarian Chamber (*Camera Agraria*) and the Court of the District Judge (*Juiz de Direito*). There are also other buildings occupied by the Government Schools, the Theatre, and the Asylum called *Asilo do Sagrado Coração de Maria,* which was founded in 1866, and has a chapel of its own. On the western side of the town there are military Barracks, built in 1811, formerly occupied by a regiment, but at present by the police and a military force, as well as the Post Office. There is a bazaar at Margão, with 74 well-provided stalls, which supplies provisions to the people of Salsette, the daily consumption being estimated at from £350 to £500. There is also an association called *Monte Pio*

.(a family pension fund), and a printing press, from which a weekly newspaper is issued.

Adjoining the chief buildings of the town rises a hill crowned by a chapel dedicated to *Nossa Senhora de Piedade*, who is regarded by the people of the locality as their special patroness. The chapel was originally constructed by the Jesuit Fathers and dedicated to the Holy Cross, with the view, as their own chronicler states, of delivering the place from the annoyances of the evil spirits by which it was then haunted. It was rebuilt in 1820, and the image of *Nossa Senhora de Piedade*, which was in the church, was transferred to the chapel in a solemn procession in which the Archbishop of Goa and the Bishop of Hieropolis took part. The chapel is well decorated and richly endowed. The top of the hill commands a beautiful view, not only of the town, but also of the sea and the surrounding villages.

MAPUÇÁ lies in 15° 36′ N. Lat. and 73° 52′ E. Long., at a distance of about eight miles from Pangim, and is bounded on the east by the river of the same name, which is a branch of the Mandovi. Occupying almost a central position in Bardez, of which province it is the capital, it is one of the most important commercial places in the whole territory of Goa. Its population consists of 12,000 souls, of whom 7,000 are Christians and 5,000 Hindus. There are about 3,151 houses in it. As a parish it comprises three village communities, the chief of which bears the same name, and the other two are known as Cunchelim and Corlim respectively: of these the first yields a revenue of about £908.

Mapuçá appears formerly to have enjoyed some celebrity among the surrounding villages, chiefly on account of a great fair held there every Friday, whence, according to some, it takes its name—from *máp*, 'measure,' and *çá*, 'to fill up,' *i.e.* 'the place of measuring or selling goods.' In other respects it does not seem to have attracted much notice.

After the Portuguese conquest of Goa, Christianity was introduced into Bardez by the Franciscans, and a church was built at Mapuça in 1594, chiefly through the exertions of Father Jeronimo de Espirito Santo, on the ruins of the chief pagoda of the place, the idol having been removed to Dargalim, in the Pernem Mahál. This church was rebuilt in 1779. Being destroyed by fire in 1838, it was constructed anew in its present form. It contains three altars, over the middle of which is seen the image of *Nossa Senhora de Milagres* (Our Lady of Miracles). This image is held in great veneration not only by the Christians but also by the Hindus. On the day of her feast, which is solemnized on the second Monday after Easter, men of every class and creed come in crowds, not only from Goa, but also from the adjoining places, bringing offerings to the Virgin in token of gratitude for the favours received through her intercession. On the same occasion a fair takes place, which lasts for five days, and is one of the best held in Goa.

In addition to this church there are six chapels, and some other public buildings very recently erected. To the west of the church is seen the Asylum of Our Lady of Miracles, where the poor and the destitute are supported by public charity. A little further lie the Jail and the Bazaar, the latter being well built and much frequented especially on Fridays by people from distant villages. To the west of the Bazaar on a little eminence stands the Town Hall, which is the best building in the place. In its principal hall, adorned with portraits of the King of Portugal and some other personages, the Municipal Chamber of Bardez holds its meetings, while in the apartment to the south on the same floor is located the office of the Collector or *Administrador do Conselho*, and to the north the Court of the District Judge or *Juiz de Direito*. In one of the apartments on the groundfloor is accommodated the office of the *Administrador das Communidades*, and in another the *Camara Agraria* holds its sittings. In front of the Town Hall runs the Royal Street, leading to Duller,—a ward which contains a range of beautiful houses newly constructed,—and passing through several villages on the northern confines of the territory of Goa.

Leaving the Town Hall and proceeding westward by the same street are seen two rows of houses, and at its extremity a large open plain through which the same road runs to the vicinity of Pangim. Near the plain stands the hill of Guirim, where formerly the Franciscans had a house, and where at present a college is built. To the west of the town are seen the Military Barracks, where a regiment was stationed from 1841 to 1871, when it was disbanded. They are now occupied by the police force, the Post Office, and several public schools. In their neighbourhood there is a chapel specially built for the use of military men, as well as a pagoda dedicated to Mároti. The aspect of Mapuçá has of late considerably improved. It was raised to the rank of a town in 1859, and is now the residence of the chief local authorities and professional men.

Polymetrical Table showing the distances of several important places from the Capital and from each other.

(The distances, as given in an official report, are calculated in leagues of 18 to the degree, and by the most frequented roads.)

	Nova Goa, Pangim.	Agoada.	Alorna.	Baga.	Betul.	Bicholim.	Cabo de Rama.	Canacona.	Chaporá.	Doddomarogo.	Gaspar Dias.	Mapuçá.	Margão.	Mormugão.	Nanús.	Pernem.	Pondá.	Quepém.	Reis-Magos.	Sanquelim.
Agoada.	1½																			
Alorna.	5⅜	5⅔																		
Baga.	2⅓	1¾	4¾																	
Betul.	9¼	10⅜	14½	11¼																
Bicholim.	3¾	4¼	2½	4¼	11															
Cabo de Rama.	10⅝	12¼	16¼	13	1¾	12¼														
Canacona.	12½	11	16½	14⅜	3¾	3⅝	3½													
Chaporá.	3	2⅝	4½	1	12	5	14	15½												
Doddomarogo.	5½	5	1	4¾	12½	1½	13½	15¼	4½											
Gaspar Dias.	⅝	2	6	2¾	9¼	4⅜	11	12½	3¾	5¾										
Mapuçá.	2½	2⅓	3¼	1½	11⅜	3	13½	15	1¾	3¼	3¼									
Margão.	5¾	7¼	10¼	8	3½	7¼	5	6⅝	8¾	8½	5¾	8¼								
Mormugão.	2⅓	3⅜	7⅝	4½	8	7⅝	9½	11	3⅓	9	1⅗	4¾	4½							
Nanús.	7⅜	9¼	7	9	10¾	4½	11¾	13	9½	6	8¼	7½	7¼	8¾						
Pernem.	5½	5⅝	2¾	3¾	14⅜	4½	16⅜	18	3	3⅝	6¼	3⅛	11¼	7⅞	9⅓					
Pondá.	5	6½	7	7¾	6¾	4½	7¾	9¾	9	6	5½	6¼	3¼	4⅗	4	9				
Quepém.	8⅓	10	11½	10½	3½	9	5¼	4¾	10½	10½	8½	11	2¾	7¼	7	13½	4½			
Reis-Magos.	⅝	⅞	5⅓	2¼	9¾	3¾	11½	13½	3	4½	1¼	2¼	6¼	3	8¼	5½	5⅝	9		
Sanquelim.	4⅓	6	3⅗	5¾	10½	1⅓	12	13½	6⅛	2⅗	8⅓	4⅓	7	7½	3¼	6	3⅗	8¼	5	
Tiracol.	6	5⅝	5½	4	15	6½	17	18⅝	3	3¾	6⅝	4½	11¾	8⅓	10¾	2¾	11	14½	6¼	7⅝

Examples.

From New Goa to Canacona	... ...	12½
,, ,, Mapuçá	... ...	2½
,, ,, Pondá	... ...	5
From Alorna to Margão	... ...	10¼
,, ,, Nanús	... ...	7

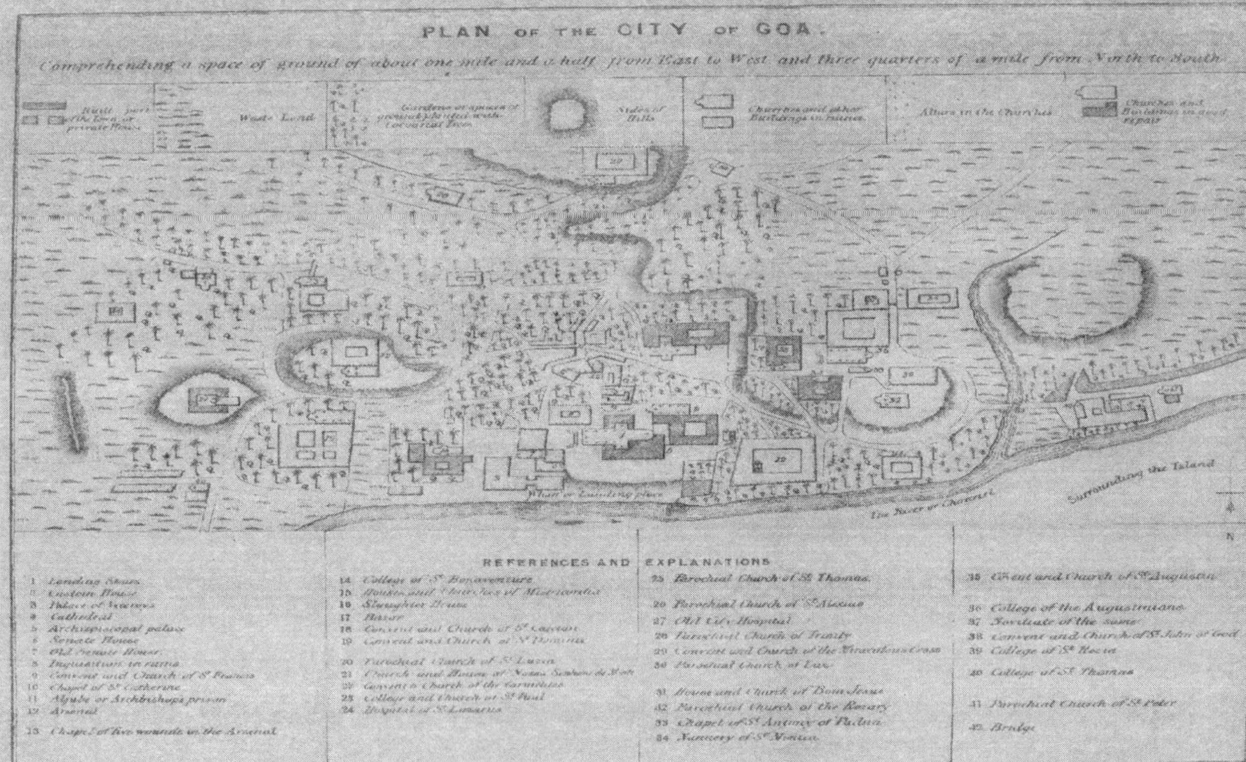
PLAN OF THE CITY OF GOA.
Comprehending a space of ground of about one mile and a half from East to West and three quarters of a mile from North to South
Waste Land
Sides of Hills
Churches and other Buildings in Ruins
Altars in the Churches
Churches and Buildings in good repair
Surrounding the Island
N
REFERENCES AND EXPLANATIONS
1 Landing Stairs
2 Custom House
3 Palace of Viceroys
4 Cathedral
5 Archiepiscopal palace
11 Aljube or Archbishops prison
12 Arsenal
13 Chapel of five wounds in the Arsenal
14 College of St. Bonaventure
16 Slaughter House
17 Bazar
23 College and Church of St. Paul
25 Parochial Church of St. Thomas.
26 Parochial Church of St. Alexius
27 Old City Hospital
31 House and Church of Bom Jesus
33 Chapel of St. Antony of Padua
35 Convent and Church of St. Augustin
36 College of the Augustinians
40 College of St. Thomas
42 Bridge

PART II.

AN HISTORICAL AND ARCHÆOLOGICAL SKETCH OF THE CITY OF GOA.

CHAPTER I.

THE ISLAND OF GOA—ITS ASPECT FROM THE HARBOUR—DERIVATION OF ITS NAME—ITS NAME AS KNOWN TO THE ANCIENT HINDUS, TO THE GREEKS, AND TO THE ARABS—THE ANCIENT HINDU CITY OF GOA, CAPITAL OF THE KÁDAMBAS—ITS CAPTURE BY THE YÁDAVAS OF DEVÁGIRI—INVASION OF GOA BY THE MUHAMMADANS—ITS CONQUEST BY THE KING OF VIJAYANAGARA.

The island of Goa, once the chief seat of the Portuguese Empire in the East, lies between 15° 31′ and 37° 50′ N. Latitude, and 74° 1′ and 75° 25′ E. Longitude. It is also known to the natives by its old name of तीसवाडी *Tísváḍi,* which means a district comprising thirty village communities.* Its form is almost that of a triangle, the base resting on the mainland, and the apex projecting into the sea. It is about nine miles long from east to west and three miles broad from north to south, the whole circuit being twenty-one miles. Its surface, comprising forty-eight square miles, is to a great extent rugged and hilly, the centre being considerably elevated. But towards the coast there are plains fringed with groves of cocoanuts, rice-fields, and orchards of mango and jack-trees, which, combined with the surrounding beautiful scenery, impart to it an aspect extremely picturesque.

The island is on both sides separated from the mainland by two rivers, the Mandovi and the Zuari, or the *Gomati* and the *Aganashini* of the Hindus, which are joined eastwards by a narrow streamlet, and discharge their waters into the

---

* It is written also Tissuary, Tissuvary or Tissuvaddy. At present it comprises thirty-one villages.

ocean, forming on both sides of the apex of the island, called the *Cabo*, two spacious anchorages in the harbour. This harbour, which Baron d'Aubonne* and Abbé Raynal† regard as one of the best in the world, was at the time of the Portuguese conquest in 1510 three and a half fathoms deep at high water and three at low water,‡ while at the present day it is half a fathom less.§ The view from the entrance

---

* *Les Six Voyages de Jean Baptiste Tavernier, Baron d'Aubonne*, Paris, 1676, Part II., p. 115.

† *Histoire Philosophique et Politique*, par Guillaume Thomas Raynal, Paris, 1780, tom. I., p. 8.

‡ *Lendas da India*, por Gaspar Correa, Lisboa, 1860, tom. II., p. 54. The author of the *Commentaries* differs slightly from the *Lendas*, and says that "they (the Portuguese pilots) found two fathoms and a half depth at low water, and three at high water": *The Commentaries of the Great Affonso Dalboquerque*, translated from the Portuguese by W. De Gray Birch, London, 1877, vol. II., p. 88.

§ *Boletim e Annaes do Conselho Ultramarino*, No. 59. Mr. Taylor in his *Sailing Directory*, London, 1874, p. 392, writes as follows about the bay and harbour of Goa:—"This place, the capital and principal seaport of the Portuguese possessions in the East Indies, has not such deep water as formerly in the bay, though the depth on the river bar is the same as represented on charts executed half a century ago. Shelter for small vessels from N.W. winds is to be had to the S.E. of the lighthouse and landing pier, in about 4 fathoms at L.W., about three cables' length from the rocky shore. Inside of 5 fathoms the bottom is mixed sand and mud, but outside of that depth there is mud. Saokari creek, round the E. end of Agoada table-land, is an excellent little refuge for small coasters....The common anchorage for large ships is abreast the fort, in 5 fathoms, mud, with the lighthouse bearing N. about ¾ mile from shore; but small vessels may go in much nearer, to 3½ fathoms, mud, with lighthouse N.W., and the E. cocoanut point of Agoada N.E. by E. The bay is doubtless a little shallower than it was fifty years ago. Some rocks, mostly above water, project a small distance seaward from Agoada S.W. point, but this side of the bay is safer to borrow on than Cabo. After the early part of May it was considered unsafe to remain at Agoada anchorage; it was usual then for the Portuguese to send their large ships, that could not go into the river of Goa, down to Mormugão, where they found shelter by mooring close under the fort walls of that peninsula, but even there, in the height of the S.W. monsoon, a swell rolls in round the point, rendering it necessary to moor the vessel head and stern, so as always to have her bow to the swell."

of the harbour is at once picturesque and imposing. To the left stands the stately fortress of Agoada,* with a series of batteries commanding the sea-coast, and with a castle and a lighthouse on the brow of a rock rising to an elevation of 260 feet above the level of the sea. In the centre of the harbour is seen the Cabo, with a beautiful palace, the summer residence of the Governors of Goa. To the right appears the fortress of Mormugão, which by its elevated position and massive structure rivals that of Agoada. Proceeding through the harbour up to the mouth of the Mandovi, we see two other forts almost confronting each other from the opposite banks of the river, and known as the forts of Reis Magos and Gaspar Dias. Further up the river lies Pangim, the modern capital of Goa, five miles distant from the harbour, and next to it the pretty little village of Ribandar, connected with Pangim by a long causeway which forms the main road over a salt marsh from the new to the old capital. The entire margin of the river from Ribandar to the ancient city was in former times flanked with a row of elegant buildings, which, together with the distant turrets and cupolas in the city and its suburbs, presented an exceedingly charming sight, of which several travellers have left graphic descriptions. At present these buildings, turrets, and cupolas have almost all crumbled to dust, but still the natural scenery which bursts on the view from all sides as we advance up the river is at once picturesque and interesting. A mere glance, says a celebrated Orientalist, at a sketch of this river will suffice to convince one that it washes an enchanted land.† The sight is indeed captivating; villages scattered all along the banks of the river, with islets floating as it were on the surface of the water, with vegetation luxuriantly growing all around, and the Western Gháṭs fading from view in the distance—these form a picture of the most diversified and pleasing character.

---

* For a description of the fortresses of Agoada, Mormugão, etc., see Part I., pp. 40 *et seq.*

† Anquetil du Perron, *Discours Préliminaire, ou Introduction au Zend Avesta*, Paris, 1771, p. cciv.

Occupying a central position on the western coast of India, and favoured by so many natural advantages, the island of Goa rapidly rose to importance in ancient times. It is to be presumed, says the celebrated French geographer D'Anville, that the island, by the advantages of its situation, must have at all times figured prominently on the Malabar Coast;* while a distinguished Portuguese historian, Diogo de Couto, assures us that it was so much frequented by the neighbouring people that they were often heard to say, "Let us amuse ourselves under the cool shades of Goa, and taste the sweetness of its betel†"—an expression which, in course of time, passed into a proverb with them.

The island of Goa receives its name from the territory of which it forms the principal part. The term Goa appears to have been derived from गोवराष्ट्र *Govaráshṭra*, the ancient appellation of the Southern Końkaṇa, and one of the seven divisions of *Paraśuráma Kshetra*,‡ which Professor Wilson surmises to be identical with गोपराष्ट्र *Goparáshṭra*, *i. e.* 'the district of cowherds or of nomadic tribes' mentioned in the *Mahábhárata*.§ This conjecture is perfectly correct, for the word *Goparáshṭra* has the same signification as गोपकपुरी *Gopakapurí* or गोपकपत्तन *Gopakapattana*, which with the aid of several inscriptions has been identified with Goa. These different designations seem to point to the conclusion, that the Aryans, who first settled in these parts, led a pastoral life.

---

* *Eclaircissemens Géographiques sur la Carte de l'Inde*, Paris, 1753, p. 91.

† Diogo de Couto, Lisboa, 1778, *Dec.* IV., liv. x., cap. iv.

‡ Paraśuráma, the sixth *avatára* of Vishṇu according to the Hindu legend, after having defeated the emperor Kártarvirya Sahasárjuna and presented the conquered land to the Bráhmaṇs, reclaimed from the sea a strip of land from the river Vaitaraṇi to Kaṇyá Kumári or Cape Comorin. This land, known as Paraśuráma Kshetra, consists of the following seven divisions, called also Sapta Końkaṇa :—Kerala, Tulanga, Govaráshṭra, Końkaṇa, Karalata, Varalata, and Barbara. For more detailed accounts about Paraśuráma see *Mahábhárata, Vana Parva, Santa Parva ; Bhagavat Puráṇa ;* and *Skanda Puráṇa*.

§ See Wilson's *Vishṇu Puráṇa*, and *Mahábhárata, Bhisma Parva.*

Diogo de Couto traces the etymology of the word *Goa* to *Goe-moat,* which, in the ancient language of the place, he says, signified a fertile and refreshing land, and which was in course of time contracted into *Goe,* and subsequently corrupted by the Portuguese into *Goa.** This explanation of the Portuguese historian, is, however, untenable, as we do not find in the Sanskrit or Kanarese languages, to which he evidently refers, any word like *Goe-moat,* while the name *Goa* was used long before the conquest of the place by the Portuguese, as will be seen from a copper-plate inscription dated Śáliváhana Śaka 1313 (A.D. 1391), translated by Major-General Sir Le-Grand Jacob.† Equally improbable is the conjecture of the author of the *Oriente Conquistado,*‡ who traces its origin to the chief local deity, *Goubat;* but this deity, as far as we know, has not even a place in the Hindu pantheon. Some again, as the author of the *Promptuario das Definiçoẽs Indicas,*§ derive the term from *Gohaladeva,* the first king of Goa, while others say that it was called after the Ṛishi *Gautama,* who is stated to have dwelt there for some time. But each of these suppositions appears to be more ingenious than correct.

The island, with the remaining territory of Goa, has from ancient times been known to the Hindus by the more familiar name of गोमन्त *Gomant.* This name occurs in the *Mahábhárata,* the *Harivanśa,* the *Skanda* and other *Puráṇas,*‖ and is associated, in the orthodox Hindu mind, with many a godly and heroic deed. For there Paraśuráma, the sixth incarnation of Vishnú, after reclaiming the whole of Surparaka¶ from the

---

* Diogo de Couto, *loc. cit.*

† *Jo. Bo. Br. R. As. Soc.*, vol. IV., p. 108; *Bo. Govt. Records, New Series,* No. X., p. 284. *Goa* is only the abbreviation of गोवा *Gova.*

‡ *Oriente Conquistado,* por Pe. Francisco de Souza, vol. I., p. 154.

§ *Promptuario das Definiçoẽs Indicas,* por Padre Leonardo Paes, Trat. 2°, cap. 3°.

‖ *Mahábhárata, Bhisma Parva,* ch. 12; *Harivanśa,* ch. 96 *et seq.*; *Sahyádri Khaṇḍa* of the *Skanda Puráṇa,* Part II., ch. iii. Goa is also known as गोमान्चल *Gománchala.*

¶ शूर्पारक A name by which the Paraśuráma Kshetra, or the land wrested by Paraśuráma from the sea, is known to the Puranic writers.

sea, established ten *munis* or sages, whom he had brought with him from the north of India.* There he performed the most solemn of all sacrifices—the *aśvamedha*, which is enjoined for the expiation of sins and the attainment of celestial bliss.† There the god Śiva, after deserting his wife, and quitting his favourite residence on the snowy heights of the Himálayas, took up his temporary abode, under the name of Gomantakesh, till he was discovered by his loving spouse, who, in the guise of a songstress, won his heart no less by her beauty than by her melodious voice.‡ There the *Sapta Ṛishis*, or seven great sages, performed penance for seven millions of years, and pleased the deity so much that he came personally to bless them in the form of Śiva.§ And there too a bloody battle was fought between Krishṇa and Jarasandha, which ended in the total defeat of the king of Magadha.‖

Kuvá, Gova and Gove are other names by which the island with the surrounding territory was formerly known. The first two, which are of great antiquity, occur also, more or less changed, in comparatively recent works, such as the *Mohit*, *Mirat Ahmedi*, and in the *Geography of Sadik Ispaháni*.¶ The name Gove is still used in a slightly modified form by the natives of the place, and it is found in many old inscriptions which have been recently deciphered, such as those of Halsi and Paṭṭadakal, in the Kaladgi District, dated Śaka 1084

---

* *Muni*, a great sage or Ṛishi. In Southern India alone there are said to have been more than forty-eight thousand of them. The following are the names of ten *munis* or sages established at Goa by Paraśuráma :—Bháradvája, Kauśika, Vatsa, Kaundinya, Kaśyapa, Vasishṭha, Jamadagni, Vishvamitra, Gautama, and Atri.—*Sahyádri Khaṇḍa* of the *Skanda Puráṇa*, Part II., chap. I.

† An interesting description of the solemnity of the *aśvamedha* sacrifice is given in the *Mahábhárata*. According to a Hindu tradition, this sacrifice was performed by Paraśuráma in the village of Haramal, in the Pernem Mahál.

‡ माङ्गीशमाहात्म्य. अ० ३. *Mangesh Máhátmya*, chap. III.

§ *Op. cit.*

‖ हरिवंश अ० ९६-९९.

¶ *Jo. As. Soc. Beng.*, vol. V., p. 464 ; Briggs's *Mirat Ahmedi*, p. 129 ; *Geography of Sadik Ispaháni*, p. 130.

(A. D. 1162).* All these three designations are analogous to Govaráshṭra, to which we have already referred.

It is not yet thoroughly ascertained by what name this island was known to the Greeks. They divided the coast into three parts,— Λαρικὴ Lariké, Αριακὴ Ariaké, and Λιμυρικὴ Limuriké, and bestowed distinct names on several places on the coast; but the identification of these places has always been a matter of dispute. D'Anville, who was the first to undertake the laborious task of comparing ancient with modern geography, identifies Goa with Νέλκυνδα *Nelkinda* of the *Periplus, Nekanidon* of Pliny, Μέλλυνδα *Melinda* of Ptolemy, and Νίνκυλδα *Nincilda* of the Peutingerian Tables. Major Rennel, however, places *Nelkinda*, the great emporium of trade in ancient times, further down the coast, and conjectures that Goa corresponds with Τύνδις *Tyndis* of the ancient Greeks. Dr. Vincent, another great antiquarian, considers the island of Goa to be identical with Αἰγιδίοι *Aigidii* of the *Periplus*, which D'Anville, Fr. Paulino, and others had identified with Angediva, on account of the similarity of names. Gosselin, Lassen, and Müller, on the other hand, differ widely from the preceding writers, the first making it correspond to the *Tricadiba Insula* of Ptolemy, and the others to the χερσόνησος *Chersonesus* of the *Periplus*.†

By what name Goa was known to the Arab and Persian writers of the Middle Ages, the successors so to speak, of the Greeks, is a question involved in less obscurity, owing to the light thrown on the subject by modern research. But it does not appear to be definitely settled. For the Arabic names of towns, ports, and districts on the coast of India differ, as

---

* *Jo. Bo. Br. R. As. Soc.*, vol. XI., pp. 219 *et seq.*

† *Antiquité Géographique de l'Inde*, par M. D'Anville, Paris, 1750, p. 83; *Eclaircissemens Géographiques, ut supra*, p. 91; Rennel's *Memoir*, London, 1793, p. xxxviii.; *The Periplus of the Erythræan Sea*, by W. Vincent, London, 1800, vol. II., pp. 391 *et seq.*; *Viaggio alle Indie Orientali* da Fra Paolino da S. Bartolomeo, Roma, 1796, p. 153; *Recherches sur la Géographie Systématique et Positive des Anciens*, par P. F. J. Gosselin, Paris, 1790, tom. 3me, p. 208; *Indischer Alterthumskunde*, von Christian Lassen, Bonn, 1852, vol. III., p. 187; Carol. Müller, *Geographi Græci Minores*, vol. I., p. 296; *Geographia Ptolomæi*, lib. VII., cap. I., tab. x., edition of 1608.

Dr. Vincent justly remarks, as widely from the names given by Ptolemy, Pliny, and the author of the *Periplus* as the latter from those known at the present day. Dr. Lee, Gildemeister, Reinaud, Badger, and other eminent authorities identify Goa with the Arabic كاوة *Káwá* or *Káwe.** Colonel Yule, on the other hand, has shown that *Káwá* corresponds to *Konva*, the *Cauvey* of Arrowsmith's great map, or *Gongway* or *Conwa* of Ritter (vol. VI., pp. 645-6), situated to the south of the Máhi estuary, and that the Arabic سندابور *Sindábúr* or *Sandábúr*, whose proximity to Goa had been pointed out by Professor Gildemeister, is identical with the island itself.† *Sindábúr* is mentioned by various writers, such as El-Masúdi, El-Edrisi, Rashíd-ud-dín, Abulfeda, and Ibn Batuta.‡

* Lee's *Travels of Ibn Batuta*, London, 1829, p. 164; Gildemeister's *Scriptorum Arabum de rebus Indicis*, Bonn, 1838, p. 46; Reinaud's *Géographie de Abulfeda*, Paris, 1848, p. cdxxvi.; Badger's *Travels of Ludovico di Varthema*, London, 1868, p. 271.

† About the identification of the island of Goa with Sindábúr, Colonel Yule writes as follows—"It is evident from Ibn Batuta's account that Sindábúr was a populous delta island, and the only such in the required position is Goa. I cannot trace the name Sindábúr in my modern map or in any of the old Portuguese accounts accessible to me. But the number of the villages mentioned by Ibn Batuta confirms the identification. For De Barros says the island of Goa, when the Moors conquered it, was called *Tiçuarii*, which is as much as to say, Thirty villages. Also in the Turkish book of navigation called *Mohit*, by the accomplished admiral Sidi Ali, of which Hammer has given a translation in the *Jo. As. Soc. Beng.*, we find a section headed '24th voyage from Kuvai Sindábúr to Aden.' The trade of Sindábúr with Aden is also mentioned by Ibn Batuta. It is curious that Masúdi refers to the abundance of crocodiles in the bay of Sindábúr; for De Barros also particularly notices their great size and numbers in the waters of Goa, and alludes to a story that they had been introduced there as a guard against surprise and the escape of slaves." (The *Indian Antiquary*, vol. II., p. 114. See also Yule's *Cathay and the way thither*, London, 1866, vol. II., p. 444.)

‡ Sprenger's *Meadows of Gold and Mines of Gems*, London, 1841, p. 346; Elliot's *History of India as told by its own historians*, London, 1867, vol. I., p. 21; Jaubert's *Géographie d'Edrisi*, Paris, 1836, vol. I., p. 179; *Géographie de Abulfeda, Texte Arabe*, par M. Reinaud et M. Le Baron MacGuckin de Slane, Paris, 1840, vol. II., p. 354; Lee's *Ibn Batuta*, *loc. cit.*; *Madr. Jour.*, vol. XIV., p. 198.

Some of them, however, confound it with سنداان *Sindán* (*Sanján*), which Rawlinson says has been corrupted into *St. John*,—the modern St. John's Point of Rennel, between Daman and Bombay.* In the *Carta Catalana* of 1375, preserved in the Imperial Library at Paris, and in the *Portulano Mediceo*, now in the Laurentian Library, *Sindábúr* is transformed into *Chintabor* and *Cintabor* respectively.† The identification of *Sindábúr* with Goa proves the ancient trade of this island with Aden and other important ports.‡

The ancient Hindu city of Goa was situated on the southern extremity of the island on the right bank of the Zuari. It is designated in the Kanarese inscriptions as ಗೋವೆ *Gove*, and in the Sanskrit as गोपकपुरी *Gopakapurí*, गोपकपत्तन *Gopakapattana*, and गोवापुरी *Govápurí*.§ It was the capital of the empire of the Kádambas, which at one time comprised not only the present territory of Goa, but also the whole of the Southern Koṅkaṇa, Palasige (Halsi), Veḷugrama (Belgaum), and many other districts comprehending upwards of 13,400

---

* Quoted in *Madr. Jour.*, vol. XIV., p. 198; Yule's *Cathay*, vol. II., p. 444.

† Yule's *Cathay*, Introduction, p. ccxxx.

‡ Yule's *Marco Polo*, vol. II., p. 376.

§ *Jo. Bo. Br. R. As. Soc.* The city of Goa is praised in the following terms in one of the Puráṇas :—

गोकर्णादुत्तरे भागे सप्तयोजनविस्तृतं ॥ तत्र गोवापुरी नाम नगरी पापनाशिनी ॥ १ ॥
गोवापुर्यां दर्शनेन पापं हंति पुरार्जितं ॥ यथा रवेर्दर्शनेन तमो याति विशीर्णतां ॥ २ ॥
गोवापुर्यां द्विजेंद्रेश स्नानार्थे मानसं यदि ॥ करोति यः सकृन्मर्त्यः संप्राप्नोति परं पदं ॥ ३ ॥
गोवापुर्या समानं च नास्ति क्षेत्रं न संशयः ॥ तत्र संत्यग्रजन्मानो वेदवेदांगपारगाः ॥ ४ ॥
मंत्रौषधितपोयोगबलेन जितमन्यवः ॥ यस्मिन्वसंति विप्राश्च षट्कर्मनिरताः सदा ॥ ५ ॥
सूत सं० अ०१६ ॥

"To the north of Gokarṇa is a *kshetra* seven *yojanas* in circumference: therein is situated Govápurí, which destroys all sins. By the sight of Govápurí the sin committed in a previous existence is destroyed, as at sunrise darkness disappears. One even by making up his mind to bathe once in Govápurí attains a high place (in the next world). Certainly there is no *kshetra* equal to Govápurí. In this place there are many Bráhmaṇs deeply read in the Vedas and Vedángas. In this place live Bráhmaṇs who are devoted to the six Karmas and have subdued their anger by means of *mantras*, herbs, penances, and *yoga*."—*Súta Saṅhitá*, ch. 16.

villages.* The city, it seems, was remarkable not only for its opulence and commerce, but also for its noble edifices and its educational and charitable institutions.† We learn from one inscription that it was full of learned paṇḍits, who passed in palanquins through its streets, displaying the valuable presents which they had received from the king; while in the hyperbolical language of another inscription the city is represented as being so beautiful and charming that it surpassed the paradise of Indra himself.‡ Some of the stately buildings of this old city were extant at the time of the Portuguese conquest of Goa,§ but neither these nor any other vestige of the city can be found at present. It is known to the natives as *Orlem Goem*, and to the Portuguese chroniclers as *Goa Velha*.||

---

* *Jo. Bo. Br. R. As. Soc.*, No. XXVII. of vol. IX., pp. 265, 301.

† *Jo. Bo. Br. R. As. Soc.*, No. XXVII. of vol. IX., pp. 262 *et seq.*; *Liv. das Monç.* (Goa Govt. Rec., MSS.), No. 93, fol. 1396; *Gabinette Litterario das Fontainhas*, Nova Goa, 1846, vol. I., p. 16; *Commentaries of Affonso d'Albuquerque*, vol. II., p. 93.

‡ *Jo. Bo. Br. R. As. Soc.*, No. XXVII. of vol. IX., pp. 273; *Liv. das Monç.* (Goa Govt. Rec., MSS.), *loc. cit.*; *Gabinette Litterario, loc. cit.*

§ *Commentaries of Affonso d'Albuquerque*, vol. II., p. 9.

|| Dr. Fryer describes thus the ancient capital of Goa in his time:—"At our landing the sea bestowed a kind murmur on the yielding sand, and cast us ashore in a place quadrated more for still retirement, than noisy commerce; there lying before its banks *Canooses* belonging to fishermen, and *baloons* of pleasure only; the *Segnioros* minding nothing less than merchandizing, and the pover employing their fish-hooks and knitting-needles to get a livelihood. So that I presume Old Goa need not complain for the loss of trade, which she never had; nor lament the deprivation of costly and spacious buildings, which she never wanted; but hath them rather as a country town (of whom she is the dame) than city, though she might claim the title of mistress; her soil is luxurious and campaign, and abounds with rich inhabitants, whose rural palaces are immured with groves and hortos, refreshed and cooled with tanks and rivulets; but always reserve a graceful front for the streets, which are broad and cleanly at this time of festivity, celebrating with triumphant arches and most pompous pageants: palenkeens pass as commonly as at Goa itself, the people as urbane, though less pestered with drunken comrades, as soldiers, seamen and ruffians; the market-place is stored with provisions,

The Kádambas who ruled in this city were probably a branch of the reigning dynasty of Vanavásipura or Banavási, which also bore the same name.* They pretended to be descended from Trinetra or Trilochanakadamba, who is said to have been born of a drop of sweat which fell from the forehead of Siva at the foot of the *kádamba* tree (*Nauclea Kadamba*), hence the name. When this personage, "half human and half divine," flourished is not sufficiently ascertained. Hindu tradition places him in the fabulous age, while Dr. Taylor conjectures that he must have lived at least 500 years before Christ.† Professor Wilson, however, judging from an inscription bearing the name, concludes that the period of his reign could not have been prior to Śálivάhana Śaka 90, or A.D. 168.‡ Of the immediate successors of Trilochanakádamba, no precise account has been handed down to us; but their power and greatness are indisputable, being attested by the

---

and the parish provided with a large church; but nothing antiquated as I could discover, by which it is easy to judge Old Goa never was deserted; but New Goa hath stoln from hence for the sake of traffick, for that purpose the river is more suitable than this bay; it may measure from one end to the other, two miles.

"Abreast of it on an hanging hill is a sumptuous structure of the Capuchins called *Sancto Pillar*, the ascent to it is by a winding staircase cut out of the rock, and railed with stone banisters; this order is discalceated also, and consanguineous to the Franciscans, differing only in superiority and austerity, their hood is long and tapering, on their scapular in fashion of a sugar-loaf; to both whom are annexed a lay fraternity, which wear the mantle and tippet, but not the vest and cord, neither are they shaved as the Fathers are: so that all degrees of them in every order are comprehended under these three classes, viz. *Patres*, Fathers; *Fratres*, Brothers; *Juvenes*, Young men: To these also belong the Sisterhood of *Sancta Clara*."—*A New Account of East India and Persia*, London, 1698, p. 154.

The Franciscan Convent of Pilar, to which Dr. Fryer alludes, still exists. It was built in 1613 and was abandoned in 1835. At present it is set apart by order of Government for the summer residence of the archbishops.

* Banavási is mentioned by Ptolemy. It was known also as *Jayantipúra.*

† *Orient. Hist. Manuscripts*, Madras, 1835, vol. II., p. 59.

‡ *Mackenzie Collection of Manuscripts*, Calcutta, 1828, Introduction, p. ci

eighteen *aśvamedhas* performed by them.* The first prince of this dynasty, whose name has been discovered from the inscriptions lately deciphered, is Gúhalladeva.† He appears to have reigned at the commencement of the 11th century of the Christian era. His successors were princes of great valour, and were involved in frequent hostilities with the Raṭṭas, Choḷas, and other neighbouring sovereigns. Many of them were, however, the feudatories of the Chalukyas who ruled at Kalyáṇa. In the reign of Jayakeśi II., a contemporary and son-in-law of the great Chalukya emperor Vikramáditya II., who held the sceptre from A.D. 1076 to 1127,‡ Goa, in common with the whole of the Koṅkaṇa, rose in rebellion against that monarch, which was soon quelled by his general Sindavanśa Mahámaṇḍleśvara Achugideva.§ On this occasion the city was reduced to ashes, as appears from an inscription on a stone at Paṭṭadakal, in the Kaladgi district.‖ A few years later, however, it was rebuilt, and attained its former prosperity under Śivachitta and Vishṇuchitta, sons and successors of Jayakeśi II.¶

The Kádamba dynasty continued in power till nearly the middle of the 13th century, when, probably through failure of successors in the male line, the throne was filled by Káma Deva, brother-in-law of Shásta Deva, the last Kádamba king.**

* *Jo. Bo. Br. R. As. Soc.*, vol. IX., pp. 231, 245. The performance of the *aśvamedha* sacrifice is believed to be the mark of independence and power: see *Indian Antiquary*, vol. I., p. 301.

† He is said to be "the eye of the universe, of extensive majesty, on account of whose brilliance the masses of the darkness of his foes took to themselves an abode in the most dreadful caverns": *Jo. Bo. Br. R. As. Soc.*, vol. IX., p. 272.

‡ *Jo. R. As. Soc.*, London, vol. IV., pp. 4, 15; Prinsep's *Useful Tables*, p. 272.

§ *Jo. R. As. Soc.*, vol. IV., p. 15; *Jo. Bo. Br. R. As. Soc.*, vol. XI., No. XXX., pp. 234, 244.

‖ *Jo. Bo. Br. R. As. Soc.*, vol. XI., No. XXXI., p. 269.

¶ *Op. cit.*, vol. IX., p. 301.

** A copper-plate grant dated Kaliyuga 4328, or A.D. 1247.

Not long after this event, Goa was taken by the Yádavas of Devágiri,* who conquered the empire of the Chalukyas.†

In 1294 A.D. Ala-ud-dín invaded the Dakhaṇ and captured Devágiri. The immense booty which he gained on this occasion prompted him afterwards, when he seized the throne of Delhi, to send frequent expeditions to Southern India, under his valiant general Malik Kafur. In the last of these expeditions Goa and other parts of Maháráshṭra were overrun by the invaders. They took back with them precious spoils, after having entrusted the government of the island of Goa to Malik Tubliga.‡

But the inhabitants of Goa, it appears, did not allow the Muhammadans to continue long in peaceful possession of the island, but were frequently engaged in hostilities with them, as well as with Jamál-ud-dín, the Muhammadan chief of Honore, who sought to attack it. The celebrated traveller Ibn Batuta, who visited India about the middle of the 14th century, and accompanied this chief in one of his expeditions against Sindábúr or Goa, writes thus :—

"I then betook myself to Jamal Oddin, King of Hinaur, by sea, who, when I came near, met me and received me honourably, and then appointed me a house with a suitable mainteuance. He was about to attend on divine service in the mosque, and commanded me to accompany him. I then became attached to the mosque, and read daily a Khatma or two. At this time the king was preparing an expedition against the island of Sindábúr. For this purpose he had prepared two and fifty vessels, which when ready he ordered me to attend with him for the expedition. Upon this occasion I opened the Koran in search of an omen, and in the first words of the first leaf which I laid my hand upon was frequent mention of the name of God, and the promise that he would certainly assist those who assisted him. I was greatly delighted with this; and when the king came to the evening prayer, I told him of it and requested to be allowed to accompany him. He was much surprised at the omen, and prepared to set out in person. After this, he went on board one of the vessels, taking me with him, and then we sailed. When we got to the island of Sindábúr, we found the people

* The modern Daulatábád.

† *Op. cit.*, vol. X., No. XIX., p. 189; vol. XII., No. XXXIII., p. 47.

‡ Briggs's *Ferishta*, London, 1829, vol. I., p. 391.

prepared to resist us, and a hard battle was accordingly fought. We carried the place, however, by divine permission, by assault."*

After this victory Ibn Batuta did not remain at Sindábúr or Goa, but when he visited it again, he found the Hindus besieging it in order to wrest it from the grasp of Jamál-ud-dín.† Nevertheless the people of Goa appear to have continued under the Muhammadan sway for some time longer, till 1367 A.D.

At this period the kingdom of Vijayanagara,‡ called by European writers Bisnagar, which had been founded some years before on the south bank of the Tuṅgabhadra, had attained a degree of power and prosperity which enabled it to cope successfully with the Muhammadans. Harihara, the Rájá of Vijayanagara, wishing to expel the followers of the Crescent from Goa, commanded his minister and general Mádhavácharya Vidyaraṇya,§ who was then ruling in Jayantipura or Banavási, to march against that city. The general promptly carried out the king's orders. He drove the Muhammadans out of the city, incorporated it with the kingdom of Vijayanagara, and re-established the ancient shrine of Saptanátha or Sapta Koṭeśvara, which had been demolished by the Moslems.‖ The victorious general remained for some time in charge of the city. He was succeeded in the government by several distinguished persons, some of whom have left their names to posterity in inscriptions commemorating grants for religious purposes. One of these inscriptions, dated Śaka 1321 (A.D. 1399), appears on a column called *Garuḍa-Kambha,* and another, dated Śaka 1334 (A.D. 1412), on a stone tablet in the temple of Víra-

---

* Lee's *Ibn Batuta, ut supra,* p. 175.

† *Loc. cit.*

‡ विजयनगर Vijayanagara (or the city of victory) was called also विद्यानगर Vidyanagara (the city of learning). To the first European chroniclers it was known as Narsinga and Bisnagar.

§ The celebrated commentator of the *Ṛig-Veda,* and author of various Sanskrit works.

‖ *Bo. Govt. Records, No. X., New Series,* p. 283; *Jo. Bo. Br. R. As. Soc.,* No. III. of 1852, p. 107; idem, No. XXVI. of 1869, p. 227; Scott's *Ferishta,* Shrewsbury. 1794, vol. II., p. 46.

bhadra situated in Hanagal Táluká, in the district of Dhárwáḍ.*

According to Ferishta, Goa continued to form a part of the kingdom of Vijayanagara till its conquest by a Sultan of the Báhmani dynasty,† but some Portuguese chroniclers relate that, previous to this event, it had thrown off the yoke of the Vijayanagara king and become independent in 1440, and that a new city had been founded in the northern part of the island, on the left bank of the river Mandovi.‡

This city is situated in 15° 27′ N. Lat. and 73° 53′ E. Long., in the village of Ela, about two miles to the north of the ancient Hindu city, and about six miles to the east of Pangim. The exact date of the foundation of this city, which is at the present day abandoned and desolate, and therefore called the old city, has not yet been correctly determined. Ibn Batuta, according to the unabridged translation of his travels published by Professor Defremeri and Dr. Sanguenetti, states that he saw two cities in Sindábúr, which, as already shown, is identified with the island of Goa or Tísváḍi, one a Hindu and the other a Muhammadan city.§ The traveller does not give the date of his visit to Goa, but it is certain that it took place between the year 1342, when he was despatched by Muhammad Togluk on an embassy to China, and the year 1349, when he returned from his travels to Tangiers, his native place. Thus, if his statement is reliable, the second city to which he refers must have been built during the first Muhammadan government established in the island, and many years before the conquest of Goa by Mádhavácharya. On the other hand, some historians place its foundation at a later period, when large numbers of Muhammadans, escaping from Honore, settled themselves in Goa under Malik Husen, forty years before the Portuguese conquest.|| The earlier and

* *Jo. Bo. Br. R. As. Soc.*, No. XXXIV. of 1876, p. 341.

† Briggs's *Ferishta*, vol. II., p. 485.

‡ *Lendas, ut supra*, II., p. 55 ; *Commentaries, ut supra*, II., p. 92.

§ Quoted by Reinaud in his *Géographie de Abulfeda*, vol. I., p. cdxxvi.

|| Barros, *Dec.* II. liv. v., cap. i., p. 434 ; Faria y Souza, *ut supra*, vol. VI., p. 129.

more trustworthy Portuguese chroniclers appear to fix the date at about 1440, the same year in which, according to them, Goa had attained its independence, and they state that the old city, then the capital of an extensive empire, was transferred to the present site because the river Zuari became shallow, while its rival the Mandovi growing deeper and broader, owing to the large streams of water which flowed into it from the Ghâṭs during the rainy season, was incapable of affording shelter to the largest merchantmen which then resorted in great numbers to the port of Goa. The inhabitants of the old city, who were very rich and engaged in commerce, perceiving the advantages of the new site, gradually removed to this place and founded a new city, where in a short time rose in every direction temples and edifices remarkable for their architectural beauty, and new docks were built for the construction of large ships intended to maintain a commercial intercourse with all ports of India. The city rapidly rose in importance, chiefly by its trade in horses imported from Ormuz, for which there was a great demand in Vijayanagara and other neighbouring kingdoms.*

At the period of which we are speaking, Goa, says the author of the *Commentarios*, was in a very flourishing state. It possessed a numerous force, both horse and foot, consisting principally of archers, whose valour, combined with their skill in using the bow, enabled them to render valuable services not only to their own but also to the neighbouring states. The city being the chief emporium of trade on this side of India, caravans of merchants constantly poured into it from different parts of the country, for the purpose of carrying on extensive commercial transactions with the natives and aliens alike. Such indeed was the prosperity of Goa that it is said to have been the only city on the coast which enjoyed at this period a revenue of £10,000.†

---

* *Lendas, ut supra,* II., p. 55; *Commentaries, ut supra,* II., p. 92.

† *Commentaries,* II., pp. 92 *et seq.*; *Lendas,* II., p. 55.

CHAPTER II.

CONQUEST OF GOA BY THE BÁHMANI KINGS—THE ATTEMPT OF THE HINDUS TO RECOVER THE CITY—DECLINE OF THE BÁHMANI KINGDOM, AND REVOLT AT GOA—ITS SUBJECTION TO THE KING OF BIJÁPUR—ITS FLOURISHING CONDITION AND COMMERCIAL IMPORTANCE.

A city so remarkable for its wealth and commerce, as well as for its advantageous situation, could not fail to excite the cupidity of the Muhammadan princes of the Dakhaṇ, who, having thrown off their allegiance to the emperor of Delhi, had founded an independent kingdom. They repeatedly invaded the territory of Goa and endeavoured to reduce it to subjection, but their attacks were successfully repelled; and we learn from Nikitin, the Russian traveller, who visited India at this time, that the Muhammadan power did not extend beyond Dábul on the coast.* Though baffled at first, the Muhammadans did not give up their design. They determined to capture Goa and other important places in the Koṅkaṇa. In 1469 the Báhmani king, Muhammad Sháh II., despatched a large force, under his general Muhammad Khvájá Gawan, to the south.† Upon this the inhabitants of Goa and the surrounding country made common cause to avert the impending danger, and hastened in large numbers to secure the mountain passes which guarded the open country. But their efforts proved

* *Commentaries, ut supra, loc. cit.*; *India in the Fifteenth Century*, Hakluyt Society, London, 1837, p. 15.

† The advantageous position of Goa had long been known to the powerful princes of the Báhmani dynasty of the Dakhaṇ. Firozsháh Báhmani, who reigned from 1397 to 1422 with a magnificence which even five hundred years afterwards was celebrated in verses by the people of the Dakhaṇ, yearly despatched ships from the port of Goa to bring down the most exquisite productions and manufactures from Arabia, Egypt, and other countries.

futile. Khvájá Gawan crossed the Gháṭs, laid siege to the impregnable fortress of Kelhna,* and captured it by stratagem. He then marched with his victorious forces on Goa, and directed the city to be closely invested both by land and sea. A fleet of 120 ships appeared at the mouth of the Mandovi, and coöperated with the land forces in reducing the city to straits. Goa was indeed strongly fortified by towers and bulwarks, especially on that side which was most exposed to the attacks of the enemy.† But it could not hold out long; it was obliged in the end to capitulate, and open its gates to the invaders, who took possession of the city and its environs.

The news of this important acquisition was received at the court of Bedar with extreme satisfaction. The long-coveted prize had at length been won. The most sanguine hopes had at length been realized. The court and capital vied with each other in celebrating the victory with pomp and festivity, and among other marks of joy the king ordered the "*nobat* to beat the march of triumph for seven days."‡

Khvájá Gawan, having left a strong garrison in Goa and supplied it with the necessary provisions, returned to the capital, where he was received by the king with the highest honours,

---

* The modern Vishalgaḍh.

† According to the Portuguese chroniclers, the city of Goa was further protected by crocodiles, with which the river abounded, and which were so enormous as to devour whole bullocks and upset large boats. As the river near the village of Gandaulim towards the east of the island was not very deep, and was fordable at ebb time, it was ordered that all the criminals condemned to death, and the prisoners captured during the Muhammadan incursions, should be cast into it, in order to accustom the crocodiles not to allow any foe to cross it.—De Barros, *Dec.* II., liv. v., cap. i., p. 433; *Lendas, ut supra,* II., p. 55; Andrea Corsali *in Ramusio,* vol. I., p. 177.

‡ Briggs's *Ferishta,* vol. II., p. 483; Scott's *Ferishta,* vol. I., p. 156; Birch's *Commentaries of Albuquerque,* vol. II., p. 95; *Lendas,* vol. II., p. 56.

dignified with the most exalted titles, and presented with a royal dress. Khush Kadam, a nobleman of considerable merit, was, at the recommendation of Khvájá Gawan, elevated to the title of Khishvar Khán, and appointed to the government of the newly conquered territory.*

But the Hindus had not yet lost the hope of recovering Goa. In 1472 Vikrama, the Rájá of Belgaum, instigated by the king of Vijayanagara, resolved to wrest the city from the hands of the Muhammadans. He was to be assisted in this enterprise by the chief of Bankápur. Muhammad Sháh, on receiving intelligence of this design, immediately put himself at the head of a large army, and, advancing by forced marches, unexpectedly appeared before the fortress of Belgaum and invested it on all sides. Assailed in his own dominions, the Rájá was forced to sue for peace after a fruitless attempt at resistance, and the design he had formed of seizing Goa was thenceforward abandoned for ever.†

The Báhmani kingdom of the Dakhaṇ had now reached its furthest extension. In 1478, with a view to its better administration, it was divided into eight *tarafs* or provinces. Each province had its own governor, and each governor had several officers under him entrusted with the management of the different parts of the province. Both the governor and his subordinate officers were apppointed directly by the king. According to this arrangement, the newly conquered territory of Goa was included in the province of Juner, and its government entrusted to Najm-ud-dín Gillání.‡

In 1481 Śiva Rája, king of Vijayanagara, despatched a powerful army to capture the city of Goa, but Muhammad Sháh, who valued his new acquisition very highly, had put it in

---

* Briggs's *Ferishta*, vol. II., p. 485 ; Scott's *Ferishta*, vol. I., p. 156.

† *Ibid.*, vol. I., p. 491 ; Scott's *Ferishta*, vol. I., p. 160.

‡ *Ibid.*, vol. II., pp. 502, 529 ; Scott's *Ferishta*, vol. I., pp. 168, 186 ; Grant Duff's *History of the Mahrattas*, p. 29.

such a posture of defence that the attempts of the Hindu prince altogether failed.*

In the following year Muhammad Sháh II. died; his son was too young to assume the government of his vast possessions. This circumstance was in itself sufficient to induce the governors of the different provinces to become independent of the central authority. The first revolt broke out at Goa. After the death of the governor, Najm-ud-dín Gilláni, one of his subordinate officers, Bahádur Khán Gilláni, seized the reins of government, and established himself as an independent ruler over an extensive territory in the vicinity of Goa. Not content with the authority thus usurped on land, he equipped a fleet for purposes of piracy at sea. He seized several ships laden with merchandize belonging to the people of Gujarát. The king of that place interposed in behalf of his aggrieved subjects. He complained to the court of Bedar of the conduct of Gilláni, and demanded his punishment. This remonstrance had the desired effect. The ministers of the Báhmani king were at length roused into action, and despatched a powerful force to reduce the rebellious officer to submission. Gilláni was defeated and slain in 1493, and the whole territory was recovered. The government of Goa was now entrusted to Malik-en-ul-Múlk Gilláni.†

The governors of the provinces, who had hitherto paid but nominal allegiance to the Báhmani dynasty, and had, through fear of the king of Gujarát, coöperated in the expedition against Bahádur Khán Gilláni, gradually declared their independence, and contributed to the dismemberment of the vast Muhammadan kingdom of the Dakhan. This kingdom was at length split into five distinct principalities, the most powerful of which was the kingdom of Bijápur, founded by Abdul Muzaffar Yusuf Adil Sháh. Yusuf was surnamed *Savái*, or Sabaio according to the Portuguese chroniclers, from the town of

---

* Briggs's *Ferishta*, vol. II., p. 517.

† *Op. cit.*, vol. II., pp. 529, 543 *et seq.*; vol. IV., p. 71; Scott's *Ferishta*, vol. I., pp. 186, 191 *et seq.*; Elphinstone's *History of India*, p. 680.

Sava, where he had been brought up in his early years.* In 1488 this prince formed a league with two other princes of the Dakhaṇ for the purpose of dividing the territory among themselves. The city of Goa and the places in its neighbourhood fell to his own share. Thereupon he exacted allegiance and submission from Malik-en-ul-Múlk-Gilláni, the officer who had, as already stated, succeeded Bahádur Khán Gilláni in the government of Goa. Malik-en-ul-Múlk thought it prudent to acknowledge Yusuf's authority, and in token of his cheerful submission caused public rejoicings to be made in the city for a whole week.† It is related that the king of Bijápur had such a predilection for this place that he not only resided there fre-

---

* Abdul Muzaffar Yusuf Adil Sháh was the son of Agá Murád, or Amurath, Sultan of the Turks (Gibbon, *Decline and Fall of the Roman Empire*, vol. XII., p. 150); after his father's death in 1451 he was saved by his mother from being put to death by his brother, who had succeeded to the throne. He was secretly delivered over to Khvájá Imád-ud-dín, a merchant of Sava, in Persia, who took and educated him till his seventeenth year. In 1459, moved by a presentiment of his future greatness, or, as the Muhammadan historian (Ferishta, vol. I., pp. 1 *et seq.*) relates, led by a dream, he set sail for India, where every bold and shrewd adventurer had a good opportunity of rising to the highest posts of honour, and even to the throne. Here he was sold, or got himself sold, to Khvájá Muhammad Gawan, the great minister of the Báhmani king and conqueror of Goa. Yusuf, surnamed *Saváí* by the Muhammadans, from the town of Sava where he was brought up, rose rapidly from a simple soldier to the command of the royal bodyguard. Invested with the title of Adil Khán and adopted by Khvájá Gawan, he was made governor of Daulatábád, and afterwards of Bijápur, where in 1489 he was crowned king.

Gaspar Correia (*Lendas*, II., p. 56) and the author of the *Commentaries of Albuquerque* (vol. II., pp. 95, 96) confound Yusuf Adil Khán with Muhammad Sháh Báhmani, both of whom are called by them *Sabaio*. The title of Adil Khán is corrupted by them, as well as by De Barros, into *Idalcão*, and is generally applied to Yusuf's son Ismail Adil Khán. The name *Sabaio* was written by some contemporary travellers—as Ludovico di Varthema (Badger's *Varthema's Travels*, p. 92)—as *Savaim*, and by others as *Zabaim*.

† Briggs's *Ferishta*, vol. III., p. 19; Scott's *Ferishta*, vol. I., p. 217. The city of Goa was well known to Yusuf Adil Khán, as it was he who had been sent by the Báhmani king to defend it against the king of Vijayanagara. —Briggs's *Ferishta*, vol. II., p. 517.

quently, but also, owing to the great advantages of its position and the beauty of its port, at one time resolved to make it the seat of his government.*

Goa was indeed at this period one of the principal emporiums of trade on the western coast of India, and the great centre which attracted people of various races and creeds from different parts of Asia. In consequence of its opulence and flourishing trade, several Eastern princes maintained amicable relations with its government.† Professor Buchot says that while Calicut, another celebrated port on the western coast, owed its importance and wealth to the veneration in which it was held by the Muhammadans, Goa was the natural entrepôt of the commerce of Asia.‡ The city was well built and fortified, and contained many beautiful edifices.§ It was the rendezvous of the Muhammadans of the peninsula, who embarked thence to proceed to Jeddah on their way to Mecca, a circumstance which, as Dr. Vincent observes, was alone sufficient to render Goa the most important station in India.|| Its fame attracted many a traveller, among whom may be mentioned Pero Covilhã, Ludovico di Varthema, Andrea Corsali, and Duarte Barboza.¶ The last named traveller describes it in these terms:—

> "It (the city of Goa) was inhabited by many Moors, respectable men, and foreigners, white men, and rich merchants, and several of them are very good gentlemen. There are also many great Gentile merchants and other gentlemen-cultivators and men-at-arms. It was a place of great trade in merchandize. It has a very good port, to which flock many ships from Mekkah, Aden, Ormuz, Cambay, and Malabar country. And the before-mentioned Sabayn Delcani lived much in this place, and he kept there his captain and men-at-arms, and no one entered or went out of this island city either by sea or by land without his permission, and all those who

* *Commentaries, ut supra*, vol. II., p. 96; *Lendas, ut supra*, II., p. 55.

† *Lendas*, II., pp. 62, 156; *Portugal*, par M. Ferdinand Diniz, Paris, 1846, p. 181.

‡ *Histoire du Portugal*, par Auguste Buchot, Paris, 1854, p. 131.

§ *Commentaries of Affonso d'Albuquerque*, vol. II., p. 96.

|| Vincent's *Periplus of the Erythræan Sea*, vol. II., p. 394.

¶ The two last travellers visited the city soon after the conquest by Albuquerque, when little change was effected in it.

entered there were registered with all their signs and particulars and from whence they came; and so with this precaution and arrangement they were allowed to return. This town was very large, with goodly edifices and handsome streets and squares surrounded by walls and towers. There is a very good fortress in it, and in the environs many gardens and orchards of fine trees and fruits, and many pools of good water. There were many mosques and houses of worship of the Gentiles. The country all round was very fruitful and well cultivated, and enjoyed much produce both from sea and land."*

This description, brief as it is, is yet sufficient to enable us to form some idea of the state of the city under the Muhammadan sway. The dimensions of the city, as given by the traveller, appear, however, to be exaggerated, for it is pretty certain that under Moslem rule the city was considerably smaller than under the Portuguese. According to Andrea Corsali its circuit was not more than a mile; † while a modern traveller, basing his estimate on his own researches and on those of Linschoten, who had seen its old ramparts, conjectures that it was no more than three-fourths of a mile in length and barely a quarter of a mile in breadth.‡ The ramparts encircling the city were not very high, but were surrounded by a ditch always filled with water. The wall towards the north extended from the Mandovi or Custom-house—a spacious edifice contiguous to the present Convent of St. Cajetan—to the Arsenal, which lay at the other extremity. Besides the gates of the Custom-house and of the Arsenal this wall had a large gate in the middle. This gate stood on the site where subsequently the Arch of the Viceroys was erected, and afforded ingress into the citadel, where Adil Sháh had magnificent apartments, with a garden full of aromatic plants. On the east the wall extended to the foot of the hill which was subsequently named the

* *A Description of the Coast of East Africa and Malabar in the beginning of the 16th Century*, by Duarte Barboza, translated by the Honourable H. E. J. Stanley, London, 1866, p. 74.

† Ramusio's *Delle Navigationi et Viaggi*, Primo vol., Quarta Editione, Venetia, 1588, p. 178.

‡ *An Historical Sketch of Goa*, by the late Rev. Denis L. Cottineau de Kloguen, Madras, 1831, p. 9; *Histoire de la Navigation de Jean Hugues de Linschot*, Amsterdam, 1638, p. 55.

hill of *Nossa Senhora de Monte,* and on the west it stretched as far as the Arsenal. On the south it reached the site of the Church of *Nossa Senhora de Serra,* which is now used as the cemetery of the Cathedral,—the Holy Hill or the Hill of *Nossa Senhora do Rosario,* and the elevated spot on which stands the convent of *Bom Jesus* lying outside this wall. Near the site of the Church of *Nossa Senhora de Serra,* the citadel had a gate, or rather a double gate, called the *Buçaes,* which led to the suburbs.* Besides the ramparts, the city was protected by strongholds erected in ancient times, as already stated, in certain parts of the island, which were called *pár* (*passos*), from the circumstance that people generally passed over thence to the main land.

Among the buildings that adorned the city, the most conspicuous were the chief mosque and the majestic palace of Sabayo (Adil Sháh), with spacious and magnificent saloons and handsome porticos supported by columns of carved wood. In front of the palace stretched a vast open square, even after the Portuguese conquest known as the *Terreiro de Sabayo.* Close to it there was a large tank of good masonry work, probably built for the recreation of the kings of Bijápur. On the side of the river, at a little distance from the tank, was a well-shaded spot where the Muhammadans generally repaired to enjoy the evening breeze.†

The private buildings in the city were for the most part single-storied, but sufficiently spacious and commodious. There were several houses of public recreation, and shops of different artizans, amongst whom the goldsmiths had the reputation of being the best in India.‡ According to De Barros the city of Goa alone yielded to Adil Sháh £5,000, besides the £20,000 or 400,000 pardaus which that monarch received from the surround-

---

* It is so called by Gaspar Correia : *Lendas,* vol. II., p. 94.

† *Lendas,* II., pp. 149 *et seq.*

‡ *Op. cit.*, p. 59 ; De Barros, *Dec.* II., liv. v., cap. ii., p. 457 ; Andrea Corsali in Ramusio, vol. I., p. 178.

ing districts which then formed the territory of Goa.* Varthema states that these pardaus were smaller in size than the xerafins of Cairo, but thicker, and had two devils stamped upon one side of them, and an inscription on the other.† This revenue was chiefly derived from customs duties, especially those levied on horses imported from Ormuz or the coast of Arabia, £2 being charged on each animal. The abovementioned *passos* yielded £110. The Government monopolized the trade in articles of daily consumption, such as vegetables, betel-nut, etc., and realized an annual profit of £1650.‡

---

* De Barros, *Dec.* II., liv. v., cap. ii., p. 455; Gaspar Correia (*Lendas*, II., p. 74) says that the territory of Goa yielded 300,000 pardaus of gold, or £15,000.

† *The Travels of Ludovico di Varthema*, translated by George P. Badger, London, 1868, p. 92.

‡ De Barros, *loc. cit.*

CHAPTER III.

THE ADVENT OF THE PORTUGUESE TO INDIA—THE CONQUEST OF GOA BY ALBUQUERQUE—HIS EXPULSION FROM THE CITY BY THE KING OF BIJÁPUR—SECOND INVASION OF GOA BY THE PORTUGUESE, AND THE FINAL CONQUEST OF THE CITY—THE POLICY OF ALBUQUERQUE.

Such was the state of Goa, when in 1498 Vasco da Gama discovered the route to India, and received at Angediva the visit of the wily Spanish Jew, commander of the fleet of Adil Sháh, who, having been foiled in his attempt to capture or destroy the Portuguese fleet, was taken prisoner and carried to Portugal, where he was baptized and received the name of Gaspar da Gama.* Twelve years after this event Affonso de Albuquerque, actuated by the counsels of Timoja, a neighbouring Hindu chief, who had gained his confidence, presented himself with a powerful fleet before the city. This great captain, swerving from the line of policy pursued by his predecessor Dom Francisco d'Almeida, the first Viceroy of the Indies, whose ambition was simply to be the master of the Indian seas, had conceived the plan of founding a vast empire on land in the East, with Goa for its capital. Situated on the western coast of the Indian peninsula, commanding a naturally favourable position for intercourse with different parts of Asia, and forming with its two splendid harbours one of the best naval stations in the East, Goa appeared to the penetrating eye and the enterprising genius of Albuquerque as admirably fitted for the realization of his most sanguine wishes. The internal state of the city was in itself favourable to the project of the Portuguese hero. The Muhammadan government was oppressive and tyrannical, and had on that account rendered itself thoroughly odious to the people; nor, by reason of the diver-

* *Lendas, ut supra,* I., pp. 125, 142.

sity of creeds and races, were the people capable of united action against a foreign invader. Moreover, the king of Bijápur was at the time engaged in consolidating his newly acquired dominions, and had consigned the city with its environs to the care of one of his favourites, Yusuf Gurgii, who, with two hundred Turks under him, practised frightful cruelties on the poor inhabitants.* All these circumstances conspired to render the city an easy prey to the first invader. Towards the middle of February 1510, the fleet of Albuquerque, consisting of twenty sail of the line and a few small vessels with 1200† fighting men, unexpectedly made its appearance in the harbour of Goa. The city, little prepared for a determined resistance, and disheartened by the predictions of a *yogi* who had foretold its conquest by a foreign people coming from a distant land, surrendered itself into the hands of Albuquerque, who celebrated his entry on the 17th of the same month with regal pomp.‡ Eight leading men presented to him on their knees the keys of the city, together with a large banner which was usually unfurled on state occasions. Mounted on a noble and richly caparisoned steed, Albuquerque entered the city amid drums beating and trumpets sounding, and proceeded to the palace of Adil Sháh, accompanied by a large number of fidalgos and captains bearing their standards, and clergymen carrying before them a gilt cross, amidst the acclamations of an immense multitude of people who hailed the conqueror, and as he passed along showered on him flowers of gold and silver.§ Having

---

* *Lendas, ut supra*, vol. II., p. 50. Besides the 200 Turks in the city, there were 400 Muhammadans in the castle of Pangim, who offered vigorous resistance to the Portuguese. De Barros, *Dec.* II., liv. v., cap. iii., p. 459.

† In this and some other points De Barros and Faria y Souza differ slightly from Gaspar Correia, whom we have generally followed.

‡ De Barros, *Dec.* II., liv. v., cap. iii. The City, according to Faria y Souza (*op. cit.*, p. 131), surrendered itself to Albuquerque on 27th February; according to the *Commentaries* (*ut supra*, p. 88) on the 29th of the same month, and according to Gaspar Correia (*Lendas*, II., p. 59) on the 1st March.

§ *Lendas*, II., p. 58 ; De Barros, *Dec.* II., liv. v., cap. iii. ; Faria y Souza, *ut supra*, p. 131.

seized the city without the loss of a single follower, the conqueror showed the greatest moderation and clemency towards all classes of the people, and issued a proclamation to the effect that equal justice and protection would be extended to all the inhabitants of the place, who were thenceforward subjects of the King of Portugal. At the same time he forbade his soldiers, on pain of death, to injure, offend, or otherwise molest the natives in the slightest degree. In vouchsafing to the people complete security of person and property, he also guaranteed to respect their rights and privileges, and promised to receive only the ancient dues, which amounted to £7,500, instead of the £15,000 which had been annually exacted by the Muhammadan government.*

Whilst Albuquerque was by these means conciliating the people and establishing his authority at Goa on a secure footing, Adil Sháh, who had at first been taken by surprise at the sudden conquest of the city by the Portuguese, made strenuous efforts to regain it.† In this he was secretly aided by the Muhammadan inhabitants of the place, who, repenting of their rashness in having delivered the city into the hands of the Portuguese, longed for the ancient domination of their co-religionists. Adil Sháh, having completed his preparations, laid siege to the city three months after its capture by Albuquerque, with an overwhelming force of 60,000 men.‡ After a short and ineffectual resistance, Albuquerque was constrained to abandon the city and betake himself with his countrymen to his fleet.

This event took place on the 23rd of May 1510, by which time the rainy season had set in.§ Owing to the

---

* *Lendas, ut supra*, II., p. 74. According to De Barros, as already stated, this sum was larger.

† According to the Portuguese chroniclers, Yusuf Adil Sháh had died before the conquest of the city by Albuquerque, but we have followed Ferishta on this point.

‡ De Barros, *Dec.* II., liv. v., cap. v., p. 490. Gaspar Correia (*Lendas*, II., p. 93) gives the number of the soldiers of the king of Bijápur as 48,000, whilst Ferishta (Briggs, III., p. 30) states it to have been only 3,000.

§ *Lendas*, II., p. 97.

stormy weather the fleet could not leave the harbour; Albuquerque therefore determined to lie at anchor during the rainy season off Pangim. Here the Portuguese had to suffer countless privations for want of provisions. Their distress was indeed so frightful that they were forced to live on rats and other loathsome food.* Though reduced to these straits Albuquerque did not lose heart. He spurned the offer of the Muhammadan prince, who, with a view to ascertain the real state of the hostile fleet, had despatched from the island a boat containing abundant provisions. Perceiving the stratagem, he ordered all the wine and biscuits which were preserved for the sick and the infirm to be exhibited from the deck, and thus presented to the messengers from the prince an appearance of cheerfulness and plenty in the Portuguese ships. He bade the messengers take back what they had brought with them, and tell their prince that the Portuguese revelled in abundance and stood in no need of foreign help, and that if their provisions should ever be exhausted, they knew well how to obtain them from the island.†

On the 15th of August, as soon as the violence of the rainy season had abated, Albuquerque started for the neighbouring island of Angediva. On his way he descried four ships well equipped coming from Portugal, which were followed by six others, constituting the second armament despatched in that year by King Dom Manuel. He was overjoyed at this unexpected succour, as well as at the welcome news which he received on his arrival at Angediva from his ally Timoja, that the Muhammadan prince had departed for the Dakhaṇ, leaving Goa under the command of his general Rasul Khán.‡ Albuquerque thereupon hastened to Cannanore, and, having there made the necessary preparations, started on the 3rd of October, with a large fleet of twenty-eight ships carrying 1700 armed men on board, for the purpose of recapturing the city

---

* *Lendas, ut supra*, II., p. 100; De Barros, *Dec.* II., liv. v., cap. vii., p. 511.

† *Lendas*, II., p. 101; De Barros, *Dec.* II., liv. v., cap. vi.

‡ *Lendas*, II., p. 121.

of Goa.* On the 25th of the same month he landed at Honore, to witness the nuptials of his friend Timoja with the daughter of the chief of Garsopa, who promised to aid him with 4,000 men. On the conclusion of these festivities he returned to Angediva, where he called his fidalgos and captains to a council of war, and in a long pathetic speech impressed on them the necessity of retaking the city. His words produced the desired effect, and his project was hailed with acclamation even by those who were at first opposed to it, all promising to coöperate heart and soul with him in the prosecution of his undertaking. Emboldened by this outburst of enthusiasm on the part of his followers, Albuquerque gave the necessary instructions for a well-planned attack on the city, and on the 24th of November, entering with his fleet the harbour of Goa with banners unfurled and trumpets sounding, cast anchor off Banguenim.

A more seasonable moment for the assault could not have been chosen. The king of Bijápur had just died, leaving his throne to his infant son Ismail Adil Sháh, who was hardly able to realize the magnitude of the danger which threatened his possessions on the coast. The defence of the city was left to the valour and genius of Rasul Khán, who had under him 4,000 soldiers in the city and 4,000 in the suburbs.† The Portuguese commenced their operations by directing an attack towards the *Ribeira* or arsenal. But they met with a vigorous resistance from within. After a long contest, they bore down every opposition, scaled the ramparts, and, planting their victorious banner on the walls, forced their way into the city, amidst deafening shouts raised in honour of St. Catherine.‡ Within the city the invaders had to encounter fresh opposition.

* *Lendas*, II., pp. 132, 140; De Barros (*loc. cit.*) and Faria y Souza (*op. cit.*, p. 137) state the number of ships to have been twenty-three.

† Briggs's *Ferishta*, III., p. 33; *Lendas*, vol. II., p. 140.

‡ The Portuguese soldier who first scaled the ramparts was called Fradique Fernandes; and it was a native Christian, by name João Corçes, who forced his way first through the door of the arsenal into the city: *Lendas*, vol. II., p. 149.

The Musalmáns fought with the courage of despair. A bloody battle ensued, in which about 2,000 Musalmáns fell on the spot. The rest were obliged to save themselves by flight through the principal gate of the Custom-house. The victors lost not more than forty men. A general consternation spread through the city. The inhabitants in their panic made towards the southern gate to effect their escape. Of these nearly 3,000, mostly Muhammadans, are said to have perished in their attempt to cross the river.* Ferishta and the author of the *Tohfut-ul-Mujahidín* attribute the capture of the city by the Portuguese to the treason of Rasul Khán and some of its principal inhabitants,† but this statement appears to be utterly groundless. It may have proceeded from a predilection for their co-religionists, over whose weakness they were naturally desirous of throwing a decent veil.‡

* *Lendas*, II., pp. 153, 155; De Barros, *Dec.* II., liv. v., cap. ix., p. 545. Camoens has sung the conquest of Goa in the following verses :—

" Que gloriosas palmas tecer vejo,
Com que victoria a fronte lhe coroa,
Quando sem sombra vãa de medo, ou pejo,
Toma a ilha illustrissima de Goa !
Despois, obedecendo au duro ensejo
A deixa, e occasião espera boa,
Com que a torne a tomar ; que esforço, e arte,
Vencerão a fortuna, e o proprio Marte."

Os Lusiadas, Canto X., v. xlii.

" What glorious palms on Goa's isle I see,
Their blossoms spread, great Albuquerk, for thee !
Through castled walls the hero breaks his way,
And opens with his sword the dread array
Of Moors and pagans; through their depth he rides,
Through spears and showering fire the battle guides.
As bulls enraged, or lions smear'd with gore,
His bands sweep wide o'er Goa's purpled shore."

Mickle's Translation, p. 377.

† Briggs's *Ferishta*, vol. III., p. 34; Rowlandson's *Tohfut-ul-Mujahidín*, p. 135.

‡ The Portuguese chroniclers give such a detailed account of this matter as to leave no doubt about the conquest being due to the valour of the Portuguese.

Albuquerque, who was watching the issue of the contest from a neighbouring hill with a select body of five hundred men, then descended from his elevated position and entered the city with the royal flag unfurled before him, and on his knees offered thanks to God for having crowned his arms with success. He then embraced all his captains as they approached him covered with wounds and bearing swords still reeking with blood, praised them for the valour and energy they had displayed on that day, and conferred on several of them the honour of knighthood.* Then turning his attention to the conquered people, Albuquerque resolved upon a course of action which has left an indelible stain on his illustrious name. Inflamed with deadly animosity against the Moslems, who had before aided the king of Bijápur in driving him out of the city, he issued orders for the massacre of the whole of the Muhammadan population, without distinction of sex, rank, or age. He let loose his soldiery on the defenceless people, and subjected them to frightful cruelties.†

For three days the town was sacked and plundered, and a considerable booty was thereby secured. Of this an estimate may be formed when it is remembered that a fifth part of it, which by the right of war was reserved for the Crown, amounted to about £20,000.‡ A far larger sum would have been manifestly due to the Crown if the soldiers had faithfully accounted for all that their rapacious hands had seized. But, as it was, they concealed more than they produced in public. Besides this ill-gotten booty, the conquerors seized 3,000 pieces of ordnance, with a vast store of ammunition.§

Albuquerque, apprehensive that the Muhammadans might, as on the first occasion, endeavour to retake the city, resolved to put it in a state of defence. He repaired the ramparts,

---

* *Lendas, ut supra*, II., p. 152.

† *Ibid.*, pp. 154, 155.

‡ *Histoire des Découvertes et Conquestes des Portugais*, par J. F. Lafitan, Paris, 1735, vol. II., pp. 109 *et seq.*

§ *Lendas*, II., p. 158.

and over the gates and in several other places erected turrets provided with embrasures. But he directed his attention principally to the rebuilding of the citadel. He entrusted the execution of the work to Thomas Fernandes, and wishing to have it finished with all possible despatch, and finding that there were not sufficient hands available for the purpose, he ordered even the chief officers of the army to take part in the work, and, to set them an example in his own person, he did not hesitate to undergo himself the toilsome drudgery of a common labourer. When at last the citadel was thoroughly rebuilt, he gave it the name of Dom Manoel, the reigning king of Portugal, and ordered a slab of stone to be put up in a conspicuous place with his own name and those of the captains who had assisted him in taking the city inscribed thereon. But each captain insisted on having his name put first in the inscription, and, as it was impossible to satisfy all, Albuquerque in pure disgust abandoned the idea, and bade only the following well-known words to be engraved on the slab :—" *Lapidem quem reprobaverunt edificantes,*" "The stone which the builders condemned."*

Albuquerque was as politic a statesman as he was a skilful general. He knew how to establish his newly acquired dominion on a secure basis. He conciliated his subjects by framing a just and equitable system of legislation. He tolerated all forms of religious belief, and made the burden of taxation as light as he could. With this, however, he was not satisfied; he aimed at cementing the union of the rulers and the ruled. He therefore encouraged intermarriages between them, by loading the married pairs with substantial gifts and favours, distributing among them the landed property of the Moslems which had lately been confiscated, and encouraging them to cultivate the mechanical arts for the benefit of the new Portuguese settlement. He also established a municipality, the first of its kind in India, composed entirely of the new settlers; organized the administra-

---

* *Lendas*, II., p. 157; De Barros, *Dec.* II., liv. v., cap. xi., p. 558; *Os Portuguezes em Africa, Asia, America e Oceania*, Lisboa, 1848, vol. I., p. 75.

tion of justice; set apart funds for the support and education of poor children, and conferred several important privileges on the city. While, on the one hand, he treated the Muhammadans with undue severity and harshness, he showed marked favour to the Hindus, guaranteeing them the enjoyment of all their customs and usages, except the horrid rite of *sati*, which he suppressed even at that early period.* He continued the practice which existed during the Muhammadan rule of farming the taxes, but punished with merciless rigour every species of oppression practised on the merchants and traders. Timoja, and after him Mádhavráv (whom the Portuguese chroniclers call Melrau), was appointed *Tanadar-mor, i. e.* the chief collector of revenues.† Persons of high birth and acknowledged merit were selected to fill important offices in the State. Rodrigo Rebello was nominated captain of the city, Francisco Pantoja *Alcaide-mor* (constable for the town), and Francisco Corvinel *Feitor* or factor.‡ In this way he laid the foundation of a benign and equitable form of government in the capital, as he intended it to be, of the Portuguese Empire in the East; but the chief seat of government was not transferred from Cochin to Goa till twenty years later.

---

* *Lendas, ut supra*, II., pp. 158, 159, 375, 376; De Barros, *Dec.* II., liv. v., cap. xi., p. 567; Faria y Souza, *ut supra*, p. 137.

† A *Tánádár* or *Thánádár* was an officer in charge of a *thána*, a place where he was posted with a small irregular force to protect the country, preserve the peace, and aid in making collection of taxes—see Wilson's *Glossary, in voce* 'Thána.'

‡ *Lendas*, II., p. 335.

CHAPTER IV.

MATERIAL PROGRESS OF THE CITY AFTER THE DEATH OF ALBUQUERQUE—PRIVILEGES CONFERRED ON THE CITY BY THE HOME GOVERNMENT—SIEGE OF GOA BY THE KING OF BIJÁPUR—FIRST OUTBREAK OF EPIDEMIC IN THE CITY, AND ITS CAUSES—THE CONSTRUCTION OF SUITABLE DEFENCES FOR THE CITY—ITS EXTENT, POPULATION, AND ASPECT IN ITS PALMY DAYS AS DESCRIBED BY SEVERAL TRAVELLERS.

Albuquerque died in 1515. Though deplored by all his followers, and even by the newly conquered people, his death did not affect the material prosperity of the city. The impulse which he had given to its substantial improvement did not die with him. Buildings began to be erected on vacant sites, both at public and private expense, which were not only an ornament to it, but also an indication of its rising greatness. In fact such buildings multiplied so fast, filling every nook and corner of the city, that there was hardly any room left for more structures. It is not, therefore, a matter of surprise that Lopo Soares, the successor of Albuquerque, should have hesitated on one occasion to grant a piece of land for the erection of a convent in addition to the three churches which were already in the city.* Being thus too small for its increasing wealth and population, the limits of the city were necessarily extended; the wide ditch that surrounded its walls was filled up, and the additional space thus created was, contrary to the royal order of 10th March 1540, assigned for new buildings. Once the old barriers were overstepped, the city rapidly grew in size in almost every direction, affording ample accommodation for its population, which, on a rough calculation, was, at this period, ascertained

* *Lendas, ut supra*, vol. II., p. 537.

to be about 200,000 souls. St. Francis Xavier was so much impressed with the beauty of the city, on his first arrival in Goa in 1542, that he speaks of it in flattering terms in a letter to a brother of his order at Rome.*

In the following year, however, cholera of a virulent type broke out at Goa, and spread so fast all over the city that, according to an eye-witness, persons of every age, rank, and sex were daily swept away in great numbers. Nay, even the stalled beast and domestic fowl could not escape its ravages. A perfect panic prevailed in the city.† The very sound of the bell tolled at the time of burial caused the affrighted people to tremble for their safety. Accordingly the Governor, Martim Affonso de Souza, forbade the tolling of the bell on the occasion of any funeral. The Cathedral being the only parochial church in the city at this time, the priests attached to it could not minister to the spiritual wants of the vast number of the sick and dying. Hence the bishop, Dom Fr. João de Albuquerque, ordered the churches of Our Lady of the Rosary and Our Lady of Light to be raised to the rank of parochial churches.‡

After the violence of the epidemic had subsided, the city began again to exhibit signs of improvement. New buildings and institutions rose on all sides, and gave it an aspect worthy of the capital of the Portuguese Empire in the East. In 1548 the number of the churches and chapels in the city and its suburbs was fourteen, whilst there were no fewer than a hundred clergymen, besides those who had no fixed residence.§ In 1557 the city was made the seat of an archbishopric. Vincent Le Blanc, a French traveller who visited Goa about this time, when the celebrated poet Camoës was also there, speaks

---

* *Letter of St. Francis Xavier* 18th September 1542, Coll., vol. I., p. 61.

† *Lendas, ut supra,* IV., p. 288. Gaspar Correia, though not a medical man, describes at that early period in clear language the symptoms of cholera morbus, and the aspect of the internal organs as shown by autopsy.

‡ *Lendas, loc. cit.*

§ *Op. cit.*, p. 669.

with admiration of the magnificence of the buildings, the luxury of the people, and the conveniences and comforts of life accessible to all in this most opulent city, as he calls it, which in his estimation surpassed even Lisbon itself.* The revenues of the city had also by this time increased considerably. As above stated, they consisted of the monopoly of all articles of retail. The *Vedor da Fazenda*, Simão Botelho, mentions in his *Tombo* (a general register) the several items of revenue.†

Goa enjoyed at this time privileges similar to those conferred

---

* *Voyages; Portugal*, por M. Ferdinand Denis, p. 251.

† The following were in 1547 the chief sources of revenue:—

	£	s.	d.
Customs revenue	2937	10	0
Betel leaves, fruits, and vegetables	187	10	0
Spices	147	1	8
Arrack	151	5	0
Revenue derived from shops—			
(*a*) Provisions	186	13	4
(*b*) Cotton cloth	44	3	4
(*c*) Silk and sundry articles	114	11	8
Exchange	71	5	9
Goldsmiths	29	11	8
Fishermen and Milkmen	22	18	4
Opium, Bhang, etc.	47	1	8
Silk-weavers	17	14	2
Washermen	11	17	6
Bread and cheese	16	17	8
Oil, milk, etc.	4	11	8

The following list of the prices of some of the articles of food in 1537 has been given by Mr. J. H. Rivara from an old official document:—

Milk at $\frac{4}{15}$*d.* per canada or 3 pints.
Pork $\frac{4}{15}$ to $\frac{14}{45}$*d.* per lb.
A Hen $\frac{8}{15}$*d.*
A Chicken $\frac{4}{15}$*d.*
An Egg $\frac{1}{32}$*d.*
A Cocoanut $\frac{1}{26}$*d.*
Plantains 2 to 12 for $\frac{1}{20}$*d.*, according to quality.
Mangoes, best, 3 for $\frac{1}{28}$*d.*, common 8.
Grapes, 1*d.* per lb.
Cucumbers, 6 to 8 for $\frac{1}{28}$*d.*

on the capital of Portugal. It had already been declared inalienable from the Portuguese Crown. It maintained direct communication with the King through its Senate or Municipal Chamber, which, as before stated, had been established by Albuquerque, and could thus lay before His Majesty not only its own wants and grievances, but also those of the other Portuguese possessions in the East. It had, besides, a special representative to plead its interests at the Court of Lisbon. In 1563 a formal proposal was made to the Home Government to establish in Goa a sort of parliament or representative assembly, where deputies from different parts of the Portuguese Empire in the East might meet together for the transaction of business affecting its welfare. But this proposal did not meet with the approval of the King, and the question appears never to have been afterwards reopened.*

During the government of Dom Antão de Noronha (1564-8) orders were received from the King of Portugal to provide the city with suitable defences, especially as it had outstepped its ancient limits, and the old walls could no longer hold or protect its teeming population. The Viceroy accordingly thought it advisable to build a wall which, commencing from the north-eastern angle of the island, might protect the whole of its eastern side, and then turning to the south terminate in the west of the city. Besides this wall, it was proposed a few years later to fortify the city itself; but this scheme was dropped, and Government applied itself to the completion of the aforesaid wall, as well as to the erection of fortresses for the defence of the harbour.†

Oranges 3 to 8 for $\frac{1}{28}$*d.*, according to quality.

Limes 6 for $\frac{1}{28}$*d.*

Arrack $\frac{1}{8}$*d.* per canada or 3 pints.

Lisbon Wine 2*d.* per canada or 3 pints.

* *Archivo Portuguez Oriental*, Nova-Goa, Fasc. I., doc. 39; II., doc. 3, 35 42; *Instituto Vasco da Gama*, Nova-Goa, 1872, vol. I., p. 136.

† *Arch. Port. Or.*, Fasc. I., doc. 18, 72; Fasc. III., doc. 35, 76, 141, 209, 243, 311.

During the progress of these works (1570) a powerful confederacy was entered into by the Muhammadan princes of the Dakhan, the king of Acheen, and the Zamorin of Calicut for expelling the Portuguese from India. Accordingly, a simultaneous attack was made on the Portuguese possessions on the coast. The city of Goa was besieged by Ali Adil Sháh with a force of 100,000 men and 2,140 elephants. There were not more than seven hundred European soldiers available at this time for the defence of the city; consequently three hundred friars and clergymen and one thousand slaves were called upon to coöperate with the regular troops. There were, besides, a number of boats stationed in the river, which were but indifferently manned and equipped. With this force, poor as it was, the city made a gallant stand against the overwhelming forces of the enemy. For ten months the besiegers invested the place without gaining any material advantage; at length, finding their numbers reduced by sickness and fighting, and despairing of making any impression on the city, they withdrew.*

At this time the Venetian merchant Cæsar Frederick was in Goa. He describes the city as grand and beautiful, and the island in which it was situated as full of "goodly gardens filled with divers trees." The prices of provisions had risen so high in consequence of the siege, that he complains of the unusually great expense he incurred in procuring means of subsistence during his sojourn at Goa. He says that an ordinary chicken cost him "seven or eight livres, which amounts to six shillings or six shillings and eight pence of English money."† In short, food became so scarce and dear that the greater part of the city was afflicted by a famine, which was followed by an epidemic fever of a virulent character.‡

This calamity, which eventually contributed in a great measure to the destruction of the city, must be traced to causes of a far deeper origin than the mere dearth of provisions occasioned

---

* Faria y Souza, *ut supra*, p. 423.

† *Hakluyt Collection of Voyages*, vol. II., p. 345.

‡ *Arch. Port. Or.*, Fasc. I., doc. 61.

by the siege. The city was in the first place surrounded by marshes and stagnant pools, emitting noxious exhalations, whilst little or no attention was paid to the hygienic conditions essential for the preservation of the public health. The muddy banks of the river outside the city were generally covered with the detritus of animal and vegetable matter, which being exposed at low tide to the tropical sun underwent putrefaction, and thereby bred the germs of disease.* Moreover, the common people, with the permission of the Government, made use of the whole of the southern margin of the river, from the Quay of the Palace of the Viceroys to that of St. Catherine, for discharging the necessary functions of nature.† It must next be remembered that the water supply of the city was remarkably deficient, especially in the hot season. The Government did not utilize the abundant stock of pure and wholesome water of Banguenim by means of pipes or aqueducts, and the poor people were obliged to make the most of the impure water which they could get from wells.‡ Lastly it may be mentioned that no measures were taken to keep the city clean. Even the principal thoroughfares were dirty, and nobody was prevented from throwing any quantity of filth he chose into the streets. This, too, was the cause of much sickness even in ordinary times, as was admitted thirty-two years later by the Viceroy, Ayres de Saldanha, in the following *alvará*:—"I make known to all who may read this *alvará* that whereas in this city of Goa the roads are not clean, and there is not that cleanliness which is necessary for health, and consequently much disease and sickness prevails, owing to the filth which its residents allow their servants to throw out, and which they without any fear leave in the lanes and public roads; and whereas it is expedient that this nuisance, so prejudicial to this city and the people thereof,

* See *Archivo de Pharmacia*, Nova-Goa, 1864, vol. I., p. 105.

† *Arch. Port. Or.*, Fasc. II., doc. 51.

‡ The Count of Linhares subsequently, in the year 1630, endeavoured to remedy this scarcity of water, by bringing it probably through an aqueduct: *Livr. das Monç.*, Goa Govt. Rec. (MSS.), No. 14, fol. 168.

should be prevented: It is hereby ordered, in the name of His Majesty, that the members and officers of the Municipal Chamber of this city of Goa do nominate a Portuguese gentleman of good life, conscience, and habits, who may serve as an Inspector of cleanliness in the aforesaid city."*

According to the author of the *Oriente Conquistado*, the city was not regarded as a very healthy place before its occupation by the Portuguese, after which its sanitary condition considerably improved. This improvement is said to have been caused in the same way as in Germany, by the introduction of Christianity into the island. He adds that the subsequent insalubrity was the result of one of two causes—either the fervour of Christianity had cooled down, or the putrefaction of the dead body of an elephant thrown into a lake near the church of *Trindade* infected the air and spread the poison all around.† What importance should be attached to the opinion of this pious writer we need not say, but it is clear from what we have stated that physical causes alone were sufficient to render the city unhealthy, and that one of them might probably have been the infection engendered by the putrefying carcass of the elephant.

The first outbreak of the epidemic in the city was of short duration. It caused, no doubt, considerable havoc, reducing the population in no small degree; but the prosperity of the city in other respects counteracted its effects. Indeed the city had by this time reached the zenith of its glory; and we pause to contemplate its greatness, such as it appears to us at this distance of time, before we proceed to show that in this very greatness are to be found the causes of its subsequent decline and fall. It is a fortunate circumstance that we have full, accurate and authentic accounts of this period in the annals of Goa, left to us by many travellers of distinction who happened to visit the city in its palmy days. Of these we may mention first John Hugo Linschot or Linschoten, a Dutchman, who, being anxious to see the fabulous lands of the East, came to Goa in

* *Arch. Port. Or.*, Fasc. II., doc. 68.
† *Orient. Conq.*, vol. I., p. 22; vol. II., pp. 53 *et seq.*

1583 in the company of the Archbishop, Dom Fr. Vicente da Fonseca, and published on his return to his native country a work called *Histoire de la Navigation*. Another traveller is Francis Pyrard, who visited Goa in June 1608, and returning to Europe two years later published his *Voyage*. We have next the authority of Ralph Fitch, an English merchant, who was for some time imprisoned in Goa, and liberated through the intercession of the Jesuit Father Thomas Estevão, the author of a *Koṅkaṇi Grammar*. We have also the excellent works of Pietro della Valle, Sir T. Herbert, and J. Albert de Mandelslo. From these and other similar authorities we can gather abundant materials for forming a correct estimate of the greatness of the city at the period we have arrived at.

According to Linschoten the position of the city was very much similar to that of Lisbon. Like Lisbon it was situated partly on rising, and partly on level ground. The city of Goa, says another traveller, stands, like imperial Rome, on several hills. Having grown to double its size under the Portuguese sway, it included at this time the *Monte Santo* in the west, the *Outeiro de Nossa Senhora de Monte* in the east, and extended towards the south as far as *Monte de Boa Vista*. The reddish soil of the city is said to have excited the curiosity and cupidity of some Italian alchymists, who hoped to extract gold from it, but were prevented by the Viceroy, lest the fame of its opulence should incite the neighbouring princes to attack and take possession of it. * The hills were crowned with elegant structures, and lower down might be conspicuously seen magnificent palaces, convents and churches, towering one above another. Pyrard tells us that it would be almost an endless task to describe minutely the numerous streets, squares, churches, convents, palaces, and other buildings both public and private, which were worth noticing in Goa. The number of the convents and churches in the city and its suburbs was found to be more than fifty.†

* Linschoten, *Histoire de la Navigation*, p. 56.

† Pyrard, *Voyage*, pt. II., p. 33.

As stated above, the city had no walls of its own, though at the time when Linschoten, Pyrard and Mandelslo visited Goa the ancient walls existed but without gates. The city was protected not only by the fortifications raised for the defence of the harbour, but also by the long wall covering chiefly the eastern side of the island, of which we have spoken above. This wall had been completed by this time. It began with a fort in the north-eastern part of the island at Daugim, and extending from that point to the church of São Braz was joined there to an old Muhammadan fort which had been rebuilt by the Portuguese; thence it proceeded to Benastarim, where it met the fortress of São Thiago.* It then took a southern direction to the fort of Mangueiral, and thence to that of São João Baptista. From that place it took a turn towards the west of the city, and terminated near the *Cuza de Polvora* at Panelim, where a battery was erected.† This wall had three principal gates, at which sentinels kept watch day and night, and as people passed through them in crossing over to the Muhammadan territory on the main-land, they were called *passos*. They corresponded with the three forts above mentioned—the *passo* of Daugim to the north-east, the *passo secco* or the ford of São Braz to the east, and that of Benastarim to the south-east. The last was most frequented by the people, especially as articles of daily consumption were carried through it from the main-land into the city. There were other *passos* also, at Pangim, at Agassaim, and at other places; but these connected the island only with the adjoining Portuguese territory. Every person who passed through those gates, either in or out of the city, paid a tax of two *baza-*

* The fort of Benastarim became very famous in the annals of Goa after the Portuguese conquest. Pietro della Valle makes special mention of it, as also of the house in which resided the then commandant of the fort, and from the balcony of which a splendid view was enjoyed of the surrounding country. In this fortress there was a huge gun which had been taken from the Muhammadans, and which was, till lately, preserved as an historical reminiscence.

† See *Promptuario das Definiçoẽs Indicas*, por Pe. Leonardo Paes, p. 131, and *Bosquejo das Possessoẽs Portuguesas no Oriente*, por J. P. Celestino Soares, Lisboa, 1851, vol. I., p. 32.

rucos,* and received a mark on the arm as a sign of payment. In this way the exact number of persons daily entering and leaving was ascertained. In this way, too, persons accused or suspected of any crime, or runaway slaves, could be detected and caught. All Portuguese were strictly prohibited from passing over to the main-land without leaving their families in Goa, lest they should accept service under any native prince.

The plan of the city given by Linschoten does not precisely determine its dimensions, because it is not drawn on a proper scale. Pyrard says, that it was nearly one and a half leagues, or four and a half miles in circuit, excluding the suburbs; but a modern traveller, after a careful study of the subject, calculates its length from east to west at a mile and a quarter, its breadth at nearly three-quarters of a mile from the margin of the river to the hill on the south, and the total circuit three miles and three-quarters.† To the east lay the suburb of Daugim, whence a row of houses continued almost without interruption to the convent of *Mãe de Deus;* to the west was the suburb of *São Pedro* in Panelim, from which another row of houses extended as far as Ribandar; to the south the dwellings extended as far as Old Goa. On almost all sides, therefore, houses and buildings were seen. Pietro della Valle writes:—"The whole of this land is thickly covered with villas and pleasure walks, and the banks of the rivers particularly are studded with houses and other buildings embosomed in delicious gardens and palm groves."‡ Barreto de Resende

---

* The *bazaruco* is worth about ·04*d*.

† Pyrard, *Voyage*, Part II., p. 16; *An Historical Sketch of Goa*, by Rev. D. L. Cottineau de Kloguen, Madras, 1831, p. 81.

‡ *Viaggi di Pietro della Valle il Pellegrino*, vol. II., p. 592. Sir T. Herbert says further: "The gardens are filled with variety of sweet and eye-pleasing flowers. Above twenty little towns (all planted with Portugals) are seen in this 30 miles compass; as also the ruins of 200 idol temples, which Viceroy de Noronha totally demolished, that no memory might remain or monuments of such gross idolatry." *Some Years' Travels into Divers Parts of Africa and Asia*, London, 1665, p. 41.

states that the number of houses* in the city of Goa was three thousand five hundred, of which eight hundred were occupied by the Portuguese. In this number were not included the convents and other religious buildings.† The population in the beginning of the 17th century is calculated according to some ancient documents at 225,000 souls, three-fourths being Christians, divided among six parishes, and the rest pagans. It seems that the clergy were not included in this number, who, as remarked by Pietro della Valle, were so numerous that one-half of them would have been more than sufficient to meet the requirements of a larger city.‡

The population was composed of men of different races and creeds. There were, according to Linschoten, merchants from Arabia, Armenia, Persia, Cambay, Bengal, Pegu, Siam, Malacca, Java, the Moluccas, China, and various other Eastern countries. There were Venetians, Italians, Germans, Flemings, Castilians, and Englishmen, but scarcely any Frenchmen. There was at this time a considerable number of Musalmáns, though in the first few years of the Portuguese rule they had been almost banished from the city. There were also Jews, who had their own synagogues and their own mode of worship, but the Hindus were not allowed the public exercise of their religion.§ The population of the suburbs must have been considerable, but we have no data from which to calculate the exact number.

The aspect of the city at this time is described by travellers in such glowing terms as to justify the appellation of '*Goa dourada*' ('golden Goa') which was given to it, and the proverb "*Quem vio Goa excusa de vêr Lisboa*," *i. e.*, "Whoever has

---

* *Fogos.*

† *Historia de Portugal,* por Uma Sociedade de Homens das Letras, vol. IV., p. 212.

‡ *Viaggi, ut supra,* p. 593.

§ Mandelslo's *Voyages and Travels,* p. 86; Linschoten's *Histoire de la Navigation,* p. 54; Pyrard, *Voyage,* Part II., p. 33.

seen Goa need not see Lisboa."* Pyrard writes about it as follows:—

"It is about a hundred and ten years since the Portuguese made themselves masters of this island of Goa, and I have often wondered at the rapidity with which the Portuguese have been able to rear stately edifices, so many churches, convents, palaces, fortresses, and other buildings, after the European fashion; at the internal order, regulations, and government which they have established, and at the power to which they have attained, everything being managed as in Lisbon itself. This city is the metropolis of the whole of the Portuguese dominions in India, and as such it commands considerable power, wealth, and celebrity. The Viceroy has his residence there, and keeps his court in the style of the King himself. Next in rank to the Viceroy is the Archbishop; we have then the functionaries of the High Court and those of the Inquisition; besides the Archbishop there is also a Bishop, so that the city is the chief seat of religion and justice in India, and every religious order has its superior there. All ships, both of war and commerce, belonging to the King of Spain [to whom Portugal was at that time subject] set sail from that port . . . As for the multitude of people, it is a marvel to see the number which go and come every day by sea and land on business of every kind. The princes of India who are on terms of peace and friendship with the Portuguese have almost all of them their ordinary ambassadors there, and often send extraordinary embassies to treat for peace; and the Portuguese also send theirs on their part. And as to the merchants continually going and coming from different parts of the East, one would say that a fair was being held every day for the sale of all sorts of merchandize, and even those princes who are not at peace with the Portuguese do not fail to send their goods and merchandise to Goa through the merchants who are on friendly terms with them . . . Thus, whoever has been in Goa may say that he has seen the choicest rarities of India, for it is the most famous and celebrated city, on account of its commercial intercourse with people of all nationalities of the East, who bring there the products of their respective countries, articles of merchandize, necessaries of life, and other commodities in great abundance, because every year more than a thousand ships touch there laden with cargo."†

The city was intersected by numerous streets, many of which were paved with stones; in the rainy season some of them became impassable; no carriages were seen; in their stead palanquins were used, borne on the shoulders of

---

* Lisbon.

† *Voyage*, Part II., pp. 16, 63.

Boyes.* Besides the *Rua Direita*, the road frequented by merchants, there were many other roads, which were called after the names of the classes of people who resided in them, sometimes also after the nature of the traffic carried on there,† so that a traveller says, "It is a great convenience that when anything is needed it is possible to know where to find it." Linschoten describes some of the streets in which pagan merchants lived, many of whom were very rich, having eighty or a hundred thousand *escus*.‡ There was one street, says he, full of shops which were crowded not only with cotton and silk dresses and China porcelain, but also with velvet and other piece-goods of Portugal; on the opposite side were other shops where clothes of all sorts and ready-made shirts were sold, for the use not only of the Portuguese, but also of slaves and poor people. In another street lived those who sold wearing apparel and ornaments worn by ladies. The Banniyas were found in another street with goods of Cambay and precious stones, and were, according to the Dutch traveller, very clever in perforating pearls and corals. There was another street for those who made beds, chairs, and other articles of joinery, which were covered with *laca*, or hard wax, of various colours, presenting a goodly appearance. The goldsmiths and other artizans had their separate streets; and those who collected rents and taxes and acted as brokers had their own square, as had also the pharmaceutics, druggists, and petty shopkeepers. There were streets and open squares or bazaars where fowls, fruits, and

* *Now called Boyás.* See Part I., p. 34.

† Some of the chief roads and thoroughfares in the city were named as follows:—Rua Direita, Rua de São Paulo, Rua de Nossa Senhora de Monte, Rua de Arvore, Rua de Surradores, Rua do Pelourinho, Rua do Bazarinho, Rua de Chapeleiros, Rua de Crucifixo, Rua do Açougue, Rua das Tres Boticas, Rua dos Ferreiros, Rua dos Ourives, Rua dos Judeus, Rua dos Banianes, Rua dos Carregados, Rua dos Guzerates, Rua dos Galés, Rua de Nuno da Cunha, Rua dos Panos, Rua da Ribeira d-El-rei, Rua de S. Jorge, Rua de Salla.

‡ About £20,000.

other eatables imported from the neighbouring continent were sold in such abundance that, according to one of the travellers, provisions were there cheaper than in any other part of the world, and "what in France cost fifty *sols* cost less than five in Goa"; in fact "a man could maintain himself with one *tanga* or five *sols* (2*d.*) a month."* These and other comforts probably induced Ralph Fitch to say, notwithstanding his sufferings at Goa, that even if he returned home, he would come back to Goa again.†

The buildings along the principal thoroughfares were in general spacious and good-looking; whilst in the interior of the city, far from the noise and bustle of the streets, were to be seen splendid mansions, surrounded by gardens tastefully laid out. Both the houses and mansions were not more than two stories high. They were built of stone and mortar, and covered with tiles.‡ The stone required for ordinary buildings was procured from quarries in the island itself, but for constructing columns and other delicate work it was ordered from Bassein. The houses were painted red or white both outside and inside; they had large staircases and beautiful windows furnished with jetties (*sacadas*). Instead of glass panes the windows had thin polished oyster-shells fitted into wooden frame-work, as is still the fashion in Goa, and were provided with lattice-work, to enable the Portuguese ladies to enjoy the view outside without being exposed to the public gaze. The inner apartments were sufficiently large to admit of free ventilation, and were moreover richly furnished; and there was an attempt at neatness and elegance which lent quite a pleasing aspect to the interior of a dwelling. The principal nobility and gentry had not only their mansions in the city, but also their villas in the suburbs, where they resided occasionally with their

* Linschoten, *Histoire de la Navigation*, p. 67; Pyrard, *Voyage*, Part II., pp. 64, 81. The last part of the statement seems hardly credible.

† *Hakluyt's Collection of Voyages*, vol. II., p. 381.

‡ According to Sir T. Herbert (*op. cit.*, p. 41) there were also terraced houses.

families, amidst orchards and groves, bowers and grottos, walks beautifully laid out, and fountains fantastically playing. Here they gave themselves up to mirth and pleasure, whiling away the time in gossiping, sporting, or playing, reclining on sofas or lolling in chairs, attended by slaves who ministered to their comfort and convenience, some fanning them, others entertaining them with the dulcet sounds of music.

There were no hotels or inns in the city; but there were boarding-houses open to the public, and frequented principally by the lower classes.* There were also gaming-houses with saloons and chambers most sumptuously furnished, and elegantly decorated. These houses were subject to a license tax, and were crowded with people of all classes, who repaired thither to enjoy their leisure hours. Those who were inordinately fond of gambling stayed there sometimes for days together, and were provided with board and lodging. They played generally at cards, dice, chess, and ball; and whilst they were playing, there were fair damsels ready to entertain them with music and dancing, jugglers to astonish them with their tricks, and buffoons to amuse them with low jests and ridiculous pranks.

It is impossible in a cursory sketch of this kind to give a very minute or detailed description of the city in its palmy days. Suffice it to say that it displayed all the activity and bustle of a great commercial city. Alluding to this circumstance, Talboys Wheeler says :—

"Every morning the sun rose at Goa upon scenes which may be easily realized. The sailors and coolies loading or unloading in the river; the busy shopkeepers displaying their wares; the slaves bringing in the supplies of water and provisions for the day. There was the palace of the Viceroy, surrounded by majestic Fidalgos giving and exchanging the profoundest courtesies. Many were perhaps making their way to the great hall of council, which was hung with pictures of every Viceroy and Governor from Vasco da Gama downwards. There was also the palace of the Arch-

* The rent of the houses was cheap; the poor Portuguese, especially the soldiers, lived in common in large apartments which were not partitioned. See Linschoten's *Histoire de la Navigation*, p. 63.

bishop, with a crowd of black-robed priests, missionaries, and clergy of every description, native as well as European. Besides these were the courts and offices of the king's council and chancery, with busy clerks labouring at their desks, but all in grave and stately fashion, after the proud manner of the noble Portuguese. Meantime, above the noise of offices and bazaars, the bells were ever ringing from the numerous churches and monasteries, and filling the whole city with an ecclesiastical clangour."*

---

* *The History of India*, vol. III., p. 438.

CHAPTER V.

THE SOCIAL MANNERS AND CUSTOMS OF THE PORTUGUESE DURING THE PROSPERITY OF THE CITY—THEIR LUXURY AND OSTENTATION—THE MODE OF LIVING OF THEIR LADIES—THEIR MANNER OF APPEARANCE IN PUBLIC, ESPECIALLY AT CHURCH—THE SOLEMNITIES ATTENDANT ON MARRIAGES AND BAPTISMS.

To complete the sketch of the city in the days of its prosperity, a short review of the manners and customs of the Portuguese seems necessary. They called themselves fidalgos or noblemen, and never cared to follow any trade or calling. They derived the greater part of their income from the manual labour of their slaves, whose earnings were entirely at their disposal.* They had abundant leisure, which they employed in various kinds of diversions, among which may be mentioned equestrian exercises, games with canes and oranges, and boat excursions. The females did not participate in these amusements, but were left at home by their husbands, whose jealousy imposed on them such restraints, that they were seldom allowed to stir out of their private apartments, and, when they did, their movements were closely watched. Such treatment brought about its natural consequences. Excluded from society, and confined within their dwelling-houses, they were not open to any of those influences which are generally at work in civilized countries in elevating the moral character. They passed their time in idle and frivolous pursuits, in singing and playing on musical instruments, gossiping with slaves of either sex, and especially devising means to elude the vigilance of their

* Pyrard, Pt. II., p. 38; Linschoten, *ut supra*, p. 57.

husbands. For this purpose they generally took into their confidence those very servants who had been kept to watch their conduct, and made them willing instruments for the gratification of their evil propensities. To such an extent did they abandon themselves to these pleasures, that we are told by almost every traveller who visited Goa at this period, that they did not scruple even to stupefy their husbands with narcotic drugs, and admit their paramours into their very bedchambers; and we are further told by Linschoten, that to give zest to those pleasures they made free use of stimulants.* Profligacy had become in fact the reigning vice among the higher classes, and their morals were hopelessly corrupt and depraved.

The rich fidalgos always kept a luxurious table, to which they had the generosity to admit their less fortunate countrymen. They treated their guests to a sumptuous repast, consisting of the richest wines and choicest delicacies served on glittering plate: the table literally groaned under the

---

* The drug much resorted to for this purpose of stupefying is said to have been the *Dutró* (*Datura Stramonium*). Pyrard (II. 69) writes as follows about the mode of administration and the effects of the same drug:—"Quand les femmes veulent jouyr de leurs amours en toute assurance, elles font boire à leurs maris de cets fruits detrempez en leur boisson ou en potage, et une heure apres ils deviennent étourdes et comme insensez, chantans, rians, et faisans mille singeries, car ils ont lors perdu toute connoissance et jugement, sans scavoir ce qu'ils font, ny ce qui se fait en leur presence. Et lors les femmes prennent leur temps de faire entrer qui bon leur semble et en user comme il leur plaist, en presence de leurs dits maris, qui n'en peuvent rien reconnoistre. Cela leur dure cinq ou six heures, plus ou moins selon le quantité de la prise. Puis ils s'endorment, et apres leur reveil croyent avoir tousiours dormy, sans se souvenir de rien qu'ils ayent fait, ouy, ou veu."

Linschoten (p. 111) also gives an almost identical description, and further remarks that the stimulants resorted to consisted chiefly of an aromatic preparation called *cachunde*. "La cachunde," he says, "a mon opinion est fait d'une espece de gallia muscata avec sus de regalisse. Les gasteaux en sont noirs, marquez de divers characteres, amers au premier goust, mais apres fort doux. Ils confortent le cœur en son avoir tres bonne haleine." (p. 65.)

weight of numerous viands, which were prepared by experts in the culinary art to satisfy their fastidious taste.* As they feasted, there were slaves in attendance, ready to fan them or entertain them with music. What most distinguished this luxurious mode of living was the fact, that even in the height of their merriment the Portuguese never forgot to use wine sparingly: feasting never bordered on rioting with them, a circumstance to which universal testimony is borne by almost all travellers who visited Goa at this time.

Mandelslo gives the following description of a dinner at which he and the English President of Surat were entertained by a Portuguese gentleman who was appointed Governor of Mozambique:—

"One of the noblest entertainments we had, was that which was made us the 15th of January (1639) by a Portuguese lord, who had been Governor of Baçim and was then newly come to the government of Mozambique. Every course consisted only of four dishes of meat, but they were so often changed, and the meat so excellently well dressed, that I may truly say I never was at the like. For with the meat there was brought such variety of excellent fruits, that by the continual change and intermixture of both, the appetite was sharpened and renewed. But what was most remarkable was that though the Portuguese ladies are as seldom seen as those of the Muscovites and Persians, yet this lord, knowing he could not any way more oblige the English than by allowing them the sight of women, we were served at table by four handsome young maids of Malacca, while he himself was attended by two pages and an eunuch. These maids brought in the meat and filled our wine, and though he himself drunk not any, yet would he have the English treated after their own way, and drink to what height they pleased. Being risen from table, he brought us into a spacious chamber, where he again pressed us to drink, and when the President was to take leave of him he presented him with a noble coverlet of Watte, a quilted covering for a horse, a fair table and a rich cabinet of lacque."†

---

* The viands among the rich consisted chiefly of beef, pork, and poultry. The poor lived on rice and fish. Fish is said to have been so abundant that in every street and lane were seen men and women frying it and pickling it for sale.—Tavernier, vol. II., p. 116; Pyrard, Pt. II., p. 64.

† *Voyages and Travels of J. Albert de Mandelslo*, London, 1669, p. 79.

At home, the Portuguese were seen in a plain loose dress. They wore a shirt and fine white breeches, with a light velvet or taffeta cap for their head-dress. The women wore a sort of loose smock called *bájú*, which was so thin as to prove a very insufficient covering for their persons. From the waist downwards they wore a fine cloth of cotton or silk. Both men and women bore round their necks, or carried in their hands, large rosaries, telling the beads continually in apparent devotion.

The rich made an ostentatious display of their wealth when they stirred abroad. They were borne in palanquins, or rode on horseback, attended by a large number of lackeys in gay and fanciful liveries, some holding large umbrellas over them, others bearing arms, and some carrying their cloaks, gilt chairs and soft cushions, when they went to church. The same pomp and display attended them when they happened to pass through the streets on foot. The most attractive portion of this pageantry were the gold and silver trappings of the steeds on which the fidalgos were mounted. The saddle was covered with a rich embroidered cloth, the reins were studded with precious stones with jingling silver bells attached to them, and the stirrups were of gilt silver.

The example of the rich was but too readily followed by persons of moderate and even slender means. They too tried, as far as they could, to make an imposing appearance in public; but were obliged to resort to several make-shifts and devices to maintain an air of grandeur and dignity about them. Those who lived together had a few suits of silk clothes in common. These they used by turns when they went out, and hired the services of a man to hold an umbrella over them as they strutted through the streets. In fact they walked with such a proud gait, and with such an affected air of importance, that, as a traveller remarked, one might be led to take them for gentlemen with ten thousand pounds a year.*

The ladies, as stated before, rarely stirred out of their

* Linschoten, *ut supra*, p. 61.

dwellings, except on festive and solemn occasions. When they went to church, they appeared in all the glory of rich and gaudy attire, with a profusion of pearls and diamonds about their persons. Pyrard gives the following interesting description of their manner of attending church :—

"Rich and noble women go seldom to church, except on the principal festivals, and when they do, they appear richly dressed after the fashion of Portugal, the dress mostly of gold and silver brocade adorned with pearls, precious stones, and with jewels on the head, arms, hands, and round the waist, and they put on a veil of the finest crape in the world, which extends from head to foot. Young maidens wear veils of different colours; whilst grown-up ladies invariably use black ones. They never use stockings. Their flowing gowns sweep along the ground. The slippers or *chapins* are open on the upper part, and cover only the extremity of the foot: the lower part is embroidered with gold and silver spangles, and the upper one is studded with pearls and precious stones. They have a sole of cork nearly half a foot in height. When they go to church they are carried in palanquins adorned as richly as possible; they take with them a valuable carpet of Persia, which they call *alcatifa*, which here (in France) would be worth five hundred *escus;* they have also two or three cushions of velvet or brocade, one to recline the head against, the other to rest the legs upon. And all these are taken with them into the church by their servants, who are either Portuguese or Eurasian. They take their children too with them in the palanquin. A number of servants and slaves follow them on foot, richly attired in silks of different colours, with large fine crape over all, which they call *mantos*. But they do not dress after the Portuguese fashion, but clothe themselves with a large piece of silk which serves them as petticoats, and have also smocks of the finest silk, which they call *bájús*. Among these slaves are seen very beautiful girls of all the races inhabiting India. And it is to be remarked that the ladies are also accompanied by pages and by one or two Portuguese or Eurasian gentlemen to assist them in alighting from the palanquins: frequently, however, they are taken into the church in their palanquins, so much are they afraid of being exposed to the public view. They do not wear any mask, but paint their cheeks to a shameful degree. It is not that the ladies fear being seen, but they are forbidden by their husbands, who are too jealous of them. One of the servants or slaves brings a rich carpet; another two costly cushions; a third a China gilt chair; a fourth a velvet case containing a book, a handkerchief, and other necessary things; a fifth a very thin beautiful mattress to be spread over the carpet; and a sixth a fan and other things for the use of the mistress.

"As already stated, these ladies, when they enter the church, are taken by the hand by one or two men, since they cannot walk by themselves on account of the height of the slippers, which are generally half a foot high and have the upper part open. One of these presents holy water to the lady, and she goes afterwards to take her seat some forty or fifty paces off, taking at least a good quarter of an hour to walk that distance, so slowly and majestically does she move, carrying in her hand a rosary of gold, pearls and precious stones. This they all do according to their means, and not according to their quality. When they take their children along with them, they make them walk before them. The female servants and slaves are very glad if their mistresses do not go to Mass, for then they go alone, and can pay court to their lovers; they neither expose nor accuse one another."*

A still more ostentatious display was made by both gentlemen and ladies at marriages and christenings. These were solemnized in after years on such a grand scale that the Government of Portugal was at length obliged to put certain restrictions on the lavish expenditure incurred on these occasions.†

The marriage ceremony was generally performed in the evening. The bride and bridegroom were accompanied to church by their respective godfathers and by a large number of friends and relatives richly dressed, the gentlemen riding on horseback, and the ladies in palanquins, followed by a crowd of pages and slaves, all moving with a slow and majestic pace. The ceremony was gone through with great solemnity at church, and when it was over, the bridal party retraced their steps homewards, amidst the sound of trumpets and cornets and other musical instruments. As they passed in procession through the streets, their friends and neighbours showered on them from their windows fragrant flowers and perfumes and fancifully wrought comfits. On reaching home, the bridal pair respectfully bowed to the whole company, thanking them for their attendance, and proceeded with the ladies to the gallery, thence to enjoy the sight

* Pyrard, II., p. 62; see also Linschoten, pp. 57 *et seq.*

† *Gabinete Litterario, ut supra,* vol. III., pp. 91, 234.

of sports in which their friends and relatives took part. These sports consisted principally of horse races and the common games of canes and oranges, to which we have already alluded. At the same time the company were entertained with the sweetest strains of music; and when the sports were over, they were led into a hall where fruits, sweetmeats, and refreshments of every kind were served—except wine, instead of which the pure and wholesome water of Banguenim was offered, the sobriety of the Portuguese in this respect being truly admirable. The company then departed, except the nearest relations, who were afterwards treated to a sumptuous banquet.

With almost equal solemnity was the ceremony of christening performed. The new-born child was taken to the church in a palanquin by the person who was to stand as sponsor, accompanied by two servants on foot, one of whom carried a gilt salver containing a few cakes and flowers, and a wax taper curiously adorned, and having fixed on it a gold or silver coin, which was to be presented to the parish priest. The other servant carried a plate with salt, a silver ewer, and a clean napkin to be used on the occasion. A large number of the friends and kinsmen of the child's parents followed in palanquins to witness the ceremony. After the child was baptized, it was brought back home, where the same games and sports were exhibited as on the occasion of a marriage.*

---

* Linschoten, *ut supra*, p. 60; Pyrard, II., p. 61; Mandelslo, *ut supra*, p. 81.

CHAPTER VI.

THE DECLINE AND FALL OF THE CITY—ITS CAUSES—DEPRAVATION OF PRIVATE AND PUBLIC MORALS—THE WAR WITH THE DUTCH, AND ITS DISASTROUS RESULT—THE SECOND OUTBREAK OF THE EPIDEMIC—THE STATE OF THE CITY AS DESCRIBED BY SEVERAL TRAVELLERS—THE INVASION OF GOA BY THE MARÁṬHÁS, FOLLOWED BY FAMINE AND GENERAL DISTRESS IN THE CAPITAL —THE GRADUAL ABANDONMENT AND DECAY OF THE CITY—THE INCREASING MISERY OF ITS INHABITANTS—THE PROJECT OF REMOVING THE CAPITAL TO MORMUGAO, AND THE CONSEQUENT DECAY OF THE CITY—A FRESH INVASION OF GOA BY THE MARÁṬHÁS, AND THEIR REPULSE—THE CONDITION OF THE CITY AS WITNESSED BY SEVERAL TRAVELLERS—THE PROJECT OF THE MARQUIS OF POMBAL TO REBUILD THE CITY—ITS IMPRACTICABILITY—THE LAST DAYS OF THE CITY AS DESCRIBED BY MANY WRITERS—THE SUPPRESSION OF THE RELIGIOUS ORDERS, AND ITS FINAL ABANDONMENT—ITS PRESENT RUINOUS STATE.

In the midst of all this pomp and splendour, this luxury and profusion, the shrewd observer could not fail to discern the seed of premature decay and dissolution. Society was almost rotten to the core. The morals of the community were extremely lax. Profligacy had become the predominant and fashionable vice, and men gave themselves up to the sensual pleasures peculiar to Oriental life. Nor was the public administration less tainted. The civic virtues of Albuquerque and Castro were supplanted by corruption and venality; justice was bought; the public offices were put up to sale; and the martial spirit of the nation degenerated into effeminacy, sloth and indolence, as in the last days of the Roman Empire.*

This demoralization was of itself sufficient, in the ordinary course of things, to bring about the decline of the Portuguese power, and with it to impair the prosperity of the capital city. But there were other causes still more powerful to accelerate its fall, the chief of which was the war with the Dutch. This brave and enterprising nation, having thrown off the Spanish yoke, began to strengthen their resources by a rapid extension of commerce, and directed their attention to the East, where they aimed at nothing less than disputing with the Portuguese the supremacy of the Indian seas. Accordingly in the beginning of the 17th century a powerful fleet was despatched to attack the Portuguese settlements in the East. Goa was blockaded in 1603; but the attempt proved abortive. The struggle, however, lasted for sixty-nine years, at the end of which period the Empire was completely shattered and dismembered; most of the Portuguese possessions fell into the hands of the enemy; and their once flourishing commerce was seriously crippled. These calamities could not but influence the destinies of Goa; they told heavily on the prosperity of the city, and led to its poverty and ruin. At the same time the epidemic fever which had afflicted the city fifty years before, broke out again in 1635 with unprecedented violence, spreading desolation and devastation all around. The Government could not, with an exchequer already drained by the expenses of the war, take proper measures to arrest the progress of the disease.† Nor were the true principles of hygiene then understood. The chief functionaries of the State contented themselves with merely joining with the clergy in imploring the Divine mercy, but the disease continued with unabated force to rage in the city, reducing and impoverishing the population. In the midst of this visitation, the Dutch appeared in 1639 in the harbour

---

* See *Soldado Pratico*, por Diogo de Couto, Lisboa, 1790, pp. 34 *et seq.*

† The Jesuits are said to have tried some measures, but they were not effectual.

of Goa with a fleet of twelve ships, and blockaded it. They, however, soon withdrew, without causing any serious damage to the city.*

But neither the fury of the epidemic nor even the collapse of the Portuguese power could blight at once the external grandeur and magnificence of the city. The rise and fall of cities, as of nations, is the work of time; and Goa was no exception to this rule. In spite of the misery that had begun to be felt by the close of the first quarter of the 17th century, the splendid buildings in the city and its suburbs excited the admiration of strangers, no less than did the ostentation and luxury of its inhabitants, even when reduced to want and indigence. J. Albert de Mandelslo, who was there in 1639, speaks of it as a noble city full of beautiful buildings and palaces. He describes the extravagance of the Portuguese fidalgos and their ladies, who were "all very richly attired in velvet, flowered satin or brocado, and adorned with an abundance of pearls and precious stones."† Tavernier also, during his stay in Goa in 1648, admired the splendour of the city, but was struck with the poverty of several Portuguese families whom he had seen on the occasion of his first visit in affluence and prosperity. He says that most of those who had six years before enjoyed an annual income of £500 were reduced at this time to the necessity of secretly begging alms; and yet they did not put aside their vanity. The ladies were particularly observed going in palanquins to seek charitable relief, attended by servants who conveyed their messages to the persons whose assistance they implored.‡

Among other travellers of the latter part of the 17th century, Thevenot in 1666 speaks in high terms of the decaying city.

---

* The city was not put to great restraint, as according to Mandelslo (p. 78) the frigates and little vessels which could go along the coast brought thither all sorts of provisions and commodities so freely that one day he saw coming in a caravan of above three hundred boats laden with pepper, ginger, cardamoms, sugar, rice, fruits and conserves.

† *Voyages and Travels*, p. 84.

‡ *Les Six Voyages*, II. 116.

He says:—"The city is great and full of beautiful churches and convents, and well adorned with palaces. There were few nations in the world so rich as the Portuguese in India before their commerce was ruined by the Dutch, but their vanity is the cause of their ruin."*

The Dutchman Philip Baldæus, who had an opportunity of seeing the state of the city at this time, writes in his book, published in Amsterdam in 1672, that there was still a good number of Europeans, Musalmáns, and Pagans of different countries, in the city; that there were still to be seen shops full of silks, porcelain, and other articles along the principal road; and that slaves were, as before, sold there by auction. Much sickness prevailed in the city, which, our traveller says, was cured by bleeding the patient five or six times a day.† Dellon, who was also about this time in Goa, speaks of the apparently flourishing condition of the city, and the terror caused by the Inquisition.‡ In 1675 Dr. John Fryer found many buildings in a ruinous state, but the city still presented a noble appearance, whilst the inhabitants made an attempt at display in spite of their increasing misery. The English doctor gives the following picture of the city and its inhabitants :—

"The city of Goa looks well at a small distance, not being to be seen far by reason of the adjacent hills and windings of the river; it is ten miles up the river, stands upon seven hills; everywhere colleges, churches, and glorious structures; it has gates to it and a wall; it is modelled but rudely, many houses disgracing it with their ruins, the streets interfering most confusedly . . . The city is a Rome in India, both for absoluteness and fabrics, the chiefest consisting of churches and convents or religious houses, though the laity have sumptuous ones all of stone; their streets are paved and cleaner than the tops of their houses, where they do all occasions, leaving their excrements there. They live with a splendid outside, vaunting in their number of slaves, walking under a street of their own umbrellas, bareheaded

---

* *Les Voyages de M. de Thevenot aux Indies Orientales,* Amsterdam, 1727, tom. 5me, p. 376.

† Churchill's *Collection of Voyages and Travels,* London, 1732, vol. III., p. 545.

‡ *Relation de l'Inquisition de Goa,* pp. 44 *et seq.*

to avoid giving distaste in not removing their hats. They being jealous of their honour pardon no affront, wherefore to ogle a lady in a balcony (if a person of quality) it is revenged with a *bocca mortis*, or to pass by a fidalgo without due reverence is severely chastised; they are carried mostly in *palankeens*, and sometimes on horseback.

"The clergy affect little of outward state, going out only *frater cum socio* in couples; they salute a father by first kissing the hem of his garment, then begging a benediction.

"The mass of the people are *Canorein*, though Portuguesed in speech and manners; paying great observance to a white man, whom when they meet, they must give him the way with a cringe and civil salute, for fear of a *stochado*.

"The women, both white and black, are kept recluse, veiled abroad; within doors the richer of any quality are hung with jewels, and rosaries of gold and silver many times double; *moneloes* of gold about their arms, necklaces of pearl about their necks, lockets of diamonds in their bodkins for their hair, pendants in their ears; a thin *lungy* or half-smock reaching to their waist, shewing their skin through it; over that, abroad, a close doublet; over their lower parts a petticoat or *lungy*, their feet and legs without stockings, but very rich slippers. Amongst them some are extraordinarily featur'd and compleatly shaped, though not of that corruscant beauty our English ladies are; and for mien far beneath them, being nurtured up in a lowly bashfulness, whereby they are render'd unfit for conversation, applying themselves wholly to devotion and the care of the house. They sing and play on the lute, make confections, pickle *achars* (the best mango achars coming from them), and dress meat exquisitely, not to put the stomack to much trouble, but such as shall digest presently; supoes, pottages, and varieties of stewes, in little china dishes or plates, which they shift before you are cloy'd, and at a common entertainment after half a dozen modes. Their relishing bits have not the fieriness of ours, yet all the pleasure you can desire; and, to speak truly, I prefer the ordinary way of ordering victuals before any others. If a stranger dine with the husband, and he consent to have the wife come in and sit at table as our women do, there is no means of persuading her, but she will be much offended if you taste not of every thing they cook. The little children run up and down the house naked, till they begin to be old enough to be ashamed."*

The city decayed rapidly after the visit of Dr. Fryer, and in 1683 it narrowly escaped falling into the hands of Sambáji. The Maráṭhás, who were plundering and ravaging every part

* *A New Account of East India and Persia*, London, 1698, pp. 149, 156.

of the Dakhaṇ, extended their incursions to the Koṅkaṇa and attacked the territory of Goa. They appeared almost at the gates of the city, and spread consternation and dismay among the inhabitants. All hopes of resistance were abandoned, and the enemy were hourly expected to enter and commence the work of sacking and pillaging, when of a sudden a powerful Moghul force was seen descending the Gháṭs, which compelled the Maráṭhás to sue for peace. The unexcepted appearance of the Moghuls, at this critical juncture, was generally ascribed to the miraculous interposition of St. Francis Xavier. *

Not long after, the people suffered much from scarcity of provisions, which, together with the epidemic and the decline of commerce, reduced the unfortunate city to misery and ruin. The more opulent families removed to the suburbs and the neighbouring villages of Guadalupe, São Lourenço, Naroá, Chorão, etc.†

The population went on rapidly decreasing, consisting at this period chiefly of the clergy, the functionaries of the State, and a scanty number of other inhabitants.‡ These last were in a deplorably wretched condition. They were reduced to such a degree of destitution that they were obliged in most cases to part with their household furniture in order to provide themselves with the bare necessaries of life; whilst many, and among them several Portuguese families which had once known better days, supported themselves by alms. In consequence of this general indigence and poverty, most of the private buildings, which adorned the city, began rapidly to decay for want of the necessary repairs.§ In an official document dated 3rd December 1687 allusion is made to this circumstance as follows :—" The greater part of Goa is abandoned, because its inhabitants cannot rebuild their houses when they have fallen; many streets once full of houses have now

* *Oriente Conquistado*, Part I., Conq. IV., Div. I., §§107, 108; *Bombay Quarterly Magazine and Review*, No. 4, July 1851.

† *O Chronista de Tissuary*, Nova-Goa, 1866, vol. I., p. 151.

‡ *Op. cit.*, p. 231.

§ *Op. cit.*, pp. 201, 202, 234.

become lonely and uninhabited; it makes the heart bleed to see the metropolis of India so destitute of means as not to be able to maintain itself on its very foundation."* This statement is borne out by a minute of the Senate of Goa, which runs thus:—' We see every day in the city houses falling into decay, not on account of the antiquity of the buildings, but for want of money, . . . which proceeds from the great poverty and general misery of the inhabitants, most of whom have not even the means of subsistence."†

The state of the city must have been sufficiently deplorable to call forth such remarks from the highest corporation of the city; remarks which are confirmed by the testimony of two eminent persons of Goa, one of whom calls it "the graveyard of the Portuguese and the natives residing there," and the other compares it to the deserted Tibur.‡

It was at this time that the Viceroy, the Count of Alvor, resolved to abandon the city and transfer the seat of government to the peninsula of Mormugão, which lies a few miles southwards. An idea of this kind had suggested itself to the ruling authorities at Goa some years before,§ but the project remained in abeyance till it was taken into serious consideration by the abovementioned Viceroy, who was apprehensive of another Maráṭhá invasion. On the 12th of January 1684 he convened in the fortress of Benastarim a council of the chief officers of the State, the heads of the religious orders, and many other eminent persons. He laid his project before them, and asked their advice. A large majority fell in with his views, as appears from their opinions preserved in the records of the Government of Goa. They urged, among other reasons, first, that the city itself was not sufficiently fortified to repel a hostile attack; secondly, that the fortifications of the island were so extensive that they required a numerous force to guard them in cases of emergency; and, lastly, that the city was too unhealthy to be

* *O Chronista, ut supra*, p. 229.
† *Op. cit.*, p. 228.
‡ *Op. cit.*, pp. 153, 155.
§ *Op. cit.*, p. 122.

fit for habitation.* The dissentients admitted the force of these arguments, but maintained that the scheme was impracticable. With a treasury so exhausted that even church property had been misappropriated to meet public wants, and with a population so miserable and impoverished that they could not preserve even their own dwelling-houses from decay, it was impossible, they said, to build a new city on a grand scale. They suggested, therefore, the advisability of making the best of their present position.† The Viceroy was, however, determined to carry out his favourite scheme, and, with the support of so many influential persons, he issued orders to lay the foundations of a new capital. In his letter of 18th January 1685 he informed the Home Government that the work was progressing favourably, and that the principal buildings were in course of erection. But his period of office had nearly expired, and when he returned home in the following year, his successor, Dom Rodrigo da Costa, took a more sober view of the matter, and ordered the work to be stopped, with the unanimous consent of all his councillors. This step did not, however, meet with the approval of the Court of Lisbon, because they were convinced, on the representation of the Count of Alvor, that unless the seat of government was changed, both the city and the little territory that remained in their possession in the East would be lost.‡ They issued, therefore, peremptory orders to the Governor of Goa to recommence the work, and apply towards its prosecution the revenue derived from tobacco. These orders were complied with, though with some reluctance, on the part of the Indian Government, and in 1693 a new Viceroy, the Count of Villa Verde, was sent with fresh instructions not only to hasten the work to completion, but at once to remove himself with all the civil and ecclesiastical authorities to the new capital. But on his arri-

---

* *O Chronista, ut supra*, pp. 145 *et seq.*

† *Op. cit.*, p. 172.

‡ *Livro das Monçoens*, Goa Govt. Records (MSS.), No. 54, fol. 1; *O Chronista*, p. 236.

val he found it extremely difficult to execute these injunctions, and, instead of removing to Mormugão, fixed his residence at Panelim, in the suburbs of the city. Thither he was followed by the Archbishop and many of the nobility. But the Count of Alvor was at this time appointed President of the Ultramarine Council in Portugal. He was naturally anxious to carry out his favourite project, and therefore insisted on a steady and vigorous prosecution of the work begun under his own auspices. The Viceroy was obliged to yield, and the work was resumed under the superintendence of the Jesuit father Theotonio Rebello.* During the next fifteen years, orders were repeatedly received from Portugal to demolish the public buildings in the city, and apply their materials in the construction of new ones at Mormugão, whilst the Viceroys were directed to transfer their residence to that place, so that their example might be followed by their subordinates and the rest of the inhabitants. These orders were generally disregarded, under several pretexts. The Viceroys were loth to change their residence, and the work made but slow progress; sometimes it so happened that parts of the work begun under one Viceroy were abandoned under another, and resumed under a third, according as they were more or less disposed to carry out the instructions of the Home Government. But during the viceroyalty of Caetano de Mello e Castro the work was pushed on with great despatch, and several buildings were completed, among which may be mentioned the Palace and the Hospital. The Viceroy himself stayed at Mormugão for a few months in 1703. Four years after, when the Count of Alvor retired from the Ultramarine Council, his favourite scheme, which he had so persistently endeavoured to carry out, was suddenly abandoned, and the work was stopped by the royal letter of 8th March 1712.† Thus ended the frantic attempt at rearing a new capital, which cost no less than £25,000 to the already impo-

---

* *Livro das Monçoens*, Goa Govt. Records (MSS.), No. 58, fol. 36; *Boletim do Governo do Estado de India*, No. 39 of 1864; *O Chronista*, vol. I., p. 272.

† *Livro das Monçoens*, No. 78, fol. 29; *O Chronista*, vol. II., p. 1.

verished State,* and which served only to accelerate the fall of the city.

For, the inhabitants in general, who had hardly sufficient means to repair their houses, neglected them altogether, when they heard of the proposed change of the seat of government. The more needy part of the population purposely allowed their houses to fall to ruin, that they might sell the materials and obtain the means of subsistence. The consequence was, that the greater part of the buildings in the city began to decay fast, and no steps were taken to arrest the progress of dilapidation. This state of things attracted at first the notice of the Government during the viceroyalty of Dom Rodrigo da Costa, who expected that the Court of Lisbon would countermand its order for the erection of a new capital. The Senate, in its anxiety to preserve the remaining buildings from the fate which had overtaken so many, appointed an officer to survey the edifices in the city at least twice a month, and compel their owners to take proper care of them. Nor was any person allowed to pull down his house, wholly or partially, without sufficient excuse. These salutary measures received the support of the local Government, but were little approved by the Court of Lisbon, which, on the contrary, ordered the buildings in the city to be demolished, and new ones erected at Mormugão with their materials. The people took advantage of these orders to destroy their buildings so recklessly, that the Viceroy, Antonio Luiz de Camara, wrote in deprecating terms, on the 20th of December 1699, to the King, informing him that, on pretence of building houses at Mormugão, the inhabitants obtained leave to pull down those in the city, but they availed themselves of this privilege only to gratify their passion for destruction to such an extent, that some actually made it a trade to demolish houses and sell their materials at a profit. In conclusion the Viceroy observed that, while the city was destroyed, Mormugão remained in the same state as before. To this the King replied

* *Livro das Monçoens*, Goa Govt. Records (MSS)., No. 107, fol. 228.

that no person should in future be allowed to demolish any building in the city, unless he bound himself to build a new one at Mormugão. The house-owners had then recourse to a cunning device. They left the roofs of their houses partly uncovered during the rainy season, so that the work of destruction might be consummated by nature, independently of permission or expense.*

Dr. John Francis Gemelli Careri, who visited the city in 1695, writes that Goa, once the centre of all the Portuguese conquests, a place of wealth and renown, and the chief mart of the East, was now reduced to a miserable condition. It had not more than 20,000 inhabitants. The Portuguese were few, but their descendants numerous, and the mulattoes constituted almost one-fourth of the population. Many of the natives were priests, advocates, solicitors, etc. The greater part of the merchants were pagans and Muhammadans, and lived apart from the Christians. The Portuguese, although fallen from their pristine grandeur, were still vain enough to parade themselves through the lonely streets in palanquins with slaves in their train holding umbrellas over them. Such slaves were found in numbers in the city, and could be had for fifteen to twenty crowns per head.†

At the period of which we are speaking, the city presented an aspect which it was truly piteous to behold. Desolation, ruin, and misery met the eye on every side. Here were whole streets deserted and abandoned. There were houses already lying in heaps of ruins or gradually crumbling to dust; whilst three-fourths of the population was fast sinking down under the pressure of want and privation; only convents and churches with a few public buildings stood out amidst this general wreck as noble and enduring monuments of the past. The Jesuit Father Francisco de Souza, in his *Oriente Conquistado*, published in 1710, exactly two centuries after the conquest of Goa by

---

* *Livro das Monçoens*, Goa Govt. Rec. (MSS.), No. 63, fol. 220; *O Chronista, ut supra*, p. 254.

† Churchill's *Collection of Voyages and Travels*, vol. IV., p. 202.

Albuquerque, calls it "the wretched capital of a poor and miserable State, so ruined and deserted that its ancient grandeur can be guessed only from the magnificence of the convents and churches, which are yet preserved with great splendour and veneration."*

These convents and churches were no doubt the only ornaments of the city at this time. The Viceroy, the Count of Ericeira, tried, by his *alvará* of 22nd August 1719, to preserve the few houses still standing in the immediate neighbourhood of the religious buildings, and to clear the roads of the ruins that obstructed them, but to no purpose. The fate of the city was already sealed. Captain Alexander Hamilton, who was in Goa at this time, says that the city contained beautiful churches and convents, but that, its climate being considered unhealthy, it was poorly inhabited, whilst in its suburbs, and specially on the banks of the river, magnificent mansions and houses were seen. He counted from a neighbouring hill nearly eighty churches and convents, and these were such as he could see from his elevated position, but there were others, as he says, both in the city and the whole territory of Goa, where thirty thousand priests lived. Each of these churches had a set of bells, one or other of which was continually ringing, and being christened, as he says, and dedicated to some saint, they had a peculiar power to drive away all manner of evil spirits, "except poverty in the laity and pride in the clergy." Some shops were still seen along the *Rua Direita* in which articles of different countries were exhibited for sale, but the native merchants were exposed to the insults and oppression of the Portuguese, who ordinarily purchased articles on credit without intending to pay for them, and when the merchants demanded payment they ran the risk of being bastinadoed. He gives a sad description of the European soldiers of the time, who committed great excesses.†

* *Or. Conq.*, vol. I., p. 21.

† *A New Account of the East Indies,* by Captain Alexander Hamilton, London, 1744, vol. I., p. 249. The number of the churches as well of the priests given by the author is exaggerated.

In 1739 the territory of Goa was again attacked by the Maráṭhás, and the city was in danger of falling into their hands. The unhappy inhabitants were seized with panic; the nuns and the other helpless portion of the population sought refuge at Mormugão.* Thither too fled the Jesuit Fathers who were in charge of the body of St. Francis Xavier, forgetting, it is said, to take it with them in their anxiety to effect their escape —a circumstance from which it was inferred that the saint did not approve of the plan of abandoning the city. At this conjuncture a new Viceroy arrived, bringing with him a sufficiently powerful force to repel the invaders. The Maráṭhás were beaten and compelled to withdraw. But they continued to be in a state of hostility till a peace was finally concluded with them in 1759, when the *Te Deum* was sung in the Cathedral. The Portuguese, however, had little reason to rejoice at this deliverance, since the foe had despoiled them of even the few possessions in India which had been spared by the Dutch, Daman and Diu alone excepted. The city was then the capital of a small territory which in its present state is called *India Portuguesa*.

It was during this period of trouble and disaster that the Viceroy, Count of Sandomil, was led to reconsider the question of transferring the capital to Mormugão; but it appears that he found the project impracticable, as he soon afterwards wrote to the King suggesting that the best way of providing against future attacks of the enemy would be to build a new city between Pangim and Cabo.†

Travellers who visited Goa during the latter part of the 18th century bear witness in unmistakable terms to the deplorably wretched state of the city. The celebrated Orientalist, Anquetil du Perron, in his preliminary discourse on the *Zend Avesta*, alludes to his visit to the city, which he found in ruins and almost abandoned, though in its suburbs on the banks of the river he saw several beautiful houses constructed with the materials of those which had once adorned the capital. The

---

* *Livro das Monçoens*, Goa Govt. Rec. (MSS.), No. 110, fol. 5.

† *Ibid.*, No. 107, fol. 228.

Portuguese were no longer distinguished by commercial activity or enterprise. Trade was chiefly in the hands of the Jesuits; and though the harbour of Goa was far the best in the Indian peninsula, its commerce, beyond that which was carried on with Mozambique, was insignificant. This fairest but poorest settlement had become a burden to the Portuguese Government, costing no less than 300,000 piastres every year, and requiring a force of about two thousand European soldiers for its defence. These soldiers were miserably paid and as miserably fed, the captains receiving each a salary of 12*s.* per month, and living only on rice and fish. As to the fleet, which once rode supreme on the Indian seas, it had dwindled down to a few ships of war.*

This account of the French *savant* is, to a great extent, corroborated by Edward Ives, a surgeon who came out to India with an English squadron under Commodore Watson and visited Goa in 1758. In the interesting work which he afterwards published, he says that the city was a heap of ruins, with hardly any dwelling-house in it, though beautiful villas graced the banks of the river in the suburbs, and that the decay of the splendid public buildings in the city showed clearly the present fallen state of the Portuguese power and commerce in India.† A description of the state of Goa and its inhabitants at this period of its decay is also given by the Dutchman Jacobus Canter Visscher. The upper classes, he says, had retreated to the environs of the city on account of the insalubrity of the climate, and the river banks and islets were adorned with flourishing farms and plantations and other fruit trees, on the profits of which the Portuguese fidalgos, who considered it a disgrace to follow any trade, subsisted. The Portuguese were devoid of any knowledge of business, but were great lovers of fine titles. High offices and military commands were all the talk among them. A post which could be filled by a small tradesman needed a

* *Zend Avesta,* Paris, 1771, *Discours Préliminaire,* p. cciv.

† *A Voyage from England to India,* by Edward Ives, London, 1773, p. 195.

general with them. For each ship of war they had a *capitão de mar e guerra,* and a levy of captains, lieutenants, and ensigns besides. Their pay, however, was out of all proportion to their titles, the captain receiving less than a Dutch sergeant. Yet they liked to make a show. Not satisfied with one umbrella carried over his head, a man of high rank required two or three, ornamented with hanging fringes and silver buttons; the bearers were Caffres or negroes clothed in red coats, and they were accompanied by other Caffres who bore long swords and acted as bravoes for their masters. There was no nation in the world so fond of sweetmeats as the Portuguese; they always handed them about on their social visits; but for wine and strong liquors they had no taste.*

---

* *Letters from Malabar,* by Jacob Canter Visscher, translated from the original Dutch by Major Heber Drury, Madras, 1862, p. 32. The translator alludes to a legend "that the old city of Goa was overwhelmed by a sudden rush of the sea, and that its houses may still be seen in calm weather below the waters." We have not heard of such a legend at Goa, but we will copy the first few lines of a beautiful poem written by him in allusion to it:—

"There was a city, glorious and free,
Built on the shore of the dark blue sea,
Where towers and spires of gilded hue,
Shone over the waves of the ocean blue,
And palace and cottage smiling told
How fair was that city in days of old!
Far, far above was the glowing sky
Where the sun shone bright o'er the turrets high,
While the cocoa shade and the graceful palm
Hung o'er the waters so lovely and calm,
Thick and numberless, side by side,
Drinking the stream of the onward tide.
But now, from that spot where the glad sun shone,
That glorious city of palms is gone,
Gone with its pride and people so brave,
Whelmed by the tide of the salt sea wave!
Yes! there below the surging deep
Fair Goa's sunken towers sleep,
All, all that once was glad and bright,
Reposing there in ceaseless night!"

In 1759 the Governor changed his residence from Panelim to Pangim; his example was followed by several persons of rank and influence. The suburbs were consequently gradually deserted. In the same year, by a Government Resolution, the Jesuits were expelled from Goa. The magnificent structures which they had reared in the city were declared the property of the State, but they were for the most part neglected and abandoned. The little commerce of the city, which had latterly been kept up, chiefly through the energy and enterprise of the Jesuits, received a fatal blow at this time.* The city thus suffered materially from the expulsion of the Jesuits. In 1775 the population was reduced to about 1600 souls, of whom there were 1198 Christians.†

In the following year the British Consul, Mr. Abraham Parson, along with Commodore Moor, visited the city. They were struck with the magnificence of several public edifices, but they found the religious houses of the Jesuits shut up. Many beautiful mansions which were built in the suburbs in the European style, they saw vacant and unoccupied: "while the Portuguese made but little figure in these parts, for, except Goa and the isle of Diu, they had no place of consequence on this side of the Cape of Good Hope."‡

It was in this state of the city, when its commerce was totally destroyed, its population reduced to a considerable extent, and its houses razed to the ground, that the Marquis of Pombal conceived the project of rebuilding it. His views on this subject appear clearly from the instructions he gave to Dom José Pedro da Camara, when he was sent out as Governor or Captain General of Goa.§ He remarks: "Divine Providence

---

* This consequence had already been foreseen by M. Anquetil du Perron. See *Discours Préliminaire*, p. ccv.

† *Boletim e Annaes*, No. 46 (Primeira Serie), p. 438. In this number were not included the friars and the *employés* of the arsenal.

‡ *Travels in Asia and Africa*, by Abraham Parson, London, 1808, p. 242.

§ See *Instrucçoens com que El-Rey D. José I. mandou passar a India, etc.*, Pangim, 1841, p. i.

having placed the city of Goa in a situation by far the most advantageous and admirably fitted to make her the capital and mistress of the whole of Asia, and the incomparable Affonso de Albuquerque having raised her to that position, which she maintained with unrivalled power and glory till the intrusion of the so-called Jesuits, she has been overtaken by such calamities that she is reduced to a heap of ruins; so that she is now a mere wreck of what she was in happier times; for those wicked men wished the city to be deserted that she might be left entirely in their hands, with none to oppose the gigantic schemes of their insatiable and restless ambition."* It will be observed that the illustrious statesman who expressed himself thus was evidently led away by his prejudice against the Jesuits, who, whatever might have been their faults in other respects, were certainly by no means responsible for the fall of the city. For, as we have seen, the misfortunes of the city were due to the insalubrity of its climate and the collapse of the Portuguese power and commerce in the East, no less than to the indiscreet conduct of the Government in attempting to rear a new capital. It was impossible, in the face of these adverse circumstances, for the city to retain its pristine grandeur. The age of Albuquerque was separated from that of the Marquis by a wide gulf, representing as each did a distinct epoch in the annals of the Portuguese Empire in the East—the one identified with the greatness, the other with the fall of the city. Any attempt, therefore, to reconcile the two could not but prove futile. And yet the noble Marquis sanguinely hoped to restore the city to its former glory. "This project was as absurd," says a Portuguese writer, "as that of the Pasha of Damascus would be if he aimed at rebuilding Palmyra because it had been founded by Solomon, and had been the capital of a flourishing kingdom, and the principal entrepôt of trade with India."†

The Government of Portugal was, however, determined to carry out the scheme of rebuilding the capital with the same

* *Instrucçoẽs, ut supra*, p. i.

† *Memorias sobre as Possessoens Portuguesas na India*, por Gonçalo de Magalhaens Texeira Pinto, Nova Goa, 1859, p. 944.

pertinacity with which it had resolved to transfer it to Mormugão. The work was commenced in 1777. The Governor of Goa wrote in the following year to the authorities at Lisbon, informing them of the progress which the work had made, and of the state of the public buildings in the city.* From this letter we learn also the plan on which the city was to be reconstructed, and the changes that were about to be made in the principal streets and thoroughfares. The Government had recourse to several measures of an oppressive character for accomplishing the work. All the village communities of the three districts of Goa were required to contribute each a certain sum of money and a certain number of workmen for the erection of houses in the city. Thus the district of the Ilhas had to pay the sum of £4,166-13-4, that of Bardez £5,833-6-8, and that of Salsette £6,500. The men who were forced to work for the State were in general poor natives living mainly on the produce of the soil they owned and cultivated. They were loth to abandon their fields and tear themselves from the bosom of their families, wherein all the solace and comfort of their lives was centred. They were, moreover, afraid of going to the city and exposing themselves to the violence of the epidemic which was raging there. But these considerations were of no avail before the duty imperatively cast on them by the State. They had to yield, or suffer themselves to be forcibly dragged to the city by the soldiers, and there made to work under the inspection of an armed force commanded by Henrique Carlos Henriques. The evil they had dreaded, at last overtook them. Most of them were seized with the prevalent disease, and not a few fell victims to it. We learn from official records of the period that out of 1,625 workmen imported from Salsette 665 fell sick and 58 died, and that too within the space of a few months, from August 1778 till the close of the year. Many and bitter were the complaints addressed to the Throne by the unfortunate people who were thus pressed into the Government service and

---

* *Livro das Monçoens*, Goa Govt. Rec. (MSS.), No. 158, f. 89.

who suffered such severe hardships. And earnestly did they pray for the redress of their grievances, which told on them more heavily than the misfortunes caused by a raid or incursion of the Maráṭhá chiefs. But neither their complaints nor their prayers were heard. The Court of Lisbon was inexorable, and insisted on a vigorous prosecution of the work. At the same time it seems to have repeated the instructions which the Marquis of Pombal had issued for peopling the city. Every fidalgo and officer of State was required to fix his residence within the precincts of the city, on pain of forfeiting the one his privileges, the other his office.* But this mandate is said to have been generally evaded by a partial compliance with it during the day-time alone.

In spite of these measures, the work of rebuilding the city made but slight progress. The ardour of the Government gradually cooled down, and as they began to appreciate the difficulties of the enterprise, they were convinced of the impolicy of prosecuting it any further. They at length abandoned it altogether, after a fruitless expenditure of £16,500, which they had exacted from the people, in addition to the sum drawn from the public treasury.

It was about this time that the celebrated poet M. M. de Barbosa du Bocage visited Goa, and being struck with the miserable state of the city gave vent to his feelings in the following touching verses† :—

> " Por terra jaz o emporio do Oriente,
> Que do rigido Affonso o ferro, o raio
> Ao gran' filho ganhou do gran' sabaio,
> Envergonhando o deus armipotente ;
> Caiu Goa, terror antigamente
> Do naire vaõ, do perfido malaio,
> De barbaras naçoes !... Ah ! Que desmaio
> Apaga o marcio ardor da lusa gente ?
> Oh seculos d'heroes ! Dias de gloria !
> Varoês excelsos, que a pezar da morte

* *Instrucçoens, ut supra*, pp. 2 ; *Memorias dos Estabelecimentos Portuguezes*, por Manoel José Gomes Loureiro, Lisboa, 1835, p. 308.

† *Poesias de Manoel Maria de Barbosa du Bocage*, colligidas por J. F. da Silva, Lisboa, 1853, tomo I., p. 232.

> Viveis na tradição, viveis na historia!
> Albuquerque terrivel, Castro forte,
> Menezes, e outros mil, vossa memoria
> Vinga as injurias, que nos faz a sorte."

J. Forbes, in his *Oriental Memoirs*, thus speaks of the city as it appeared to him at this period:—"On landing I beheld magnificent structures mouldering into ruin, the streets were faintly traced by the remains of their forsaken mansions, and squares and markets once populous were now the haunt of serpents and noxious reptiles; the few inhabitants were priests, monks, half-starved soldiers, and low mechanics. Notwithstanding the general decline of Goa, the churches and the convents retained their grandeur, and were in good repair."*

W. Franklin, who was in Goa towards the close of the 18th century, says that though the city was still adorned with fine churches and handsome convents, it was quite fallen and in no estimation with other powers, and that to defray the current expenses of the Government, the Court of Lisbon was obliged to send out annually a very large sum of money, which was swallowed up by the convents and soldiery. The traveller then remarks:—"The glorious times of Albuquerque are no more; power and wealth have long since taken their flight from the discoverers of the East."†

In the beginning of the 19th century the city of Goa attracted the attention of strangers chiefly by its religious buildings, many of which were still preserved in great splendour. Dr. Claudius Buchanan wrote in 1808 that the magnificence of the churches in Goa far exceeded the idea he had formed of them from the descriptions given by travellers. Goa, says he, is, properly speaking, the city of churches, and the wealth of all its provinces appears to have been spent in their erection. These specimens of ancient architecture are unrivalled in taste as well as in grandeur by any that can be witnessed in these days in any part of the East.‡ They present a striking contrast to

* *Oriental Memoirs*, by J. Forbes, London, 1834, vol. I., p. 187.

† *Voyages and Travels in all parts of the world*, by J. Pinkerton, London, vol. IX., p. 234.

‡ *Christian Researches in Asia*, London, 1811, p. 163.

the gloom and misery that surround them. In fact with the exception of these convents, the decay of the city in other respects was by this time complete. Texeira Pinto writes in 1823 that though no decree had been passed for the destruction of the city, like that of the senate of Rome, *de delenda Carthagine;* though no irruption of barbarians had threatened her with ruin; though no fury of conquerors, like Alexander, had been directed against her as against Persepolis; though no deluge, no earthquake, no natural calamity had overtaken her, still little or nothing remained of the city of Albuquerque except the soil on which she stood. The population in her suburbs was hardly a twentieth part of what it had been. The parishes which had from twelve to thirty thousand inhabitants were almost deserted.* The city presented a scene of desolation and ruin; there were only convents and churches with their ecclesiastics and their dependants. The superior of the Augustinian convent said four years after (1827) to the Abbé Cottineau de Kloguen, who was in Goa at this time, "Il ne reste plus de cette ville que le sacré, le profane en est entièrement banni," "Nothing remains of this city but the sacred, the profane is entirely banished."†

The Abbé himself has left us by far the best description of the city in the last days of its existence. He says: In the midst of its ruins the old limits of the city could be distinctly traced. The public squares and thoroughfares were still distinguishable, and most of them were still bordered on both sides with low and mouldering stone walls. But there was not a single decent-looking house in the city; a few wretched huts were scattered here and there at a considerable distance from each other. It was a vast solitude. The greater part of the city was covered with cocoanut trees, which were a source of revenue to the church and convents and to private individuals. The suburb of Lower Daugim or of Santa Luzia on the east was also very much in decay; it contained only about fifty common

---

* *Memorias sobres as Possessoens Portuguesas na Asia*, p. 171.

† *Instituto Vasco da Gama*, vol. III., p. 151.

houses on both sides of the streets, inhabited by Muhammadans and Hindus, but the suburb of Panelim or of São Pedro on the west was in a better condition, having a row of elegantly constructed houses facing the river and extending to Ribandar. The total population of the city and its suburbs was about 3,200, two-thirds of which belonged to Panelim.* The city was found much in the same state by the Rev. Joseph Wolff in 1833, and by Dr. John Wilson in 1834.†

In the following year the Home Government adopted a measure which proved a deathblow to the city. A resolution was passed for the suppression of all religious orders throughout the Portuguese dominions. Accordingly the friars, who were at this time the only inhabitants of the city, were obliged to abandon their convents, and settle elsewhere. The majestic buildings which they had raised with exquisite skill and preserved with unceasing care, and which had excited the admiration of all travellers and strangers who visited Goa, were now destined to share the fate which had overtaken so many other edifices in the city, both public and private. They became State property, but were either neglected and suffered to decay, or purposely demolished to furnish materials for the construction of new buildings at Pangim, which had already become the seat of government. At the same time the valuable property, both moveable and immoveable, which belonged to these convents was sold, and the proceeds were made over to the public treasury.

With the suppression of the religious orders, and the fall of the convents, the last spark of life in the city became almost extinct. The proud capital of the Portuguese Eastern Empire was humbled to the dust. It was reduced to a heap of ruins, and turned into a wilderness, infested by venomous snakes and reptiles. The spot hallowed by the fame of Albuquerque and St. Francis Xavier, which had witnessed so many triumphs of the sword and the Gospel, which had absorbed

---

* *An Historical Sketch of Goa, ut supra*, p. 80.

† *Researches and Missionary Labours*, by the Rev. Joseph Wolff, London, 1835, p. 478; *Oriental Christian Spectator*, Bombay, 1834, vol. V. (First Series), p. 119.

the wealth and commerce of the East, and had attained an almost classic name, now presented a piteous spectacle of wide-spread desolation and decay. The spacious squares and piers along the river-side, so full of life and activity,—the crowded bazaars stocked with the varied products of different climes and regions,—the public thoroughfares thronged with men of every race and creed,—the noble edifices both public and private, religious and secular, rivalling in grandeur and beauty some of the best structures in Europe,—the palaces and churches and convents with their lofty spires and turrets,—these and other distinguishing features of a great and flourishing city were gradually swept away, till at length they have been almost completely obliterated. It is difficult to trace them with any accuracy amidst scattered ruins, overgrown with thick shrubs and bushes, and half-buried in cocoanut groves. A few religious buildings, happily preserved from the general wreck, stand in the midst of this awful solitude to attest the departed glory of the old capital. A few priests break the sepulchral silence which reigns all around by the melodious hymns they chant; a few individuals occasionally break in on the lonely scene to contemplate the noble remains of a fallen city.

In surveying its ruins, the tourist cannot help being struck with the decay and desolation which meets his sight in all directions. Dr. Russell, who lately accompanied the Prince of Wales on his visit to the city, speaks of the ruins thus:—"The river washes the remains of a great city—an arsenal in ruins; palaces in ruins; quay walls in ruins; churches in ruins—all in ruins. We looked and saw the site of the Inquisition, the Bishop's prison, a grand Cathedral, great churches, chapels, convents, religious houses, on knolls surrounded by jungle and trees scattered all over the country. We saw the crumbling masonry which once marked the lines of streets and enclosures of palaces, dockyards filled with weeds and obsolete cranes."*

---

* *The Prince of Wales' Tour*, by William Howard Russell, 2nd ed., London, 1877, p. 230.

CHAPTER VII.

DESCRIPTION OF THE PRINCIPAL QUARTERS AND BUILDINGS OF THE CITY—QUAY OF THE VICEROYS, AND RIBEIRA DAS GALE'S—QUAY OF ST. CATHERINE—ARCH OF THE VICEROYS—PALACE OF THE VICEROYS.

Before concluding the sketch of the city, it is necessary to describe its principal quarters, with the squares, quays and buildings which once adorned them; for then only can we form at this distant day some faint idea of the splendour and magnificence which lies entombed under the ruins of the old capital.

Quay of the Viceroys, and Ribeira das Gale's.—On landing we find ourselves within the Quay of the Viceroy's Fortress. A luxuriant but lonely grove of palm-trees stands now on the site of this once busy pier, which was also known by the name of *Terreiro,* and measured about seven hundred paces in length and two hundred in breadth. Numerous ships that came laden with merchandize from various parts of India touched at this pier, which was consequently crowded with people. Here stood the *Bangaçal,** a large building where the cargo was stored; and the *Peso,* where it was weighed. Here was the *Alfandega* or Custom-house, which a traveller, writing in the beginning of the 17th century, compares with the *Palais Royal* of Paris. Here too were the lodgings of Government officers and contractors.† Of these buildings, there is at present no trace to be found, whilst the Custom-house has long since been removed to Pangim.‡

* *Bangaçal* formerly meant a place of sale or store, but it is now restricted to a place where only timber is sold.

† *Voyage de François Pyrard,* Part II., p. 28.

‡ The Custom-house during the Muhammadan government was called *Mánḍvi* or *Mandovi,* a name which was subsequently given also to the adjoining river. A duty of six per cent. was paid on almost all the articles imported and exported. The Custom-house appears to have been rebuilt during the government of Dom Constantino de Bragança. See *Arch. Port. Or.*, Fasc. I., doc. 3.

To the east of the pier lay the *Bazar Grande,* or the Great Bazaar, which is now transformed into a wilderness. To the west was seen another square, spacious, well built, and jutting out into the river, called *Ribeira das Galés.* It was the mooring-place of almost all the galleys of Goa, and contained everything that was necessary for equipping them. Here the convicts were condemned to undergo hard labour. Here sentries kept constant watch, and no one had access to this place except on business. From this spot, too, ships started for Portugal laden with merchandize.*

Quay of St. Catherine.—Close to this square there was another, equally large and beautiful, which extended as far as the Arsenal, and was bounded on the north by the walls of the Royal Hospital, to which passengers arriving sick from Portugal were taken, without much trouble, from on board. Here the cargo was often landed amidst a large crowd of Christians, pagans, and negroes. The goods were carried from the place in a somewhat peculiar manner; they were suspended from a long bamboo stick supported on the shoulders of two or four men, who, to lighten their burden, sang humorous songs as they passed along. It was called *Caes de Santa Catharina* (the Quay of St. Catherine), and was the chief place of embarkation and landing.† The pier now called *Caes de Arcebispo* is a work of recent date, and must have formerly been part of the Quay of St. Catherine. There is nothing at present to show the once flourishing condition of these places. Instead of the bustle which once prevailed here, a complete silence now reigns, broken only by the wind whistling through the branches of the palm-trees which grow luxuriantly on the spot.

Arch of the Viceroys.—Returning now to the Quay of the Viceroys, we see at a little distance from the landing-place an elegant and lofty portico, which formed the principal entrance

* Pyrard, *ut supra,* Part II., p. 27.

† It was also called the *Fish Bazaar,* as fish brought for sale was landed there. Pyrard, *loc. cit.*

to the city, and was called *Arco dos Vice-reys* (the Arch of the Viceroys). It stands on the site of the principal gate through which people entered the city, and which was decorated on the occasion of the entry of every new Viceroy. In 1599, during the government of Dom Francisco da Gama, the great-grandson of Vasco da Gama, this portico was built of black stone by order of the Senate of the city of Goa, with the twofold object of saving the expense of decoration and of perpetuating the name of the famous discoverer of the sea route to India. A statue of St. Catherine, patroness of the city, made of gilt bronze, was placed in an upper niche, and in a lower one the statue of the great argonaut, dressed in the fashion of his time. The former has lost much of its freshness, and the latter has its features a little defaced by time. The façade of the door was adorned with elegant paintings representing the Portuguese wars in the Indies, which are now, by the use of whitewash, altogether effaced.* The inauguration of this monument was celebrated with great pomp; Diogo de Couto, the famous Portuguese historian, himself took part in the proceedings. There is nothing at present remarkable in the portico except an inscription dedicated to the Immaculate Conception of the Virgin Mary, and commemorating the emancipation of Portugal from the Spanish yoke in the following words :—

"Legitimo e verdadeiro Rei D. João 4, Restaurador da Liberdade Portugueza. 1656."

---

* *Boletim do Governo do Estado da India*, 1851, p. 322; Pyrard, Part II., p. 21. Faria y Souza writes about the statue of Vasco da Gama as follows:—"In the year 1600 Ayres de Saldanna arrived at Goa as viceroy to supersede the Count de Vidigueira, who was universally disliked by the Portuguese inhabitants. The marble statue of the great Vasco da Gama, his grandfather, stood over the principal gate of the city, fastened to the wall by a strong bar of iron. At the instigation of some enemies to the count, a French engineer named Sebastian Tibao applied to the iron bar during the night *a certain herb* that has the quality of eating iron, so that the statue fell down next night, and its quarters were hung up in different parts of the city." (*A General History and Collection of Voyages and Travels*, by Robert Kerr, vol. VI., p. 486.) If the statement of the writer be true, the statue now existing is different from the original.

Translation.

"The lawful and true King Dom João IV., Restorer of the Portuguese liberty. 1656."

Palace of the Viceroys.—On passing through the portico the ruins of the Palace of the Viceroys on the left at once meet the sight. This palace was so close to the Quay of the Viceroys that it commanded a full view of the river with its shipping, and of the square with all its bustle and activity.* Here was formerly the castle or fortress of Adil-Sháh, or the Sabaio, which after the Portuguese conquest was rebuilt, as they say, by Albuquerque. The first Captain of the city, Rodrigo Rebello, and subsequently captains of the ships, used to live in it.† In 1554 the Viceroy, Dom Pedro Mascarenhas, being extremely old, and unable to ascend the staircases of the palace of the Sabaio, where the Viceroys lived before him, removed his residence to this fortress, which, partly retaining its old name, was called the Palace of the Fortress, or the Fortress of the Viceroys.‡ His successors continued to live there till the year 1695, when the Count of Villa Verde, on account of the epidemic, fixed his abode in Panelim, but the most important public business of the State was still transacted in this palace. In the course of a century and a half, during which the Palace of the Fortress was the residence of the powerful Viceroys, it was wholly remodelled in its aspect and dimensions. Tavernier and other travellers speak of it with admiration.§ According to Pyrard, it was very magnificently built, and as it stood on an eminence (probably the ancient fortress) it was the most conspicuous building in the city. The palace looked towards the south, and in front of it stood a large square, called *Terreiro do Paço*, surrounded by beautiful

---

* Pyrard, Part II., p. 28.

† *Lendas, ut supra*, vol. II., pp. 158, 176.

‡ Diogo de Couto, *Dec.* VII., liv. I., cap. iii.; Pyrard, *ut supra*, p. 28; *Diccionario Historico-Explicativo á Viagem de duas mil legoas*, por F. N. Xavier, Nova-Goa, 1848, p. 101.

§ *Les Six Voyages*, vol. II., p. 115.

houses. From this square a large staircase of stone led to a spacious hall of the palace, which was adorned with the pictures of the ships that had come out to India since the time of Vasco da Gama, with their names and those of their captains written below.* The number of these pictures must have been very great, for as early as 1612, 806 vessels had left Portugal for the East.† This hall opened into another still more spacious, which contained the life-size portraits of all the Viceroys and Governors, bearing their names and exploits. It was in this hall that the Viceroy received ambassadors from the princes of India, held his council, and transacted the most important affairs of the state. The palace had many other apartments, and contained, as the abovenamed traveller states, chapels, water reservoirs, and even part of the royal treasury.‡ Here the Viceroy lived in regal splendour, maintaining his court in a style almost rivalling that of the greatest Eastern potentate. His first entry into the city was a real ovation, and people of all classes vied with each other in celebrating the occasion amid great rejoicings. Majestic arches were erected from the pier to the cathedral, whence, after the usual ceremony of installation, the Viceroy was escorted to the palace amidst the acclamations of the people and the deafening roar of cannon. Here he was welcomed by the ambassadors of the Indian princes, who offered him valuable presents. The halls of the palace were constantly thronged by fidalgos, who, with the hope of obtaining lucrative offices, presented him with large sums of money, which enabled him to amass upwards of £100,000 during the short tenure of his office.§

---

* Pyrard, *ut supra*, p. 30; *Historia de Portugal*, por uma Sociedade de Homens de Letras, vol. IV., p. 213.

† *Boletim e Annaes do Conselho Ultramarino*, No. 155, p. 41.

‡ Pyrard, *ut supra*, p. 30.

§ Pyrard, *ut supra*, p. 49. Milburn, in his *Oriental Commerce*, London, 1813, p. 306, says :—"Some of the Viceroys returned to Portugal with £300,000, several of the Governors and Generals with £100,000, and many subordinate officers, both civil and military, with from £20,000 to £50,000."

Twice a week the Portuguese and native Christians, who were destitute of the means of subsistence, besieged his palace, and his almoner was ordered to distribute alms among them. It was on rare occasions that the Viceroy stirred out of his palace, and when he did, he made a royal progress, as it were, through the city. A day previous to his appearance in public, drums were beaten and trumpets sounded, as a signal to the noblesse and the gentry to accompany him on the following day. Accordingly early in the morning about three or four hundred fidalgos and courtiers appeared in the *Terreiro do Paço* clad in rich attire, mounted on noble steeds with gold and silver trappings glittering with pearls and precious stones, and followed by European pages in rich livery. With such a splendid cavalcade did the Viceroy show himself in public. On ordinary days he had in his palace a guard of a hundred Portuguese dressed in uniform, who accompanied him when he went out attended by the fidalgos. It is easy to imagine the bustle* which on these occasions prevailed in the square in front of the palace, and the magnificence which was displayed within its walls on gala days. No trace now remains of its former grandeur. It commenced to decay when the city was abandoned. In 1774, when the question of rebuilding the old city was mooted, it was also thought advisable to repair the palace, but the whole scheme was given up as impracticable. The Governors, however, according to Abbé Cottineau, continued till 1812 to use its great hall, on public and festive occasions.† In the same year an estimate was made of the expenses attendant on the repair and preservation of a certain portion of this palace, and it is said to have amounted to £2,732-15-10, but as this portion was considerably dilapidated, it was shortly afterwards ordered to be demolished by the Council of the Public Treasury in 1820.‡ The remain-

* Linschoten, *ut supra*, pp. 65 *et seq.*; Pyrard, *ut supra*, p. 45.

† *An Historical Sketch of Goa*, p. 88.

‡ *Diccionario Historico-Explicativo*, p. 101.

ing part stood for some time longer, and the aforesaid writer speaks in 1827 with admiration of its grandeur.* This part, too, gradually fell into decay, and is now lying in ruins covered with creepers and shrubs. In front of this palace stood the High Court; on its right the chief Jail, called *Tronco*; and the royal Magazines to the left. Of these and other buildings, once so conspicuous in this quarter, hardly any vestige is left at present.

---

* *Inst. Vasco da Gama*, vol. III., p. 234.

CHAPTER VIII.

RUA DIREITA—THE CATHEDRAL—THE ARCHIEPISCOPAL PALACE—THE SENATE-HOUSE—PALACE OF THE INQUISITION, AND AUTO DA FE'—CONVENT AND CHURCH OF ST. FRANCIS OF ASSISIUM.

Rua Direita.—The road is still to be seen which once led straight from the Palace of the Viceroys to the Church of *Misericordia*, and which was therefore called *Rua Direita*. This road was the principal thoroughfare of the city, lined on both sides with stately buildings where bankers, jewellers, and other traders of different countries transacted business. It was densely thronged by people who attended auction-sales held there from morning till noon; on which account it was also called *Rua dos Leilões*. Linschoten gives in his work an excellent description of this street. It is astonishing, says he, to see here the crowd of sellers and buyers during the market hours. Persons of all creeds and races mingle together, with large umbrellas in their hands, which protect them from the heat of the sun in the hot season, and from the rain during the monsoons. Here too execution-sales take place by order of the law courts: the revenues are farmed; the valuable articles of India the noble horses of Arabia and Persia, and slaves of both sexes are exhibited for sale. Many of these slaves are well skilled in music, embroidery, and several other useful arts, and fetch a price proportionate to their accomplishments, no less than to their personal charms.*

The Cathedral.—Midway in the *Rua Direita* stands the Cathedral or *Sé Primacial*, one of the most ancient and celebrated religious buildings of Goa, and at present the only one where

* Linschoten, *Hist. de la Navigation*, p. 57; Pyrard, *Voyage*, Part II., pp. 30 *et seq*.

religious service is regularly held every day on a somewhat grand scale. The project of erecting a church in the city was started by Albuquerque himself when he took it from the Muhammadans. Gaspar Correia says that soon after its capture the conqueror embraced his colleagues, knelt down to thank St. Catherine, on whose festival day his arms had been crowned with success, and vowed to erect a church in her honour on the spot where he stood, near the river-side. The vow was speedily fulfilled. A few days after, he ordered a church, or rather a chapel, to be built, and an altar raised with a picture of St. Catherine hung over it. As the chapel was not sufficiently large and commodious, and as it was built of mud and covered with straw, which rendered it liable to catch fire, Mass was celebrated in the spacious veranda of the castle in the city.* Albuquerque, who was anxious to have a better church built on the spot, left instructions to enlarge the chapel on his departure for Malacca. These instructions were carried out in his absence in 1511 by his friend Diogo Fernandes, a wealthy fidalgo.† To this church (which the aforesaid chronicler calls in anticipation the cathedral of Goa, as De Barros also does) were transferred the bones of Dom Antonio de Noronha, a gallant soldier, nephew of Albuquerque, who had been mortally wounded in the attempt to capture Goa, and had been buried in the neighbouring island of Divar.‡ In 1538, when Dom João de Albuquerque came out as Bishop of Goa, the Church of St. Catherine had already been raised to the rank of Cathedral by a Bull of Paul III., issued on the 3rd November 1534. The ceremony of the bishop's installation in the new Cathedral was performed with great pomp. Subsequently canons and other functionaries were appointed. Every canon received the sum of £4-3-4 per annum, and the bishop £100.§ In 1546 there were more than thirty

* *Lendas, ut supra*, tom. II., pp. 146, 154, 158.

† *Op. cit.*, pp. 199, 200.

‡ *Op. cit.*, p. 109; De Barros. *Dec.* II., liv. VII., cap. IV., p. 128.

§ *Lendas*, tom. IV., p. 89.

canons and chaplains, who enjoyed a higher salary.* Before this date, in 1530 or 1531, the original building appears to have been enlarged, as the King, in a letter dated 26th March 1532, addressed to the Senate of Goa, says that he is aware of the Cathedral having been completed by means of public and private donations.† This fact is corroborated also by Simão Botelho, the *Vedor* of the Treasury.‡ But Gaspar Correia, who relates many incidents connected with this cathedral, such as the solemn reception of Dom João de Castro and his son Dom Alvaro, and the celebration of the nuptials of the daughters of the Governor, Garcia de Sá, makes no mention of the enlargement of the original building: he says indeed that the Cathedral of St. Catherine cost £833-6-8, which may perhaps be owing to its enlargement.§ We think, however, that the church, if enlarged at all, could not have been considerably increased in size, as it was soon afterwards rebuilt. Up to 1542 the Cathedral was the only parochial church in the city, and in 1557, was made the archiepiscopal metropolitan church of India by a Bull of Pope Paul IV. While buildings for religious and secular purposes were being erected at this time in a magnificent style in all quarters of the city, it could not be expected that the principal church in the East would be left in the original simplicity of its construction. Accordingly, in the reign of Dom Sebastião, the Viceroy, Dom Francisco Coutinho, Count of Redondo, caused a more splendid cathedral to be built in 1562, out of the

---

* *Op. cit.*, pp. 89, 669. The salary of the Bishop in 1554 was £111-2-2⅔, and that of the Chapter £72-14-5⅓: *Subsidios para a Historia da India Portuguesa*, Part II., p. 68. Since 1561 the Dean received £11-2-2⅔, and the *Cantor*, Treasurer, Archdeacon, and *Mestre-Escola* £8-6-8 each, 10 Canons £6-18-10⅔ each, Quartenarians £5-11-1⅓ each, the Sub-Treasurer £4-3-4, the *Sub-Cantor* £1-7-9⅓, 12 Chaplains £4-3-4 each, 4 Choristers £1-2-2⅔ each, besides £0-5-6⅔ every two years for a red gown for their use. *Arch. Port. Or.*, Fasc. V., doc. 343. This money was paid out of the income accruing from the lands in Bardes. *Op. cit.*, doc. 743.

† *Arch. Port. Or.*, Fasc. I., doc. No. 2.

‡ *Subsidios para a Historia da India Portugueza*, Pt. II., p. 52.

§ *Lendas, ut supra*, vol. IV., tom. II., pp. 577, 591, 601, 618, 650, 669, 673.

proceeds of the sale of such property as escheated to the Crown whenever a Hindu or any other infidel died intestate and without heirs.* The work seems to have been begun at once, as Pyrard, who was in Goa in 1608, says that he found it in an unfinished state, though it had been prosecuted for fifty years past, its design being too grand to be carried out.† It has occasionally been stated that the new church occupies the site of the old one. But this is clearly a mistake, as we have seen that the old church stood near the river-side, close to the Royal Hospital, whilst the present church lies at some distance from it. It is said to have been built on the ruins of a Hindu temple or a Muhammadan mosque—probably the latter, because the former would not have been allowed to stand close to the palace of a Muhammadan prince which was situated there. The work was delayed for many years for want of funds, although the Home Government gave every assistance for its successful prosecution, authorising the grant of considerable sums of money by the *alvará* of the 9th March 1571, and directing the authorities of Goa to avail themselves of the services of the eminent architects Antonio Argueiros and Julio Simão, Chief Engineer to the State of India, who then superintended the construction of an important building of the Jesuits in the city.‡ In 1595, under the supervision of the last named engineer, the

---

* *Arch. Port. Or.*, Fasc. III., doc. 23; Fasc. V., doc. 435.

† Pyrard, Pt. II., p. 31. There is a difference of three or four years between the date quoted above and the date given by Pyrard, which is probably due to a mistake of the latter.

‡ *Arch. Port. Or.*, Fasc. III., doc. 25. 59, 79, 686; Fasc. V. doc. 526. Julio Simão was born in India, as stated in doc. No. 79 quoted above; his grave is in the Cathedral in the transept below the steps of the sanctuary, with the following epitaph:—"Sepultura de Julio Simão, Quavaleiro fidalgo da caza delrey nosso Senhore seu Engenheiro mór deste Estado, Mestre Arquitecto das obras desta Se, e de sua mulher Caterina de Bustamante e erdeiros," i. e. "Grave of Julio Simão, Knight Fidalgo of the household of the King our Lord, and his Chief Engineer in this State, Master Architect of the works of this Cathedral, and of his wife Caterina de Bustamante, and heirs." The Arch of the Viceroys was also erected by him.

work was pushed on very vigorously.* But the building was far from being completed, as the Bishop of Cochin, Dom Fr. André de Santa Maria, who was then acting as Archbishop of Goa, wrote in the same year to the King that, although a considerable outlay had been made, much still remained to be done, and it would be long before the Cathedral could be wholly built, as its walls were large and massive.† This opinion is perfectly in accordance with that expressed by Pyrard, about fourteen years later, in the extract from his book quoted above. The work was even suspended for a short time for want of funds, but was afterwards resumed, under instructions received from Portugal.‡ Notwithstanding several difficulties, the body of the church was at last finished in 1619, and the Blessed Sacrament placed on the altar on the feast of the Guardian Angel, amidst great solemnities and rejoicings, as stated in a letter of the Governor, Fernão de Albuquerque, of the 14th February 1620. The building was however completed in the year 1631, as we learn from the *alvará* of the Viceroy, the Count of Linhares, of 21st May of the same year; and the outhouses were constructed in subsequent years during the archbishopric of Dom Fr. Francisco dos Martyres (1636-52). This probably accounts for an inscription, which will be presently noticed, wherein it is said that the Catholic Kings, successors of Dom Sebastião, ordered the work to be continued up to that period.

This cathedral, which was in course of construction for upwards of three-fourths of a century, and which witnessed the rise and fall of the Portuguese power in the East, is a really majestic edifice. Dr. Fryer, who visited it in 1675, says that it is hardly surpassed in grandeur by any church in Great Britain; Dr. Buchanan writes in 1808 that it is worthy of one of the principal cities of Europe; and Dr. Russell, who visited it lately with the Prince of Wales, testifies to its "vast

---

* *Arch. Port. Or.*, Fasc. III., doc. 204.

† *Op. cit.*, Fasc. III., doc. 210.

‡ *Op. cit.*, Fasc. III., doc. 312, 369.

and noble proportions."* It is situated to the west of the great square called *Terreiro de Sabaio,* and has its façade turned to the east. Its beautiful courtyard is approached by a flight of steps. The building is not very imposing in its outward appearance; the height of the frontispiece, including the cross on the top, is 115$\frac{2}{3}$ feet, and the breadth 100$\frac{4}{5}$ feet; its total length is 250 feet, and breadth 181$\frac{1}{5}$ feet. It is externally built in half Tuscan half Doric style, internally in the Mosaic-Corinthian. It has three large portals. On the top of the middle portal is a large slab with the following inscription, in two columns, with a tiara and keys, the insignia of the Pope in the middle:—

" Rein^{do} o Mui Cat^{co}
Rey D. Seb^{am} m^{dou}
Fazer esta SSe
. . (†) . o anno do
S^{r} de 562 sẽdo
Administradores
Della os Arcebpos
Primazes
Os catolicos Reis seus
successores

A mandaram conti-
nuar a custa
De sua Real Fa-
z^{da} ate o prezente
Q' he o Arcebpo Pri-
maz D. Frey Fran^{co}
dos Martyres e
Vizo Rey deste
Estado . . . . "†

Translation.

"In the reign of the very Catholic King Dom Sebastião this Cathedral was ordered to be erected . . . . . † in the year of our Lord 1562, the Archbishops and Primates being the Administrators. The Catholic Kings his successors ordered it to be continued at the cost of their Royal Treasury up to the time of the present Archbishop Primate Dom Frei Francisco dos Martyres, and Viceroy of this State . . . ."

* *A New Account of East India and Persia*, p. 149; *Christian Researches in Asia*, p. 158; *The Prince of Wales' Tour*, p. 232.

† Here space is left, probably for the insertion of the name of the Viceroy.

This cathedral has now only one lateral tower, the other towards the north having fallen down on the 25th July 1776; the sum of £2,083-6-8 was calculated as necessary for its reconstruction. This sum was to be raised by means of a tax levied on marriages, but the project was never carried out. The tower now existing being of considerable height, overlooks the whole city, and commands a beautiful view of the surrounding villages. In this tower are hung five bells, one of which is very large and is tolled about five times a day, and also on the death of the Pope, the King, the Governor, the Archbishop, and any Canon. On the occasion of the principal festivities, as also at times when the Governor, the Archbishop or the Chapter come to the church, all the five bells are rung. On other minor festival days the four smaller are rung. Every day two are tolled for half an hour to summon the Canons to the choir. Four of these bells, mentioned in the Royal Letter of the 26th March 1532,* may possibly have belonged to the old Cathedral. The great bell is the same that used to be tolled on the occasion of the *auto da fé* in the time of the Inquisition, and its thrilling sounds still awaken in the mind strange reminiscences of the past.

Mr. Thomas Ribeiro, the present Minister of Portugal, has written some excellent verses on the principal bell of the Cathedral from which we transcribe the following :—

É noite lobrega! o sino,
o sino d'oiro da sé,
dá badaladas soturnas
chamando ás preces nocturnas!...
Quem chama o sino?...quem é?!
Pois d'estas cryptas sombrias,
d'estas funerarias urnas
quem se levanta? quem vê
coar-se o raio divino
da luz das mysticas lampas
pelas janellas do templo
como o olhar casto da fé?

---

* *Arch. Port. Or.*, Fasc. I., doc. 2.

Só se das marmoreas campas
resurgem por horas mortas
os heroes de mil batalhas,
naufragos de cem procellas
da sorte nos invios mares,
e vão depor nos altares,
em vez de rasgadas velas,
ensanguentadas mortalhas!

Tange, sino d'oiro, tange
na velha torre da sé,
que se o teu som se refrange
nos ecos da solidão,
se das abobadas rôtas
que estão ruindo a pedaços
te responde o furacão,
talvez que aos heroes d'Ormuz
de Chaul, Diu e Ceylão,
quebres o sêlo da morte
e acordes o coração.
Era tão grande! tão forte! . . .
Poderam com tantas máguas
e ganharam tanta gloria
sobre o terra e sobre as aguas
e são tão vivos na historia!
. . . . *

The interior of the church is very magnificent, and has a vaulted ceiling. Its body, excluding the four chapels on each side, is 142$\frac{3}{5}$ feet long and 69$\frac{1}{5}$ broad, and is divided by two rows of pillars into a nave and two aisles, the nave 72 feet high, and each of the aisles 57$\frac{1}{2}$. At the entrance, besides the two marble basins for holy water inserted in the columns, we see the baptismal font, which is of black stone and of considerable size. It belonged to the old Cathedral, as stated in the following inscription on its border :—

"Esta pia mandou faser Jorge Gomez, e a deo a esta Sé em onra e louuor do Senhor Deos em 1532."

---

* *Jornadas*, Part II., p. 229.

Translation.

"George Gomez ordered this font to be made, and gave it to this church in honour and praise of the Lord God in 1532."

It is probable, as a writer suggests, that in this font the Apostle of the Indies, St. Francis Xavier, may have baptized a great number of the natives of India. Another remarkable object in this place is a large picture representing St. Christopher with the Infant Jesus on his shoulders. On the 25th July of each year, the day dedicated to the commemoration of this holy martyr, the Chapter offers thanks to the saint for having saved through his intercession the rest of the Cathedral from destruction when one of its towers fell down.

Turning to the right we see four chapels; the first dedicated to St. Anthony, the second to St. Bernard, the third to the *Cruz dos Milagres*, and the fourth to the Holy Ghost. The chapel of the *Cruz dos Milagres* deserves attention on account of the cross, which, according to a legend hereafter to be mentioned, the common people believe to have miraculously grown in size before it was located in this chapel. Its present length is 20⅗ feet.

Of the four chapels on the left, the first is dedicated to *Nossa Senhora de Necessidades,* the second to St. Sebastian, the third to the Blessed Sacrament, and the fourth to *Nossa Senhora de Boa Vida.* Of these the chapel of the Blessed Sacrament is the most spacious and beautiful and has its own vestry; its altar is elegantly wrought and decorated. The Blessed Sacrament is kept there, while in other churches it is always on the principal altar. This chapel is 72 feet long and 21½ broad. Proceeding further into the interior we find the transept 36 feet by 90⅓. It has six altars, three on each side, those to the right dedicated respectively to St. Joseph, *Nossa Senhora das Dores,* and St. Peter ; those to the left to *Nossa Senhora de Angustia,* St. George, and *Nossa Senhora d'Esperança.*

Near the altar of St. Joseph there is a slab in the wall covering the bones of the first Archbishop of Goa, Dom Gaspar de Leão Pereira, in whose time the erection of the present cathedral was commenced. This prelate, having died in 1576, was buried in the convent of *Mãe de Deus* in the suburb of Daugim, which he had founded, but, the convent being in a decayed state, his bones were removed in 1864 to this place. On the same side of the transept lies the vestry. We see there various pictures of St. Catherine and of the twelve Apostles. The vestments, though very rich and formerly highly spoken of, are now worn out. There are valuable gold vessels, especially a monstrance worth £500.

The principal chapel, with its high altar, has an imposing appearance, and is 38 feet long and 34⅓ broad. The altar-piece is very large, and richly adorned with engravings, pillars, pilasters, and other embellishments. It has three niches in the centre, one above another, in which stand three images, one of St. Catherine, another of *Nossa Senhora d'Assumpção*, and the third of Christ crucified. Over the last image there is the figure of a dove, symbolizing the Holy Ghost. On both sides of the altar-piece stand, on high pedestals, images of St. Peter and St. Paul; besides these there are four engravings representing the martyrdom of St. Catherine. The altar-piece appears to be very old, and its gilding has lost its freshness. The choir, which rises three steps high, is of the same breadth as the nave, and extends from the foot of the high altar to the railings, which separate it from the nave. On the epistle side there is a large and rich ebony stand, which belonged once to the Convent of St. Francis. On either side of the choir there are chairs and seats for the canons. The throne of the Archbishop is on the gospel side; its canopy is lowered when the archbishopric is vacant. The chair of the Governor, without a canopy, is placed within the railings, after the chairs of the canons. Masses are daily said at different altars, and the canons meet in the choir twice a day, at half-past eight in the morning and at three o'clock in the afternoon, to say divine office. In the morning they sing at High Mass, and recite prime, terce, sext, and nones, and in the evening compline, matins, and lauds. On certain festival days they sing part of the service. The High Mass is accompanied with the music of the organ in the adjoining gallery: there is also another organ, which belonged to the Convent of St. Francis. On Sundays and feast days the choristers of the cathedral come to sing, and a sermon is preached from the pulpit, which is in front of the Governor's chair. Both the pulpit and the gallery are approached through the vestry. A few canons and other functionaries of the Cathedral reside in the old city; most of them live in São Pedro, in the island of Piedade or Divar, and other neighbouring places. All, however, are bound to attend service daily, unless prevented by illness or some other cause, or during vacation, which they are entitled to take by turns. Two of the dignitaries of the chapter being employed by the Archbishop in his palace are exempted from daily attendance at the choir. Nevertheless, like the other canons, they are allotted their week, during which they are supposed to be present, being replaced by semi-canons and quaternarians, who have their own weeks. The Archbishop attends during the Holy Week, and on Maundy Thursday consecrates the holy oils, and celebrates Pontifical Mass on Easter Sunday, Epiphany, Whit Sunday, Corpus Christi, Assumption-day, Christmas, and the feast of St. Catherine. He is attended on these occasions by the first four dignitaries, who sit by his side round the throne. In the absence of the Archbishop on certain festivals the Dean acts for him, and, in the absence of other dignitaries, the other canons act in the order of seniority. Besides this chapter, the cathedral, which is at the same time a parish church, has its curate, who acts as vicar. This parish is now reduced to a miserable state. In 1600, when there were many parishes in the city, the cathedral had more than 80,000 parishioners, in 1720 this number was reduced to 1,858, and now there are scarcely 80 parishioners. The curate is appointed by the Archbishop, but the chapter and the other functionaries are selected by the King and confirmed by the Archbishop, and paid from the public treasury.

Archiepiscopal Palace.—To the north-west of the Cathedral lies the Palace of the Archbishops. It is a two-storied edifice; the upper story, being of tolerable height, admits of free ventilation, and commands a beautiful prospect. In style the structure is chaste, and devoid of ornamental work. Its entire length is 230 feet, and its extreme breadth 108 feet, exclusive of the space occupied by the compound and the garden. Dr. Gemelli Careri, who visited this palace in 1695, testifies to its magnificence and spaciousness, as well as to the elegance of its apartments and the beauty of its numerous galleries.*

On the whole, the building has not suffered much from the ravages of time, and still retains not a little of its former dignity. Some of its upper apartments are spacious and cheerful, while those on the groundfloor wear a sombre and melancholy aspect. It was in one of the former that the Archbishops used to be entertained with the same sumptuousness as the Viceroys; and there too a celebrated prelate, who was distinguished by his piety and humility, daily admitted to his own table twelve poor persons, selected by his servants from among a large number who strove to render themselves worthy of enjoying such a marked distinction. The courtyard in front of the apartments of the Archbishop was daily thronged with men of all ranks, who came on business or for the purpose of paying their respects to him. When the Archbishop went out of this palace to any part of the city, he was accompanied by many mounted noblemen and ecclesiastical personages in palanquins, attended by their respective pages and lackeys on foot.†

All the apartments mentioned above are unfurnished and uninhabited, with the exception of the groundfloor, which is

---

* Churchill's *Voyages and Travels*, vol. IV., p. 205.

† Pyrard, Pt. II., p. 52; *Historia da Fundação do Real Convento de Santa Monica da Cidade de Goa*, Lisboa, 1699, p. 14.

occupied by the curate. In one of the corridors are hung the portraits of all the Archbishops, many of whom had in former times resided there. Attached to this building is a chapel, erected for their use. The palace appears to be as old as the Cathedral, or even much older: for Pyrard, who visited Goa in 1608, alludes to this palace as being the residence of the Archbishop,* though, as we have said before, the Cathedral was far from being completed at that time.

The Archbishops continued to reside in this palace till the year 1695, when, in consequence of the epidemic which was then raging all over the city, the Archbishop as well as the Viceroy abandoned their respective palaces and removed to Panelim, in the suburbs of the city. Some of the prelates, however, specially Dom Fr. Manoel de Santa Catharina, after this event occasionally resided in the old palace for a short period, spending the rest of their time at the palace of Panelim or that of Santa Ignez. The present Archbishop also stays there occasionally.

Senate-house.—Opposite the Cathedral, at the extremity of the *Terreiro de Sabaio,* stood two other edifices, the *Stanco Real de Tabacco* (Royal Depôt of Tobacco) and the Senate-house. In the latter building, which was well constructed and commodious, the Senate of Goa held its sittings till the year 1835, when the Municipal Chamber of the Ilhas, which represents the ancient Senate, transferred, by Government order, its sessions to Pangim. As this edifice was abandoned, it began to decay, and consequently ten years afterwards, when the same Chamber again desired to hold its sittings there, it could not do so beyond a year, for fear the building might give way, and was obliged to return to Pangim, where up to the present day it transacts business in a new building erected for the purpose. The old edifice is now merely a heap of ruins.

Palace of the Inquisition.—Near the Cathedral, to the south of its courtyard, stood the celebrated Palace of the In-

---

* Pyrard, Pt. II., p. 31.

quisition so contiguous to it that one of the angles of its foundation still appears to meet the walls of the former building. This magnificent palace, so designated by the Marquis of Pombal, was flanked on both sides by two high-roads, one of which, to the east, was the famous *Rua Direita*.* It was, as already stated, the residence of the Sabaio before the Portuguese conquest, and subsequently of the Viceroys and Governors, till 1554, when they removed to the Palace of the Fortress. Six years later, on the establishment in India of the tribunal of the Inquisition, the vacant palace was appropriated for its use. The Inquisition made such changes in the edifice as were necessary for its purposes. It contained many halls and chambers, in one of which, known as the *Meza do Santo Officio*, and decked with curtains of green taffeta, stood a huge crucifix (now removed to the chapel attached to the Governor's palace at Pangim) leaning against tapestry work, and so elevated as almost to touch the ceiling. According to a tradition current among the inhabitants of Goa, every individual charged with witchcraft, or any offence against the Catholic religion, was placed before this crucifix, when all of a sudden a thrill appeared to pass through his whole frame: he trembled from head to foot, and at last dropped senseless on the ground, incapable of fixing his eyes on it any more. In the middle of this chamber a daïs was raised about a foot high, on which a table nearly fifteen feet long and four broad was placed, with chairs for the Inquisitors, the Secretary and other officers, when they examined the culprits brought before them.† The edifice had also galleries, a chapel, quarters for the residence of the principal Inquisitor, and a great number of prison cells.

This palace was, according to the testimony of all travellers, a stately and superb edifice. It had three stories, and a beautiful façade which appears to have been of black stone; for Captain Franklin, who visited it, says, "its black outside

---

* *Instrucçoẽs, ut supra*, p. 1.

† Dellon's *Relation de l'Inquisition de Goa*, pp. 48 *et seq.*

appears a fit emblem of the cruel and bloody transactions that passed within its walls."* Pyrard describes it as a vast edifice built of fine stone, with a large and magnificent hall surpassing in grandeur even the splendid hall of a royal palace.† But a more detailed description of it is given by Dellon, who was confined as a prisoner in one of its cells in 1674. He writes thus :—

"The house of the Inquisition, which the Portuguese call *Santa Caza* (Holy House), is situated at one of the sides of the great square in front of the Cathedral dedicated to St. Catherine. This is a large and majestic edifice, having in front three doors, the central one being the largest, and the hall I have spoken of is reached after ascending a staircase by this door. The side doors lead to the chambers of the Inquisitors, each of which is sufficiently large to contain suitable furniture. Besides these there are many other apartments for the accommodation of the officials of the house. Proceeding to the interior, a large two-storied building is visible, divided into many partitions, and separated by a courtyard. Each floor has a gallery in the shape of a dormitory of seven or eight cells, each ten feet square. The number of cells rises to two hundred.

"The cells of one of these dormitories are dark for want of windows, and are lower and smaller than those of the other dormitories; when I complained one day of harsh and severe treatment, these cells were shewn to me, with a view to make me understand that I might have been placed in a much worse situation. The other cells are square-vaulted, whitewashed and clean, into which the light of day is admitted by means of small grated windows without shutters, and placed so high that the tallest man could not reach them.

"The walls, on the whole, are five feet thick; the cells are shut by means of two doors, one opening into them, the other opening out. The former has two strong iron handles, and when the lower half is left open exhibits a kind of railing with a small window upwards, to allow of the prisoner's being supplied with food, clothes, and other necessary articles, which were thrown in. This window has a small shutter secured by two strong chains. The other door is neither so strong nor so thick, and is made of a single plank without an opening. It generally remains open from six to eleven in the morning, for ventilation and for purifying the air in the cells."‡

---

* *A General Collection of the best and the most interesting Travels*, by John Pinkerton, vol. IX., p. 234.

† Pyrard, Pt. II., p. 31.

‡ Dellon, *ut supra*, p. 51.

Many of the changes and additions to the old edifice which Dellon here describes were gradually effected. The increased number of the cells was due to the increasing number of arrests made by the orders of the Inquisition. The expenses attending their construction were borne by the public treasury. By a royal letter dated the 26th March 1620, the Viceroy was authorized to apply for the purpose the fines imposed by courts of justice. But as these were not adequate to meet the necessary outlay, the Viceroy, the Count of Linhares, signified to the King, on the 10th February 1630, his intention of devoting to the construction of the cells the income till then set apart for the benefit of the Cathedral, which was by this time nearly completed. Notwithstanding this, it would appear that the Viceroy did not at once endeavour to put his plan into execution, because in the following December he wrote again to the King that with the funds available from the public treasury and by means of a loan he had succeeded in completing fifty additional cells, which cost £308-6-8, a considerable sum when the cheapness of materials at this time is taken into consideration.

Nor was this all: with other funds certain improvements were effected in the apartments intended for the *Mesa do Santo Officio* and for the senior Inquisitor; while a project was formed for adding other cells. The Viceroy, however, not having at his disposal the necessary funds to carry out these additional works, was obliged, as will be seen from an *alvará* dated the 21st May 1631, to revert to the plan, already noticed, of devoting to the construction of these cells and the repairing of the fortress the income originally set aside for the erection of the Cathedral, for he said that both these works, viz. the prisons and the fortress, "should be undertaken with promptitude and energy, since His Majesty had recommended it by several despatches, and since the royal treasury was so low that it could not meet half the demand that was made upon it."

From time to time several other additions continued to be made to the Palace of the Inquisition, so that it became at length the largest of all the palaces of Goa, containing such ample accommodation that it was once under contemplation to transfer to that building eleven large public offices.

The tribunal of the Inquisition having been abolished by a royal letter dated the 10th February 1774, the Marquis of Pombal ordered that, on the rebuilding of the city, the palace should be occupied by the Viceroys and Governors, as in the first years after the conquest, insinuating at the same time that the removal of their residence to the *Casa de Polvora* (Powder House), situated at Panelim, a quarter of a league distant from the city, was the work of the Jesuits, who, he says, planned this removal lest the Palace of the Viceroys should throw into the shade the edifices belonging to their order.* Dom José Pedro da Camara, who was Governor and Captain General at the time, pointed out, however, the unfitness of the palace for the residence of the Viceroys, and the extreme inconvenience to which they would be put on account of the alterations that had been made for the accommodation of the late tribunal, not to speak of the expense attendant on the demolition of the numerous cells (which would involve an outlay of £1,000); whilst the remodelling of the building to render it suitable to the Viceroys would, without affording any commensurate advantage, cost so large a sum as £1,515.† In lieu of this the noble Governor proposed to transfer to the palace some of the public offices, removing himself and his suite to the Palace of the Fortress, which required but little expense to render it habitable.

On the death of Dom José I., the Marquis of Pombal lost his influence at court, and his project of converting the Palace of the Inquisition into the viceregal residence fell to the ground. The Inquisition being re-established in the reign of Donna Maria I., in 1779, the palace was again set apart for its use. But, though revived, it did not retain

---

* *Instrucçoẽs comque El Rey Dom José*, etc., p. 1.

† *Instrucçoẽs do Marquez de Alorna*, Nova-Goa, 1856, p. 90; *Dic. Hist.-Explic., ut supra*, p. 101.

its original powers, which were considerably curtailed, and was finally abolished in 1812. Thus this famous Palace of the Inquisition was once more closed, and the sum of £1,351-3-4 which was found stored in its coffers was removed to the public treasury, while its rare archives, with some other valuable articles, were transferred to the Arsenal. Dr. Buchanan, the last traveller of distinction, who visited the palace in 1808, just on the eve of its being closed for ever, says that, on entering the spacious hall where the prisoners used to be arrayed before they joined the procession of the *auto da fé*, he could not fail to be reminded of the tragic scenes which must have been enacted in that very hall. Thence he proceeded to some small rooms, and next to the vast apartments of the First Inquisitor. He was not, however, permitted to penetrate into the secret-house, nor descend into any of the prison cells.* At the time of his visit the Palace was not in a decayed state, though it required some repairs, which were about to be effected when the order for closing it was received; whereupon the Viceroy, the Count of Sarzedas, confined himself to the execution of such only as were absolutely necessary. The edifice being afterwards completely abandoned, began to show signs of dilapidation in 1815, and the decayed parts were pulled down in 1820.

The Abbé Cottineau, who visited Goa in 1827, could not fail to discern its original grandeur even amidst its ruins. He says: "Its front, adorned with three lofty vaults and ascended by large stone steps, must have been very handsome; it is now raised one story above the groundfloor. The breadth is about seventy feet, and as to the length it cannot be ascertained, being surrounded with walls covering about two acres of ground . . . At present the whole is fast decaying; there are no doors nor window-cases now existing; shrubs, thorns, and rubbish choke up the entrance, and the interior must be filled with serpents and other reptiles."† The edifice, such as it was about the period of Cottineau's visit,

* *Christian Researches in Asia*, p. 152.

† *An Historical Sketch*, p. 107.

would have stood a little longer, had it not been razed to the ground in 1828-30 by order of the Government, its materials being employed to erect another building at Pangim. The *débris* was suffered to remain on the spot till it was removed in 1859, on the occasion of the exposition of the body of St. Francis Xavier. The labourers who were employed in its removal discovered a subterraneous staircase, and human bones buried under a thick piece of lead of the shape of a whale or a boat. Part of the *débris* can even now be seen on the spot where once the Palace of the Inquisition stood, an object of terror and dismay to the common people of Goa, who trembled at the mere mention of its name, and, not daring even to point the finger at it, spoke of it as *Orlem gor*, or the Great House.

It does not fall within the scope of this work to attempt anything like a minute and detailed account of the proceedings of the Inquisition transacted within the walls of this palace. We shall therefore restrict ourselves to a delineation of its principal traits.

The *personnel* of the Inquisition consisted ordinarily of three Inquisitors, who were the principal functionaries entrusted with the direction of the *Santo Officio*, a designation commonly applied to the Inquisition. These functionaries had their deputies in Salsette and Bardez, as well as in all the important places subject to the Portuguese Crown in the East. Under the immediate control of the Inquisitors served various officials, both stipendiary and honorary, among the last being included the *Familiares de Santo Officio*. These were taken from all ranks of the people, especially from amongst the nobility, and wore a gold medal stamped with the coat of arms of the *Santo Officio* when proceeding to arrest the persons accused of any offence cognizable by the tribunal. Besides these there were *Revedores* or *Qualificadores*, whose business it was to examine every book that was published, and bring to the notice of the Inquisitors any expression or passage which they found contrary to the Catholic faith. There were, besides, deputies who assisted at the trial and examination of the accused and studied their cases, one promoter, four notaries, two attorneys to defend the prisoners, one sexton and three assistants, one bailiff, four guards of the secret prisons, one porter, three solicitors, one steward, two physicians, one surgeon, one chaplain, one guard of the penitential prisoners, and one barber. This establishment, framed in accordance with the general regulations of the Inquisition of Portugal in 1640, underwent several modifications with regard to its officials and their salaries. In 1565, five years after the institution of the Inquisition in Goa, there were only five functionaries, whose salaries, paid from the public treasury, amounted annually to £71-7-9⅓.* In 1682 their number was raised to thirty-two, and the cost, including the grant of £4-3-4 sanctioned for the poor prisoners of the *Santo Officio*, consequently increased to £387-7-2. In 1800, a few years before its abolition, the number was forty-seven, and the amount spent, including the abovementioned grant, £422-17-1⅓.†

As regards the treatment generally given to the prisoners in this palace, it appears that the rigour of the Inquisition was not carried to such a frightful extent as is generally believed. In fact the prisoners were, in point of food and clothing, far better off than those in the civil jails. Each prisoner was confined in a separate cell, and was provided with a bedstead and a mattress, and, if he was a European, with a quilt. There were besides in his cell two earthen vessels filled with water, for washing and drinking purposes, a broom to clean the cell, an empty dust-basket, and a large basin for necessary purposes, which was removed every four days. All prisoners were served daily with three meals:—breakfast at six o'clock A.M., consisting of rice-gruel for natives, and a three-ounce loaf, fried fish, fruits, and sometimes sausages for the Europeans; dinner at ten A.M., and supper at four P.M., consisting of rice and fish. The Europeans were better provided for, as they had bread and meat twice a week for dinner, and bread, fried fish, rice and fish or egg curry almost daily for supper.

* *O Chronista de Tissuary*, vol. IV., p. 51.

† *Narração da Inquisição de Goa*, pp. 79, 82, 84.

By way of discipline the prisoners were enjoined to maintain perfect silence, and for any disturbance they ran the risk of being whipped by the guards, who incessantly watched them from the galleries. But in cases of undue oppression or ill-treatment at the hands of these sentinels, they had full liberty to make a complaint to the Inquisitor, who, accompanied by his Secretary and an interpreter, visited them twice a month. Similarly they were allowed to make known whatever wants or privations they suffered. Sick prisoners were tended with the utmost care. They were visited by physicians or surgeons, and were provided with everything that was necessary for their relief and comfort. On their deathbed they had confessors, but were not admitted to the participation of the other sacraments which, according to the ritual of the Catholic Church, are administered, during the closing hours of life, to its orthodox members. After their death they were interred within the precincts of the palace, without any religious ceremony whatever. When a prisoner died during his trial, if the charge brought against him was capital and substantiated, his bones were disinterred and burnt on the occasion of the next *auto da fé*.*

The *auto da fé* was a solemnity which generally took place once in every two or three years. On the day of its celebration, early in the morning the prisoners were taken out of their cells and conducted to the spacious gallery of the palace, clad in a flowing black dress, with white stripes on its outside, which reached down to their ankles; those who were condemned for offences against the Catholic faith wore over this garb a large scapular called *sambenito*, made of yellow cloth with crosses of St. Andrew painted in red over it. Others, again, who were doomed to be burnt alive, wore a different kind of scapular, called *samarra*, of greyish colour, bearing their own representation amidst firebrands and demons, with their names and the nature of their crimes. The heads of these prisoners were covered with pasteboard caps, called *carochas*,

---

* Dellon, *ut supra*.

which had also similar figures painted over them. The prisoners, thus attired, issued from the Palace of the Inquisition at the sound of the large Cathedral bell, which announced to the eager multitude who flocked to the place from all quarters of the city that the ceremony of the *auto da fé* was about to commence. Then a solemn procession was formed, headed by Dominican friars, with the standard of the Holy Office borne in front, which represented a richly embroidered effigy of St. Peter the Martyr, founder of the confraternity of the Inquisition, holding in one hand a sword and in another an olive-branch with this inscription, "*Justitia et misericordia.*" In the rear of these friars marched the culprits with lighted torches in their hands, accompanied by their respective sponsors, who were always persons of distinction. Nor was this all. The effigies of deceased prisoners, dressed in the abovementioned *samarras* and *caruchas*, together with as many cases enclosing their bones, also formed part of the procession. After passing through some streets of the city, in about an hour the procession slowly moved to the Cathedral or to the Church of St. Francis, which still exists. Here, on a side of the high altar, two dais were raised, one to the right for the Inquisitor and Councillors, and the other to the left for the Viceroy and his staff, the criminals and their sponsors sitting on benches in a sort of gallery, three feet broad, erected for this purpose, and extending along the whole length of the church. When all were seated, a sermon was preached, and the proceedings of the Inquisition relating to each prisoner were read. Then ensued the confession of the faith and absolution from excommunication granted to those prisoners whose lives were to be spared, and these formed generally a large majority. Those who were sentenced to death were made over by the Inquisition to the secular authority, which burnt them, after previously strangling such as confessed themselves to be Christians, on the *Campo de São Lazaro*, in the presence of the Viceroy and his staff. On the following day, the portraits of the criminals who were burnt, with their names, nationality and crimes, were hung in the Church of St. Dominic.* Thus ended the ceremony of the celebrated *auto da fé*.

The prisoners who were neither burnt nor absolved were sentenced to different kinds of punishment. Dr. Fryer says: "As we rowed by the Powder-Mills we saw several the Holy Office had branded with the names of *Feticeiros* or Charmers, or in English, Wizards, released thence (from the prison of the Inquisition) to work here, known by a yellow cope, weed or garment, like our city poor pensioners, sleeveless, with an hole for their neck only, having a red cross before and behind."†

It has not yet been possible to ascertain the precise number of the *autos da fé* held in Goa from the establishment of the Inquisition till it was abolished; but according to a book published in Portugal in 1845 concerning this institution, seventy-one *autos* took place from 1600 to 1773. But as to the number of persons actually condemned on those occasions the book is silent. As regards a few of the *autos*, however, it is said that 4,046 persons were sentenced to various kinds of punishment, of whom 3,034 were males and 1,012 females. Those that were condemned to the flames were 105 men and 16 women: 57 were burnt alive, and 64 in effigy. The *Chronista de Tissuary* gives the following dates of some of the *autos*:—13th May 1764, 29th May 1768, 7th May 1769, 3rd February 1771, 7th February 1773; but the number of the condemned is not given.‡

Convent and Church of St. Francis of Assisium.—At a little distance from the ruins of the Palace of the Inquisition,

* Dellon, *ut supra*, pp. 139 *et seq*. *Narração da Inquisição de Goa*, Nova Goa, 1866, pp. 143 *et seq*.

† *A New Account*, p. 155.

‡ *O Chronista*, vol. II., p. 161; *Historia dos Principaes Actos e Procedimentos da Inquisição em Portugal*, Lisboa, 1845, p. 38. F. N. Xavier, in the *Gabinette Litterario*, vol. III., pp. 89 and 280, states that four persons were condemned to the flames in the *auto da fé* in 1650, and eighteen persons accused of heresy on 14th December 1653. He remarks that these were the first and second *autos* held at Goa, which is not true. The same writer gives the following dates of some of the *autos da fé*: 1612, 1650, 1653, 1655, 1676, 1681, 1683, 1685, 1687, 1711, 1736. See *Instrucção do Marques d' Alorna*, p. 92.

to the west of the Cathedral, is seen the Convent, with the Church, of St. Francis of Assisium. This convent, venerable alike for its antiquity and its historic associations, is erroneously believed to have been the first religious building erected in Goa after the Portuguese conquest, on the ruins of an ancient mosque, where Mass was celebrated for the first time. But we have already shown where the first church was built, and where the first Mass was said. The Portuguese chronicler, who was an eye-witness of the first exploits of his countrymen in these parts, clears up every doubt about the origin of this convent. According to him, in 1517 Fr. Antonio de Louro, a Franciscan friar, brought to the Governor, Lopo Soares d'Albergaria, a royal letter from Portugal by which he and his eight colleagues were permitted to erect a convent in the city at the public expense. The Governor, in obedience to the royal mandate, made over to the Franciscans some houses belonging to a deceased Thánádár, João Machado, which they had themselves selected. These houses occupied a considerable space of ground, and had a garden attached to them. The friars at once made the necessary changes in them for their temporary accommodation. They formed a chapel with three altars and a choir, and made their cells on the side of the garden. This space being, however, found insufficient for a convent such as they contemplated, they obtained, on a further representation to the King, additional ground, where they commenced to erect a building after their own design. But it soon became clear that the structure would attain such proportions as to obstruct the access of light to the neighbouring houses through their windows. Their owners consequently took alarm, and entered into a long litigation with the friars. This circumstance, added to his anxiety for the completion of so grand and stately an edifice, and the displeasure of the Governor which he had incurred on account of its exorbitant cost, gradually undermined the constitution of Fr. Antonio, and accelerated the close of his mortal career before the realization of his long-cherished scheme. His colleagues prosecuted the work with the same ardour and solicitude, and in a short time had the satisfaction of seeing their labours crowned with success. Thus the first convent in Goa sprang into existence at a cost of 60,000 pardaus in gold, or £6,000, and the Franciscans immediately removed their residence thither, after demolishing the building erected for their temporary accommodation.* It is said that in 1529 the convent underwent material repairs;† but it does not seem likely that within so short a time after its completion it could have stood in need of renovation. In 1548 the great convent of the Franciscans, as St. Francis Xavier calls it in a letter addressed to the members of his Society, afforded shelter to forty friars, to whom the Government, by the directions of the Sovereign, gave every protection.‡ In accordance with an order of the Viceroy, Dom Antão de Noronha, in 1565, these friars were supplied with a few articles of daily consumption, at the expense of the State, to the value of nearly £100 per annum, besides which they received a monthly subsidy of 8*s.* 4*d.* for the sick.§ Some years later the Government granted them some small houses adjoining their establishment.|| After the lapse of a century and a half, the convent began to show signs of decay, in consequence of which many of its cells were repaired between 1762 and 1765. Several other improvements conducive to its neatness and elegance were also effected through the fostering care of its Provincial, Fr. Antonio de Padua.

In 1835 this great house of the Franciscans was closed by the peremptory orders of the Government, thus expelling from the shelter of its roof twenty-seven of its pious inmates; while

---

* *Lendas, ut supra*, vol. II., p. 537; vol. IV., p. 669.

† *Op. cit.*, vol. III., p. 306.

‡ *Letter of St. Francis Xavier* of 18th September 1542, Coll. vol. I., p. 61; *Lendas*, vol. IV., p. 669.

§ *O Chronista*, vol. IV., p. 71; *Arch. Port. Or.*, Fasc. III., doc. 90. Simão Botelho, however, instead of the annual subsidy of 2,000 pardaus or 260,000 reis, gives in his *Tombo* only the sum of 135,000 reis, or about 450 pardaus. See *Subsidios para a Historia da India*, p. 70.

|| *Arch. Port. Or.*, Fasc. III., doc. 25, 59, 77, 163, 335.

the State appropriated all its property, to the value of £13,350-14-6⅝. From this period the edifice, which Pyrard* did not hesitate to call the richest and most beautiful in the world, with its cloisters, whose embossed walls portrayed the chief incidents in the life of St. Francis of Assisium, painted in gold, blue, and other colours, was neglected and abandoned. At present it is considerably decayed, and threatens to become a complete ruin. Its vast corridors, however, its numerous cells, its spacious refectory and many other apartments, though unfurnished, are still objects of universal admiration. A long staircase of black stone leads to the upper floor of the building, whence by another staircase the highest story, called *Ghâṭ* by reason of its elevation, is reached. The apartment for the novitiate of this convent was on the lower pavement of the principal corridor, which lay opposite the gate and overlooked the churchyard. This pavement is built over the vault of the mosque, where it is erroneously conjectured that Mass was said for the first time. It does not, however, appear to have been other than a vault, intended perhaps for keeping the ordinary utensils.†

The Church, which is contiguous to the Convent, was begun to be erected at about the same time with it, completed in 1521, and especially dedicated eighty-two years later by the Archbishop, Dom Fr. Aleixo de Menezes, to the Holy Ghost. It appears that the church was not repaired during this interval, and consequently began to decay. It was therefore demolished in 1661, and re-erected by means of the voluntary contributions of the Catholics of the place. But though rebuilt it retained the old gate, the same by which St. Francis Xavier and several other personages, celebrated in the annals of Portuguese history, entered. It is of black stone exquisitely carved, and is probably the only relic, met with in the East at the present day, of the Portuguese architecture of the beginning of the 16th century.

---

* Pyrard, *ut supra*, P. II., p. 31.

† A minute description of the supposed mosque is given in the *Resumo Historico da Vida de São Francisco Xavier*, by F. N. Xavier, *Nova Goa*, 1861, p. 25.

Thus the church, with its portals, represents two epochs in the annals of the Portuguese Eastern empire—the epoch of its prosperity under Dom Manoel, and the epoch of its decline and fall under Dom Affonso VI.* This church recalls to memory the numerous triumphs which were commemorated within its walls amid pomp and pageantry, the solemnity with which crowds of proselytes were baptized, the *autos da fé* celebrated in the presence of the Viceroy and his court, and the funeral obsequies of many illustrious persons, from the brave Christovão Britto and the heroic Dom João de Castro, to the noble Dom Manoel da Camara, whose remains lie buried there. It is a vast edifice, and has in its courtyard an old large cross made of black stone. Its external architecture belongs to the Tuscan order, and the internal to the Mosaico-Corinthian. Its length is about 190 feet, and its breadth 60 feet. The pavement is covered with quaint epitaphs adorned with various coats-of-arms. Gemelli Careri, who visited it in 1695, speaks of it thus:—"It is one of the best churches in Goa, with a roof curiously adorned with fretwork, and it is like one entire mass of gold, there being so much of this metal on its altars."† The gold here spoken of by the traveller refers probably to the rich gilding of the altar-piece, as the splendid decorations with which it was ornamented were all of silver.

This church, which in the days of Pyrard‡ was so much frequented, is at present completely deserted. There are no longer found the Grey Friars of whom Dr. Fryer has left the following graphic description—" We saw the convent or church of the Franciscans or Grey Friars, with cords instead of girdles about their middles, sandals instead of shoes; they wear grey broad brimmed hats, as countrymen do, as well as cowls abroad, their habit being borrowed of the rustics; they touch not money, but carry one with them

* *Ensaio Historico da Lingoa Concani, por J. H. da Cunha Rivara Nova Goa*, 1858, p. 415.

† Churchill's *Voyages and Travels*, vol. IV., p. 205.

‡ Pyrard, *ut supra*, Pt. II., p. 31.

that will, and are mendicants."* The side altars have been stripped of their frames, and the great organ, which the Provincial, Fr. Antonio de Padua, had placed there, has been removed to adorn the church of Margão. Of the nine altars which the church once possessed, three only with their wooden pieces are left, two in the transept and one in the chief chapel. The latter is indeed of exquisite workmanship, and is in keeping with the grandeur of the finest part of the building. It is still well preserved, and has not altogether lost the freshness of its gilding. The large tabernacle is delicately carved, richly gilt, and painted in blue. It is supported by figures of the four Evangelists, and is of an octagonal shape, with small doors which used to be withdrawn to exhibit the Holy Sacrament when publicly exposed. Above the tabernacle and high on the altar is placed a huge image of Christ crucified, about 6½ feet high, one hand of which is represented as embracing an equally large image of St. Francis of Assisium kneeling on a daïs, on which are written the three vows or virtues of that great saint—poverty, humility, and obedience.

Of late, by order of the chief authorities of Goa, an effort has been made to keep the church in a decent state, especially as it is well preserved and promises to stand for a long time. The convent, with the church, is at present entrusted to the care of a priest, who occupies one of its apartments.

---

* *A New Account of East India and Persia*, p. 150.

CHAPTER IX.

THE CHAPEL OF ST. CATHERINE—CHAPEL OF ST. MARTIN—ROYAL HOSPITAL—ALJUBE, OR ARCHBISHOP'S PRISON—ARSENAL—COLLEGE OF ST. BONAVENTURE.

Chapel of St. Catherine.—In front of the Church of St. Francis there runs a steep narrow road which leads to the Chapel of St. Catherine—the self-same road in which a hard-fought struggle took place between the Portuguese and the Muhammadans when the city was captured by Albuquerque. The chapel is a small building, important only as an historical monument of the times in which the martial spirit of the Portuguese was blended with their religious enthusiasm. It was erected immediately after the conquest of Goa in 1510, in honour of St. Catherine, on the spot where formerly stood a gate by which the Portuguese entered and took possession of the city. The Governor, Jorge Cabral, had it enlarged in 1550, and decorated with a new altar-piece for the celebration of Mass on the festival of the saint, which was annually solemnized with a brilliant procession in which the Viceroy with the principal nobility took part.* This solemnity continues, slightly altered, at the present day, the procession going from the Cathedral to the Chapel.

Over the door of the Chapel there was a slab of stone whereon the following inscription was engraved in gold letters, as stated by Pyrard† :—

"Aqui neste lugar estava a porta porque entrou o Governador Affonso d'Albuquerque e tomou esta cidade aos mouros em dia

---

* *Lendas, ut supra*, vol. IV., p. 716; Pyrard, Pt. II., p. 31.

† Pyrard, *loc. cit.*

de Santa Catharina anno 1510, em cujo louvor e memoria o Governador, Jorge Cabral, mandou faser esta caza anno 1550 á custa de S. A."

Translation.

"Here was the door by which the Governor, Affonso d'Albuquerque, entered and took this city from the Muhammadans on the day of St. Catherine in the year 1510, in whose honour and memory the Governor, George Cabral, ordered this Chapel to be built in the year 1550, at the expense of His Highness" (the King).

The Chapel seems to have been subsequently rebuilt for the third time, when the slab just mentioned was removed from its original place and fixed in the wall near the side door, where it is seen at present.

Chapel of St. Martin.—Close to the Chapel of St. Catherine and contiguous to the Royal Hospital there was another chapel, dedicated to St. Martin, which was almost as large as a church. It was connected with an equally important historical fact. When Dom João de Castro returned victorious from Diu in 1547, the people of Goa, wishing to celebrate his triumph with great pomp, demolished a portion of the wall of the city, as the gate was too narrow for such an occasion, and covering the spot with brocade and velvet of different colours, erected over it an arch with a brazen flag bearing the image of St. Martin, on whose festival a signal victory had been gained over the King of Cambay. To commemorate this event, a slab with an inscription in gold was fixed in this wall.* Here Dom João de Castro, after his reception, ordered an altar to be raised, over which, not long after, the abovementioned chapel was built. In the last century the chapel having probably fallen down with the Royal Hospital, the slab was transferred to the Chapel of St. Catherine. This slab represents St. Martin mounted on horseback and giving part of his garment to a beggar, with the following inscription :—

* *Lendas*, vol. IV., p. 637 ; Diogo de Couto, *Dec.* VI., liv. IV., cap. vi. ; Or. Conq., Part I., Conq. I., Div. i., § 37.

"Por esta porta entrou D. João de Castro, Defensor da India, quando triumphou de Cambaya e todo este muro lhe foi derrubado. Era de 1547 A.

Translation.

"By this door Dom João de Castro, Defender of India, entered when he conquered Cambay, and this whole wall was destroyed for him. Era of 1547 A."

Royal Hospital.—Adjacent to the Chapel of St. Catherine stood the Royal Hospital, facing towards the north the pier of the same name. This far-famed institution was, like a few others, founded immediately after the conquest of Goa by the Portuguese. Having established his authority in the city on a firm basis, Albuquerque erected a long range of low buildings where he lodged his sick soldiers, for whose benefit a supply of medicines and other articles of necessity was purchased at the public expense.* The hospital, having thus sprung into existence, continued always to engage the attention of the great Captain even when he was called away from India on distant expeditions. On one occasion when he sent his Secretary, Antonio da Fonseca, in 1515 from Ormuz to India on some errand, he is said to have expressly directed him to look after the welfare of his favourite institution.† The King of Portugal himself, with the intense interest which the Lusitanian sovereigns of those times took in the affairs of the East, sent instructions that all the sick lying in the hospitals of India, especially of Goa, should be tended with the utmost care.‡ Accordingly a regulation was framed in 1520, placing the infant hospital on a firmer basis, and providing a systematic regimen, followed by various other directions for its proper management.§ About this time the edifice appears to have been considerably improved and enlarged, as it was found to afford but scanty and ill-suited accommodation. In 1524 the hospital became an

* *Lendas, ut supra*, vol. II., p. 158.

† *Op. cit.*, p. 445.

‡ *Arch. Port. Or.*, Fasc. III., doc. 77; Fasc V., doc. 48.

§ *Op. cit.*, Fasc. V., doc. 10, 35, 55.

object of attraction to the Portuguese, many of whom procured admission into it, through the favour of the authorities, even when suffering from no disease, or on pretext of being cured of slight injuries sustained in broils in which they had involved themselves. To check these abuses Dom Vasco da Gama, who then held the viceregal authority, was forced to take stringent measures.* About this time the administration of this useful institution was in the hands of the *Santa Casa de Misericordia* (the Holy House of Mercy), which received annually for its maintenance from the public treasury, a sum of nearly £164-11-8, which was in 1552 increased to £208-6-8, and in 1565 to £278.† The *Santa Casa* continued to manage its affairs with great care, vigilance, and zeal till 1591, when it was placed under the superintendence of the Jesuits, who in 1585 had framed appropriate rules for its management, and who, though frequently requested to assume its administration, had, with various excuses, declined to undertake the charge.‡ At this time the average number of patients is said to have been between four and six hundred every year, and the Viceroy, Mathias d'Albuquerque, finding it expedient to increase proportionately the subsidy for defraying the expenses, assigned for this purpose certain revenues of the city which yielded about £500 annually.§ The King, Dom Felippe, in his letter of the 25th February 1595, expressed his great satisfaction that the Jesuits had taken the direction of the hospital into their hands, and in another letter, written in the following year, ordered the Viceroy to hand over to them regularly the amount necessary to keep up the establishment; but, this direction having been disregarded by the authorities in Goa, the Jesuit Fathers, after a period

---

* *Lendas*, vol. II., p. 819.

† *Subsidios para a Historia da India Portugueza*, p. 70; *O Chronista*, vol. IV., p. 83.

‡ *Arch. Port. Or.*, Fasc. III., doc. 33, 59, 77, 97; Fasc. V., doc. 838.

§ *Op. cit.*, Fasc. III., doc. 91, 119; Linschoten, *Histoire de la Navigation*, p. 70.

of about five years, severed their connection with the institution, which was again made over to the *Santa Casa*.*

The edifice appeared at this time to be falling into decay, and as it was evident that, unless the necessary repairs were made, the whole structure would crumble to pieces, it was resolved to rebuild it on the same site out of the funds accruing from the fines imposed in the High Court. But these not being sufficient for completing the new building, which was in design very vast and magnificent, the Viceroy, in obedience to a royal mandate, applied in its erection the money realized from the licence granted to certain merchants to make a voyage to China.† The edifice was completed in a few years, under the direction of the Jesuits, who once more undertook the administration of the hospital in 1597, having received assurances‡ of greater punctuality in the payment of the amount necessary for its maintenance, which was in a few years increased to £1,000, a very large sum considering the cheapness of articles and the insignificance of wages in those times.§

---

* *Op. cit.*, Fasc. III., doc. 175, 210, 240.

† *Op. cit.*, Fasc. III., doc. 119, 140, 163, 175, 241.

‡ *Alvará* of the Viceroy, Dom Francisco da Gama, dated 12th July 1597.

§ *Arch. Port. Or.*, Fasc. III., doc. 175; Fasc. V., doc. 838.

To give an idea of the monthly salaries of the officers of this Hospital, we give the following list, found in the records of the institution :—

	£	s.	d.
Physician attending on the Hospital	1	0	10
Surgeon	0	16	8
Treasurer	0	13	$10\frac{2}{3}$
Clerk	0	10	0
Hospital Attendant...	0	10	0
Gatekeeper...	0	10	4
Bleeder	0	4	2
Purveyor	0	3	4
A servant for enema	0	4	2
A native assistant	0	2	6
Steward	0	4	2
Each servant attending on the sick, besides food ...	0	1	4
Washerman, besides food and about ½ pint of arrack per day	0	2	1

It was during the period of its administration by the *Santa Casa*, and especially while it was under the fostering care of the Jesuits, to whom its management was confided for upwards of a century and a half, that the Royal Hospital acquired the celebrity which rendered it an object of universal admiration. Travellers, who visited Goa in the 16th and 17th centuries, speak in such flattering terms of the elegance of the structure, and of the order and magnificence prevailing therein, that we should hardly have credited them, had not their testimony been unanimous and corroborated by official documents still extant. Vincent Le Blanc, who was a patient in this hospital about the middle of the 16th century, says that it was beautiful in appearance and the best provided in the world with everything necessary for the comfort and convenience of its inmates, and in wealth, neatness and usefulness rivalled that of the Holy Ghost in Rome and the Infirmary of Malta. Linschoten speaks highly of the internal management and order prevailing in the hospital in 1583.* Pyrard, who, like the first mentioned traveller, was treated in this hospital in the beginning of the 17th century, writes thus :—"This hospital is, in my opinion, the best in the world, whether as regards the elegance of the edifice and its appurtenances—everything being arranged in the best manner—or as regards the good order and discipline maintained there, the cleanliness that prevails, the great care taken of the sick, and the assistance and consolation they receive in every way they can wish, both in reference to

	£	s.	d.
Each cook when sleeping in the hospital on account of the sick, beside food	0	2	6
Otherwise only	0	2	6
Boy assisting the Gatekeeper in conveying messages to the sick...	0	0	10
Servant assisting the Purveyor	0	0	5
Servant in charge of the almirah of surgery, with extra allowance	0	2	0
Vedor	0	7	6
Receiver	0	5	10

* *Voyage de Vincent Le Blanc*, Linschoten; *Histoire de la Navigation*, p. 70.

medical attendance, medicines, and diet, for the cure of their bodies, and in point of the spiritual comfort obtainable at any hour."*

The hospital was a two-storied edifice, and resembled, according to some writers, a palace. Its façade bore the royal arms and the inscription "*Hospital Real.*" It was long and spacious, containing many halls, chambers, galleries adorned with Scripture paintings, porticos, and gardens interspersed with lovely parterres, where its convalescent inmates usually repaired in the evening to enjoy the fresh air, with a beautiful and spacious courtyard in the middle paved with stone. Besides the numerous apartments for the sick and their attendants, there were separate rooms used as repositories for articles of daily consumption and for clothing, such as trowsers, shoes, drawers, and night-gowns. Each room was entrusted to a ward-boy, who had possession of its key, and who was held responsible for the safety of the articles lodged therein.† Albert de Mandelslo, who saw this hospital when he accompanied the English President of Surat to Goa in 1639, after alluding in glowing terms to its saloons and galleries, says: "The noblest apartments of the hospital were the kitchen and the apothecaries' shop, both well furnished with all things necessary for the accommodation of the sick."‡

According to Pyrard fifteen hundred dead bodies were annually removed from the hospital; and the number admitted, which consisted wholly of Europeans, was very large. The maximum number of admissions was about three thousand, especially when fresh ships arrived from the mother-country, while the minimum seldom fell under three hundred.§ Rich and noble persons frequently repaired to this hospital, prefer-

---

* Pyrard, *Voyage*, Part II., p. 3.

† *The Voyages and Travels of J. Albert de Mandelslo*, p. 81; Pyrard, *Voyage*, Part II., p. 9; *Regimento do Hospital Real da Cidade de Goa*, Fasc. V., doc. 838.

‡ Mandelslo, *loc. cit.*

§ Pyrard, *ut supra*, p. 8; Linschoten, (*op. cit.*, p. 70) says that in his time the annual number of dead amounted from four to five hundred.

ring it to their homes, as it contained a complete supply of all that could be desired.

The internal management of the hospital may be gathered from the writings of these and other travellers, but more precisely from its rules and regulations still preserved in the archives of the Goa Secretariat, and published a few years since. The institution was placed under the care of a Superintendent (*Mordomo*), who was one of the most distinguished of the Jesuits; all persons connected with the establishment were under his control, and all business was conducted under his personal inspection. The superior officers belonged to the ruling class, the inferior to the mass of the people, slaves being selected to perform the meanest duties. At five o'clock every morning a bell was rung, at the sound of which the chief officers were required to proceed to the chapel to hear Mass. Then the Physician and the Surgeon, who were generally the best men of their profession at Goa, and also attended on the Viceroy in cases of illness, visited, in company with the Superintendent and a few other officers, the wards of the sick, who were lodged in separate rooms according to the nature of their diseases. A hospital attendant then personally administered medicine to each patient, while the Superintendent took care that the directions of the physicians were strictly followed. At seven o'clock bread and some other light food were served to each patient on a table kept near his bedstead. At ten dinner was served on china porcelain dishes, and sometimes, as stated by Le Blanc, on silver plates; and it consisted of roasted or boiled fowl and other meat, bread and rice, with sweets for dessert. The sick were also allowed to invite the friends who came to visit them, to partake of these viands. Dinner was followed by a *siesta*. At four in the afternoon the medical attendants once more visited the patients, while the Superintendent with a subordinate officer went through the same round of duties as in the morning. Supper was served at five o'clock, and, like the dinner, was regulated according to medical directions. Soup and other nutritious food were also provided, if prescribed, to the sick. After supper, as after dinner, the hospital authorities asked the patients whether their wants had been fully satisfied. Before eight in the evening all retired to rest. The bedsteads were painted in different colours, and even gilt. They never exceeded the number of the sick, being removed into the repositories whenever their occupants left the hospital. Each patient was provided with a fine mattress, pillows and coverlets either of silk or cotton. The bed-sheets were of excellent fabric. The sick were often visited by priests, who ministered to their spiritual wants, and occasionally by the Viceroy, the Archbishop, and the highest functionaries of the State, who distributed among them large sums of money. Not unfrequently the patients were allowed to remain for some time in the hospital during convalescence, and on their departure, in cases of necessity, were supplied with a complete suit of clothes and a shilling, besides the articles brought by them to the hospital, and which were registered on their admission in the inventory kept by the hospital authorities.

The dying were removed into a separate room, that their agonies might not frighten their fellow-patients, and there they received every solace which the Catholic religion affords during the last moments of earthly existence, at the hands of a priest, who did not quit their bedside till they had breathed their last. After death they were allowed a decent burial, even when they had left nothing to defray the expenses of interment.

In the hospital the greatest cleanliness was observed. The visitors, as some travellers remark, could not but feel the liveliest interest and the greatest satisfaction at beholding an establishment so grand, useful and elegant, with apartments wonderfully neat, and galleries exquisitely decorated. Every room was swept clean and fumigated with incense twice a day, and whitewashed thrice a year. The clothes of the sick were changed twice a week, and oftener when necessary. All the cooking utensils and other vessels were rinsed and tinned with the utmost care. The servants were obliged not only to treat the patients with great care, attention, and civility, but also to appear before them in a neat and clean dress. It was, besides, a part of their duty to wash the sick according to the directions of the physicians.*

The fame of this hospital, where the sick were treated with so much solicitude, and almost pampered with the dainties of luxurious living, began to wane gradually with the decline of the city. By the middle of the 17th century it had already suffered in public estimation, for Tavernier, who visited it at this time, writes that this hospital, which was once so much renowned, began to be ill managed about the time of his second visit, in consequence of which the sick who entered there left it only to be carried to their graves. The treatment adopted then contributed in a great measure to this result, for the patients were bled thirty or forty times, and as often as the noxious blood was supposed to circulate in the system. During the first twelve days after this operation, the patients were compelled to swallow thrice a day a loathsome beverage of cow's urine, a mode of treatment supposed to have been adopted from the pagans. The celebrated traveller also remarks that, in lieu of the rich and strong viands formerly allowed, the convalescents were obliged to content themselves with a spare diet consisting of beef-tea and rice-gruel, butter and meat being considered as poison. Nor was this all. Such was the corruption noticed in the administration of the hospital that the attendants, unless they were bribed, refused to give even a glass of water to the thirsty, on the pretext that it had been prohibited by the physicians.†

Dr. Fryer, who visited the hospital in 1675, partly corroborates the statement of Tavernier. He writes : "The physicians here are great bleeders, insomuch that they often exceed Galen's advice *ad deliquium* in fevers, hardly leaving enough to feed the currents for circulation, of which cruelty some complain

---

* *Arch. Port. Or.*, Fasc. III., doc. 838 ; Pyrard. II., pp. 2 *et seq.* ; Mandelslo, *Voyages*, p. 81. The Regulation of the Hospital of 1586 differs in some incidental points from the statements made by the travellers, owing to the alterations subsequently introduced into it.

† *Les Six Voyages* de J. B. Tavernier, Part II., p. 123 ; Harris' *Voyages and Travels*, vol. II., p. 359.

invidiously after recovery."* During this period the administration of the hospital passed, by a royal letter of the 20th February 1688, to the members of the order of St. John of God,† but, after some years, reverted to the Jesuits, who retained its superintendence till their expulsion from Goa in 1759. About this time the epidemic raged most furiously, depopulating the city, which was in consequence wholly abandoned. By the latter part of the 18th century the hospital had altogether lost the excellent management for which it had once been celebrated. There was no longer to be seen the cleanliness which was once observed, nor the attention and care which was once paid to the patients. The hospital was, in consequence of the decay into which the majestic edifice had fallen, temporarily removed in 1760 to the College of St. Roch, and thence to Panelim in the Palace of the Viceroys, who about that time had transferred their residence to Pangim. From this place the institution was transferred to Pangim in 1842. It now bears the title of the Military Hospital, and is under the direction of the Chief Health Officer.

The magnificent edifice of the old city, now hastening to decay, was abandoned and fell into ruin, so much so that hardly any traces of it exist at present, the site on which it stood being comprehended within the walls of the Arsenal.

Aljube or the Archbishop's Prison.—To the north of the Royal Hospital was the *Aljube*, or the Archbishop's Prison, in which were confined, by the order of that ecclesiastical dignitary, those who transgressed the disciplinary canons of the Catholic Church. Dellon, who was imprisoned there for two days before he was cast into the prison of the Inquisition, has left a horrible picture of it. He says: "This prison is the most filthy, dismal and hideous of all that I ever witnessed, and I doubt if there can be any other in the world more repulsive and more loathsome. It is a kind of vault to which the light of day has hardly any access through a small aperture,

---

* *A New Account of East India and Persia*, p. 151. About the decline of the hospital at this period see also *O Chronista*, vol. I., pp. 203, 233.

† *Liv. das Monç.*, Goa Gov. Rec. (MSS.), No. 53, f. 61.

through which the most subtle rays of the sun can with difficulty penetrate. The stench is unbearable, for there being no cloaca, its place is supplied by a ditch on a level with the ground in the midst of a subterraneous passage, where the prisoners go for necessary purposes, but it being almost impossible to get to it, the greater part of the prisoners sit near it. At nightfall I could not persuade myself to lie down, for fear of worms generated by putrid and filthy matter, of which the dungeon was full, especially its pavement. I had thus to pass the night reclining against the wall."*

It appears that in course of time the state of the prison was gradually improved, for Cottineau writes in 1827 thus:—"The *Aljube*, of which Dellon gives a frightful description, is now much altered for the better; it is a neat stone building with a court towards the south of it. The *Provisor* of the Ecclesiastical Court has the superintendence thereof, and visits it regularly once a month, or oftener if necessary. It very seldom contains any prisoners."† Dr. John Wilson, who visited this prison in 1834, says, however, that he heard there "a good deal of scolding," and that he saw a canon sign an order of imprisonment for an individual, from which he concludes that the *Aljube* is a kind of substitute for the Inquisition. He also describes it in the following terms:—"It is not merely used for the purpose of imprisoning priests, but it is used as the place of the Archbishop's Court. This Court has the power of inflicting punishment by fine and imprisonment, as well as by suspension, excommunication and penance. Its decisions are not at present characterized by any great degree of severity, but it must be evident that its powers are incompatible with civil and religious liberty."‡ The conjecture of the learned traveller was, however, erroneous, the *Aljube* not being an ecclesiastical court, nor its discipline in any way so severe as that of the Inquisition, for which it never was a

* *Relation de l'Inquisition de Goa*, p. 47.

† *An Historical Sketch*, p. 108.

‡ *Oriental Christian Spectator*, vol. V., First Series, p. 124.

substitute. This edifice, which, according to a despatch of the Governor, Dom José Pedro da Camara, dated the 3rd May 1778, was fit to be demolished rather than reconstructed, was subsequently reduced in dimensions, and the *Camara Agraria* of the Ilhas held its sittings there for some time. At present, however, this Chamber meets in Pangim, and the prison is wholly abandoned.

Arsenal.—To the west of the *Aljube* and of the Royal Hospital lay the *Ribeira Grande*, which in the first days of the Portuguese conquest was merely called *Ribeira*, or *Ribeira das Naus*, or *Ribeira das Armadas*, and subsequently the *Arsenal*. It included, besides the Docks, various important public establishments, such as the Mint, and the Gun-foundry, where everything requisite for the army and the once renowned and formidable navy was manufactured.*

The origin of this vast arsenal, which contained so many establishments and had a chapel attached to it, or rather a parochial church as it is termed in ancient documents, can be traced to the times preceding the capture of Goa by Albuquerque. De Barros describes it as the place where the Muhammadans had, when that great captain conquered the city, drawn ashore their ships; and through the gate of which, dedicated subsequently to St. Catherine, the Portuguese first entered the city. The extent of this celebrated arsenal of Adil Khán must have been considerable, for the spoils which the Portuguese found on the capture of the city in its docks consisted of forty large ships, twenty-six brigs, and a large number of *fustas* or pinnaces, and in its magazines forty heavy guns, fifty-five pieces of ordnance called falcons, two hundred muskets, and a large quantity of powder, pitch, naphtha, oil, steel, iron, copper, cannon balls, with a variety of other articles.† After the conquest of Goa, Albuquerque made the necessary improvements in the Arsenal and appointed Francisco Corvinel, a Floren-

---

* Tombo Geral (MSS). p. 48.,

† *De Barros, Dec.* II., Liv. V., cap. ix.; *Commentaries, ut supra*, p. 99; *Hist. dos Descobr. e Conq. dos Port.*, Lisboa 1786, Tom. II., pp. 52, 53.

tine, as its Superintendent, with the title of *Feitor.** This officer was afterwards superseded by the *Vedor da Fasenda* (Overseer or Controller of the Public Treasury). Affonso Mexia, the then *Vedor* of the treasury, framed in 1526 a set of rules for its proper management.† In 1540 there were seven hundred persons employed on various works in this establishment, but little care was taken in selecting them, or in regulating their salaries. This irregularity was removed by the Viceroy, Dom Antão de Noronha, who in 1565 issued a resolution fixing the amount of the salaries of the principal officers employed in the Arsenal at £35-11-6.

The Arsenal was towards the close of the 16th century in a most flourishing state, keeping pace with the rapid growth of the Portuguese power in the East. The celebrated French traveller Pyrard, who visited it some time after this period, gives a lively description of it. According to him it was well arranged, and had terreplains and palisades mounted with artillery to defend the river. Its commandant was the *Veador* or *Vedor da Fasenda,* who had there a beautiful and well-fortified residence, which had one gate towards the city, and another towards the river. These doors were closed at night, not so much for fear of an enemy as of robbers from the city. The *Vedor* exercised supervision over the public treasury, and over everything relating to land and naval forces, and in many respects was next in rank to the Viceroy himself. Opposite the residence of the *Vedor* there stood, in the same square, a beautiful church of the *Cinco Chagas,* richly decorated, to which two priests were attached. In a wing of this church there was a space enclosed with an iron railing, where every day the *Vedor* sat with other officers of state for the transaction of business. All these officials, especially those who looked to naval armaments, resided there in public buildings during their tenure of office. It was in this *ribeira* or square that money was coined, cannon were cast,

* *Lendas,* vol. II., p. 176; De Barros, *Dec.* II., liv. v., cap. ii.

† *Arch. Port. Or.,* Fasc. V., doc. 55, 56.

and other work connected with war vessels and merchantmen was done. It was astonishing to behold the number of artizans who laboured there at every sort of work, without observing either festivals or holidays, under the directions of a Portuguese foreman who derived his name from the particular trade which he supervised, with the addition of a *mor*, and who had under him several native artizans of his own craft. They received their pay every Sunday morning. It was the most pleasant thing in the world, says the traveller, to see there the great number of ships, some lying in the dock, others hauled ashore. There were smithies, foundries and other workshops provided with rooms for artizans and workmen. All these were of stone, to provide against fire.

From his verandah the *Vedor* could see all that passed in the arsenal and on the river, and every night a strict watch was kept to guard the ships from fire. The sentinels were either Hindús or Christians, and were called *Naiques.* They were numerous and were relieved every day; they were also employed in executing the orders of the *Vedor*, carrying his messages and performing other duties. The muster roll of the artizans was called twice a day, and there was a *Contador* (accountant), who paid their wages, as also an *Apontador* (overseer), who watched them and noted the number of days each artizan worked.

It is in this place that the prison denominated the *Sala* was erected, where criminals, especially those who were under the immediate control of the *Vedor*, were confined. The *Vedor* had two *Meirinhos* (constables) and a clerk under him. These officers, according to the above traveller, often combined together to extort money from the people.

The *Vedor*, being next in rank to the Viceroy, used to amass as large a fortune as the Viceroy himself. Superintending all matters connected with the exportation and importation of goods, and the equipment of the fleet, he had abundant opportunities to enrich himself. At both gates of this square or *ribeira*, the porters and guards, ever vigilant, allowed no one to enter or leave the place without searching him in order to see if he possessed stolen property. This square was very long and broad, the breadth being nearly 200 paces. It had a vast store of valuable articles belonging to the State.*

On the 9th June 1753, this vast establishment, together with a great portion of the shipping, was destroyed by fire. But a few years later it was rebuilt, and by an *alvará* of the 28th April 1773 was considerably improved, its designation being changed to that of *Arsenal de Ribeira de Naus,* and the post of the *Vedor da Fazenda* being abolished and substituted by that of *Intendente da Marinha e Armazem.*†

Notwithstanding the rapid decline of the Portuguese power and navy, the expenses of the establishment amounted to an enormous sum, and the number of workmen employed therein to 861.‡ Subsequently, however, efforts were made to reduce the expenditure, but nevertheless the outlay was more than could be borne by the exhausted treasury. According to the estimate made in 1841-2, the *personnel* of the Arsenal consisted of 475 *employés,* and the aggregate sum spent in the payment of their salaries and the purchase of the requisite articles amounted to £15,009-3-10⅗. By a Government Resolution of the 29th November of the same year, these expenses were curtailed to £10,666-3-10⅗, which sum the treasury continued to pay until the Governor, the Viscount of Torres Novas, by an order dated the 4th July 1856, gave it almost a death-blow by reducing its establishment, and altered its designation to *Arsenal do Exercito,* and the title of the officer, who was at its head, to that of Inspector.§ It was maintained, however, for a few years longer, and at length abolished in 1869, its vast offices being razed to the ground. At present hardly anything remains of the arsenal except its crumbling walls and a heap of ruins. Thus disappeared this "monument

---

* Pyrard, *ut supra,* Part II., p. 24.

† *Liv. das Monç.* (MSS.), No. 153, f. 268.

‡ *Esboço d'um Dic. Hist. Adm.,* por F. N. Xavier, Pangim, 1850, p. 196.

§ *Bol. do Governo do Estado da India de* 1856, No. 54, p. 333.

of the power, politics, and social status of the Portuguese since the sixteenth century."*

College of St. Bonaventure.—A few paces from the Arsenal to the west, and on the margin of the Mandovi, was the College of St. Bonaventure. It was a vast building, remarkable above all for its grand cloister, supported by beautiful arches and columns, and divided by two long corridors. The dormitories, as Gemelli Careri observed in 1695, were indifferent.† Closely attached to it was the church of the same name, which was small and had nothing in it worth mentioning. The college was erected in 1602, at a cost of £8,333-6-8, by Fr. Miguel de São Boaventura, Provincial of the Franciscans. This sum was originally subscribed by the noble matrons of Bassein with the object of founding a monastery for the nuns of the Franciscan order of St. Clare. The Archbishop, Dom Fr. Aleixo de Menezes, not having consented to this, the sum was applied to the erection of a building in which the young professed friars of the order of St. Francis might study philosophy and theology. By the royal *alvará* of the 16th April 1617 an annual sum of £41-13-2 was granted for its support. The building, having in course of time fallen into decay, was repaired and improved in 1765 by the Provincial, Fr. Antonio de Padua, but was almost entirely abandoned when the friars transferred their educational establishment to the convent. After the suppression of the religious orders in 1835, the college was placed under the administration of a friar of the same order, the treasury having appropriated its moveable and immoveable property of the value of £2,700-14-10½. It was also deprived of almost all its utensils; and an excellent image of St. Francis of Assisium,

---

* For an interesting description of the building and the offices of this Arsenal a few years before it was abandoned and fell into decay, see *Bosquejo das Possessoẽs Portuguezas no Oriente*, by J. P. Celestino Soares, p. 188. The late Governor, Viscount Sergio de Souza, proposed to convert the vast enclosure formerly occupied by the Arsenal into a farm for practical instruction in agriculture.

† Churchill's *Voyages and Travels*, vol. IV., p. 206.

similar in attitude to that in the convent of St. Francis, was carried to the church of Nagoá in Bardez, where it is placed on a separate altar. The committee appointed by Government in 1870 to inspect the public buildings of the city was of opinion that the College of St. Bonaventure, which was finally used as barracks, was not in a condition to be preserved, and it was consequently demolished, no trace whatever now remaining of it.

CHAPTER X.

SANTA CASA DE MISERICORDIA—CHURCH OF NOSSA SENHORA DE SERRA —RETREATS OF NOSSA SENHORA DE SERRA AND OF SANTA MARIA MAGDALENA—SQUARE OF OLD PELOURINHO.

Santa Casa de Misericordia.—Having examined all the principal buildings to the north-west of the city, let us return now to the *Rua Direita* near the Cathedral. To the south, at a distance of a few paces, there was an elegant group of buildings dedicated to certain charitable institutions, which were under the administration of the *Santa Casa de Misericordia* (Holy House of Mercy), a pious association of laymen—similar to that of Lisbon—established in Goa some five or six years after its conquest. The *Santa Casa* had here its own building, with its meeting-hall, secretariat, etc. It had also its own chapel, where historians relate that various religious ceremonies were frequently held,* and whence Pietro della Valle saw in 1624 a very solemn procession set out on its way

* *Lendas, ut supra,* vol. IV., pp. 591, 604, 618, 650, 660. Mr. J. H. da Cunha Rivara states in a note (p. 43) of his translation of Pyrard that in the time of the traveller the church of *Serra* was used as a chapel to the House of Mercy; but this does not appear to be the fact, according to Pietro della Valle, and especially the author of the *Lendas,* who at p. 591 says that Dom João de Castro, in his triumphal entry into the city of Goa after the conquest of Diu in 1547, " reaching the House (Chapel) of Mercy, left the pall below which he was walking alone, and stepping in said a prayer and offered a piece of brocade; he did the same in the Church of *Nossa Senhora de Serra,* where he threw holy water over Affonso d'Albuquerque."

to the Church of *Nossa Senhora da Luz.** This chapel seems to have subsequently been converted into the elegant church, spoken of by Hamilton,† the ruins of which still excite admiration. Pyrard mistook this chapel for the Church of *Nossa Senhora de Serra.*‡

Church of Nossa Senhora de Serra.—This old and beautiful church was erected in 1513 by Affonso d'Albuquerque, in fulfilment of a vow which this pious and gallant captain had made when his vessel *Nossa Senhora de Serra* was in great danger in the Red Sea, over the ruins of the principal gate of the city, through which the Muhammadans used to go to the suburbs, and through which many of them effected their escape during the battle which ended in the capture of Goa. It was vaulted, and had towers which could be used for purposes of defence in cases of emergency. The founder ordered forty-eight shops to be built in its vicinity, near the place usually called *Pelourinho,* where the roads crossed each other, in order that a part of their income might be applied to the support of the church and of a clergyman who was charged to say one mass daily for the repose of his soul after death, and the residue to the maintenance of a few Eurasian orphans, as well as to remunerating the judges of the city, who

---

* Pietro della Valle says :—

" La confraternita della Misericordia fece in Goa la solita processione la sera al tardi, che suol fare ogni anno in tal giorno, partendo dalla sua chiesa ed andando con due feretri fin alla chiesa di Nostra Signora de la Luz a pigliar le ossa di tutti gl'impiccati e giustiziati in quell'anno, i quali nel medesimo giorno portati dalla sepoltura che sta sotto la forca, molto fuori della città da quella chiesa, di là poi dalla detta confraternita della Misericordia sono portati con solennità in processione alla loro chiesa per seppellirli, dove anche si fanno loro solenni esequie. Io non aveva veduto questa processione l'anno passato, perchè mi trovava nel Balagat; però ne ho fatta qui ora menzione. Il due novembre. La sera al tardi i padri Domenicani fecero con molta solennità la lor processione del Rosario, e così anche la mattina seguente che dovevan fare la prima settimana di ottobre, trasportata un mese più tardi per evitar le pioggie che nel mese di ottobre sogliono talvolta disturbarla."—*Viaggi*, vol. II., p. 785.

† *A New Account of the East Indies,* vol. I., p. 249.

‡ Pyrard, Part II., p. 30.

had to audit the accounts triennially. On his death Albuquerque was buried there, in accordance with the directions contained in his last will. There his obsequies were celebrated with great pomp amid crowds of people who bewailed his loss as almost a national calamity. And there too the natives repaired in after times to implore his favour and protection whenever they were oppressed by his successors.* His remains were, however, conveyed to Portugal in 1565. This church, one of the most elegant and richest in the city, was gilt in the interior, and had over its portal a gilt stone statue of the conqueror, which was afterwards transferred to Pangim.† This edifice, which appears from its architecture to have been rebuilt in comparatively recent times, is still standing, and is converted into a cemetery for the use of the almost deserted parish of the Cathedral; it is now overrun with creepers, and, except the sanctuary, is quite roofless.

Retreats of Nossa Senhora de Serra and Santa Maria Magdalena.—The Archbishop, Dom Fr. Aleixo de Menezes, having founded in 1605 two *Recolhimentos* or Retreats for females, ordered suitable buildings to be erected close to the churches of *Serra* and *Misericordia.* One was called the Retreat of *Nossa Senhora de Serra,* the other of *Sancta Maria Magdalena.* The first afforded shelter to the orphan girls of noble families. At the time of their marriage they were provided with dowries, which were sometimes in the shape of public appointments conferred on their husbands. In this Retreat also the jealous fidalgos left their wives when they were obliged to go abroad, on public or private business. The other Retreat was specially set apart for such females as sincerely wished to make a thorough atonement for their past frailties, and thenceforward to lead a pure and virtuous life. A year after the suppression of the convents of Goa in 1835, these Retreats were transferred from their tottering buildings

---

* *Lendas,* vol. II., pp. 376, 457, 460; De Barros, *Dec.* II., liv. v., cap. ix., p. 542.

† Pyrard, II., *loc. cit.*

to the untenanted Convent of St. Augustine. This convent, being one of the largest buildings of the city, necessitated so much expense for its use and preservation, that the *Santa Casa* was obliged in 1841 to remove the Retreats to the comparatively modest Convent of the Carmelites at Chimbel, near Ribandar, where they are still to be found. The buildings originally erected for these Retreats fell into ruins after they were altogether abandoned.

Square of the Old Pelourinho.—Close to these buildings was the square of the *Pelourinho Velho* (Old Pillory), just in the centre of the city, where six or seven streets crossed one another. It was so called because formerly a pillory was erected there, for the punishment of criminals. Here during the day the bazaar was filled with all sorts of fruits and eatables, and at night with stolen articles, which, being sold at a very cheap price, gave it the name of *Baratilha*. Here too sat all the bleeders, who, like the surgeons and apothecaries, were native Christians, and whenever wanted were sought for there. Close to this square there was a large building in which justice was ordinarily administered, and another which served as a police station. There was also a slaughter-house.* All these buildings have disappeared. The square is now completely changed in its aspect, but it is the only spot at present where some wretched huts and petty shops are to be seen.

---

* *Op. cit.*, pp. 32, 40.

CHAPTER XI.

THE CONVENT AND CHURCH OF ST. CAJETAN—CONVENT AND CHURCH OF ST. DOMINIC—CHURCH OF SANTA LUZIA, AND THE SUBURB OF DAUGIM—CHURCH OF NOSSA SENHORA DE MONTE— CONVENT AND CHURCH OF THE CARMELITES.

Convent and Church of St. Cajetan.—Retracing our steps by the *Rua Direita,* and proceeding to the north-eastern quarter of the city, we come across several buildings erected there in its happier days. The first we meet with is the small Convent and beautiful Church of St. Cajetan. It is so close to the ruins of the Palace of the Viceroys that Dr. Buchanan mistook it for its chapel.* Towards the north it borders on the Quay of the Palace of the Viceroys. The convent, with the church, was built by some Italian friars of the order of the Theatines, who in 1640 had been sent by Pope Urban VIII. to preach Christianity in the kingdom of Golconda; but, as they were not allowed to enter the kingdom, they settled in Goa under their superior, Fr. Pedro Avitabile, in the neighbourhood of the old College of St. Paul, whence they removed to two different quarters of the city, and at length, by a royal letter of the 22nd March 1655, obtained the present site, near the *Terreiro do Paço,* for the erection of a convent. From the establishment of this religious order in Goa till 1750, fifty-six friars and three novices started from Europe for India, of whom twenty-three only reached their destination. On account of this difficulty of bringing new friars to Goa, Dom Carlos José Fidelis, who was at this time the prefect or superior of the convent, obtained permission from his superior at Rome to admit natives

---

* *Christian Researches in Asia,* p. 157.

into their order. Accordingly from 1750 to 1804 about thirty-nine natives took the vows, and one joined the convent as a lay brother.* When Cottineau visited Goa, there were about fifteen Theatines.† At the time of the suppression of the convent in 1835 sixteen left it, and the public treasury appropriated its property, to the value of £8,834-10-3. It is still preserved, and has been fitted up for a temporary palace of the Governors since the time of the Viscount of Torres Novas. A clergyman resides in it, under the title of Administrator. The building, though smaller than the other convents, has beautiful halls and corridors.

The church is also small, but it exceeds in beauty the Cathedral itself. It is said to have been built after the style of the Basilica of St. Peter in Rome; Gemelli Careri, however, says that it is in imitation of St. Andrea della Vella in the same city.‡ Its length is 121 feet, and breadth 81 feet. The external architecture is of the Corinthian order; the interior of the Mosaic-Corinthian. Its beautiful façade looks towards the west, and with its cupola presents a majestic appearance. An excellent spiral staircase of fifty steps leads to its towers, where the bells are hung. The church is vaulted, and on the threshold the following words o Christ are painted in bold letters:—"*Domus mea, domus orationis.*" The body is divided into a nave and two aisles: the latter have each three chapels or altars, in addition to the large altar in the sanctuary. In the middle of the nave, directly underneath the beautiful cupola, which is raised over four large arches elegantly carved, there is a well or tank with a small opening in its covering closed with a square slab. To its exhalations people attribute the green spots which appear on the inside of the cupola. About this reservoir of water within the church there are different opinions. Some say that it was a sacred tank or *tírtha* wherein the Hindús bathed; others relate that the architect who superintended the construction

* *Resumo Historico da Vida de São Francisco Xavier*, p. 376.

† *An Historical Sketch*, p. 130.

‡ Churchill's *Voyages and Travels*, vol. IV., p. 205.

of this church was blind; that twice were his labours rendered fruitless by the fall of the walls, which had been partially raised; that, when thus disappointed, he resolved to lay the foundation of the edifice deeper and on a more secure footing; and that, with this view, he ordered a portion of the ground to be dug up, that he might ascertain by touching the earth taken out how deep the foundation should be laid. This tradition may perhaps be a creation of the imagination, while the first appears to be probable, because although the church was a building erected in the middle of the 17th century, at which period the Hindús were prohibited from publicly celebrating their religious rites in the city, and could not therefore have had their *tírthas* there, it is just possible that a sacred well might have been shut up, that its water might remain undefiled. This presumption is strengthened by the circumstance that the Hindús of Goa, and even of the neighbouring districts, still try to obtain a few drops of the same water, some even offering to pay a large sum of money.

The principal chapel is remarkable above all for its altar-piece, which is admirably wrought and tastefully gilded. Dr. John Wilson says that he never saw anything like it.* Under the altar there is a vault wherein are deposited the embalmed bodies of the Baron of Candal, Tavares de Almeida, and Viscount Sergio de Souza, three of the Governors of Goa, who died in 1840, 1877, and 1878 respectively. Here was also preserved the body of the Governor, Baron of Sabroso, who died in 1838, before it was taken to Portugal. The door of the vault is closed from the outside, since a thief once made his way through it into the church.

Convent and Church of St. Dominic.—At a little distance towards the east of the Convent of St. Cajetan stood the magnificent Convent of St. Dominic, with its church, erected by the Dominicans, who arrived in Goa in 1548. These friars, six in number, brought with them letters from the King, Dom João III., to the Viceroy, ordering him to grant them a sufficient piece of ground, with a sum of £5,000, for the purpose

* *Orient. Christ. Spectator*, vol. V. of First Series, p. 119.

of establishing in the city a convent according to a plan which they had already prepared in Portugal. Consequently the Governor, Garcia de Sá, allowed them to choose a spot for themselves at the foot of the hill of *Nossa Senhora de Monte*, near a small spring, where, to make room for their convent, they had to demolish several huts, besides a large house belonging to a Portuguese gentleman, Pedro Godinho, who was with difficulty prevailed upon to give up possession of it. Under their superior or vicar-general, Fr. Diogo Bermudes, they built a church of earth and a house for temporary use, admitting fifteen or twenty young men of noble families, who helped them with pecuniary sums, in addition to £62-10-0 per annum which they received from the treasury.* The new building of the convent, with its church, was begun on the 30th April 1550 with the funds allowed by the King, and was completed in 1564. The *Vedor* of the Treasury, Simão Botelho, though once threatened with excommunication by the vicar-general of the Dominicans, extols, in his letter of the 30th January 1552 to the King, the labour and care taken by this virtuous priest in prosecuting the work of the building, which attained larger dimensions than had been contemplated in the plan above referred to.† This convent afforded shelter to the negro slaves. The Dominicans formed them into a confraternity, and exhorted their masters from the pulpit to give them kind treatment. The slaves, fancying themselves emancipated, abandoned their cruel masters, and fled in such numbers to the sacred asylum that the charitable friars were obliged to moderate the tone of their sermons, as it was impossible to maintain so large a number with the limited funds at their disposal.‡

The convent continued to flourish for about twenty years, when the friars complained of the unhealthiness of the locality, and requested the King, through the Archbishop Dom Fr.

* *Lendas, ut supra,* vol. IV., p. 669.

† *Subsidios, ut supra,* Part III., p. 36.

‡ 600,000 to 800,000 reis. See *Subsidios*, p. 70 ; *O Chronista*, vol. IV., p. 71.

Vicente da Fonseca, to grant them permission to build a college in another place, where the young members of their order might be instructed. They also prayed that the rents of the pagodas of the island of Goa should be transferred to them from the Jesuit Fathers, most of whom had removed themselves to Salsette.* The Viceroy, Dom Duarte de Menezes, complying in part with their wishes, ordered in 1584 a spacious college to be built at Pangim on the hill where the church now stands. This college did not, however, satisfy the friars, on account of its situation on a height infested with the deadly cobra de capello.† The building was therefore demolished, and a new one constructed in 1596 in the neighbourhood of the church of St. Peter, in the suburbs of the city. The original convent was however the chief seat of the Dominicans, and the centre from which their missionaries spread themselves over different countries of the East. In 1636 their number was 250. The festivals of the convent were celebrated with great pomp, and are still highly spoken of. In the nave over the principal door of its church were hung up representations of the culprits burnt by the orders of the Inquisition on the occasion of the *auto da fé*, with their names and those of their parents and their native country, as well as the nature of their crimes, written beneath, that they might serve as so many trophies, according to Dellon,‡ consecrated to the glory of the *Santo Officio*, of which the Dominicans were Inquisitors *ex officio*, but, according to these friars, as a warning to the Christians who were wanting in faith.

Both the church and the convent were splendid buildings, of which travellers speak with great admiration. Dr. Fryer wrote about them in 1675 in these words:—"We were brought to the college (convent) of the Dominicans, the seat of the Inquisidor, who is always one of this order; a magnificent front to the street ascending by many steps, being a huge fabric; the church surpassed the Cathedral, the pillars from

* *Liv. das Monç.*, Goa Gov. Rec. (MSS.), No. 3, fol. 19; *Arch. Port. Or.*, Fasc. III., doc. 9.

† *Arch. Port. Or.*, Fasc. III., doc. 210, 265.

‡ *Relation de l'Inquisition de Goa*, p. 159.

top to bottom being overlaid with a golden wash, and on the walls the martyrology of their order. In the sacristan were massive silver candlesticks and other vessels very rich; the dormitories elegantly contrived in upper and lower walks, and the whole without compare to others that fell in our ken:—*Erasm. vincit opibus Parathalassium tot candelabra argentea, tot statuæ aureæ, baptisteria, etc.* The habit is a white vesture with a crochet under a black gown or cowl like nuns. Their college was well replenished with devotees, and commanded a blessed prospect."* Gemelli Careri, who wrote some twenty years later, says that the church had a nave and two aisles formed by six columns on each side, and that on its arches, especially in the choir, the gold glittered in abundance. The convent, says he, was magnificent, containing many dormitories, cloisters, and spacious chambers, as well as delightful gardens.† These buildings had not entirely lost their original splendour in the first quarter of this century, before they were destroyed. Cottineau in 1827 happened to dine there with the vicar-general, and in his account compares the *socate* according to the Chinese fashion, which he tasted there, with the soup *au vermicel* he had tasted with the Bishop of Bombay, adding that nationality is always recognized even in the most ordinary things. He speaks with admiration of the size and splendour of the convent, and of the magnificence of its cloisters. The church, which in his time needed some repairs, was neat and charming, and its façade the best of all.‡

---

* *A New Account of East India and Persia*, p. 149.

† Churchill's *Voyages and Travels*, vol. IV., p. 205.

‡ *Inst. Vasco de Gama*, vol. III., pp. 155, 257; *An Historical Sketch of Goa*, p. 118.

On another occasion Cottineau, when he dined in this convent, says:—

"Après la messe nous avons eté à St. Dominique pour y passer le reste de la journée, comme j'en étais convenu avec le Père Vicaire Général j'ai dit mes petites heures avant diné dans la cellule que m'avait été preparée; j'avais demandé à diner au refectoire avec les Religieux au nombre de dix-sept, tant prêtres, que profès et novices et un frère convers; on a chantée les prières avant le repas, et le lecteur a chanté l'homelie sur l'evangile du jour, mais bientôt le Père Vicaire, qui était assis au haut de la table

The last traveller of importance who visited the convent and church of St. Dominic was Dr. John Wilson. He also bears testimony to its beauty and spaciousness, and to the valuable pictures of Italian artists adorning its interior, the best of which represented the trial of Christ. This picture, he says, could not bear the test of historical criticism, one of the lictors being represented with a pair of spectacles in his hand.*

At the time of Dr. Wilson's visit there were twenty-five friars in the convent, which having been closed in the following year, the treasury obtained both moveable and immoveable property of the total value of £16,812-19-10¼. This was the first convent that was demolished in 1841, by an order of the Governor, Lopes de Lima. The materials were mostly carried to Quepem and used in the construction of barracks, some of its bars and massive columns of black stone being made available for the pavilion erected for the statue of Affonso d'Albuquerque in Pangim. The beautiful altar-pieces were neglected; the majestic image of St. Dominic, 7⅝ feet in height, which stood on the chief altar, was removed to the Arsenal, and its great bell was carried to a distant village called Moirá in the province of Bardes. The other articles were either sold or destroyed. Amidst the ruins of this vast building stood the magnificent façade of the church, which was recently demolished. There still stands, however, amidst thickly entangled shrubs, the great cross which adorned its church, attesting the past glory of the Dominican friars in the city of Goa.

Close to the Convent of St. Dominic there was an open space, where they trained horses, and behind it a beautiful

---

avec le Prieur à côté de lui, a frappé sur la table, pour faire cesser, et a permis de parler : outre Antoine et moi il y avait quatre laics à table : le diné était bien servi à la mode du pays, mais pas par portion. Je ne dois pas oublier de remarquer que le refectoire est vouté et superbe. Après diné on a chanté les graces, et on s'est rendu à l'eglise ; après quoi chacun a été se reposer."—*Instituto Vasco de Gama*, vol. III., p. 283.

* *Orient. Christ. Spect.*, vol. V., First Series, p. 123.

fountain, the waters of which were conveyed by pipes to a small chapel of delicate structure, whose interior was adorned with shells in a curious manner and which was dedicated to St. John the Baptist.* It is now in a decayed state, and the image of the saint is missing. Pyrard says that the fountain was conveniently situated, and had reservoirs for the washing of clothes. Its water was inferior to that of Banguenim.†

Church of Santa Luzia and the Suburb of Daugim.—At a little distance from the Convent of St. Dominic, to the north-east and in the suburbs of Daugim, was situated the parish church of Santa Luzia, founded about the year 1544. The priest attached to it received, according to the Rules framed by the Viceroy, Dom Antão de Noronha, in 1565, the annual sum of £1-13-4. The inhabitants of the parish at the most flourishing period of the city must have been numerous, but in 1775 it was reduced to 194. This number was further reduced, there being in 1827 not more than 55 parishioners. Cottineau, who celebrated Mass in this church on the birthday of his mother, says that it was large and well adorned, though its funds were limited.‡ In 1864 it became a chapel, and the parish was incorporated with that of St. Braz. Subsequently, requiring considerable repairs, it was demolished, and at present its ruins only are to be seen. Further in the Upper Daugim there was the Franciscan convent of *Mãe de Deus,* built by the first Archbishop of Goa, Dom Gaspar d' Leão Pereira, a pleasure-house with a garden for the Viceroys, a palace of the Senate, and the church of St. Joseph. All these edifices, as well as the splendid private mansions which once existed there, are now in ruins, except the church of the convent of *Mãe de Deus*. This however is in a tottering condition ; the image of the Virgin which adorned its chief altar, and is held by the people of Goa as miraculous, has been removed to the newly built church at Saligão in the province of Bardez.

* Pyrard, Part II., p. 41.

† It was sold at three *bazarucos* for a pitcher.

‡ *Instituto Vasco de Gama*, vol. III., pp. 258, 259.

Church of Nossa Senhora de Monte.—To the south of the ruins of the Church of Santa Luzia, and close to the site of the Convent of St. Dominic, there is a hill which commands a picturesque view of the whole city and its environs. Its summit is reached by a flight of steps built of stone. High on the hill stands a chapel dedicated to the Blessed Virgin, and called by the name of *Nossa Senhora de Monte.* This hill is frequently mentioned by the first Portuguese historians of India, since there the Musalmáns had placed some pieces of ordnance which made terrible execution among the forces of Albuquerque when he captured Goa. The chapel was erected soon after the conquest, and is mentioned by Gaspar Correia.* It was probably reconstructed once or twice in subsequent times, and had, according to Pyrard† and some other travellers, the dimensions of a beautiful church. The present building, which is vaulted, is well preserved and has three altars, over the middle of which is seen an image of the Virgin. The chapel has outhouses, where some years ago lived a chaplain of the Cathedral, who was in charge of it, but it is now closed throughout the year, and Mass is not said in it even on Sundays; only one annual festival of *Nossa Senhora de Monte,* with novenas, is celebrated in it.

Convent and Church of the Carmelites.—Contiguous to the hill of *Nossa Senhora de Monte* there is an eminence, on which there was a convent with a church of the Barefooted Carmelites. According to the *Oriente Conquistado* this building was erected in 1612, but according to other writers in 1607 or 1630. The last date, however, cannot be accurate, because Pietro della Valle, who was at Goa in 1623, and dwelt at the foot of the eminence, makes mention of the convent, which, being situated on a height, he says, enjoyed a beautiful prospect.‡

This writer also alludes to the pomp with which the Carmelites commemorated in this chapel the canonization of St. Theresa, the foundress of their order. This ceremony took place

* *Lendas,* vol. II., pp. 93, 193, 195.

† Pyrard, Part II., *ut supra,* p. 41.

‡ Viaggi, *ut supra,* vol. II., p. 596.

on the 20th May 1623, on which occasion two Portuguese boys, mounted on horseback and attired in travelling costume, were sent to the Viceroy's palace to announce to him in verse the news of the canonization. After this the two boys ran through the whole city singing, with a flourish of trumpets, other verses intimating the same tidings; meanwhile bells were rung not only in the church of the Carmelites, but also in all other churches. At night the city was illuminated at the request of the Fathers, and a masquerade held, at which Pietro della Valle, who had known the saint personally and regarded her with great veneration, appeared in the garb of an Arab of the desert. There was also a kind of dramatic performance, in which an image of the saint was exhibited surrounded by twelve persons bearing devices and mottoes in twelve different languages. Next morning a solemn mass was celebrated by the Carmelites in their church, and an eloquent panegyric delivered by a friar of the convent of St. Augustine before a very large congregation, composed of the Viceroy, the fidalgos, and people of all ranks and classes.*

In this church many festivals, especially that of *Nossa Senhora de Carmo,* were solemnized by the Carmelites with great pomp. The friars were remarkable for their zeal and devotion, and succeeded in securing the patronage of several rich and influential persons, who materially contributed to render their convent one of the richest and most flourishing at Goa.

As the Carmelites were foreigners, the Portuguese Government had no confidence in their loyalty, and therefore insisted on their taking the oath of allegiance to the King, which, it is said, they refused to do. They were consequently expelled from Goa in 1707, and the convent with all its property was bestowed by the King on the Priests of the Congregation of St. Philip Neri, who established their college there.† It is also said that when Pedro Paulo, the Preposito or Superior of this Congregation, took pos-

* *Viaggi di Pietro della Valle il Pellegrino,* vol. II., p. 603.

† *Chronologia da Congregação do Oratorio de Goa* (MSS.), liv. IV., cap. 7.

session of it two years later, the money and other valuable articles of gold and silver belonging to the convent were found missing, and that at that time there was only one Carmelite, Fr. Leandro de São Francisco Xavier, who made over the convent and its landed property, yielding an income of £51-15-10, of which £36-7-6 was charged with various pious duties.* The Carmelites of Rome made great efforts to recover possession of the convent and its estates, which they alleged to be of great value, but they could not succeed, and the members of the Congregation of St. Philip Neri continued in possession of it till the suppression of the religious orders in Goa, when the public treasury appropriated its property of the aggregate value of £4,991-1-3.

This convent was inferior to the other convents in size, but the church was comparatively larger and more beautiful. Tavernier says that the convent of the Carmelites was situated in the most healthy place, and that it had two galleries, one over the other.† Dr. Fryer writes about it as follows:— "The college of Carmelites is on an high mountain, prospecting the whole city; it is a fine building; these are begging friars too, eat only fish, except in sickness; clothed with a coarse russet tippet, coat and vest, girt about with a cord; in their hall where they repast, at the upper end of the table, is placed a death's-head; over their cells, sentences denoting each virtue, which were wrote in capital letters of gold over the doors, as fortitude, patience, and the like. Here we left many devout old men on their knees praying fervently and living piously."‡

Gemelli Careri gives a still better description of the convent in the following terms:—" On Friday, the 8th (1695), I went to see the Church of the Italian Carmelites, standing on a pleasant hill. Though small, it is very beautiful, and arched, as are all the churches in India, with six chapels and a high altar well

---

* *Chronologia da Congregação do Oratorio,* (MSS.) *loc. cit.*

† *Les Six Voyages*, vol. II., p. 122.

‡ *A New Account of East India and Persia*, p. 150.

gilt. The monastery is handsome and well contrived with excellent cloisters and cells, and a delicious garden in which there are Chinese palm-trees, which yield a pleasing shade with their low and thick leaves; there are also two cinnamon trees like those of Ceylon."*

Both the convent and the church were in a good state of preservation for years after these travellers had visited them, but fourteen years after the suppression of the religious orders, their roofs were removed by orders of the Government, and the buildings, which were vaulted, were abandoned to the inclemency of the weather, in consequence of which they are now reduced to a heap of ruins, except only the façade of the church. In a half-ruined wall on the north side was lately discovered a large slab with an inscription in gold, somewhat defaced, surmounted by the bust and decorated with the arms of a nobleman to whose memory it was dedicated. This slab was probably a monument raised to Dom Pedro Mascarenhas, who, as stated by the Count of Linhares in his letter of the 15th April 1634, had offered £833-6-8 to the Church of the Carmelites on condition of their erecting in its principal chapel a sumptuous monument in his memory with his arms engraved on it.† At present the place is difficult of access, because of the thick shrubs and bushes that surround it.

---

* Churchill's *Voyages and Travels*, vol. IV., p. 251.

† *Livros das Mouçoens*, Goa Gov. Rec., MSS., No. 20.

CHAPTER XII.

THE COLLEGE AND CHURCH OF ST. PAUL—CHAPEL OF ST. FRANCIS XAVIER—HOSPITAL OF ST. LAZARUS—CHURCH OF ST. THOMAS.

College and Church of St. Paul.—To the south of the Convent of the Carmelites, and bordering on the high road, are seen the noble ruins of the famous College of *Santa Fé* or of St. Paul. It is impossible to approach this spot without being reminded of the early history of the Catholic Church in the East, and of the glorious deeds of the Apostle of the Indies, who made it the chief place of his abode in India for a considerable time. The college was established for the purpose of instructing the new converts of all races and nationalities of Asia in various arts and sciences, and qualifying them for preaching the Gospel in their own languages in different parts of the country. It was founded chiefly through the exertions of Diogo Borba and Miguel Vaz, both of whom took a deep interest in the propagation of the Catholic religion. They had, with the assistance of several influential laymen, formed a pious association called the Confraternity of *Santa Fé* or Holy Faith, and obtained from the Viceroy, Nuno da Cunha (1529-38), a grant of the income of the pagodas of the Ilhas for the purpose of establishing and maintaining a college.* The foundation-stone of the building was laid on the 10th November 1541, over the ruins of a great mosque near the road called *Rua De Carreira de Cavallos,* and subsequently the Road of St. Paul. The college with its church was completed towards the close of 1542.† The church being consecrated on the 25th January

* *Lendas, ut supra,* vol. IV., p. 289.

† *Op cit.,* vol. II., p. 93. The date is mentioned by Gaspar Correia, who in this as in a few other points differs from Father Francisco de Souza: compare *Lendas,* vol. IV., p. 289, with the *Oriente Conquistado,* vol. I., pp. 31 *et seq.*

1543, the day of the conversion of St. Paul, was called after him, and mass was celebrated there for the first time amidst great rejoicings, in the presence of the Governor, the nobility, and the gentry. On this occasion two of the native pupils of Father Borba acted as acolytes, and the rest as choristers.* During the first period of its existence, the college trained about eighty Indian youths, some of whom made great progress in their studies, preached the Gospel to their countrymen in the vernacular dialects, and converted many to Christianity.† It was endowed, as already stated, with the rents of the demolished pagodas, which, according to the *Oriente Conquistado,* amounted to £80 per annum, and, according to Gaspar Correia, at first to £75 and subsequently (in 1543) to more than £400.‡ In addition to this endowment the college enjoyed the patronage of several persons of rank, who took a deep interest in its welfare. It rose however to great importance when St. Francis Xavier, in 1544, came to reside there at the request of Father Borba, on whose death the Apostle took charge of the college and all that belonged to it, in the name of the Society of Jesus, which had about this time been established in Goa. The King of Portugal not only approved of the foundation of an institution which fully realized one of the chief objects of the discovery of the route to India, viz., the propagation of the Christian faith, but also endowed it with a special allowance of £111-2-2. He also confirmed the grant of the whole property of the pagodas made in 1550 to the College by the Governor George Cabral.§ Thus supported on all sides, the institution enlarged its scope, in

* *Lendas*, vol. IV., p. 289.

† *Op. cit.*, vol. IV., p. 291. According to the *Oriente Conquistado*, vol. I., p. 31, and *Historia da Vida do Padre S. Francisco Xavier*, by Lucena, Lisboa, 1878, vol. I., p. 141, the number of the students was respectively sixty and seventy.

‡ *Orient. Conq. I.*, Div. I., § 25 ; *Lendas*, vol. IV., p. 290. See also *Arch. Port. Or.*, Fasc. V., doc. 75, where the rents of the pagodas are said to have been 768 pardaus; and the *Subsidios para Historia da India Portugueza*, Part II., p. 70, where they are given as amounting to 600,000 reis.

§ *Arch. Port. Or.*, Fasc. V., doc. 100, 115.

consequence of which the old building was demolished, and in its stead a new one erected with sufficient accommodation for the residence of the Jesuit Fathers and of about a hundred students.* About the same time new rules were framed for the management of the College, and the ablest teachers of the Society selected for its direction. It was divided into two classes, in one of which elementary instruction was imparted to about a hundred students, the more promising of whom, seventy-two in number, were promoted to the other class, where they learned Latin, music, rhetoric, philosophy, and theology; during leisure hours they also visited and served the sick, attended the funerals of the poor, and taught the people catechism. The rest, who were unfit for higher studies, were dismissed, or employed in other affairs suited to their capabilities. The College, as stated by Father Lucena, who was thoroughly acquainted with its management, might stand comparison, as regards the dimensions of the building, the efficiency of its tutorial staff, and the soundness of its instruction, with the best colleges of Europe.† Under the direction of Fathers Antonio Gomes, Paulo Camerte, Antonio Criminal, Nicolau Lancelloto, and Affonso Cypriano, who were selected by St. Francis Xavier, the college became the chief institution of the disciples of Loyola in India, to which more than three hundred churches with their colleges in different parts of Asia were subject.‡ The Jesuit Fathers, with their pupils, who were carefully instructed in the principal tenets of the Catholic Church, exerted themselves so strenuously in propagating the new faith, that the common people looked upon this institution with a kind of awe mingled with admiration; they were known all over India by the name of *Paulistas,* from the College of St. Paul, which was the basis of their operations.

---

* According to the *Oriente Conquistado,* vol. I., pp. 61, 62, two distinct buildings were erected, one for the accommodation of the students, and the other for the residence of the Jesuits.

† *Historia da Vida do Padre Francisco Xavier,* by João Lucena, vol. I., p. 144; see also *Oriente Conquistado,* vol. I., pp. 61, 101.

‡ *Historia da Vida do Padre Francisco Xavier, ut supra,* vol. I., p. 147.

This college was connected with many an important event in the annals of the Catholic religion in India. It was in its Church that the first jubilee for India granted by the Pope at the request of St. Francis Xavier was announced in 1551 by Father Gaspar Berzeo. It was there that the *Santos Passos,* or a representation of the passion of Christ now exhibited during Lent in Catholic Churches in India, were first introduced. There the ambassador of the king of Cambay, the three first Japanese who embraced Christianity, many nobles, and a vast number of pagans were baptized. There St. Francis Xavier preached the Gospel to crowds of people, and there his body was first deposited when brought from China. There too subsequently were the remains of the Jesuit martyrs of Cuncolim buried. In 1560 this Church, showing signs of decay, was demolished, and on the 25th of January of the same year the foundation-stone of a new one was laid, with solemnities such as had never before been witnessed in India, by Dom João Nunes, a Jesuit and Patriarch of Ethiopia, with the assistance of Father Antonio de Quadros, the Provincial of the Jesuits. The new building was grand and beautiful, but some years after a crack was noticed in one of its walls, and it was therefore supported from the outside by three arches, built under the direction of João de Faria, a Jesuit well-known for his skill in architecture. These arches were so wide and lofty that a high road passed beneath them, and so handsome that the building was called after them the Church of St. Paul of the Arches.

The College of St. Paul daily rose in public estimation, and in process of time the building was found hardly sufficient to accommodate all the institutions connected with it. In 1568 there were eighty-eight Jesuit Fathers residing within its precincts and giving instruction to more than three thousand pupils.* There were besides a Novitiate and an Hospital for the native poor, for the maintenance of which a subsidy of

---

* *Oriente Conquistado,* vol. II., p. 42.

£12·10-0 was allowed from the public treasury during the government of Dom Antão de Noronha.* In 1570, when the city was afflicted with the epidemic, the locality in which the college was situated became so unhealthy that fifty-eight fathers are said to have fallen victims to it.† For these reasons, especially for the last, the Society purchased in 1578, on the hill of *Nossa Senhora de Rozario*, which was regarded as a very healthy spot, a house for the residence of the sick members, which subsequently became the New College of St. Paul. Another building was erected for professed members on the *Terreiro dos Gallos*. The old college, not being however at once abandoned, continued for some time longer to be the principal institution of the Jesuits in India. Pyrard says that it was attended in 1608 by the same number of students as before, all of whom received instruction gratis. They were distributed into several classes, and, as an inducement to work, were occasionally entertained with theatrical performances as well as with mock fights, in which they were arrayed as soldiers in order of battle, and divided into companies of foot and horse. The students before beginning their school work, heard mass in the Church of St. Paul, and when returning home walked together in groups, each group consisting of those boys who lived in the same locality, singing in the streets the catechism and prayers in a loud voice. This practice spread at that time through all the villages of Goa, and is still kept up in some of them. Every Sunday evening the three thousand students were formed into groups according to their respective classes, and went in procession with their masters and other Jesuit Fathers to the Church of *Bom Jesus*, carrying crosses and flags, and chanting hymns all along the road. Crowds of people swelled this procession, which must have presented a truly imposing spectacle. When the procession entered the church, a clergyman taught catechism and preached a sermon.

* This hospital was founded by Father Paulo Camerte in 1551; in process of time it was transferred to Margão, and thence to Rachol.

† *Orient. Conq.*, vol. II., p. 85.

The chief festivals were, however, celebrated by the students in the church attached to their own college, especially the feast of St. Paul, on which occasion the Viceroy, accompanied by two or three hundred fidalgos mounted on horses richly caparisoned, went to this church, where he was received by the students, who in costly silk clothes marched in rank and file before him. On this day he was entertained by the Fathers with a sumptuous dinner, followed by the sports and amusements of the students.*

By 1623, when Pietro della Valle visited Goa, all the bustle and activity had disappeared from the college, together with the festivities in the church. In fact the college was abandoned, and the schools were transferred to the new building on the hill of *Nossa Senhora do Rozario*.† Tavernier makes particular mention of the old college which he saw in 1640; ‡ but he does not describe the building. Dr. Fryer says that it was in 1675 the seat of the Provost (*Provincial*) of the Jesuits, "who is independent and rules *suo jure*."§ Gemelli Careri states that only two fathers resided in 1695 in the college, which was partly ruined; and that in the church, once equally magnificent, were instructed catechumens, "for whose mainteuance the King contributed four hundred pieces of eight a year."‖ In the time of Cottineau in 1827 both the college and the church were in so ruinous a state that only a small part of the former remained, and of the latter a façade of the Doric order, the side walls, the choir cloister, staircase, and the arches. Around the building there grew palm-trees and shrubs that rendered the place very difficult of access. "Nous avons," says the abbé, "penetré avec difficulté dans le jardin tout rempli de cocotuers et d'autres arbres, et dont le terrain

---

* Pyrard, Part II., pp. 34, 48.

† *Viaggi di Pietro della Valle*, vol. II., p. 759.

‡ *Les Six Voyages*, Part II., p. 122; Harris' *Collection of Voyages*, vol. II., p. 359.

§ *A New Account of East India and Persia*, p. 150.

‖ Churchill's *Collection of Voyages and Travels*, p. 206.

est. couvert d'arbustes et herbes, la retraite des serpents."* The remains of the college and church, as well as a majestic cross of black stone, were demolished by order of the Government some four or five years after Cottineau's visit, with the view of using the materials for the buildings that were being erected in Pangim; but, having been found useless, they were abandoned, and are still to be seen lying there, overgrown with thick shrubs. The façade of the church, however, escaped the general wreck, and exists at present in a somewhat decayed state, and is the only relic of the famous College of St. Paul.

Chapel of St. Francis Xavier.—Within the enclosure of the above college stood, on a small eminence, the celebrated chapel of St. Francis Xavier. It is related that on one occasion the saint, whilst at prayer, was so much overpowered by devotional fervour that he felt himself almost suffocated, and then, opening his soutane near the chest, burst into an exclamation "*Domine sat est*," "Lord, it is enough." The author of the *Oriente Conquistado* states that, according to a tradition, this chapel was erected to commemorate the above incident, on the very spot where it occurred, and that every year on a Friday in Lent high mass was celebrated, attended by the gentry of the city, but that, on the other hand, some writers, especially Father Manoel Xavier, affirm that the saint himself caused this chapel to be built, and was in the habit of saying mass there. The same author conjectures that this chapel was one of the two that stood within the enclosure of the college, of which one was dedicated to St. Anthony, and the other to St. Jerome, and that possibly, after the abovementioned incident, the latter may have been dedicated to St. Francis Xavier.† At any rate it is clear, both from traditional and historical evidence, that this chapel was particularly hallowed by the presence of the Apostle of the

---

* *Instituto Vasco da Gama*, vol. III., p. 182.

† *Oriente Conquistado*, Conq. IV., Div. ii.

Indies, in consequence of which it was held in great veneration by the Catholics of Goa, and was kept in a decent state for a long time. It is said that on its walls all the important incidents in the life of the Apostle were beautifully painted. Subsequently the edifice appears from its architecture to have been improved and enlarged. When the College of St. Paul was abandoned, this chapel was to a certain extent neglected, but was nevertheless well preserved till the close of the 17th century.* Later on, when the city was deserted, the building began to decay. In 1827 there were, besides the sanctuary, a small portico with seats on both sides and a well-wrought façade, the nave which stood unroofed and presented on the top only one timber beam, and the vault of the choir, all of which gave unmistakable signs of approaching ruin.† At present there exists only a small roofless building about thirty feet long and twelve broad, with the pavement overgrown with grass. Previous to the exposition of the body of St. Francis Xavier in 1859, the Government ordered the chapel to be repaired, and the shrubs hedging it to be removed, with a view to render it easily accessible. During the exposition people flocked there in crowds, and many afflicted with various diseases came from distant places and remained there for some days in hopes of regaining health. In course of time the chapel fell again into neglect, and continues still in this state, notwithstanding the endeavours of many Catholics of Goa to repair it by means of a subscription, and the recommendation to the same effect of a committee appointed by Government in 1870 to inspect the buildings of the old city.

There is a tradition current in Goa that at the foot of this chapel the saint had planted a jack-tree, the bark of which possessed the power of healing various maladies. A traveller says, however, that he saw in 1695 in the garden of St. Paul's College two jack-trees and some mango-trees planted by the

---

* Churchill's *Voyages and Travels*, vol. IV., p. 206.

† *Instituto Vasco de Gama*, vol. III., p. 182.

same saint.* Whether he planted one or more trees, it is not certain, but it is undisputed that the tree near this chapel was greatly prized by the Catholics of Goa, in common with many other objects connected with the memory of the saint. Chips of this tree and images made of its wood received marked respect. In a chapel dedicated to St. Rita in the village of Curtorim, in Salsette, there is a cross made of the same jack-tree, which formerly belonged to the Convent of St. Francis, and which is highly esteemed by the common people. This jack-tree must have long since disappeared, but on the occasion of the last exposition of the body of St. Francis the trunk of a similar tree was discovered in the neighbourhood of the chapel of the Saint, and people, fancying it to be the same that was planted by him, were anxious to obtain even small chips of it. Close to the same chapel there are two wells, the water of which is spoken of as possessing rare properties. It is believed that the saint used to wash his feet in the well which lies on the left side of the road leading to the chapel and has a flight of steps hewn out of a rock leading to the level of the water, and that he used to drink the water of the other well, which is on the right side of the road and is a little deeper. There is however no foundation for such a tradition.

Hospital of St. Lazarus.—Leaving the spot which was the favourite abode of the Apostle of the Indies, and forcing our way through shrubs and bushes towards the eastern boundary of the city, we arrive at the ruins of the Hospital of St. Lazarus, where St. Francis Xavier, on his arrival from Europe in 1542, used to tend the lepers. It was founded about the year 1530 or 1531, as appears from a letter of the King of Portugal dated the 26th March 1532, in which, after stating that he was aware of the foundation of this hospital, he alludes to the privileges and rules which were asked for it, similar to those of the hospital at Lisbon.† The institution was maintained at the public expense, and was under the superintendence of the Senate or Municipal Chamber, and the *Santa*

---

* Churchill's *Voyages and Travels*, vol. IV., p. 206.

† *Arch. Port. Or.*, Fasc. I., doc. 2.

*Casa de Misericordia.** It had a parish church which received a contribution of £1-13-4.

The hospital was a beautiful and well furnished edifice, and the church had an elegant chapel dedicated to St. Louis of France. The esplanade in which these buildings were erected was very spacious, called *Campo de São Lazaro,* and also sometimes *Campo de São Thiago,* because it led to the fortress of São Thiago.† On this esplanade the Portuguese grandees and noblemen had their favourite equestrian games with canes and oranges on the festivals of St. John and St. James. Pietro della Valle gives the following description of the solemnities which were held during the feasts of the two saints :— "On the feast of St. John, as is usual in Goa every year, the Viceroy and many other Portuguese gentlemen went out in disguise but without masks, in groups of twos or threes; and, having heard mass in St. John's Church, passed through St. Paul's street, which is also called the race-course, and is the best place of Goa. Several groups of native Christians passed through the streets with banners, tambourines, and arms, dancing and performing mock fights with bare swords; these were pedestrians; then came the horsemen with Moorish javelins and ran two races, *i.e.* from St. Paul's Church towards the town and back again, always in groups of twos or threes, according to their costumes and previous arrangement; and once again they came downwards from St. Paul's, all going together. This over, they proceeded to do the same and in the same order in the square of the Viceroy's palace, which brought the festivity to a close. I went to see this spectacle in St. Paul's street from the house of one who is called king of the Maldives, which are numberless small islands all in a row and connected together towards the west and not far away from the coast of India. . . . On the feast of St. James, the patron saint of Spain, the same festivities and

---

* *Op. cit.*, Fasc. II., p. 273.

† Pietro della Valle says that the road which led from Santiago to the city was very fine, and passed through a beautiful plain covered with verdure, villas and pleasure walks.

masquerades as those described above were held in the morning, differing only in this, that the Viceroy and the rest of the company heard mass in St. James' church."* The esplanade was also used as a parade-ground by native Christian soldiers.† It was there also that the criminals sentenced to capital punishment by the Inquisition were burnt. In the time of Cottineau the Hospital of St. Lazarus was still in existence, and admitted not only lepers, but also poor patients. A secular priest acted as superintendent of the house, and also as chaplain.‡ Since 1840, when the hospital was closed, the building has rapidly fallen into decay. It is now completely in ruins, there being hardly any vestige left of its former grandeur. The image of St. Lazarus is at present preserved in the parish church of Corlim.

Church of Saint Thomas.—Close to the Church of St. Lazarus stood other edifices, of which the most noteworthy was the church of St. Thomas, one of the twelve Apostles, who is said to have preached the Gospel in India. Ever since the discovery of the route to India, the Portuguese had been searching for the body of that saint, which, according to a tradition, had been buried at Meliapur. The Viceroy, Dom Francisco de Almeida, sent in 1507 four persons to the Coromandel coast in search of it, but it was only in 1522 that the body was discovered by Manoel de Frias, who was in charge of the Portuguese settlements on that coast. The Government of Goa, in accordance with instructions received from Portugal, ordered the church where it was found buried to be repaired. The remains of the saint, together with a spear with which he was killed, were, according to an eye-witness, deposited in a richly decorated case which was hidden by Father Alvaro Penteado in some secret part of the church, from which it was again removed in 1533 by Father Ugo Nicclay to another equally unknown part, to prevent it from being stolen or profaned.§ To deposit the

* *Viaggi di Pietro della Valle il Pellegrino*, vol. II., p. 606.

† *Arch. Port. Or.*, Fasc. II., doc. 47.; Pyrard, Part II., p. 32.

‡ *An Historical Sketch*, p. 91.

§ *Lendas*, vol. II., pp. 722, 778, 786; vol. III., pp. 419 *et seq.*

relics in a completely secure spot, where they might receive the veneration due to them, the Viceroy, Dom Constantino de Bragança, acting upon the instructions of the Home Government, ordered them to be removed in 1560 to Goa. The Christians of Meliapur, who were devoutly attached to the saint, would not however allow his bones to be translated thither: consequently the delegates who were sent to fetch them could only succeed in bringing with them a bone with a few other relics of the saint. These were enshrined with great solemnity in a church which had been erected in the city for their reception, and which was consequently named after the saint. This church, which Pyrard describes as belonging to a large parish,* began to decay in process of time, and was called Old or Broken St. Thomas. In 1720 the number of its parishioners dwindled to 493. In 1827 Cottineau describes the church as follows:—"The Church of St. Thomas the Apostle is in the great street of St. Paul's College, at a furlong distance from it and on the same side. It was made a parish after the two preceding churches (of the *Rozario* and *Luz*), but never became a collegiate. It is now very poor and in ruins, as well as the adjoining presbytery, or priest's house. The vicar does not reside in Goa, and mass is celebrated only on Sundays and festivals. On St. Thomas's day, the 21st December, the canons of the Cathedral and deputations of the convents come hither in procession after the high mass of the Cathedral is over, and before that of the church commences, bringing back the reliquary of the saint, which is carried to the Cathedral on the eve of the vespers, by the members of a confraternity attached to this parish. The number of its communicants amounts to twenty-four. The vicar's salary is seventy-five rupees, like that of all the others in the diocese."†

Shortly after his visit, this church fell completely into ruin, and there are hardly any traces left of it at present.

---

* Pyrard, Part II., p. 32.

† *An Historical Sketch*, p. 102.

To the south of this sacred edifice, at a short distance, there was an incomplete building dedicated to the same saint, which was called New St. Thomas. Dr. Fryer speaks of the same, and of the place in which it stood, in the following terms:—"Coming again to Goa I lodged at the house of a French physician in the camp of St. Thomas, which the city overlooks in the same manner as old Rome did the Martian Vale. I saw there an unfinished piece of the St. Thomas Christians, but the troubles of their Prince called them back before it could be perfected; others say prevented in it by thunder and lightning. The great traders of this place for diamonds are the two Martins, both Jews, yet to carry on their designs permitted to live as Christians, they constantly frequenting Mass, and at table every meal during our stay had hogs' flesh served up."*

Near it lay a large well excavated out of a rock. Pietro della Valle, speaking of it, says that it was the work of the former heathen rulers of the land, being one of the largest that he had seen; it was round, having, according to him, a diameter of twenty ordinary paces, and was very deep; it was surrounded by a parapet with two doors, and had flights of steps leading to its very bottom.† On the same side, which formed the south-eastern boundary of the city, there was a beautiful lake frequented by waterfowl, as Linschoten and Pyrard tell us, amidst charming villas with gardens belonging to Portuguese fidalgos. The terrible epidemic which broke out in the city in 1570, is said to have been caused in a great measure by the poisonous effluvia issuing from this lake.‡ Near the lake, in the outskirts of the city towards the south, stood the gallows.

---

* *A New Account, ut supra*, p. 183.

† *Viaggi di Pietro della Valle*, vol. II., p. 609.

‡ Linschoten's *Histoire de la Navigation*, p. 56; Pyrard, *Voyage*, Part II., p. 32; *Orient. Conq.*, vol. I., p. 53.

CHAPTER XIII.

THE CHURCH OF ST. ALEXIUS—HOSPITAL OF ALL SAINTS—CHURCH OF THE HOLY TRINITY—CONVENT AND CHURCH OF THE CRUZ DOS MILAGRES—CHURCH OF NOSSA SENHORA DA LUZ.

Church of St. Alexius.—Returning now by the main road, which runs close by St. Thomas' Church, and proceeding to the west, we come again to the site of St. Paul's College, and passing by the same, we see, a few yards off, traces of two buildings. The one to the north of the street at the foot of the Convent of the Carmelites was the parish church of St. Alexius, which was erected by the Archbishop Dom Fr. Aleixo de Menezes towards the close of the 16th century. This church was at first in a very flourishing state, but within a quarter of a century from the date of its erection it began to show signs of rapid decay, and about the year 1775 could count only 158 parishioners. Not long after, it crumbled to dust. The image of the saint was removed to the Cathedral, while the cross in the courtyard is the only relic of the building.

Hospital of All Saints.—Directly to the south of the Church of St. Alexius, along the road leading to the Church of the *Cruz dos Milagres,* stood the second of the two buildings mentioned above, the Hospital of All Saints, founded in 1547 by the *Santa Casa de Misericordia* for the relief of the poor, as stated in a document found among the records of that institution. In 1681 it was amalgamated with the Hospital of *Nossa Senhora de Piedade,* on the understanding that the Senate or the Municipal Chamber which established the latter should contribute £5 per month, besides the interest accruing from

£500 given to the same by the Viceroy, Count of Linhares. The building in which the hospital was accommodated began to decay in 1822, in consequence of which it was transferred to the old house called *Real Stanco do Tabaco,* and thence successively to the Convents of St. John of God and St. Barbara at Morombim. Between 1842 and 1843 it was proposed to be removed to the College of St. Thomas, but the project was not carried out. It was however finally transferred in 1851 to Ribandar, where it still exists, and is called the Hospital of the Poor or of the *Santa Casa de Misericordia.**

Proceeding further to the south, by a road now almost lost among shrubs, we find a small reservoir of water. It is the celebrated *Tírtha of Brahmapuri,* sacred to *Śiva,* who, according to a Hindu legend, dwelt there thousands of years ago. This *tírtha,* before the Portuguese conquest of Goa, attracted annually crowds of pilgrims from different parts of India, but under the new *régime* pilgrimages to this spot were at first strictly prohibited. This severity however was considerably relaxed in later years, so that we now find a number of Hindus annually visiting this *tírtha* in the month of Shráwan (August).

Church of the Holy Trinity.—Close to this *tírtha* lies the site of the parish church of the *Santissima Trindade* (The Most Holy Trinity), which is believed to have been built on the ruins of the pagoda of Śiva by the Archbishop Dom Fr. Aleixo de Menezes, about the same time that the Church of St. Alexius, of which we have already spoken, was erected.

The parish of this Church, which in 1614 had about 12,000 souls, was so much deserted that in 1775 there could be found hardly thirty-two persons; consequently the church was neglected and was allowed to fall into ruin.

Convent and Church of the Cruz dos Milagres.—At a small distance from the above church, towards the west, are seen on a hill called *Monte de Boa Vista,* from the excellent view it commands of the city and its environs, the half dilapidated

* For further description, *vide* p. 328.

Church of the *Cruz dos Milagres* (Cross of Miracles), and the Convent of the Congregation of the Oratory. The church owes its existence to a miracle said to have been wrought on its site on the 23rd February 1619. We may be allowed to detail at some length the particulars of this miracle from an old manuscript in our possession, as it caused great sensation at the time, and is still a frequent topic of pious conversation in many a household in Goa. It is said that a priest named Manoel Rodrigues had set up a cross of teakwood on a rock on that hill. On the 23rd February 1619 people were surprised to see from the city several flags of crimson hue playing in the air near this cross. They were still more surprised on the following morning to witness a human figure nailed on the cross, with a halo of light around him. This spectacle, bursting on their view from a distance, tempted several persons to approach the spot, but by the time they arrived there everything that had struck them from a distance had disappeared. They then returned to the place whence they had seen the extraordinary spectacle, and again observed a figure nailed on the cross, with the head uplifted, hands stretched out, feet fastened together, a white towel encircling the waist, the body covered with wounds and stained with blood, and a crown of thorns around the head. The whole figure appeared to be wrapped in an ethereal flame of dazzling splendour which reached the skies. At this sight the whole city was astonished. Thereupon the Archbishop, Dom Fr. Christovão de Lisboa, ordered the cross to be conveyed in a solemn procession to the neighbouring church of *Nossa Senhora da Luz* on the shoulders of the canons and the chief public functionaries. Subsequently a canonical investigation was made in regard to the supposed miracle, and as it was reported that many miraculous cures had been effected by simply touching the cross, a committee of theologians and medical men was appointed to report on the matter, and their opinion was that these cures were supernatural. Another miracle connected with the cross is said to have taken place on the 5th March 1619, when a stream of water issued from the rock on which it stood, for a day and night together. The Archbishop then ordered fasts and public prayers in all the churches and convents, and appointed a committee of theologians, selected from among the friars of every convent, to give their opinion upon this matter. The committee finding no cavity in the rock capable of holding such a large quantity of water, arrived at the conclusion that the event was miraculous. Upon this a solemn festival was held in the Cathedral, and a church was erected to commemorate the miracle by means of contributions raised from the people. A slab with the following inscription in gold letters was also placed on the spot where the miraculous cross stood:—

"Neste logar estava a Santa Cruz, quando nella appareceu Jesus."

Translation.

"In this place stood the Holy Cross when Jesus appeared on it."

When the cross was about to be removed from the Church of *Nossa Senhora da Luz* to the church specially built for it, it is stated to have grown in size, since it could not pass through the door by which it had formerly been taken in, and it was found necessary to widen the entrance and to separate the horizontal bar of the cross from the main stem. The Church being built of weak materials, could ill withstand the fury of the elements to which it was exposed, and fell on the 8th August 1659, when the miraculous cross was taken back to the Church of *Nossa Senhora da Luz.** In 1669 an Augustinian friar, named Agostinho dos Reis, commenced to rebuild the church on a grander scale, and placed the cross in it after its completion in 1671. A miraculous image of *Nossa Senhora de Bom Successo* (Our Lady of Good Success), which was in the cell of a friar in the convent of St. Augustine, was also removed thither in a solemn procession. Regarding this image it is

* See *Chronica da Congregação do Oratorio* (MSS.), Livr. I., Cap. IV.; *Promptuario das Definições Indicas*, por Padre Leonardo Paes, p. 48; *Anno Historico*, por Padre Francisco de Santa Maria, p. 243; Churchill's *Voyages and Travels*, vol. IV., p. 206.

said that the friar had prayed before it to be cured of a disease of a virulent character, and that to satisfy himself that he enjoyed the favour of the Virgin Mary, he begged the cloth which covered the image to be removed and the image revealed to his sight. The prayer was heard, and the image stood before him stripped of its covering.* A few years later, the church was made over to some native priests who had formed themselves into a religious community called the Congregation of the Oratory of St. Philip Neri, in the Retreat of St. John of the Desert, in the parish of Guadalupe, in Batim.

In 1685 Rev. José Vaz, a native of Goa and venerated as a saint, joined the congregation and erected a little house contiguous to the church, and submitted its rules to the Pope for approval, which was accorded in 1707. This community lived there till the suppression of the religious orders in Goa, when thirty-six of its members left it, and the public treasury appropriated its property, of the aggregate value of £14,424-7-9½. The miraculous cross was removed afterwards on the 3rd May 1845, by orders of the Governor, J. F. Pestana, to the Cathedral, where it is at present.

The church was small, but well constructed and vaulted. The convent, which after the death of Rev. José Vaz had been enlarged by the addition of various cells and dormitories, was spacious and beautiful. These buildings commanded a picturesque view not only of the city, but also of the whole island and harbour of Goa. When they were abandoned, they gradually fell into decay, and were ordered to be demolished in 1846. Some of the walls might even now be seen in a mouldering state, amidst a frightful wilderness, the abode of venomous snakes and reptiles, but it is difficult to approach them and observe the relics of the last religious edifice of the city.

Church of Nossa Senhora da Luz.—Close to the Church of the *Cruz dos Milagres*, towards the west, there was, as stated above, the Church of *Nossa Senhora da Luz* (Our Lady of Light). This church was very old, and had been raised to the

* *Chronica da Congregação do Oratorio, loc. cit.*

rank of a parish church, together with that of the Rosary, in 1543, when cholera was raging in the city.* It was subsequently turned into a collegiate church, and received from the public treasury the sum of £14-1-7 per annum,† of which £3-16-0 were for petty expenses, £2-15-7 for the vicar, who had the title of Prior, £6-13-4 for four priests who served in it, and 16*s.* 8*d.* to the treasurer. This church is frequently mentioned in the Portuguese chronicles of the 16th century. It was here that Dom João de Castro, on learning of the heroic defence of the fortress of Diu in 1546, offered thanks to God, and deposited the flag which had been taken from the king of Cambay.‡ In 1614 this church had 30,000 parishioners; but in the first quarter of the 18th century this number was reduced to 109, and a hundred years after to 8. At the time of Cottineau's visit it was closed except on Sundays, when mass was said there.§ It fell completely into ruins soon after, and no trace now remains of it except a cross on the outside, like that of the Church of St. Alexius.

---

* *Lendas, ut supra,* vol. IV., p. 289.

† According to the Regulations framed by Dom Antão de Noronha; but according to the *Tombo* of Simão Botelho only 92,715 reis.

‡ *Lendas*, vol. IV., pp. 456, 571.

§ *Instituto Vasco de Gama*, vol. III., p. 229.

HOUSE AND CHURCH OF BOM JESUS.

CHAPTER XIV.

THE HOUSE AND CHURCH OF BOM JESUS—CHAPEL AND TOMB OF ST. FRANCIS XAVIER.

House and Church of Bom Jesus.—Returning to the main road, and proceeding a few paces westward, we meet again in the centre of the city the old *Pelourinho.* Close to it there lay a spacious square called *Terreiro dos Gallos,* from the fact that people were here entertained with cock-fights—a spectacle once very popular, but prohibited in 1594 under grave penalties.* On this site was built the *Casa Professa,* or the Professed House of the Jesuits, who were about to erect this building in 1585, when they met with such opposition from the Senate or Municipal Chamber of the city, the *Santa Casa de Misericordia,* and the Franciscans, that but for a device to which they had recourse, they would probably have been compelled to abandon the project. It is related that on the night previous to the day on which they expected they would be legally restrained from building on the spot, they took possession of a small house situated between two bakeries, converted it into a temporary church, inscribing on the door the word "Jesus," by which the institution was to be thereafter named, and placed there, with the greatest secrecy, two Jesuit Fathers, and two lay brothers, provided with the vestments and sacred vessels necessary for celebrating mass. Early on the next morning the door of the house was thrown open and a bell rung, at the sound of which the neighbours were attracted to the place, where they were surprised to find a priest about to

* *Arch. Port. Or.*, Fasc. III., doc. 157; Pyrard, Pt. II., p. 32, explains in a different way the origin of the word *Terreiro dos Gallos.* He says: "L'appelent *Terreiro dos Gallos*—c'est à dire, le lieu des coqs, à cause de la volaille et l'autres vivres qu'on y vend."

say mass. The news of this incident spread rapidly through the whole city, and the Jesuits had the satisfaction of thus baffling their opponents, who could not dislodge them from the house.

The missionaries then proceeded, with their characteristic activity, to enlarge the building and make the requisite accommodation for their residence, which they fixed there on the 12th January of the following year.* Their adversaries, foiled in their opposition and unable to obtain redress from the Viceroy or the Archbishop, both of whom seemed inclined to favour the Jesuits, laid their complaints repeatedly before the King of Portugal, praying him to interpose on their behalf, and stop the further progress of the building which the Jesuits were rearing with speed and energy; but they were mortified to find that their supplications failed to move the august sovereign. In 1589 the edifice was well-nigh completed, at a cost of about £833-6-8, as appears from a royal letter.†

Some writers, observing the portrait of Dom Fr. Sebastião Pinto Pimenta, Knight of the Order of Christ, over one of the portals of this House of *Bom Jesus*, have been erroneously led to conjecture that it was founded by that Portuguese nobleman; but from a document‡ lately discovered among the records of the Secretariat at Goa, it appears that Pimenta was the founder of the College of the Jesuits in Chaul, and that his portrait, which had long graced the hall of that college, was removed to the House of *Bom Jesus* on the cession of that city to the Maráṭhás. The house had really no particular founder, but owed its origin mainly to the united efforts of the Jesuit Fathers at Goa. It was erected under the supervision of Domingos Fernandes, a lay brother and an architect of considerable merit, and of Julio Simão, who was at that time the Chief Engineer of Goa.§ This edifice, like almost every

* *Orient. Conq.*, vol. II., p. 222.
† *Arch. Port. Or.*, Fasc. III., doc. 25, 59, 64, 77.
‡ *Alvará de 10 de Março de 1648.*
§ *Orient. Conq.*, vol. II., p. 230; *Arch. Port. Or.*, Fasc. III., doc. 79.

building of the Jesuits, was vast and splendid, and excited the admiration of every spectator. The celebrated Orientalist Anquetil du Perron says, "I cannot help admiring the house of the Jesuits, a superb building, which would have been regarded in Europe as one of the most beautiful religious houses."*

A traveller who visited it in 1639 and dined there, describes in glowing terms its several halls and apartments adorned with valuable pictures, representing the most celebrated members of the Society of Jesus and their pious deeds. In speaking of the hospitality of the Jesuits, he says: "They brought us into their refectory, where the tables were placed all along the walls, as we had seen them in the professed house, and in so great a number that there was room enough for two hundred persons. Yet were there only four of the chief among them that dined with us, while all the rest stood and waited on us. We were as well treated by these as we had been by the others; but I must confess these gave us the best Canary that ever I drank. Of all the moral virtues, there is not any the Jesuits endeavour more to practise than sobriety, insomuch that drunkenness is a vice they can the least of any be charged withal, and yet at this time they often called on us to drink—I conceive, purposely to engage us, to make it appear that it was not out of pure compliment we commended their wine. After dinner they carried us up to the steeple, whence we could take a view of all the city, the sea, the river, and all the adjacent champion (champaign), as far as the mountain, much better than we could have done from the fourth story of the professed house."†

The building, as it stands at present, is but a part of the original edifice, some of its long corridors and spacious apartments having been destroyed not only "by the corroding tooth of Time," but also by the raging flames of a great fire which

---

* *Discours Préliminaire ou Introduction au Zend Avesta*, p. ccxiv.

† Mandelslo's *Travels*, p. 81. It must be remarked that the traveller confounds the Professed House with the New College of St. Paul.

consumed a great portion of it.* Even in its present state its aspect is majestic and imposing. It has three stories with an elegant façade, and is ascended by two excellent staircases, one of which is in front, and the other towards the vestry. The stories above the groundfloor contain each two saloons, eighteen cells and a parlour, besides spacious corridors and other accommodation for the comfort of its inmates. After the expulsion of the Jesuits in 1759 from Goa, this house was placed under the care of the Archbishop. The Marquis of Pombal, who was a relentless foe of the Society of Jesus, imagining that the house was larger than it really was, ordered, by his *alvará* of the 15th January 1774, that this vast and magnificent college, as he called the House of *Bom Jesus*, should be used as the Palace of the Archbishop, the Chapter Hall, the Ecclesiastical Court, and the residence of the canons and other ecclesiastical dignitaries.† But the Governor of Goa, convinced of the impracticability of this measure, kept the order in abeyance, and the house was occupied for some time afterwards by one of the seminaries established for the instruction of the clergy. When the seminary was abolished, the house was entrusted to the care of a canon, who, under the title of Administrator, still resides there.

Attached to the professed house, and parallel to the road running from Panelim to São Thiago, stands, on a spot 4⅓ feet high, the stately Church of *Bom Jesus*. This church was begun to be built on the 24th November 1594 out of the funds bequeathed for the purpose by Dom Jeronimo Mascarenhas, and was consecrated by the Archbishop, Dom Fr. Aleixo de Menezes, on the 15th May 1605. Pyrard, who saw it when it was almost completed, states that it was at first destined for administering the sacraments, and baptizing the pagans.

---

* According to Tavernier (Part II., p. 123) a great part of the house was burnt in 1663 by an accident at night, and was again rebuilt at the cost of 60,000 *écus;* it is said that subsequently the house suffered from a similar accident.

† *Instrucções, ut supra*, p. 2.

On a festive occasion he observed there 1,500 natives of either sex in a solemn procession, with palm-branches in their hands, ready to be baptized.* This church is a superb edifice, much admired for its architectural beauty. Albert de Mandelslo considers it one of the most stately buildings that were raised in Asia by the Jesuits, and says: "The structure is vast and magnificent, and the ornaments are so suitable to the greatness thereof, that it were not easy to imagine anything more noble."† This statement has been corroborated by several other travellers. Its façade, looking towards the west, is an elaborate piece of workmanship, and by its grandeur, no less than by the exquisite combination of the Doric, Corinthian, and Composite styles in its architecture, excites the admiration of the spectator. It is built of black granite, and is $78\frac{1}{2}$ feet high and $75\frac{3}{5}$ broad. The façade may be divided into four parts: the lowest containing three elegant portals; the part immediately above having three large windows corresponding to the portals; the third three circular windows; while the fourth forms a quadrangle richly embellished with arabesques. All these portions, adorned with pillars, rilievos, and rich carvings, give the façade a magnificent appearance.

The interior of the church, built in the Mosaico-Corinthian style, is remarkable for its charming simplicity. Its length is $182\frac{4}{5}$ feet, its breadth $55\frac{1}{2}$, and its height $61\frac{1}{5}$. On each side there are three rows of windows rising one over another, besides those of the choir, and corresponding circular ones. Those in the second row have attached to them a projecting gallery skilfully carved and richly gilt and painted, intended apparently for the accommodation of persons of rank on rare and solemn occasions. The walls are not now wholly gilt, as they appear

* Pyrard, Pt. II., p. 34. The traveller also states having seen in the same church a cross of massive gold, three feet long and four inches broad, which the Jesuit Fathers had caused to be made with a view to offer it to the Pope. It was beautifully wrought, and was studded with various kinds of precious stones; it was worth more than 100,000 *écus*.—*Ib.*, p. 33.

† Mandelslo's *Travels*, p. 80.

to have been in Pyrard's time, nor are they adorned with those admirable paintings *du plat fond* to which Tavernier alludes in his travels.* They are painted in white and greyish colours, and decorated with gilt lining. The pavement is matted; while the ceiling, repaired in 1863 at a cost of £2,500 and embellished with exquisite decorations, imparts additional beauty and elegance to the interior of the edifice. The body of the church is spacious, and has underneath the choir, on the left side, an altar on which is placed a glass case containing the relics of the martyr Saint Pauline arranged in the form of a human body, with a certificate of her canonization passed by the Prefect of the Sacred Relics in Rome and identified by the Archbishop of Goa on the 23rd October 1784. The pillars supporting the choir bear the two following inscriptions, in Latin and Portuguese, relating to the consecration of the church:—

"Hanc Ecclesiam Jesu solemni ritu consecravit Reverendissimus et Illustrissimus Dominus D. Aleixius Menesius, Archiepiscopus Goensis, Indiæ Primas. Anno Domini M.D.C.V. Id. Ma."

Translation.

"The Most Reverend and Illustrious Lord Dom Aleixo Menezes, Archbishop of Goa and Primate of the Indies, consecrated this Church of Jesus with solemn rites on 15th May 1605 A.D."

The inscription in Portuguese runs thus:—

"Esta Igreja de Jesus se começou a 24 de Novembro de 1594, e consagrou-a o Reverendissimo e Illustrissimo Senhor D. Fr. Aleixo de Meneses, Arcebispo de Goa, Primaz da India. Anno do Senhor 1605, 15 de Maio."

Translation.

"This Church of Jesus was begun to be built on the 24th November 1594, and the most Reverend and Illustrious Lord Dom Fr. Aleixo de Menezes, Archbishop of Goa and Primate

* Pyrard, *Voyage*, Pt. II., p. 33; Tavernier's *Voyages*, Pt. II., p. 123.

of India, consecrated it in the year of our Lord 1605, on the 15th May."

On the wall near to the side door on the north is the cenotaph of the founder of the church, the apex of which, made of bronze richly gilt, and supported by two figures of lions, is surmounted by the arms of the pious captain with a dragon, his exploits being represented on the cenotaph in basso-rilievo on four plates, and the following inscription engraved on a slab, also in relief:—

"Sepultura de Dom Hieronimo Mascarenhas, Capitão que foi de Cochim e Ormuz, e a cuja custa se fez esta Igreja; em gratificação a Companhia de Jesú lhe dedicou este logar. Faleceu no anno de 1593."

Translation.

"The grave of Dom Hieronimo Mascarenhas, late Captain of Cochim and Ormuz, at whose cost this Church was built; out of gratitude the Society of Jesus has dedicated this place to him. He died in 1593."

In the transept there are two altars and two chapels. The chapel on the northern extremity of the transept is dedicated to St. Francis Borgia, the patron saint of Portugal and its dependencies; while opposite to it, towards the south, lies the chapel now occupied by the splendid sarcophagus of St. Francis Xavier. The main altar, which is 54 feet high and 30½ broad, is dedicated to the Infant Jesus, from whom the church derives its appellation. The statue is, as the name imports, small, but by way of contrast there stands, in the centre of the altar, a colossal image of St. Ignatius of Loyola, the founder of the Society of Jesus, which, from its conspicuous position, attracts the attention of every visitor. The attitude of the saint is, as justly remarked by a traveller, full of dignity, and inspires awe mingled with veneration, the expression of his face wearing the appearance of an inspired person, and his right hand being uplifted like that of a general charging his soldiers to advance, but at the same time pointing towards heaven. It is said that this was exactly the attitude of the saint when in an ecstasy he exclaimed, "*Quam sordet mihi tellus quum cœlum aspicio!*" *i. e.* "How doth the earth disgust me when I lift my eyes to heaven!"

Remarkable as these chapels and altars are for the beauty of their decoration, yet, when compared with the sanctuary and the magnificent mausoleum which enshrines the remains of the Apostle of the Indies, they dwindle into insignificance. The chapel where the celebrated tomb lies, being frequently visited by innumerable pilgrims, is particularly interesting and demands special attention.

Chapel and Tomb of St. Francis Xavier.—A few years after the erection of the Church of *Bom Jesus*, the Jesuits of Goa, being informed of the canonization of the saint, determined to commemorate this event with great solemnity, and to remove his body to this church from St. Paul's, where it had been originally deposited after it was brought from Malacca. The translation of the body, which took place in 1624, was an occasion of great public rejoicing and brilliant festivities, which are vividly described by the celebrated traveller Pietro della Valle, who was at the time at Goa.* It was deposited at first in the Chapel of St. Francis Borgia, and in 1655 was transferred to the chapel where it now lies. This chapel stands, as already stated, at the southern extremity of the transept of the church. The space under its principal arch is filled up by a species of lattice-work, exquisitely wrought and richly gilt, which separates it from the transept. Under this arch on the side of the church is raised an altar, supporting a graceful silver image of the saint 4¾ feet high and weighing 100 lbs., the gift of a pious Genoese lady, relict of Urbano Durazo, who spent £300 on its execution. The head is crowned with a golden diadem (another present made

---

* *Viaggi di Pietro della Valle il Pellegrino*, vol. II., p. 763.

about the same time), which cost upwards of £100.* On the pedestal is the following inscription :—

"Sanctissimo Indiarum Apostolo
Francisca De Sopranis Patritia Genuensis,
Urbani Duratii olim uxor,
Nunc Maria Francisca Xavieria
In celeberrimo Incarnationis Monasterio
Christi Sponsa,
Peregrino Celesti
Peregrini Amoris votum et monumentum,
P. P.† Anno Domini 1670."

Translation.

"In honour of the most holy Apostle of the Indies,
Francisca De Sopranis, a Patrician lady of Genoa,
Formerly the wife of Urbano Durazo,
Now Maria Francisca Xavieria,
Spouse of Christ
In the most celebrated Convent of the Incarnation,
Caused (this image) to be placed
As an offering and token of a pilgrim's love
For the Heavenly Pilgrim,
A.D. 1670."

The image is seen with a staff in each hand, one of which, the pilgrim's staff, with which the saint is always represented, is made of silver, and the other of Indian cane. The latter is taken by the Governors of Goa previous to assuming charge of their office, as an emblem of authority, in exchange for the one they offer to the saint, to secure his protection over the Por-

* *Orient. Conq.*, Part. I., Conq. IV., Div. I., § 109. According to Mandelslo (*Travels*, p. 80) it appears that on the altar there was formerly a wooden image which was a faithful representation of the saint. He says, "The first thing we were shown was the high altar; but though it were one of the noblest I ever saw, yet came it not in wealth near another lesser one, which had been built in honour of Saint Francis Xavier, whom they call the Apostle of the Indies. We were shown his image which was upon wood drawn according to the life, and we were told his body was still to be seen in that church in the same posture as it was at the time of his departure."

† P. P. seem, as suggested to us by the Rev. Dr. J. Willy, S.J., to stand for "*ponere procuravit.*"

tuguese territories. The origin of this ceremony is attributed to a miracle by means of which, according to a popular tradition already alluded to, the saint is believed to have saved Goa from falling into the hands of the Maráṭhás. On the 24th November 1683 Sambáji invaded Goa with an overwhelming army, and made himself master of the island of Jua or Santo Estevão, which is separated from the old city by a very narrow tributary of the Mandovi. All hopes of a successful resistance having been given up, the then Viceroy, Count of Alvor, terrified at the impending evil, resolved, as a last resource, to invoke the protection of St. Francis. With this view he is said to have forthwith repaired, with some Jesuit Fathers of the professed house, to the chapel of the saint, where having remained for some time deeply absorbed in prayer, and having undergone voluntary flagellation by way of penance, he caused the coffin wherein the body of the saint is preserved, to be opened, and deposited in it his staff, the letters patent relating to his nomination to the post of Viceroy, and a petition written by himself, in which, in the name of the king, he implored the saint to defend and save Goa, as well as to accept its government. Scarcely had this invocation been finished when, it is stated, a powerful army of the Moghuls was seen descending the Gháṭs, at the sight of which the Maráṭhás patched up a peace and retired, to the great exultation of the Portuguese.

The entrance to the passage leading to the Chapel of St. Francis Xavier is by the door which lies to the right of the altar on which his silver image stands, and not by the railings which cover the arch, and which are not opened save on the day on which the feast of the saint is celebrated. This chapel is entered by three doors, looking to the east, west, and south respectively. Over the last door is hung a beautiful picture, $5\frac{7}{10}$ feet by $4\frac{1}{3}$, which is said to be a faithful likeness of the saint.* The face is serene and noble, and the com-

* The description of the picture of the saint, as well as of his tomb and chapel, is chiefly derived from the *Jornal da Santa Igreja Luzitana do Oriente de* 1846, No. 6.

plexion ruddy, such as the Apostle is believed to have had when he first came out to India. He appears in the black habit of his order, a grey cloak and a staff, with his eyes raised to heaven, his right hand on his breast, and his left pointing to his heart burning with divine love. Below the picture is seen, in golden letters in relief, the following distich :—

"Dimidium cernis, quem magnum suspicit orbis :
Xavier est : totum nulla tabella capit."

Translation.

"The half of him you see whom the world admires as great,
Xavier he is : the whole no tablet holds."

The interior of the chapel is richly gilt and embellished with twenty-seven choice pictures representing the life and miracles of the Apostle. Eight of these on the left side of the shrine belong to the Italian school, and are arranged in three rows. In the first row there are two pictures, one of which represents the Hospital of the Invalids in Venice, and Xavier kissing the loathsome ulcer of a patient; the other, his interview at Figem with Duarte da Gama and other Portuguese gentlemen receiving him with deep respect and veneration. The second row presents three pictures. In the first Xavier is seen with a surplice and a stole praying, apparently for the cessation of a terrible plague which had then broken out in the island of Manar; the second illustrates his visit to the king of Bungo, in Japan; and the third shows Pope Paul III. pronouncing his apostolic benediction on the eve of his departure to India for the purpose of preaching the Gospel to the heathen nations. Of the remaining three, in the last row, those on the two extremes exhibit Xavier first as a servant of certain Japanese knights, and secondly as standing in a fit of ecstasy, while the middle one represents his glorious death at Sanchan. There were also at one time in this chapel twelve large silver lamps, which were kept burning day and night. Of these only four remain, weighing 152½ lbs., the rest having been seized, along with other articles of gold, by the Government in 1840, and converted into coin. The magnificent sarcophagus which lies in this chapel was, according to the author of the *Oriente Conquistado,* a gift of the Grand Duke of Tuscany in return for the pillow on which the head of the saint reposed for many years after his death, and which was presented to him by Father Francisco Sarmento, Provincial General of the Jesuits.* Originally it appears to have been of far greater dimensions than it now is; but, owing to the chapel being too narrow and ill suited for a monument so sumptuous, it was somewhat reduced in size. Nevertheless this superb shrine is universally admired as a masterpiece of art, and it is said that, with the exception of the far-famed Táj Mahál erected at Agra by the emperor Sháh Jahán, there is no other mausoleum in India, or even in Asia, which can equal it in grandeur and magnificence. One of the latest travellers, who visited Goa some years ago, says: "I hastened to the shrine of the celebrated Francis Xavier, of which I had heard much. It surpassed all my expectations, and certainly excels anything of this kind which I had before seen."† The tomb is generally believed to have been placed in the chapel in 1655, but the following extract from the travels of Gemelli Careri shows that it had not reached Goa before 1695:—" Thursday the 7th April (1695) I went to visit the body of St. Francis Xaverius at the Church of *Bom Jesus*, or Good Jesus, being the professed house of the Jesuits........... It (the church) has an high altar, with two on the sides, all well gilt, and on the left a chapel where the precious body of St. Francis lies. It was in a crystal coffin within another of silver, on a pedestal of stone; but they expected a noble tomb of porphyry stone from Florence, ordered to be made by the Grand Duke."‡ But Dr. Fryer, who had visited Goa twenty years before, speaks of the tomb and its venerable and precious con-

---

* *Orient. Conq.*, Conq. IV., Div. I., § 109.

† Dr. J. Wilson in the *Oriental Christian Spectator,* vol. V., First Series, p. 121.

‡ Churchill's *Voyages,* vol. IV., p. 250.

TOMB OF St. FRANCIS XAVIER

tents in the following manner:—" We paid a visit to the *Domo of Bom Jesu*, the church an admirable piece, the repository of St. Xaverius, the Indian Apostle, where is a famous tomb in honour of him who first spread the Gospel as far as China, and sealed it with his martyrdom, near two hundred years ago, leaving his body a miraculous relic of his better part, it still retaining its vivid colour and freshness, and therefore exposed once a year to public view, on the vespers of his festival."* This English traveller probably refers to the "crystal and silver coffin on a pedestal of stone" spoken of by Gemelli: for it is evident that the latter, who is considered as one of the most trustworthy travellers, and who saw and kissed the body of the saint, could not have erred about a point so important. This conjecture is further strengthened by a short description of the supposed tomb given by Dr. Fryer on the occasion of the feast of St. Francis, in a different part of his work. He says: " We left Goa on the eve of St. Xaverius' feast; the tomb therefore was richly set out; and as Erasmus relates of Thomas à Becket that nothing could be seen baser than gold, so truly here silver was the meanest; pearls and precious stones, as well as gold, cast forth their lustre by the reflection of the virgin flambeaux upon them"—a description which evidently refers to the coffin, as will be seen below.†

The first sight of this tomb from the entrance of the chapel strikes the spectator with admiration. It is constructed of rich marble of variegated colours, and consists of three steps or stages besides the silver coffin.

The first or lowest stage is of jasper. Its bottom is of reddish and purple colours marked with white stripes, and the borders are of white stone with yellow stripes. The flourishes, festoons, arabesques and various other rilievos with which it is embellished, together with the figures of eight large cherubs at the four angles and on the sides, and of four small cherubs on the

---

* *A New Account*, &c., p. 150.

† *Op. cit.*, p. 183.

edges, as also the four edges themselves, are of the finest Carrara alabaster. This stage is $4\frac{1}{3}$ feet high, $19\frac{1}{10}$ long, and $9\frac{2}{3}$ broad, and resembles an urn.

The second stage, $5\frac{2}{3}$ feet high, $11\frac{1}{2}$ long, and $5\frac{1}{3}$ wide, is a regular quadrangle. It is also made of the finest jasper stone; its base is of greenish colour variegated with white, black and ash-coloured spots; its borders and friezes and the frames of its plates are of yellow jasper striped with white and black, and of a polish equalling the transparency of glass. In the centre of each of its four sides is seen a rich bronze plate with a beautifully wrought edge on either side, which is of black jasper marked with white spots and decked with small bouquets of lilies inlaid thereon. Each of these plates is painted black, and represents various incidents in the life of the saint. Each has over it an emblematic figure of blue polished stone, which is supported on either side by an angel of the size of a child of four to five years of age delicately wrought out of the whitest alabaster, and holding a motto. There is also a corresponding emblematic figure below each plate. The plate on the west side of the tomb represents the saint barefooted in the habit of a Jesuit with a surplice, a stole, and a crucifix in his left hand, baptizing with his right a large crowd of the savages of the Moluccas, variously clad, the men with a girdle of feathers or a piece of linen round their loins, and the women in a garb almost European, the children being naked; on one side is seen also a catechist. The emblematic figure over it exhibits the sun in the meridian, and bears the motto "*Ut vitam habeant,*" "That they may have life." There is another below it which shows a book with several crosses falling from above. The plate on the north side of the shrine represents the glorious apostle preaching to the savages of the Moluccas, all clad in the same manner as in the plate already described, save one man, who stands aloof from the others, dressed in a sort of tunic reaching as far as the knees, with slippers on his feet, a sword or scimitar hanging from his belt, and a club in his hand. It is surmounted by an emblematic figure representing the rising sun, with the motto "*Nox inimica fugata,*" "Hostile night is put to flight." Corresponding to this figure there is another below the plate representing the sun with luminous circles. The plate on the south side represents St. Francis crossing precipitately a river on a rafter to escape from the fury of the savage islanders of Moro, who pursue him with arrows and stones. The emblematic figure over it bears the picture of a lion overtaken by a furious tempest, and the motto "*Nihil horum vereor,*" "I fear none of these things." The lower one shows a heart emitting flames. The plate on the east refers to the death of the saint at Sanchan. He is represented as lying down in agony on a mat in a wretched hut between two of his disciples, Antonio and Christovão, and surrounded by angels. He is barefooted and dressed in his usual habit, embracing firmly a crucifix, his hat and staff lying on one side, and a water-pitcher near his feet. The emblematic figure over it shows the setting sun, with the following motto:—"*Major in occasu,*" "Greater in setting," while the lower one displays the sky overcast with clouds, and thunderbolts shooting through the air and overthrowing a mosque crowned with a crescent.

The third and the highest stage is exquisitely wrought. It is $9\frac{2}{3}$ feet long, $3\frac{2}{3}$ broad, and $2\frac{1}{3}$ high. It is surrounded by a beautiful railing of red jasper marked with white spots. This railing is adorned with pretty figures of angels; its middle portion is graced with columns elegantly carved and standing at equal intervals. The intervening spaces are surmounted with arches, and have several incidents in the life of the saint represented on them. The friezes of its four lateral columns are of black stone with white stripes, while the plinths are of yellow jasper. On the top of this stage lies the far-famed coffin, overlaid with silver, in which the remains of the saint are deposited.

This coffin appears to have existed in the times of Drs. Fryer and Gemelli Careri, as seen from the extracts already cited, and could not therefore have accompanied the mausoleum presented by the Grand Duke of Tuscany. It measures $6\frac{4}{5}$ feet in length, $2\frac{9}{10}$ in breadth, and $3\frac{3}{10}$ in height exclusive of the lid, which bulges out in a curvature of $1\frac{1}{2}$ feet on each side. It is crowned by a beautiful cross which is $2\frac{1}{2}$ feet high. The cross stands on a pedestal graced with the figures of two angels on either side, the one near the head of the saint holding a heart surrounded with a halo, and the other near the feet bearing the motto "*Satis est, Domine, satis est!*" "It is enough, O Lord, it is enough!"—words which the saint used to utter when he felt his heart overpowered with love to God. The silver envelopment of the coffin, so skilfully wrought, is attached to a velvet lining and adorned with brilliant stones of divers colours. The coffin is on each side divided into seven panels, each of which has two plates one over the other, so that there are fourteen on each side, besides two at each extremity, representing in rilievo some important incidents in the life of the saint. Each space between the panels is surmounted by the figure of an angel twelve inches high, with an appropriate emblem in its hand. There are besides, in several parts of the coffin, cones of different sizes, which are embellished with gilt flowers and studded with brilliant stones. There were also formerly a variety of rich ornaments, which were appropriated by the Government. This coffin weighed 600 silver *marcos* (300 lbs.), which, at the rate of £1-13-4 per *marco*, amounted in value to £1,000. The present value of the coffin is £788-8-9, but its delicate workmanship is inestimable. The chief excellence of this workmanship lies in the thirty-two plates mentioned above, which we shall endeavour to describe in their order, commencing with those near the head of the saint.

The first plate represents Xavier bound hand and foot with strong cords which are miraculously cut asunder. In the second we find him kissing a loathsome ulcer in an hospital of Venice. In the third, whilst sick in the hospital of Vicentia, he is visited by St. Jerome, to whom he had a special devotion. In the fourth, in an hospital at Rome he foresees in a vision all his missionary labours. In the fifth, his sister, who was an abbess, has a vision of his future career. In the sixth, he saves the Secretary and a domestic of the ambassador Dom Pedro Mascarenhas. In the seventh, he raises a sick man from his bed. In the eighth, he baptizes a great multitude of idolaters. In the ninth, at Cape Comorin he restores to life a boy drowned in a well. In the tenth, he suddenly cures a sick man. In the eleventh, he frightens and puts to flight the Badejas in Travancore. In the twelfth, he restores to life two boys in two different places. In the thirteenth is shown the miracle of the coins at Meliapur. In the fourteenth, he effects two miraculous cures in Malacca. In the fifteenth is seen a crab restoring his crucifix, which had dropped into the sea. In the sixteenth, he preaches to a great throng of people. In the seventeenth, whilst preaching in the cathedral of Malacca on the 4th December 1547, he announces the victory of the Portuguese against the king of Acheen. In the eighteenth, he reclaims in Khárepaṭan a Portuguese who had accompanied him from Goa. In the nineteenth, he assists a sick man in his dying moments, and puts to flight the devils that had got hold of him. In the twentieth, the saint, in a kneeling attitude, has on his shoulders an infant, perhaps the one he is said to have cured of a swelling. In the twenty-first, bearing his luggage on his shoulder, he travels on foot from Amanguchi to Meaco. In the twenty-second, he restores speech to a dumb man and cures him of palsy at Amanguchi. In the twenty-third, he cures a deaf Japanese. In the twenty-fourth, Xavier is praying during a storm in the ship of Duarte da Gama. In the twenty-fifth, he baptizes three princes of the Maldives. In the twenty-sixth, he cures, on his return from Japan, a friar who was on the point of death in the College of St. Paul. In the twenty-seventh, he sweetens a quantity of sea-water on his voyage from Malacca to China. In the twenty-eighth is seen the apostle in his last moments at Sanchan. In the twenty-ninth, he appears after his death to Catherina de Chaves, as he had promised when parting from her. In the thirtieth, the body of the saint in sacerdotal vestments is exposed to public veneration and works miracles. In the thirty-first, he is seen elevated about two feet above the level of the altar. In the thirty-second, the saint is represented as standing in a niche at Chaul surrounded by lighted tapers.

The inside of the coffin is covered with yellow damask studded with 124 precious stones cut in the shape of stars. From its top hang in two rows by golden chains six tassels of ambergris, one of which is now missing. Several valuable ornaments formerly adorning the coffin, besides being removed to the Mint, as stated before, have been sacrilegiously abstracted. Thus, in the place of a silver railing was substituted another of lead, and instead of 473 precious gems we have as many false stones.* The coffin is $5\frac{1}{10}$ feet in length, and $1\frac{5}{8}$ in breadth, and is opened with three keys.† It is lined with the richest tissue interwoven with flowers of various colours, which have not lost their original freshness. The body of the saint is still, after the lapse of upwards of three centuries, in a well-preserved state.‡ But it is somewhat shrunken, being only $4\frac{1}{2}$ feet in length. In an official report made by the chief surgeons and physicians of Goa, who were commissioned to examine the body on the occasion of its last exposition in 1859, they say "the cranium on the right side is covered with scalp still bearing hair, though scanty, and on the left side completely denuded of it. The whole of the face is covered with a dark dry integument, with an opening on the right side communicating with the maxillary fossa, and apparently corresponding to the place of the contusion referred to in the report drawn up on the 1st of January 1782. Of the front teeth only one of the lower incisors is wanting.

* *Boletim do Governo do Estado da India*, No. 78 of 1860.

† These three keys had been lost, and could not be found on the occasion of the last exposition of the body of the saint in 1859. New ones were therefore made and given respectively in charge of the Governor, the Archbishop, and the Chief Secretary to Government. None of them was ever sent to Portugal, as is generally believed.

‡ Our drawing represents the body of the saint as it is at present.

S FRANCIS XAVIER

A P Cortes & Co Litho. Bombay

Both the ears exist, but the right arm is wanting.* The left hand, including the nails, is entire, just as it is described in the abovementioned report of 1782. The abdominal walls are covered with an integument dried up and somewhat dark in colour, the abdominal cavity not containing any intestines.† The feet are covered with an integument equally dried up and dark in colour, the prominence of the tendons being distinctly marked. The fourth and fifth toes of the right foot are wanting.‡ Some remnants of the integument and phalanges of one of these toes are in a very spongy condition."§

The venerable body of the saint is clad in the richest vestments, elegantly embroidered and studded with large and valuable pearls, the gift of Dona Maria Sophia, wife of Dom Pedro II., King of Portugal, made about the year 1693.‖ The head is uncovered; his *barrete*, of which mention is made by the author of the *Oriente Conquistado*,¶ was sent to the abovementioned queen, who, to secure the intercession of the saint, placed it on her head at the time of her confinement.**

* The right arm of the saint was cut off by order of the Pope on 3rd November 1614, and divided into four parts, the greater of which was sent to Rome.

† According to Lucena (*Historia da Vida do Padre São Francisco Xavier*, vol. IV., p. 401) and Vieira (*Sermão, Xavier Acordado*) the intestines of the saint were found in their natural state two months and a half after his death. See also *Peregrinação de Fernaõ Mendes Pinto*, Lisboa, 1829, tom. III., p. 292. Dr. Cosme Saraiva, chief physician to the Viceroy, who examined the body of the saint in 1556, about four years after his death, certifies also that he found the intestines still in the abdomen, and that through a hole in it fresh blood could be taken out.

‡ One of these toes was bitten off when being kissed, in 1554, by a Portuguese lady called Dona Isabel de Carom, who was anxious to possess a relic of the saint.

§ *Boletim do Governo do Estado da India*, No. 80 of 1859, p. 528.

‖ See the *Carta Dedicatoria* of P. Balthazar Duarte in vol. VIII. of Padre Antonio Vieira's *Sermons*. Of the vestments the chasuble bears the arms of the Queen embroidered over with the following inscription:—"*Suo S. Xaverio Maria Sophia Regina Portugalis.*"

¶ *Orient. Conq.*, Conq. IV., Div. I., p. 108.

** Vieira, *loc. cit.*

On his right side lies a staff studded with 194 emeralds, and towards his feet hangs a gold medallion bearing on the obverse the arms of Portugal with the following inscription :—"D. Francisco Xav. Indiarum Apost. et in Orient. Defensore recens assump. duc. An. D. M.M.D. CXCIX.," and on the reverse the effigy of Dom Pedro II. with the words "Petrus, Rex Portugalis."

The body of the saint was formerly very frequently exposed for public veneration by the Jesuits, who had charge of it. According to the above extract from Dr. Fryer, it appears that in his time (1675) the body used to be exposed once a year, and that it retained its original freshness. This exposition generally took place on the day of the festival of the saint, which was solemnized with great pomp and *éclat*. He says: "From the tops of the towers belonging to the Jesuits we beheld lamps at night striving to vie with the stars for number and lustre, which appeared gloriously on the water as we rowed down the river to our ship."* Twenty years later, when Gemelli Careri visited Goa, he found, from inquiries made, that for nine years the people had not enjoyed the benefit of the annual view of the body, as will be seen from the following extract:—"Since with the Pope's leave the saint's arm was cut off, the rest of the body has decayed, as if he had resented the loss, and therefore the Jesuits for nine years past do not show it to any but the Viceroy and some other persons of quality. Being told as much at my first coming to Goa, I so far prevailed as to have the Viceroy use his power with the Provincial; and he, not knowing how to refuse him, would at least defer the favour till that morning, showing me the holy body, with the church shut, clothed in his habit, which is changed every year."† The conjecture of the traveller does not appear to us to be

---

* *A New Account*, p. 150. In 1632 the Government ordered that every year on the vespers of the feast of St. Francis the city should be illuminated. *Livro das Monçoens*, MSS., No. 47, f. 127.

† Churchill's *Voyages*, vol. IV., p. 250.

quite correct. It is true that about the time of his visit the body was less frequently exposed than before, but this was not because the body had begun to decay, as he puts it, ever since the arm was cut off. If, however, this had been the case, the precautionary measure would have been taken long before, and the body would not have been so often exposed. As it was, it appears that, some time before Gemelli's visit, the practice of publicly exhibiting the body was stopped, on account of the eagerness of the populace to possess themselves of some relics of the saint, which could not fail to injure the body. A few persons of high rank alone were privately allowed to see it. But even this privilege was afterwards withdrawn by the royal letter of the 2nd April 1755, probably because they too, in their indiscreet devotion, had caused some damage to the body, and since then the body is not shown without express orders from the Government of Portugal. Accordingly, within the last hundred years the body has been only twice exposed to the public—in 1782 and again in 1859. Of the first occasion very little is known; but of the second a full account, even to the minutest details, can be gathered both from public and private sources.* The ceremony commenced with great solemnity and pomp on the 3rd December, the day on which the Catholic Church celebrates the feast of the saint. On that and the following days there was so large a concourse of people desirous of kissing the feet of the great apostle that it was found necessary to keep the church open day and night. The crowd of devotees from different parts of the country increased every day, and the authorities were obliged to prolong the period of exposition for a week more. And yet numbers went away disappointed, without having either kissed his feet or caught sight of the saint. It is computed that nearly 200,000 persons of various races and creeds from several parts of India approached the shrine to honour the Apostle of the Indies. Indeed, as observed in the report published in the

---

* See *Resumo Historico da Maravilhosa Vida de São Francisco Xavier*, por F. N. Xavier, Parte II., Nova-Goa, 1861.

*Boletim do Governo,** the ancient city of Goa appeared at this time to have risen from its ruins full of life and glory, such as it displayed in the days of its prosperity, when it was the chief emporium of trade in the East. Thousands of portraits in miniature of the saint were daily sold with incredible rapidity. The offerings in money to the shrine of the saint amounted to nearly £1,000. A few Hindus, hearing of the miracles wrought, are said to have embraced Christianity, and many Christians who were suffering from incurable diseases to have been restored to health. The miraculous cures reported to have been effected through his intercession created such a sensation in the country that a committee was appointed, composed especially of several skilful physicians, to inquire into the matter. They unanimously pronounced these cures supernatural. The exposition was closed on the 8th of January, amidst the deafening roar of guns from all the fortresses, and the ringing of bells in all the churches of Goa. On the whole, the spectacle presented by the Church of *Bom Jesus* on this occasion was the grandest and the most affecting of all that had been witnessed there in the present century.†

Before leaving this church let us cast a cursory glance at its magnificent vestry, situated near the Chapel of St. Francis. In stateliness and beauty it stands unrivalled in Asia, while its dimensions are those of an ordinary church. The entrance door is elegantly carved with figures of saints and other ornaments in bas-relief. It has a vaulted roof adorned with fine stucco-work. The walls are decorated with elegant pictures, amongst which the one overhanging the door is from the pencil of Murillo, and represents Magdalene inflamed with divine love, which is beautifully expressed by the following text from Scripture :—

"Fulcite me floribus, stipate me malis,
Quia amore langueo."

---

* *Boletim do Governo do Estado da India de* 1860, No. 4, p. 20.

† The body of the saint has once more been exposed since the 3rd December of the present year, with great pomp and solemnity. The exposition will continue till the 6th January.

"Stay me up with flowers, compass me about with apples,
Because I languish with love."

Standing against the walls there are on either side three large chests of drawers elegantly carved, with gilt labels indicating their contents. The vestry communicates with its chapel by means of an arch which is gilt and painted in fresco. On each side of this arch there stand inserted in the walls two chests carved and gilt in the same fashion as those mentioned here. Under the arch is seen the grave of the pious founder of the vestry, with the following inscription:—

"Sepultura de Balthazar de Veiga, á cuja custa se fez esta sachristia; a Companhia de Jesus, em gratificação desta boa obra, e de outras que fez a esta caza, lhe dedicou este logar para seu jazigo. Faleceu a 14 de Janeiro de 1659."

Translation.

"The grave of Balthazar de Veiga, at whose expense this vestry was built. The Society of Jesus, out of gratitude for this and other benefits done to this house, has set apart this site for his resting-place. He died on the 14th January 1659."

CHAPTER XV.

THE HOLY HILL—CHURCH OF NOSSA SENHORA DO ROZARIO—CHAPEL OF ST. ANTHONY—CONVENT AND CHURCH OF SANTA MONICA—CONVENT AND CHURCH OF ST. AUGUSTINE—CONVENT AND CHURCH OF ST. JOHN OF GOD—NEW COLLEGE OF ST. PAUL, OR ST. ROCH.

Holy Hill.—A few paces towards the west from the Church of *Bom Jesus* rises the Mount of Rosary, which is called the Holy Hill, on account of a group of religious buildings which were once erected there, and some of which still exist. This hill, as stated by the author of the *Oriente Conquistado,** was uninhabited till 1526, when it was purchased by Pedro de Faria, ex-Captain of Malacca, who fixed his own residence there, assigning the remainder of the hill for the erection of private buildings and of two churches. These churches were dedicated to *Nossa Senhora do Rozario* (Our Lady of the Rosary) and St. Anthony respectively, in accordance with a vow which Affonso de Albuquerque had made, when he was stationed on the hill with a portion of his army before his entry into the city on the occasion of its final conquest.† The vow of the conqueror does not seem to have been fulfilled till after his death.

Church of Nossa Senhora do Rozario.—The Church of *Nossa Senhora do Rozario* (Our Lady of the Rosary), or Santa Maria do Rozario, as it is called by Gaspar Correia, stands on the western part of this hill. It was raised to the rank of a parochial church in 1543, as already stated,‡ along with that of *Nossa Senhora da Luz,* and was entrusted to the

* *Oriente Conq.*, vol. II., p. 154.

† *Lendas, ut supra,* vol. II., p. 151.

‡ *Op. cit.*, vol. IV., p. 289.

care of the Dominicans. It was held in great veneration by the public, and it was there that St. Francis Xavier used to teach catechism every evening to an immense crowd of persons, who flocked together at the sound of a little bell he rang. Soon after, it was made a collegiate church, having four beneficed clergymen, receiving in 1565 from the public treasury £14-1-6$\frac{3}{8}$, distributed in the same way as the amount sanctioned for the Church of *Nossa Senhora da Luz.*

The feast of the Rosary was celebrated with great pomp and a grand procession. Pietro della Valle, who was present at it on one occasion, describes it in the following manner :—" On the evening of the 30th September the Dominican Fathers, with the members of the Society of the Rosary, made a solemn procession in Goa with many chariots and statues dressed up and jewelled, according to their fashion. All the streets through which the procession passed were decorated with evergreens, and the windows with tapestry. The whole population of the city flocked together to see this spectacle, which takes place every year on the feast of the Rosary, on the 1st Sunday of October. There is one procession on the evening previous to the feast, after the vespers; and on the morning of the feast another, on a lesser scale, halting at the door of the church, but in other respects accompanied with all the ceremonial, and also with the Blessed Sacrament."* This parish, one of the most populous in the city, had not more than 196 parishioners in 1720, which number was in 1775 further reduced to 182, dwindling finally in 1827 to 6. By this time the church had ceased to be a collegiate church, though it still retained this title. Its vicar, who was called Prior, received in 1827 an annuity of £10, but did not reside in the church, which always remained closed, except at mass.† It ceased in 1869 to be a parochial church, being reduced to the rank of a chapel affiliated to the Cathedral. The building, which now appears old, is not very large. It has five altars, the

* *Viaggi di Pietro della Valle il Pellegrino*, vol. II., p. 786.

† Cottineau's *Historical Sketch*, p. 107.

chief of which bears the image of *Nossa Senhora do Rozario*. Among others there is the grave of the king of Tanor, who had embraced Christianity. At present it is opened only on Wednesdays, when a priest of the cathedral comes to say mass. The annual feast is solemnized on the first Sunday of October, the chapter being in attendance.

Royal Chapel of St. Anthony.—The Church or rather the Chapel of St. Anthony, which lies to the south of the Church of Nossa Senhora do Rozario, was built at the same time as the latter, and was called the Royal Chapel. The Portuguese held this chapel in great veneration, as it was dedicated to their national saint. St. Anthony was regarded as the captain of the army, and as such his salary was drawn by the chaplain in addition to his pay, which amounted to nearly £9. Besides this, the public treasury contributed some necessary articles for the use of the chapel. Pope Alexander VIII. granted a plenary indulgence to those who visited it on the feast-day of the saint. It was administered by the Chapter of the Cathedral, but in 1606 the management passed, by orders of the Archbishop, Dom Fr. Aleixo de Menezes, into the hands of the Augustinian Friars. Soon after the suppression of the religious orders it was closed and abandoned. The building, however, still exists, and is in charge of the superintendent of the Convent of St. Francis. It is small, and has its façade turned towards the east.

Convent and Church of Santa Monica.—Contiguous to the Chapel of St. Anthony, to the north, is the great Convent and Church of Santa Monica, in which the nuns lived. The foundation of a convent for nuns in Goa had long been desired, but was not sanctioned by the sovereign till 1598.* The Archbishop, Dom Fr. Aleixo de Menezes, by whom many other important institutions were established, took upon himself to erect this, and the foundation was laid by him on July 2nd, 1606, but the building was not completed

* *Arch. Port. Or.*, Fasc. III., Nos. 140, 163, 243, 246, 254, 365.

till 1627, and it cost nearly £20,000. The convent began to be occupied when only a portion of it was built, and in the very year of its foundation (1606) twenty-one ladies from the Retreat of *Nossa Senhora de Serra* joined it in a body. The most distinguished of them were Dona Felippa Ferreira and her daughter Dona Maria de Sá, of Tanna, who, on taking the vow, were known as Soror Felippa de Trindade and Soror Maria do Espirito Santo. The convent was large enough to accommodate a hundred nuns. The rules compiled by the Archbishop, on the model of those of St. Augustine, for the régime of the convent, were approved by Pope Paul V. in his brief *Ut ea quœ pro religiosarum personarum* of the 27th November 1613, and received the sanction of the King, who, by the *alvará* of the 26th March 1636, accepted its patronage, whereupon the convent was called the *Royal Convent of Santa Monica.* Fr. Agostinho de Santa Monica, in his *Historia da Fundação do Real Convento de Santa Monica da Cidade de Goa,* published in Lisbon in 1699, describes the origin, administration, and the internal arrangement of this religious institution. This vast building was provided with everything necessary for the comfort and convenience of its inmates. All the apartments were fitted up for distinct purposes, and known by distinct names. The groundflocr has a gate, *Portaria de fora,* from which visitors are allowed to hold communication with the inmates. This gate opens into the apartments called *Aposentos de Porteira* and *Locutorio de fora.* To these follow *Portaria de clausura* and *Casa de Rodo,* where a nun remained in charge of the keys, in consequence of which she was called *Rodeira.* The door between these two apartments is called *Porta de prohibição,* signifying that it is strictly forbidden to any one to enter through it. Any visitor having anything to say to a nun could only do so in the presence of the doorkeeper.

This floor has an open space in the centre, which is the principal courtyard, called "*valle dos lirios,*" "the valley of lilies." The passages leading to it have each a separate name. In the cloisters on the eastern side of this floor there is an infirmary with a chapel of the *Assumpção da Mãe de Deus,* a seminary, and various other apartments. On the north side there is the Chapel of St. Augustine, denominated the Chapel of Our Father, with cells and dormitories, many of which are called after the name of the saint, whose rules were followed by the nuns of Santa Monica. On the southern side lies the church, and the corresponding cloister, called the Cloister of the Church, and, among other rooms, there are the *confessionario* and *Casa do commungatorio,* where the nuns used to confess and receive communion. Towards the west is seen the Chapel of the Divine Saviour, and nearly all the cells, dormitories and other apartments contiguous to it bear his name.

The apartments on the second floor have also special names. The southern wing of this floor, which looks towards the church, is called *Crasta do Monte Calvario,* where the sufferings and death of Christ used to be represented. This exhibition is made even at present, on the first Friday of Lent, and the inmates pass in procession through the interior of the convent. There are also four different vestries bearing different names; an altar; an organ, etc. The cloister on the east side, with its dormitories, cells, etc., is called *Claustro de Belem,* &c.; there is also a dining-hall, with some other apartments. On the west side there is a chapel dedicated to the Mother of God, with a dormitory, cells and other rooms bearing her name. A corridor on this side leads to a chamber called *Deposito,* where all papers relating to the property of the convent were kept. It has a grated aperture in one of its walls, through which rents were received, and sometimes, contrary to the rules of the convent, communication was held with visitors. The third floor has apartments similar to those on the second. The dormitory bears the name of St. Clare, and its cells are denominated *Cella de Ostia Tiberina* and *Cella do Valle dos Lirios.* There are four other small cells, called *Casas de penitencia* (or 'places for penance'), where refractory nuns were confined. There is also the *Noviciado,* an apartment where novices were trained.

This convent, as stated by the Viceroy, the Count of Linhares, in his letter of the 4th January 1630, was larger even than any of those in Portugal with the exception of that of Odivellas.* Some of the apartments are now in ruin. Within the enclosure of the convent the grounds are laid out in walks and parterres, called by different names.

This was the only convent in Goa which was open to nuns, not only of European, but also of Eurasian and native extraction. Like friars, they took the three vows of poverty, chastity, and obedience, put on a white habit, and were under the guidance of a Prioress, chosen from among themselves every third year. They had their novitiate, and as soon as they took the vows, renounced the world, and were for ever forbidden to step beyond the threshold of the building. No male is allowed access to the convent, save a physician in cases of sickness, or a priest to administer extreme unction, and the Archbishop, who, accompanied by two or three priests, annually visits it as superior. Even women are not easily admitted, except as servants, the number of whom was formerly very large, and who had assigned to them two dormitories, one called *Dormitorio das Africanas* for negro servants, and the other called *Dormitorio de S. Thomé* for Indian servants. Besides, there were lay-sisters having a distinct dormitory for themselves, called *Dormitorio de S. Guilherme.*

After the foundation of the convent, many ladies sought admissicn into it with great zeal and enthusiasm. Their number increased day by day, and the convent, too, rose in public estimation. People loved to speak with interest and admiration of the godly life led by the nuns, and an event soon occurred which confirmed the public opinion. This occurrence is not merely popularly believed, but is also found narrated in the official records of the Secretariat of the Government of Goa.† Sister Mary of Jesus, daughter of a German nobleman, who before assuming the veil had been known as Dona Maria de Crom, widow of

* *Liv. das Monç.* (MSS.), No. 13, fol. 18.
† *Ibid.*, No. 47, fol. 291.

Dom Manoel de Souza, died in the convent on the 2nd January 1683, at the advanced age of seventy-eight years. It was discovered that she had marks of wounds on her hands and feet resembling those of Christ. The Prioress having communicated this fact to the Chapter, which then acted for the Archbishop, an inquiry was ordered to be made into the matter by a committee of three of its canons, who examined the wounds and caused them to be washed with vinegar and salt, but finding no change came to the conclusion that they were supernatural; she was buried, but the Ecclesiastical Provisor, seeing that the case called for further investigation, ordered, with the sanction of the Chapter, the grave to be reopened on the next day, and the dead body to be examined by the chief physician, Dr. S. de Azavedo, and other surgeons, as well as the superiors of the religious orders of the city. The wounds were subjected to a fresh examination and trial, but remained unaltered. Moreover, on the breast of the lady they noticed the mark of a wound such as might be inflicted with a spear, which having been washed appeared fresher than before. This committee, deeming the case an extraordinary one, reported it to the Viceroy, the Count of Alvor, who on the same day convened in the monastery, besides the physicians and surgeons of the place, the Chapter, the Ecclesiastical Court, the members of the Inquisition, the chief civil authorities, and many noblemen, and caused a further inquiry to be made in his own presence. The result was that they too were convinced that the wounds were of a supernatural character. The Viceroy then gave orders to bury on the following day the body, which is said to have been as fresh, soft and flexible as that of a living person, with great pomp and solemnity. On that day the convent was besieged by a large multitude striving to obtain permission to see the body of the supposed saint. It being impossible to resist their solicitations, the body was taken out and carried through the streets near the convent, the wounds it bore being exposed to public view. The streets were lined on both sides with soldiers, and the procession slowly passed along, the Inquisitors and the superiors of the religious orders bearing the body on their shoulders. When they reached the church of the convent, the Chapter announced to the people that, in accordance with the rules of the Apostolic See, the deceased could not be allowed to be honoured as a saint, but might receive the respect which was due to her on account of the miracle wrought on her body. These proceedings were caused to be faithfully recorded, not only by the Chapter, but also by the Viceroy, who sent a report to the Home Government with an official letter dated the 24th January 1683, and ordered a copy of it to be kept in the Secretariat. Gemelli Careri, who was at Goa twelve years afterwards, refers to this occurrence, and adds that the forehead bore also marks of slight wounds as if caused by thorns.*

The convent, where this and some other miraculous events are said to have occurred, rapidly declined in importance when the city was abandoned on account of the epidemic. In 1804 there were sixty-one professed nuns and four novices ; in 1827 there were not more than thirty ; and in 1835, when all the convents were closed except this, admission was refused to novices. Consequently the number of the nuns rapidly decreased. In 1856 not more than seven or eight nuns were found living within its precincts. This number was reduced in ten years to four, and at present there is only one, considerably advanced in years. There are also living in the convent several female servants, most of whom are old, and their business is to make rosaries, scapulars, and preserves of fruits, syrups and sweets of different sorts, which are sold for the benefit of the convent and have a great reputation in the country.

This convent had formerly considerable landed estate yielding a large income, but sustained a heavy loss when the Maráṭhás conquered the Portuguese territory to the north of Bombay, where some of the lands were situated. According to an official estimate made in 1804 the estate was worth £11,070, and yielded an income of £568-6-8,

* Churchill's *Voyages and Travels*, vol. IV., p. 205.

which is now considerably reduced. The property is now under the administration of a committee appointed by the Archbishop, and will probably, after the death of the only nun now left, be appropriated by the State, while the convent, built at a great cost by the first Primate of the East, will, like the others, be abandoned to its fate.

The Church of Santa Monica is attached to the convent to the south, and is not very spacious. Its external architecture is a combination of the Tuscan, Corinthian and Composite orders, and the interior belongs to the Doric and Composite. Its greatest length is 175 feet, and breadth 36 feet. The nave is divided into two parts. The first makes up the principal part of the church, with two side altars, the one on the right dedicated to *Divino Jesus*, the other on the left to *Virgens Africanas;* the altar of the principal chapel contains the image of Santa Monica, mother of St. Augustine, the renowned doctor of the Church, to whom the convent and the church are dedicated; the other part, which is the *Capitolio*, is separated from the first large arcade by a double iron railing. The nuns used to hear mass from the choir, which is in the inner part of the chapel, and through the railings could see the priest at the altar without being seen by the people outside. There is nothing remarkable in this church, except an image of Christ, reputed to be miraculous, which was formerly in the choir, and is now placed in a tribune in the nave of the church, having on the right side the epitaph of Diogo de Santa Anna, a friar of the order of St. Augustine and Administrator of the Convent of Santa Monica, who died on the 26th October 1614. It is stated that on the 8th February 1636, the second Friday of Lent, this image opened its eyes and was seen moving, while from its wounds blood appeared to flow as though it were living. The miracle is said to have occurred again on the 12th of the same month, in the presence of the Viceroy and fidalgos, as well as many other people. The Rev. Professor Francisco de Santa Maria says that the Bishop, Dom Fr. Miguel Rangel, who then governed the diocese of Goa, the Inquisitors, and other persons of rank witnessed the occurrence, and after a thorough inquiry into the matter came to the conclusion that it was miraculous.* The image was thenceforward held in great veneration, and Pope Benedict XIV. granted the privilege of a special prayer to be recited in its honour in the diocese of Goa. Its feast is celebrated to this day with pomp on the last Sunday of November, and the treasury annually contributes the sum of £10 for the purpose of having a lamp burning before the image at night all the year round. It is 6½ feet in height. It is also said that several defects which had previously existed in its workmanship miraculously disappeared.

Convent and Church of St. Augustine.—In front of the Convent and Church of Santa Monica rose the Convent of St. Augustine, which, a celebrated traveller of the 17th century says, looked from a distance like one of the noblest palaces in the world;† it had two stories, and a magnificent staircase leading to them. According to another traveller this convent was by far the most beautiful and stately building in the city. Few cities in Europe, says he, can boast of possessing within their precincts such a magnificent building. The cloisters, the pillars, the galleries, the halls, and the cells are all very fine.‡ Gemelli observes that this convent, with its vast dormitories, its numberless cells, and other apartments, had spacious gardens "always green and beautified with the best trees India produces."§ Dr. Buchanan, who was a guest in the convent at the invitation of the Provincial, Fr. José das Dores, a very learned clergyman, speaks in equally high terms of it, and says that at the sight of its extensive library he felt as if he had been suddenly transported to one of the libraries at Cambridge.|| Lastly, Dr. Wilson, after comparing the splendid apartments of this convent with those of the University of Edinburgh, speaks with admiration of the excellent

---

* *Anno Historico* por Padre Francisco de Santa Maria, Lisboa, 1714, pp. 174-86; *Promptuario das Definições Indicas*, por P. Leonardo Paes, p. 39.

† Mandelslo's *Voyages and Travels*, p. 81.

‡ *An Historical Sketch* by Cottineau, p. 122.

§ Churchill's *Voyages and Travels*, vol. IV., p. 205.

|| *Christian Researches in Asia*, p. 159.

pictures that adorned its walls, and which represented the martyrdom of several members of the order of St. Augustine; the learned Doctor was so much moved at their sight that he said, "I could not but think with admiration of their (the martyrs') devotedness, and wish that more of it were exhibited among Protestants."*

The convent was erected in 1572 by twelve Augustinian friars immediately after their settling in Goa under Fr. Antonio de Paixão, who was their first Provincial. A few years later, on their application, the King of Portugal, by the royal letter of the 2nd March 1587, made them a grant of money, which was subsequently increased.† Ten years after this date the convent was rebuilt, chiefly through the endeavours of Fr. Gaspar de São Vicente, and dedicated to *Nossa Senhora de Graça.* The ceremony of laying the foundation-stone was very grand, and attended by the Viceroy, the Count of Vidigueira, the Archbishop, Dom Fr. Aleixo de Menezes, and a number of noblemen. It was soon afterwards completed, and in course of time became one of the richest convents in Goa. When suppressed in 1835, it was in a good state of preservation. Fifty-nine friars left it on that occasion, and the public treasury appropriated its moveable and immoveable property, worth £43,236-16-3$\frac{3}{10}$.

Close to this convent, to the north, was the Church of St. Augustine, a very spacious building, with its façade looking to the west. A long and beautiful staircase led up to it. It had two towers which were very high, and contained bells of enormous size. It had a nave, with a vault which was the best constructed in Goa, and was therefore admired by strangers. Captain

---

* *Orient. Christ. Spect.*, vol. V., First Series, p. 121.

† This annual allowance consisted of eight casks of wine, one cask of oil, twenty *khaṇḍis* of wheat, twenty-five packages of rice, eighteen *khaṇḍis* and five *mans* of coarse rice, fifty sawfish, one *khaṇḍi* of butter, half a cask of wax, one *khaṇḍi* of cocoanut oil, one hundred and twenty pieces of cloth, two bags of sugar, and ten boxes of marmalade. In 1596 a cask of wine, a *khaṇḍi* and fifteen *mans* of coarse rice, five packages of fine rice, three *khaṇḍis* of wheat, one of cocoanut oil, and half a *khaṇḍi* of wax were added to it. *Arch. Port. Or.*, Fasc. III., doc. 170, 204.

Franklin says that the building of the choir belonged to the Gothic style.* The edifice had eleven altars, all richly adorned, but the main altar is said to have been a masterpiece of workmanship. This beautiful church was erected almost at the same time as the convent; and there is a curious tradition about it. An Italian architect, who was entrusted with the construction of its vault, twice built it, but his labours were on both occasions rendered fruitless by its fall. Being reduced to despair, he rebuilt it a third time, and to try its stability placed himself and his only son directly under it and ordered a heavy cannon to be fired near the building, choosing rather to lose his life in the event of the vault falling through than to undergo a fresh disappointment. Fortunately the vault resisted the shock; he was satisfied as to the durability of the work, and received a suitable remuneration for his pains. This church was closed along with the convent; the valuable articles belonging to both were sold or lost, and the principal bell, which weighed 4,800 lbs., was removed to the fortress of Agoada.

To the south of the convent was situated the Novitiate of the Augustinians, which may be said to have formed part of the same. Opposite to this building, to the west, there was the grand college called *Collegio de Populo.* It was erected in 1600 by the Provincial, Fr. Pedro da Cruz, and was destined for the training of the younger brethren of the same order. It was connected with the Novitiate by an arch spanning a broad street called *Rua dos Judeus*, Street of the Jews.

This noble group of buildings, belonging to the Augustinians, which, as a traveller remarks, presented a magnificent spectacle, was abandoned in 1835. Soon after the closing of the convent, some charitable institutions of the *Santa Casa de Misericordia* were, as already stated, transferred to these buildings. But on their removal to another place, the buildings fell into neglect, and gradually became dilapidated, their ruin being precipitated by the fall of the sumptuous vault of the

* Pinkerton's *Collection of Voyages and Travels*, vol. IX., p. 234.

church, on the 8th September 1842, which buried under its *débris* the colossal image of St. Augustine, founder of the order, and that of *Nossa Senhora da Graça,* patroness of the church. The Council of the Public Treasury ordered the sale of the materials in the following year. It is said, however, that the *Collegio de Populo* remained in a good state of preservation till 1846, when it was demolished, under Government orders. Nothing now remains of all these buildings but a heap of ruins, amidst which stand the arch and the lofty tower, whose gloomy aspect prepares the traveller at a distance for the desolation and misery which is to be witnessed in the once opulent city.

Convent and Church of St. John of God.—In front of the ruins of the Convent of St. Augustine, to the east, there is the half-decayed Convent of St. John of God, with its church dedicated to *Nossa Senhora de Bom Successo.* It was a small building, and had nothing particularly interesting about it. It was erected in 1685 by some members of the order of St. John of God, on a spot which they had partly purchased, and partly received as a grant from the Government. The public treasury contributed 6*s.* 8*d.* per diem for the support of eight brethren, some of whom served in the Royal Hospital after the expulsion of the Jesuits, and the rest lived on the above allowance. In the time of Abbé Cottineau their number did not exceed twelve,* and it fell off gradually till the final suppression of the order in 1835. The convent was afterwards used as a Hospital for the poor when the establishment of the *Santa Casa de Misericordia* with its two Retreats was, as already stated, transferred to the Convent of St. Augustine. In 1844 the building of the convent was purchased by the nuns of Santa Monica for the residence of the chaplains, confessors, and other persons employed in their behalf. In 1850 the roof of the church was removed, for want of the necessary funds to keep it in repair ; it is still found in this condition, along with its abandoned convent, of which only a portion of the front is now standing.

---

* *An Historical Sketch,* p. 130.

New College of St. Paul.—On the other side of the Convent of St. Augustine, on the western verge of the hill, rose the New College of St. Paul, or, as it was generally called, the Convent of St. Roch. This superb edifice, four stories high, was much admired not only for its vast dimensions, but also for the magnificent style of its architecture. Dr. Fryer says that this college was the largest religious building in Goa.* It was erected, as stated elsewhere, upon the ruins of a house purchased by the Jesuits on the Holy Mount when the locality of the old college became unhealthy and inadequate for all the institutions which were under their charge. This house had been built by Pedro de Faria, ex-Captain of Malacca, after he had purchased the hill in 1526. It then came into the possession of the Captain of Ternate, and lastly of the General Ouvidor, Dom Francisco de Marques Botelho, who sold it to the Jesuit Fathers in 1578. It was used as a sanitarium till 1585, after which it was enlarged and converted into a professed house. On the latter being transferred to the building on the *Terreiro dos Gallos*, it became the Novitiate of the Jesuits. In 1610 it was changed into a college under the title of the New College of St. Paul, as distinguished from the old one. This house had a chapel which was differently designated at different times, according to the purposes to which the house was dedicated. It was called Chapel of St. Roch when the house was used as a sanitarium, Chapel of *Nossa Senhora da Conceição* when it became a Novitiate, and Chapel of St. Paul when it was converted into a college. To the common people, however, both the college and chapel of St. Paul were almost always known by the original name of St. Roch.

The removal of the Jesuits to the New College of St. Paul met with greater opposition than their previous removal to the professed house of *Bom Jesus*. They had obtained permission for this purpose both from the Goa and Home Governments on several conditions, some of which were that they should not raise

* *A New Account of East India and Persia*, p. 149.

the building so high as to obstruct the light and air, as well as the view of the sea, enjoyed by the neighbouring buildings, and secondly that they should not build a large church with confessionals, etc., so as to prejudice the interests of the neighbouring parishes; but, disregarding these restrictions, they raised a lofty church and a majestic college. The consequence was that the friars and nuns who had their convents on the hill, as well as the priests who were in charge of parishes, laid complaints before the Senate of the city against the Jesuits. They also incited the people to expel the Jesuits by force from their new residence, and the struggle would have terminated in actual violence, had not certain influential persons interfered, and persuaded both parties to refer the matter to the decision of the Viceroy, who was then absent from Goa.* In spite of all this opposition, the Jesuits continued in possession of the college, as we learn from Pietro della Valle, who visited Goa in 1623.† He says: "The Jesuits up to this date have prevailed over the city, which wishes them to return to Old St. Paul's for the convenience of students, and also over the Augustinians, and the King himself, who several times ordered them to leave that place and to destroy the new college, and they have remained, notwithstanding all the opposition made against them, in possession of their new and splendid building, and are even enlarging it, calling it New St. Paul's, because they wish that all their colleges in India should be dedicated to St. Paul, the doctor of the Gentiles."‡ Tavernier also alludes to the dispute, and says that the Jesuits eventually won the suit.§

The Jesuits had also to struggle against another more powerful foe. According to the *Oriente Conquistado*, this magnificent college was on five different occasions a prey to

* *Liv. das Monç.*, Goa Gov. Rec. (MSS.), No. 12, fol. 240.

† The King by his royal letter of the 8th February 1611 had ordered that the Jesuits should not transfer their College to the new building, but they had already done so a year before. *Arch. Port. Or.*, Fasc. I., doc. 79.

‡ *Vioggi di Pietro della Valle*, vol. II., p. 760.

§ *Les Six Voyoges*, Pt. II., p. 122.

flames and suffered considerable damage. On the 1st January 1591 the Novitiate was utterly reduced to ashes. On the 26th of June 1617 the College was entirely destroyed. On this occasion the Rector, Dom Jeronimo Xavier, a relative of St. Francis Xavier, and a man of great piety and virtue, was burnt to death. On the 15th December 1663 an upper corridor, together with its cells, was consumed by fire. On the 6th January 1675 the roof of the college was destroyed in a similar way; and lastly, in 1698, the wardrobe was struck down by a thunderbolt.* Though man and nature appeared to have been thus at first leagued together against the founders of this college, they did not lose heart, but with dauntless resolution and indefatigable industry succeeded in making it the foremost institution in Goa.

Dr. Fryer says that it was built in the form of a cross, and bore the appearance of a seraglio on the water. It had a suite of apartments fitted out with every accommodation necessary for its inmates. It had a rich and extensive library, and an hospital with a well-furnished dispensary, where Gaspar Antonio, the inventor of the famous Goa stones,† secured a yearly income of more than £2,000 on behalf of the college. This lay-brother was a native of Florence, and at the time of Dr. Fryer's visit was old and blind, but he was very much respected for his great skill in medicine, in consequence of which he was consulted by the well-to-do people of all classes in the city.‡

* *Orient. Conq.*, vol. II., p. 154.

† The Goa stones, or *Pedra Cordial*, as it appears from the Royal letter of the 21st March 1691, were the monopoly of the Jesuits, who not only sold them in India, but exported them to Portugal in large quantities and with great profit. After the death of Gaspar Antonio, these stones were manufactured by Jorge Ungarete, and subsequently by several Jesuit Fathers. Their composition is not exactly known, but it is said to have been much similar to that of the following formula:—Re. Coral branco, vermelho e pedra bezoar ana 2 onc. Rubins, jacintos, topazios, saphiras e aljofar, ana 1 onc. Esmeralda ½ onc. Ambargriz e almiscar 2 escrop. Folhinhas de ouro No. 4. *Livro das Monçoens*, No. 56; p. 79, *Archivo da Pharmacia*, vol. I., p. 48.

‡ *A New Account of East India and Persia*, p. 150. We may repeat here what we have stated elsewhere, that the traveller mistook the College for the Professed House.

Father Francisco de Souza, Pietro della Valle, and various other authors give a highly interesting description of the teaching and scholastic *fêtes* that used to take place in this college. It was conducted by the most learned members of the Society of Jesus, such as Alexandre Lin, who had been a professor in one of the most renowned institutions of Italy, Pantaleon Venceslau, a profound mathematician from Germany, Christopher de Giovanni, an eminent scholar in Greek and Arabic, Joseph Massagna, a famous naturalist.* By far the most interesting account that has been written of the college is that left by Mandelslo, who accompanied the President of the English settlement at Surat to Goa. He testifies to the magnificence, order, and economy, which prevailed in this college under the management of the Jesuits, as well as to the festive entertainments which were held there on solemn occasions. We give the following long extract, which we trust will prove acceptable and interesting to our readers :—

"The next day, being the 16th, we dined at the professed house of the Jesuits, who had invited us to a sumptuous feast. There were in this house a hundred and fifty fathers, and at least as many scholars or students, yet did not that great number nearly fill that noble structure, which was four stories high, and had the pleasantest prospect in the world as well towards the sea, as on the land side. They first showed us all the conveniences of the house, their wealth, and the order they observed in their economy. Then they brought us into a fair arched hall, as big as an ordinary church, which was beset with tables placed all along the walls. The cloth was laid with the trenchers, the drinking cups and earthen pots, and they had brought in bread and fruit. In the midst of the hall there was another little square table, covered and furnished as the rest, for those who were to do penance for their having done anything contrary to the discipline of the order. In the midst of the entry to this hall there was a pillar, out of which issued a spout of water for the washing of their hands. Then they carried us up to the third story to another hall, which was not as large as that below, but so richly furnished as might become the apartment of a very noble house, as well in point of tapestry, as other things. The table prepared for us was very large, and placed in the midst of the hall, covered with a noble cloth, beset with fruit and bread and china dishes, which persons of quality

* *Oriente Conquistado, Conq.* 1, *Div.* 11, § 13; *Viaggi di Pietro della Valle,* vol. II., p. 596.

in those parts do prefer before those of silver. The Father Provincial, having given the President the precedence, sat down by him, and afterward ordered all our company to be so placed, as that between every two, there were two Jesuits to entertain and discourse with us; the rest standing behind to wait on us. The meat was brought in little dishes of porcelain, to every man his own dish; and this for several courses, both of flesh and fish, all excellently well dressed. The desert was suitable to the rest of the entertainment and consisted in tarts, florentines, eggs drest after the Portuguese way, admirably well perfumed, marchpains, and conserves both dry and liquid.

"At our rising from table, they conducted us into several chambers, where they left us to take the ordinary repose, during the greatest heat of the day. There were in every chamber three beds, and in the midst upon a table a great vessel of porcelain full of fair water. Then they came and carried us into a hall, where we were to have the divertisement of a ball, which was danced by the children of certain Indians, whom they had baptized and instructed in the Roman Catholic religion. The Archbishop of Goa, who was Primate of all the Indies, was there also in person, as well to participate of the divertisement, as to entertain the President, by order from the Viceroy. The dancing-master made the first entrance along, and did pretty well for a Portuguese. The habits of the dancers were very rich, but they had no visards on, nor anything upon their heads but a crown of flowers. The noblest entrance, and that which discovered the subject of the ball, was that of fifteen persons who came in bringing along with them some pieces of a broken pillar, some garlands of divers flowers wherewith they adorned the pillar after they had, after several turnings, absolutely set it together, all performed with observance of the music. At the upper end of this pillar came out a flower, made like a tulip, which opened of itself while they danced; till at last there came out of it an image of the Blessed Virgin with her child in her arms, and the pillar itself opened in several places to cast out perfumed waters like a fountain. After they had danced a while, they took the pillar asunder, after the same manner as they had put it together, and went out of the room in very good order. The Jesuits told us that by that invention they represented the pains they had taken in planting among the Pagans and Mahometans of these parts, the Church of God, whereof our Saviour is the only pillar or corner-stone. After this there was an entrance of twelve youths, who sung and played every one upon a different instrument, all done in exact measure. There came in also some *morris-dancers*, who danced to the castagnets, and kept measure with the music so exactly that I never saw anything like it. There came in also one man alone who was covered with birds' nests and clothed and masked according to the Spanish mode, who began the farce of the comedy by ridiculous and fantastick postures; and the ball was concluded with the coming in of twelve boys dressed like apes, which they imitated in their cries and postures. The ball being over, we stayed there a while to hear their music, which was altogether after the Portuguese way. As we took leave of our entertainers, they told us that they made use of those divertisements as well to induce the pagans and Mahometans of those parts to embrace the Christian religion, by that kind of modern devotion, as to amuse the children and divert them after their studies."*

This famous college appears to have declined in course of time from its original splendour. At the end of the 17th century there were seventy fathers in the college, and twenty-five in the professed house.† After the expulsion of the Jesuits from Goa, the college was closed. The building was for a time, as already stated, occupied by the Royal Hospital before its removal to the Palace of Panelim, and was some years later used as barracks when an attempt was made to rebuild the city. Towards the close of the 18th century the college showed signs of decay, and the cost of repairing it was estimated at £4,733-6-8, but the Government being unwilling to spend such a large sum, the majestic building gradually crumbled to dust. The Viceroy, Count of Sarzedas, wrote in 1810, to the Government of Portugal that the college building, for which an offer of more than £8,000 had once been made when it was in a tolerably good condition, was now reduced to a heap of ruins, while all the valuable articles in it had been stolen.‡ These ruins existed in the time of Abbé Cottineau,§ and were an object of admiration to travellers. They were subsequently removed, and the materials used for the building of military barracks at Pangim. There is at present no trace of this college, the greatest and the most splendid building of the Jesuits in the city of Goa.

---

* Mandelslo's *Voyages and Travels*, p. 79. We may repeat here what we have stated elsewhere, that the traveller mistook the New College of St. Paul for the Professed House.

† Churchill's *Voyages and Travels*, vol. IV., p. 205.

‡ *Liv. das Monç.* (MSS.), No. 190, fol. 741.

§ *Instituto Vasco de Gama*, vol. IV., p. 153.

CHAPTER XVI.

THE SUBURB OF SAO PEDRO—FOUNTAIN OF BANGUENIM—COLLEGE OF ST. THOMAS—CHURCH OF ST. PETER—PALACE OF THE ARCH-BISHOPS—CASA DE POLVORA—RIBANDAR—HOSPITAL OF THE POOR—CHURCH OF NOSSA SENHORA DA AJUDA—RETREATS OF NOSSA SENHORA DE SERRA AND SANTA MARIA MAGDALENA AT CHIMBEL—CAUSEWAY OF RIBANDAR.

Suburb of Sao Pedro.—Descending the Mount of the Rosary by a declivity close to the site of the New College of St. Paul, and crossing a small bridge, we reach the parish of São Pedro, the western suburb of the city. This parish comprises two villages, Banguenim and Panelim.

Fountain of Banguenim.—Banguenim was famous for its pure water, which was supplied to the whole city. Pyrard gives the following interesting description of this fountain, which according to another traveller represented Lucrecia, out of whose wound ran the water highly valued by people of all classes :—

"With regard to the water which is ordinarily drunk in the city and its suburbs, the best and the most wholesome, as well as the lightest, in my opinion, is the one which is sought for at a quarter of a league's distance from the city, where lies a great fountain of pure and limpid water called Banguenim, which issues from the rocks. The Portuguese enclosed it with a wall, and by means of pipes the water was brought down to large reservoirs, where a great number of men and women used to wash clothes. They were called *mainatos* or washermen. There were other reservoirs for bathing purposes, so that the road was much trodden and frequented, although it was rugged, because one had to climb and descend three or four high mountains. Nothing else is here seen except people on their way to, and from, this fountain, even as late as ten o'clock at night. Many persons go together to bathe there armed with weapons, and dressed only in their shirts and pantaloons.

"The water is sold in the city; the slaves supply it in all quarters of the city in great earthen vessels, each of which contains two pots, and they sell the pot at five *bazarucos*, which is nearer six *deniers*. They stand with their vessels in fixed localities, without crying 'water' in every street. It would have been far better if the Portuguese had brought the water of the fountain to the city through pipes and aqueducts, but they say that their mode of bringing water gives at once profit and employment to their slaves, and that otherwise foreigners would use this good water without paying for it; because there are more foreigners than Portuguese and natives, and for these reasons they do not like to have the water conveyed to the city."*

This fountain is now in a dilapidated state, but its water is still considered as wholesome.

College of St. Thomas.—The first remarkable building which was seen in Banguenim was the college of St. Thomas Aquinas, situated on the margin of the river close to the bridge which has been just mentioned. It had been erected by the Dominican Friars, as stated above, at Pangim, but owing to certain inconveniences it was demolished, and with its materials the College, which we are now describing, was commenced to be built in 1596 through the efforts of Fr. Francisco de Faria, Vicar General of the order. It was completed soon after the arrival of the Viceroy Dom Francisco da Gama, Count of Vidigueira, in the following year.† In this college the younger members of the Dominican order received instruction, and here too resided the aged and sick brethren of the same order. The college received from Government an annual supply of some of the necessary articles of food and raiment, as it did when it was at Pangim.‡ But subsequently a fixed sum of money (£43-15-4) was allowed to it by the *Alvará* of the 3rd November 1599. In 1626 the building was partly destroyed by the explosion of some barrels of powder which had been kept by order of the

* Pyrard, Pt. II., p. 41.

† *Arch. Port. Or.*, Fasc. III., doc. 925.

‡ These articles consisted of sixteen *khaṇḍis* of wheat, twenty of rice, four casks of wine, eight oil-vessels, and some pieces of cloth: *Arch. Port. Or.*, *loc. cit.*

Government in its cellars, on which occasion some of the friars were burnt to death. It was however repaired and was in a good state of preservation in the time of Gemelli, who writes about it as follows:—"Wednesday, the 2nd of March 1695. I went to the Church of St. Thomas of the Dominicans, a good fabric on the bank of the channel. It has seven altars; the monastery is large and beautiful, inhabited by twenty-five fathers."*

The Abbé Cottineau too found it in 1827 in a pretty good state. He says:—"The college of St. Thomas Aquinas in the suburb of St. Peter is likewise spacious, but not so much as the convent (of the Dominicans). It is, however, in a much more healthy situation, whence many of the elder members of the order retired from the office and exempted from the duty of daily assisting at the choir, prefer this residence; besides the young professed members who are instructed in this college, seculars are also admitted to the lectures."†

It was closed along with the other religious buildings in 1835, the public treasury appropriating its property, worth £5,240-17-3¼. No further care being taken of it, the roof fell in 1844, and as the building seemed to be in a tottering condition, it was demolished two years later during the governorship of Postana; there is at present no trace of it, and the spot where the Dominicans prepared themselves to preach the Gospel in different countries of the East is desolate and covered with palm trees.

Church of St. Peter.—Close to the site of the College of St. Thomas to the west, there is the parish church of St. Peter. It is very old, and appears to have been erected about the year 1542 or 1543, at the expense of the public treasury, by Portuguese architects, as we learn from an official document.‡ Some think it to have been erected by orders of the Archbishop Dom Fr. Aleixo de Menezes, but this opinion may be shown to

---

* Churchill's *Voyages and Travels*, vol. IV., p. 206.

† *An Historical Sketch*, p. 119.

‡ *Bosquejo Historico das Communidades*, Nova Goa, 1852, Part II., p. 130.

be erroneous by the following clause in the regulations framed in 1565 by the Viceroy, Dom Antão de Noronha—"The priest who serves as curate of St. Peter's house, which is in Banguenim, and which is also a parish, will receive a yearly salary of £1-13-4." From this it is clear that the church could not have been built by the Archbishop, who commenced to govern the diocese in 1595. Besides, the question of precedence which arose between this church and that of St. Thomas, erected, as already stated, in 1560, corroborates the above documentary evidence. The church wears now an antique appearance and has nothing remarkable about it. It is small in size and in one of its altars is seen an image of St. Peter, the Prince of the Apostles, to whom it is dedicated. On the floor are seen four or five inscriptions almost effaced, that at the entrance bearing the name of João Rodrigues Machado. The population of the parish which, during its most flourishing period, must have been very considerable, was reduced in 1720 to 1,997 souls and in 1775 to 1,794. This number was still further reduced in 1827 to 860, in 1857 to 504, and has now dwindled to 261.

Palace of the Archbishops.—Proceeding a little further we approach the splendid palace of the Archbishops, situated at Panelim, which formed, as stated above, a part of the parish of St. Peter. It stands on the slope of a hill to the south of the main road, and is about five and a half miles distant from Pangim, and a quarter of a mile from the old city. It enjoys a picturesque and widely extended view, and is approached by an excellent stone staircase. Cottineau, who was a guest there in 1827 of the Archbishop S. Galdino, says that it looks from outside like a double-storied building, but has only one floor above the level of the ground in the shape of a square cloister in the finest style, of vast dimensions and in an excellent condition. At the entrance was a chamber adorned with the life-size portraits of all the Archbishops and opening into the audience-hall, which was tastefully furnished. Here were seen the arms of the Prelate, the portrait of the reigning

King of Portugal, geographical charts, and a likeness of Leo XII. The same traveller speaks also of the chapel and the library of the palace, which Dr. Wilson says contained about 2,000 volumes. Its gardens extended up to the road which led to the city. In this palace the Archbishops maintained to some extent the style and splendour to which they had been accustomed in the old palace in the city, and when they stirred out, although they did not, as formerly, take in their train a large number of attendants, they still preserved a certain degree of state. "When the Archbishop goes out," says the Abbé, "on festivals and for public purposes, he is always preceded by a young clergyman, bearing a large silver cross. Like the Governor, he has only two sorts of conveyances—a *palki* after the Bombay fashion, and a boat suitably painted and ornamented. In the first case, the clergyman bearing the cross goes in an open *palki* before him, and in the second the cross is fixed to the prow of the boat."*

The Archbishops transferred their residence to this palace in 1695, on account of the epidemic which raged in the city, but when the disease spread to the suburbs where this palace stood, it was abandoned, and the successors of the Archbishop S. Galdino resided at Santa Ignez or Pangim. Being thus neglected, it naturally began to decay, and one of its wings fell in course of time. Its principal halls are still standing, but they are in so tottering a condition that nobody can safely approach them. A few of its apartments are, however, in a tolerably good condition, and since 1866, under the orders of the Home Government, they have been used as office rooms of the *Camara Pontificia* (the Pontifical Chamber) and the *Tribunal da Relação Ecclesiastica* (the Ecclesiastical Court). The committee appointed in 1870 to examine the buildings of the old city found that these apartments were ill-fitted for these purposes, and

---

* *Instituto Vasco da Gama*, vol. III., p. 128; Cottineau's *Historical Sketch*, p. 100; *Orient. Christ. Spect.*, vol. V., First Series, p. 121.

recommended the removal of these establishments to the House of *Bom Jesus.*

Casa de Polvora.—Another remarkable building still existing at Panelim is the *Casa de Polvora,* or gunpowder-factory. It is not very far from the archbishops' palace and stands close to the river-side. It was erected by the Viceroy Dom Francisco da Gama, great-grandson of Vasco da Gama, as may be seen from the following inscription on its entrance door over an image of St. Catherine—

"Reinando em Portugal o Catholico Rei D. Filippe 3 mandou a cidade fazer toda a fabrica desta caza de Polvora do dinheiro de hum por cento, sendo Vice-Rei deste Estado Francisco da Gama Conde Almirante, o qual principiou e acabou e fez aperfeiçoar, emque ora está o Vice-Rey D. Miguel de Noronha Conde de Linhares anno de 1630."

Translation.

"When the Catholic King Dom Phillippe III. was reigning in Portugal, the (senate of the) city ordered the construction of this powder factory out of the proceeds of the duty of one per cent., the Viceroy of this State being Francisco da Gama, Count Admiral, who commenced, completed and improved (the edifice) where now resides the Viceroy Dom Miguel de Noronha, Count of Linhares. Year 1630."

The manufacture of gunpowder in this building has been stopped for some years past. In the compound attached to the building there is a stone reservoir which is supplied with water brought by an aqueduct from Banguenim.

Near the *Casa de Polvora* was a palace for the recreation of the Viceroys, where, on account of the epidemic in the city, the Count of Villa Verde and his successors resided since 1695. Though much inferior to that in the city, it had spacious and commodious apartments, which, according to Gemelli, had been added at various intervals.* When the residence of the Viceroys was removed to Pangim in 1759, during the

* Churchill's *Voyages and Travels*, vol. IV., p. 251.

government of the Count of Ega, the Royal Hospital was transferred from the city to this palace. At the end of the first quarter of this century the building was in a good state of preservation, and the number of patients that were treated here exceeded sixty. The members of the order of St. John of God, six of whom resided in it, were in charge of this hospital.* About this time natives of Goa also served in it as physicians. The Royal Hospital, now called the Military Hospital, having been transferred to Pangim in April 1842, it was suggested that the two retreats of *Nossa Senhora de Serra* and *Santa Maria Magdalena* already described, should be brought into the vacant building, but the scheme not having been carried out, it was abandoned. In 1850 the roof was pulled down by orders of Government, and the materials were sold; in 1855 a lofty arch which overhung the street, and some other houses in the neighbourhood, were demolished; however, two large apartments of the palace, which had before been used as infirmaries for the officers, were reserved. They are now incorporated with the *Casa de Polvora.* In 1856 the ruins of the palace were ordered to be removed by the Governor Viscount of Torres Novas, and there is at present hardly any trace of it left.

Close to the *Casa de Polvora,* communicating with it from the interior, there were the Military Barracks, now in a dilapidated state. There were also at Panclim some other buildings, and many splendid houses of fidalgos and noblemen. In fact the suburb of São Pedro, when it was made the residence of the Viceroy and the Archbishop, became at the same time the chief place of abode of officers of state and other Portuguese gentlemen, who, following the example of the chief authorities, abandoned the city. This suburb some time afterwards became almost as unhealthy as the city itself, and was consequently deserted in its turn, so that it is now in nearly as desolate a condition as the latter.

---

* Cottineau's *Historical Sketch*, p. 130. According to Loureiro (*Memorias dos Estabelescimentos Port.*, p. 361) there were twelve members of the order of St. John of God in the Hospital.

Ribandar.—Leaving Panelim and proceeding further, we arrive at Ribandar, a pretty little town which forms at present the second division of Nova Goa. Ribandar was anciently called *Raibandar* or the royal landing place. It was at first corrupted into Rabandar, then Rebandar, and finally into Ribandar.* In 1510 the Muhammadans, having retaken the city from Albuquerque, built here a redoubt. After the second capture of Goa by the Portuguese, a house was built at Ribandar for a *Thanadhar* at a cost of £4. This officer was enjoined to keep watch on the goods which passed through the river on that side and to collect taxes, and had in 1554 under him one naique and nine peons. In 1572 he was allowed his share in sundry articles which he had to inspect.†

Ribandar has been the residence of many Portuguese noblemen ever since the city and the suburb of São Pedro became unhealthy. The Christian population of Ribandar was estimated in 1775 at 3,092 souls, which number in 1828 was reduced to 2,434, and is at present about 2,200.

Hospital of the Poor.—The first building which we see just on the borders of Ribandar near the river side, is the Hospital of the Poor. It has a pretty appearance, but has scanty accommodation for the establishment which was transferred there by the *Santa Casa de Misericordia* in 1851. In every ward, whether set apart for male or female patients, a crucifix is hung. There is a chapel, with a chaplain residing in the house. The hospital is not in a flourishing condition, and is only resorted to by the natives of the neighbouring villages of the Ilhas. The number of patients treated in this hospital is given elsewhere.‡

Church of Nossa Senhora da Ajuda.—At a little distance from the hospital lies the Church of Ribandar, dedicated to *Nossa Senhora da Ajuda*. Its erection is, according to a

* Compare *Lendas, ut supra*, vol. II., pp. 94, 97, 99, 167; *Subsidios ut supra*, Pt. II., p. 75; *Arch. Port. Or.*, Fasc. 50, p. 869; *O Chronista*, vol. IV., p. 69.

† *Lendas*, vol. II., p. 99; *Subsidios*, Pt. II., p. 76.

‡ See Part I., p. 61.

tradition, attributed to the miraculous appearance of the Virgin Mary to save a Portuguese ship from being drowned in the river, or, according to some, in the sea. Hamilton, alluding to this, says—"At a certain time, but God knows when, a ship of Portugal coming to India, got the length of *Cabo de Bona Esperanza*, and then met with such a violent storm, that drove the ship so violently before it, that it was past the pilot's skill to keep her to rights in her course; and who should come to their assistance in that critical juncture, but *Senhor Diabolo*, who took the helm, and managed it very dexterously; and the Virgin Mary, to show her kindness, stood a whole night on the forecastle, directing the devil how he should steer, and behold, to the great admiration of all concerned, the ship was high and dry in the morning, in a valley on the south side of the river of Goa, about half a mile within the land. The ship sailed very well, for on that night she ran, according to a moderate computation, 1,500 leagues. And in commemoration of this miracle there is a fine church built where the ship anchored so safely, and the structure is just the length, breadth and height of the ship. The church I have often seen as I passed up and down the river. And this story is so firmly believed at Goa, that it is dangerous to make any doubt of it."* This church, built in honour of the Virgin out of gratitude, soon became a parochial church. By the Rules framed by Dom Antão de Noronha in 1565, a sum of £1-13-4 was annually granted from the public treasury for the support of its vicar. It was in this church that the body of St. Francis Xavier was first deposited when brought from Malacca, during the short time necessary for the preparation of its reception in the city.† The church was rebuilt in 1711, and provided in 1841 with an altar-piece brought from the *Collegio de Populo*. It is a pretty large building, embellished with paintings of some saints on its ceiling; it has four altars, on the chief of which is seen the image of the Virgin.

---

* *A New Account of the East Indies*, vol. I., p. 257.

† *Peregrinação de Fernão Mendes Pinto*, tom. III., p. 297.

Retreats of Nossa Senhora de Serra and Santa Maria Magdalena at Chimbel.—About two miles to the south of Ribandar, in the village of Chimbel, of which that place forms a part, are situated the two retreats of *Nossa Senhora de Serra* and of *Santa Maria Magdalena*. The former building is spacious, and was originally a convent of the Carmelites of the third order. It was begun to be erected in 1747; and the friars came to live there three years after; but their rules were not approved by the Pope till 1790. It had a church dedicated to Our Lady of Mount Carmel, which still exists. In 1835 the Government ordered the convent to be closed, when twenty-three friars left it, and its moveable and immoveable property, amounting in value to £7,857-4-0, was seized by the public treasury. The Retreats, as stated before, were subsequently transferred to this building in 1841. They are under the management of respectable ladies, who not only look to the good behaviour of the grown-up inmates supported there by charity or at their own expense, but also of the girls who are entrusted to their care. None of them are allowed to go out without permission, and no males are admitted within. Marriageable girls are sometimes visited by gentlemen who wish to marry them. In one of the outer rooms of the abovementioned building, the Committee of the *Santa Casa de Misericordia*, by whom the Retreats are administered, holds its sittings; it is adorned with the portraits of three of its patrons, viz., Salvador Antão, a convert from the Bráhman caste and a native of Rachol, who died in 1647, and who is represented with flowing hair and trousers like those of Zouaves; João Pero Morato, a Portuguese priest, who died in 1653; and a Portuguese nobleman, Christovão Luiz Andrade, who died in 1756. There is also the portrait of the Archbishop Dom Fr. Manoel de Santa Catharina, which belonged probably to the Carmelite Convent, of which he was a patron. The Retreat *Santa Maria Magdalena*, which is to the right of the former one, is a small building, and has a chapel of its own.

To the south of the convent of the Carmelites, in the village of Morombim, was formerly situated the Conventual House of

Santa Barbara, where the Dominican friars used to go during convalescence for change of air. It had moveable property of the value of £1,742-9-4, which was appropriated by the Government when the house was abandoned. It is now in ruins.

Causeway of Ribandar.—Returning now to Ribandar, and proceeding by the main road to its western border, we see the long causeway which connects it with Pangim. It was begun by the Viceroy, the Count of Linhares, in 1633, and completed the next year, at a cost of £3,333-6-8. Popular tradition attributes the work to the supernatural power of the Jesuits, who are said to have constructed it in one night with the light of a single lamp. Possibly the tradition arose from the help which they rendered in the construction. The causeway is 9,542 feet long, and is supported by three arches on the eastern side in the middle, and thirty-eight on the western side. Here in a quadrangular column is read the following inscription :—

"Reinando a Magestade do Catholico Rei D. Filippe 3° N. S. Governando este Estado o V. R. D. Miguel de Noronha, Conde de Linhares, mandou a cidade faser esta Ponte de dinheiro de hum por cento, e se começou o anno de 633 e se acabou o anno 634."

Translation.

"During the reign of His Majesty the Catholic King Dom Filippe III., Our Lord, and the government of the Viceroy Dom Miguel de Noronha, Count of Linhares, the city ordered this bridge to be erected out of the money of one per cent., and it was begun in the year 633, and finished in the year 634."

By the *alvará* of the 22nd June 1634 all the ground adjoining the causeway was granted by the Government to the Senate or municipal chamber of the city, which took upon itself the responsibility of keeping it in proper repair for the benefit of the public. That the Senate actually fulfilled this engagement at its own expense, can be seen from the two following inscriptions, the first of which is on the large arch at its eastern portion, and the second in its middle portion on a cross :—

"No anno de 1699 sendo João Rodrigues da Costa Vereador do Senado da Camara da Cidade de Goa, mandou reedificar este arco."

Translation.

"In the year 1699, João Rodrigues da Costa being *Vereador* of the Senate of the Chamber of the City of Goa, this arch was ordered to be rebuilt."

"Sendo Governador e Capitão General deste Estado Illmo. e Exmo. Sr. D. João José de Mello, se renovou esta ponte á custa do nobre Senado da Camara no anno de 1771."

Translation.

"In the time of the Governor and Captain General D. João José de Mello, this bridge was repaired at the expense of the noble Senate of the Chamber in the year 1771."

The causeway was also repaired in 1859, during the administration of the Viscount of Torres Novas.

THE END.

BOMBAY: PRINTED AT THE EDUCATION SOCIETY'S PRESS, BYCULLA.